WALKER'S
REMODELING ESTIMATOR'S
REFERENCE BOOK

A Reference Book Setting Forth Detailed
Procedures and Cost Guidelines
For Professional Contractors
Involved In Estimating
Residential Remodeling

SECOND EDITION

Written by
HARRY HARDINBROOK
Revised & Edited
by
P. J. SAMMARTINO

FRANK R. WALKER COMPANY

Publishers
Lisle, Ill.

We will be grateful to readers of this volume who will kindly call our attention to any errors, typographical or otherwise, discovered therein. We also invite constructive criticism and suggestions that will make future editions of this book more complete and useful.

FRANK R. WALKER COMPANY

TABLE OF CONTENTS

Chapter 1
How to Use This Book 1

SECTION I/Major Projects 4

Chapter 2
"Kitchens" 5

Chapter 3
Baths 25

Chapter 4
Room Conversions 43

Chapter 5
Room Additions 55

SECTION II/Interiors 78

Chapter 6
Flooring and Stairways 79

Chapter 7
Drywall, Paneling and Ceiling Tile 109

Chapter 8
Painting and Wallpaper 141

Chapter 9
Plumbing 171

Chapter 10
Electrical 185

Chapter 11
HVAC 207

SECTION III/Exteriors 224

Chapter 12
Roofing, Gutters and Downspouts 225

Chapter 13
Siding and Exterior Painting 251

Chapter 14
Windows and Doors 289

Chapter 15
Porches and Decks 313

List of QUICK REFERENCE CHARTS for Labor Factors

Page

Chart 1 - Rough Framing 76–77

Chart 2 - Installing Stairs 107

Chart 3 - Plastering 134–35

Chart 4 - Interior & Exterior Trim 136

Chart 5 - Interior Millwork 137–39

Chart 6 - Insulation 248

Chart 7 - Roofing 249

Chart 8 - Sheet Metal 250

CHAPTER 1

HOW TO USE THIS BOOK

Today it is common knowledge that the biggest change in residential housing has been the growth in the remodeling market. And, the growth has been explosive. Annual growth isn't even talked of in millions of dollars, today it's billions. And, it will continue to grow at that rate for a number of years to come.

In compiling a book of estimating and cost data that is used throughout the world, it is impossible to quote material prices and labor costs which apply universally. Some computations are required on the part of the reader to make this book an accurate estimating reference in your construction area.

Here is the method by which labor costs were developed:

The hours worked divided by the production rate equals hours per unit of material.

$$\frac{\textbf{HOURS}}{\textbf{RATE}} = \text{LABOR HOURS PER UNIT}$$

For example:

A carpenter should be able to frame and erect 375-425 fbm of lumber per 8-hour day at the following labor cost per 1000 fbm:

Assume he can do the larger amount, 425 fbm. To find the labor hours per unit, in this case fbm, divide 8 by 425 which equals .0188 hours.

$$\frac{8 \quad \textbf{(hours)}}{425 \quad \textbf{(rate)}} = .0188 \text{ Hours Per Unit}$$

To find out how long it will take to do 1000 fbm, multiply 1000 by .0188 or move the decimal 3 places to the right. It will take 18.8 hours to install 1000 fbm.

To find out how long it will take to install 100 fbm, multiply 100 times .0188 or move the decimal 2 places to the right. It will take 1.88 hours.

With this method of figuring labor hours per unit, you can easily figure square feet, cubic feet, lineal feet or any other unit of measure that you will need for estimating purposes.

By using the Walker estimating table, the cost per ft., b.m. is determined as follows:

	Hours	Rate	Total	Rate	Total
Carpenter (1000 f.b.m.)	18.8	—	—	$20.60	$387.20
Cost per 100 f.b.m.		—	—		38.72
Cost per f.b.m.		—	—		.39

In order that this table will be of the utmost value to you, blank rate and total tables have been left for you to insert your local wage scale. Thus, assuming the labor rate in your area is $19.81, your cost per ft. would be:

	Hours	Rate	Total	Rate	Total
Carpenter (1000 f.b.m.)	18.8	$19.81	$372.43	$20.60	$387.20
Cost per 100 f.b.m.		—	37.24	—	38.72
Cost per f.b.m.		—	.37	—	.39

In the case of the examples set forth in the product chapters, where there is a range, the average of the two figures shown is used. Therefore, when the amount of material placed is shown as 1700–2200 sq. ft., the figure used is 1950 sq. ft. Where decimal fractions occur, those greater than one-half are rounded up to the next highest figure and those less than one-half are rounded off as is. For example: $0.0565 is rounded off to 6¢; $0.0532 is rounded off to 5¢.

The hourly rates used in this book were taken from the U. S. Department of Labor, Bureau of Labor Statistics as reported in the 1980 summary. They reflect national averages including fringe benefits. Therefore, they would not necessarily apply in any individual market and should not be used in making your estimates.

However, as has been mentioned previously, space has been provided for you to insert your local figures for materials and labor—including fringe benefits. By inserting and using your figures in the proper place, this book can be a time-and money-saving reference in estimating in your market. You will thereby eliminate estimates which are too high or too low. Remember, however, to revise your figures as your local labor and material rates change.

The profitability of your business depends on the accuracy of your estimates . . . you cannot be too careful!

QUICK REFERENCE CHARTS FOR LABOR COSTS

The *Quick Reference Charts*, which are found at the end of key chapters in this book, are a fast and convenient way to figure labor costs for many types of work. The experienced estimator knows that the productivity of workers is influenced by many conditions—job site and weather conditions, quantities of work involved, size and mix of crews and experience of workers. Eventually, it will be necessary for the estimator to develop his or her own cost data, based on field experience and the company's cost records. The cost data in this book serves as a starting point for the beginner and a quick reference for the established estimator, but he must understand that, as with any publication of this type, figures are based on average job conditions. Production rates in a given situation could be higher or lower.

Once you have estimated materials quantities, the *Quick Reference Charts* will help you to figure labor costs quickly and efficiently. Each chart lists the types of work, the unit of measure used for pricing and a multiplying factor, which represents the labor production rate per unit. Here's how it works:

For example, you have figured the board footage of lumber required for walls studs in a room addition. Now, you want to know the labor cost of setting the studs. Turn to *Quick Reference Chart # 1* at the end of Chapter 5, "Room Additions". The second line of the chart gives the labor factor for studs:

Item Description	Unit	Factor
Studs	BF	.02000

The unit of measure is Board Feet (BF). The multiplying factor is .02000, which represents the manhours required to set one (1) board foot of studs. Let's say that you figured 500 board feet of lumber are needed. To determine the labor cost, multiply

Total board feet of x Factor x Hourly Labor Rate = Labor Cost
    Lumber

500 x .02000 x $20.60   = $206.00

The *Hourly Labor Rate* should be an average rate. For example, the work described is to be performed by one carpenter and one helper. The carpenter is paid at the rate of $20.60 per hour. The helper is paid $15.45 per hour. You need to find the average Hourly Rate. The average rate is figured by totaling the sum of all wage rates and dividing by the number of workers. In the example above:

(20.60 + 15.45) ÷ 2 = 36.05 ÷ 2 = $18.03 Average Hourly Rate

A list of the *Quick Reference Charts* appears at the front of the book after the Table of Contents. For a more detailed breakdown of the components of labor cost, refer to the cost tables given in the text, the ones described at the beginning of this chapter. The successful remodeling estimator knows the importance of accurate labor pricing and understands the different methods for figuring unit costs on any project.

SECTION I/Major Projects

The relationship of the kitchen to many remodeling contractors is much the same as the kitchen to the home . . . it's the focal point of their business. Although some might argue that family/"rec" rooms or baths command greater interest, it's a moot point, and remodeling of those areas will be taken up in subsequent chapters.

The biggest advances in kitchens in recent years have taken place in two areas, design and appliances. Kitchens are opening up and flowing into adjacent rooms. In addition to new appliances, like garbage compactors and built-in barbecues, the selection of convenience and work saving appliances is growing every day. And when it comes to design, it is not so much the allocation of space, it's the selecting and placing of the functional elements for efficient use as well as aesthetic appeal which will make a kitchen successful.

When an architect or designer is involved, placement is their responsibility. Otherwise, it's the contractors.

But, regardless of whose responsibility it is, the contractor should be aware of basic kitchen design if for no other reason than to answer questions which are bound to arise.

Central to the design and function of all kitchens are three work centers, the sink, the refrigerator and the range. Together these three elements form what is called the "work triangle."

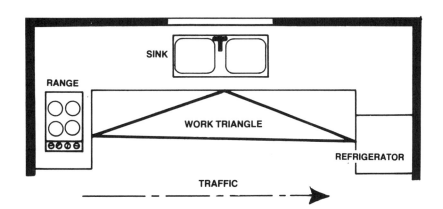

You'll have a happy client if the total length of the "work triangle" is not more than 22 feet or less than 13 feet. It has also been suggested that the minimum length of a leg of the "work triangle" be no less than 4 feet. Keeping within those parameters will save the housewife a lot of unnecessary steps and make meal preparation in the kitchen a more pleasurable operation.

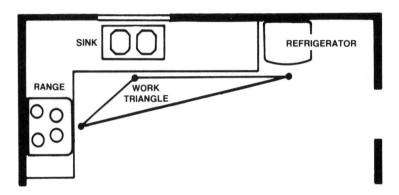

Nor should you ignore the fact that in some homes the kitchen is more than just a place to prepare meals. For some it becomes an entertainment center or even a type of family room and the "work triangle" should be planned so that traffic patterns from these activities interfere minimally or not at all.

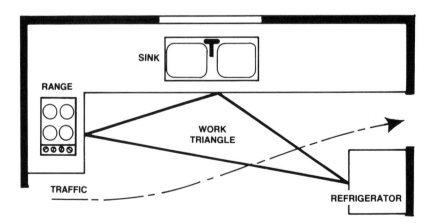

Additionally, you should consider whether doors should open from the left or right. Do they interfere with traffic or the "work triangle"? Adequate counter space should also be allocated around each of the work centers, otherwise meal preparation or clean-up cannot be carried out efficiently.

Care should also be taken to allow sufficient space between walls, or counters to open drawers without having to step aside and permit another person to pass by.

For maximum efficiency, the pantry, refrigerator and staples storage cabinets should be closest to the entry door where the staples can be brought in; normally the garage door, side door or back door.

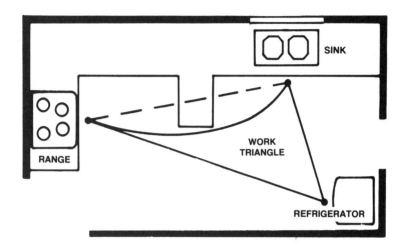

Also for efficiency, and to be sure food brought to the table is as hot as possible, the range/oven/microwave should be in that part of the kitchen closest to the family room table, breakfast nook or door to the dining room.

Be sure that the refrigerator door swings to the proper side (both right and left swinging models are available) so that food going in or coming out can conveniently be placed on the counter alongside the open door (next to the handle). On double door model refrigerators it is best to have counter space on both sides of the appliance.

The kitchen work flow is generally from staples storage or refrigerator to sink for washing, addition of water for cooking, etc. to range top or oven. For this reason, the sink should be between the refrigerator and stove.

How you resolve these problems will be influenced to some extent by the kind of kitchen layout selected. However, by giving careful attention to the "work triangle and traffic pattern" many of these headaches can be eliminated.

Today, there are four basic kitchen designs. To those you can add penninsulas and islands. By so doing you can create an attractive and efficient kitchen which will appeal to the most discriminating homeowners.

Although each has pluses and minuses, the selection of the basic design

Courtesy Merillat Industries, Inc.

Regardless of the kitchen style, there is sufficient variety of cabinets today to please the taste. Wood, such as in these oak cabinets is much in demand.

will be influenced to a great extent by the amount of space and the shape of the space available.

Although some say that none of these designs is any better than any other, two, the U-shaped and the L-shaped provide the greatest flexibility. The reason being that "work triangles" can be planned so that they have the least traffic interference. Their only drawbacks: there may not be sufficient space for a good U-shape, while the L-shape may minimize counter and cabinet space. When the latter occurs, it can affect both the "work triangle" and the traffic pattern.

Of the remaining two, the single wall and the corridor, the corridor is the most desirable. The big plus is that it can be a real step-saver in the "work triangle", and the key cabinets and counters can be near at hand. The biggest drawback for both is the traffic pattern right through the "work triangle". A second drawback for the single wall layout is lack of space. And obviously, depending on overall space, neither is well suited for entertainment or family activities.

However, the good contractor can work around these limitations and by so doing create a kitchen that is both efficient and aesthetically appealing.

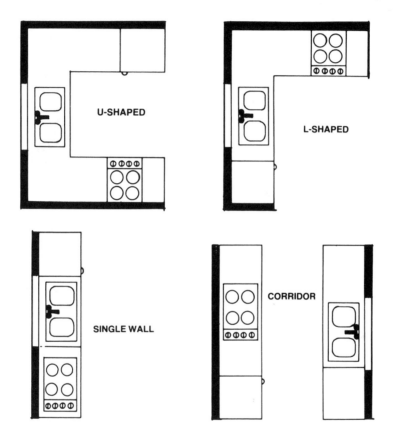

FUNCTION AND COLOR

After the "work triangle" has been decided there's still another key step to kitchen efficiency . . . providing proper storage in a convenient location. This means that cooking utensils should be near the stove, food preparation utensils near the sink, storage containers near the refrigerator and dining utensils as close as possible to that section of kitchen where meals will be consumed. This means that in selecting cabinets not only is the kind important, so is the placement.

Courtesy Ashland Builders

In this remodeling job, the kitchen design eliminated the need for a "work triangle". Instead, it is laid out in a highly functional straight line.

Where storage space is limited, consideration should be given to using additional cabinets above the wall cases. Custom made cabinets can be designed to utilize the soffit space and thus add additional storage area.

However, manufacturers of pre-assembled cabinets offer what are known as "short cabinets". They require a minimum of 15" of usable space.

Color is the key word for the '80's, and whether it's appliances, wall treatments, cabinets or floor coverings, there's sufficient variety to indulge the taste and personality of the most demanding homeowner.

Decorators and designers suggest that a single base color be selected, such as brown. It can be the brown in the floor covering, the cabinet

Courtesy Merillat Industries, Inc.

A corridor kitchen can be a real step-saver in the "work triangle". Key cabinets and counterspace can be near at hand.

facing, counter top or an appliance. Start simply and build up in layers, for example, yellow and beige, to which you can add contrasting brilliant colors as accents. As many as four or five colors can be used which compliment or enhance the base color.

Texture is another element. One manufacturer offers 108 choices in decorative surfacing ranging from tile to leather, from woodgrain to marble. Counter tops can be in simulated wood, like butcher block, and floor coverings in simulated brick. Or, cabinet facings in simulated wood like dark hickory and counter tops in simulated leather. Most have low maintenance and high eye appeal.

Thus, today's remodeling contractor has at his disposal, a greater variety of high quality materials and appliances which, if he does his job carefully, will help justify the costs he must charge if he is to make a profit in today's construction market.

Even though the reader's remodeling contract may call for redoing only a portion of a kitchen, he may wish to review that section in this chapter. For remedial jobs involving rewiring, replumbing or simply cosmetic changes, such projects are covered in more detail in the chapters covering a specific trade.

Before commencing work, the contractor should make allowances for the following:

- arrange for protecting the adjacent area

- removal of rubbish and salvage

- restrictions during normal working hours

- daily clean-up involved

- are plans of original structure available showing mechanical and structural details involved?

- check building codes in order to determine if there is work required beyond that which has been ordered, such as fire or window exits or strengthening structural members

- before fully uncrating or unpacking any appliances or fixtures visually inspect them for damage

REMOVING CABINETS AND APPLIANCES

Sink Removal.   The following procedure involves one man removing a two-well sink without garbage disposal. Turn off water lines and disconnect drain. Remove trap and drain. Disconnect fixtures and lift sink out.

	Hours	Rate	Total	Rate	Total
Plumber	1	—	—	$20.55	$20.55

If the sink is supported by a wall hanger or joined to the countertop with a trim ring, add 15 minutes to the above time. If a garbage disposal is to be removed add another 20 minutes.

Installing Shut-Off Valves.   Each water line requires its own shut-off valve. Where a dishwasher is to be added, the valve will require a dual outlet. Figure both valves at $6.00 each, and one plumber to install them allowing ½ hour per valve.

	Hours	Rate	Total	Rate	Total
Plumber	.5	—	—	$20.55	$11.25

Removing Range Tops and Ovens. If electric, turn off power at circuit breaker box. If gas, turn off at outside meter or shut-off valve if inside. Lift range top out and disconnect gas or electric fittings being sure power is off. Remove oven faceplate and slide out. Disconnect electric or gas fittings.

	Hours	Rate	Total	Rate	Total
Electrician	.5	—	—	$22.51	$11.26
Plumber (gas)	.5	—	—	20.56	10.28

If this is the only work performed, Journeymen will normally charge at least 1 hr. minimum.

Removing Base Cabinets and Tops. Base and wall cabinets are best removed by reversing the order in which they were installed. Thus it is easiest to remove the base cabinets first. Then the wall cabinets. To remove standard cabinets or countertops, figure 1/6 hour carpenter time for each lin. ft. of cabinet at the following labor cost per lin. ft.:

	Hours	Rate	Total	Rate	Total
Carpenter	0.17	—	—	$20.60	$3.50

REMOVING TRIM AND FLOORING

Removing Baseboard. One man should be able to remove 200 lin. ft. per hour of one-member baseboard at the following rate per linear ft.

	Hours	Rate	Total	Rate	Total
Carpenter	0.5	—	—	$20.60	$10.30
Cost per 100 lin. ft.			—		$10.30
Cost per lin. ft.			—		$ 0.10

Removing Sub-flooring. Where existing sub-floors require removal, a carpenter and laborer can remove 100 sq. ft. in 1.5 hrs. at the following cost per 100 sq. ft.:

	Hours	Rate	Total	Rate	Total
Carpenter	1.5	—	—	$20.60	$30.90
Laborer	1.5	—	—	15.67	23.51
Cost per 100 sq. ft.			—		$54.41
Cost per sq. ft.			—		$ 0.54

Prior to the installation of any new fixtures and appliances being relocated, water, drain lines and electrical outlets should be roughed in. For estimating data, see pages 192 and 173, Electrical and Plumbing.

No Roughing In.   Where no roughing in of water lines or drain is required, a plumber can place and connect a double kitchen sink in 3 hrs. For extensive remodeling or where increased electrical service is to be brought into the kitchen, some removal of drywall to expose studs may be necessary. It may be possible to remove only that portion of the wall to be covered by the new base cabinets. However, the amount can vary from job to job. In order to minimize duplication of estimating information, the cost to remove and replace drywall is covered in Chapter 7, "Wall Coverings", Page 118.

Changing Interior Doors and Openings.   When remodeling, sometimes either an additional opening or changing the entrance is desirable. Smaller kitchens can appear larger by opening a wall and adding a counter on the family room side.

To close off an existing opening, using 2 x 3" or 2 x 4" framing with drywall on both sides, allow one carpenter 4 hrs. to close the opening. If the opening was where a door previously existed, allow an additional hour to remove the framing.

To cut a new door in a non-load-bearing wall without electrical, heating ducts or plumbing, allow one carpenter 4 hrs. to cut and frame the opening.

However, if any of the previous services exist, re-routing is difficult to estimate. Charge time and materials.

Doors may vary from solid to louvered to cafe. See Chapter 14, Page 301 for installation. To move windows see Chapter 14, Page 295.

HANGING WALL CABINETS

Because of their variety and mass, cabinets generally set the tone for the entire kitchen, be it colonial or rustic, contemporary or ethnic. They also set the color pattern. Latches can be friction catch, magnetic catch, touch latch or even sliding. They can be made of wood, metal, plastic, even glass in a variety of widths and depths. And whether they are factory or custom built, they come with doors attached ready for installation.

Wall cabinets should be installed before base cabinets for easier installation, and to avoid damage due to reaching and dropping. Single-door units measure 9 to 27" wide, double-door units 24" to 48" in three inch increments. Heights range from 12" to 48". Depths, from 12" to 14". Special depth cabinets are also available for above the refrigerator. Filler strips are used where the distance, wall-to-wall is not an even multiple of 3 inches.

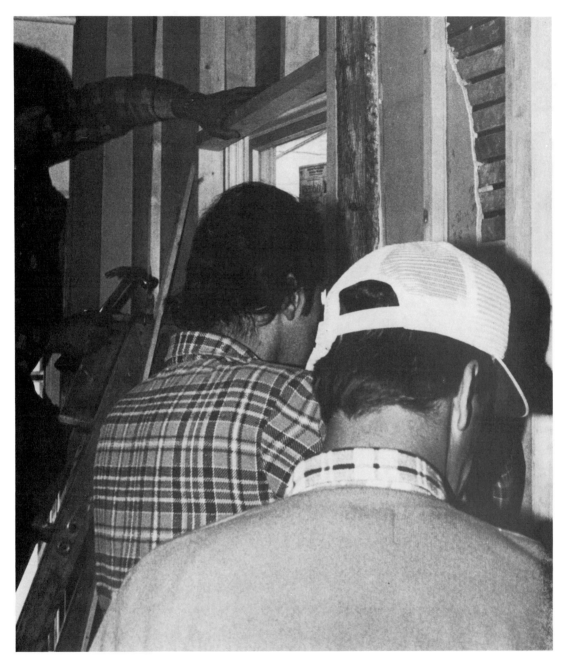

Courtesy Ashland Builders

Notice old wood lath from which plaster had to be stripped before installing new wall.

Courtesy Ashland Builders

This kitchen remodeling job involved closing the opening on right and creating a new doorway where window is on left.

Fixtures and Cabinets   Unit Prices

Counter Tops (4', 6', 8', 10', 12' lengths)

Satin, velvet, solids	$ 5.49 lin. ft.
Slate colors	7.99 lin. ft.
End cap kits	5.89 each
End splash kits	9.55 each
Built-up kits	3.99 each
Mitre kits	4.49 each
Additional mitres	4.49 each

Double Roll Bar Tops

Satin, velvet, solids (26" wide)	$ 6.49 lin. ft.
Satin, velvet solids (36" wide)	10.88 lin. ft.
Slates (26" wide)	7.99 lin. ft.
Slates (36" wide)	13.22 lin. ft.
Top caps	3.50 each

Bar Sink

Stainless steel, 15" x 15" (complete)	$63.95

CABINET DIMENSIONS

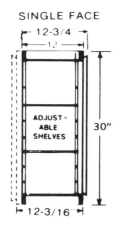

SINGLE FACE

12-3/4

12

ADJUST-
ABLE
SHELVES

30"

12-3/16

DOUBLE FACE
Frame to Frame Dimension

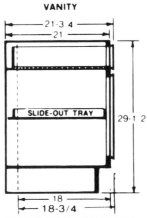

VANITY

21-3 4

21

SLIDE-OUT TRAY

29-1 2

18

18-3/4

SPACE SAVER VANITY

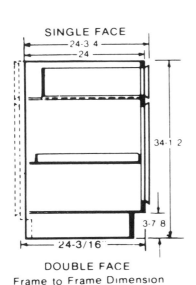

SINGLE FACE

24-3 4

24

34-1 2

3-7 8

24-3/16

DOUBLE FACE
Frame to Frame Dimension

REMOVABLE
TOP PANEL

66"

OVEN CABINET

OC2766S

24

24-3/4

Courtesy Merillat Industries, Inc.

Kitchen Faucets

Washer-type (without spray)	$19.95
Washerless (with spray)	34.95 to 43.95

WALL BLIND CORNER CABINETS

BASE BLIND CORNER CABINETS

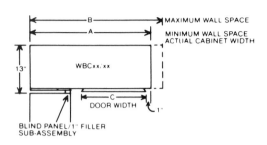

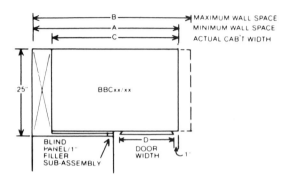

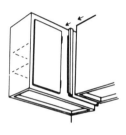

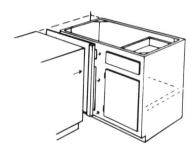

Courtesy Merillat Industries, Inc.

When installing base or wall blind corner cabinets or when "turning a corner" with regular base as wall cabinets, it is necessary to use a filler in the corners. This will provide adequate clearance for opening doors a full 90° and unobstructed pulling out of trays and drawers.

Kitchen Sinks
Porcelain on steel (double-well, 32" x 21")

White	$34.95
Color	39.95
Rim	8.95
Stainless Steel (double-well, 32" x 21")	39.95
Basket Strainers (stainless steel)	5.89
Sink (SS or china)	35–50
Faucets	35–75
Garbage disposal	50–150

Cabinets (laminated finish)

Wall Cabinets

30" high (no mullion)	$ 56–100
Dbl. door (no mullion)	92–143
(w/mullion)	109–174
18" high (no mullion)	65–114
(w/mullion)	76–131

15" high (no mullion)	67–110
(w/mullion)	72–113
12" high (no mullion)	63–106
(w/mullion)	68–121
30" Dbl. faced (no mullion)	101–176
Dbl. door (no mullion)	152–258
(w/mullion)	186–302
18" Dbl. faced (no mullion)	111–209
(w/mullion)	133–239
30" blind corner (no mullion)	72–168
Diagonal corner	107–175
Dbl. faced corner	119–162

Base Cabinets

Regular bases	$ 75–125
Two-door (no mullion)	132–186
(w/mullion)	152–220
Sink base (no mullion)	95–152
(w/mullion)	117–178
Drawer base (w/drawers)	134–178
Corner base unit	101–267
Double faced base	130–209
Two-door (no mullion)	215–320
(w/mullion)	242–367
Sink front, with floor (no mullion)	80–133
(w/mullion)	94–152
Oven cabinet	196–315
Finished ends (each)	30
Utility cabinet	157–316
Finished ends (each)	20–30
Adjustable shelves	30
Counter top (vinyl)	$5.50–10.00 per foot
(butcher block)	12.00 per foot

To Install Wall Cabinets. Locate relevant studs, draw plumb lines. Check walls for high spots, eliminate where possible. Mark upper and lower position lines and attach temporary support cleats. (Note: Where rangehood exhausts behind soffit and not through attic, cut wall opening before hanging cabinets. Install ductwork before hanging soffit.) Hang corner cabinets first.

New oven cabinets should be installed as part of the wall cabinets even though they extend to the floor.

A carpenter and laborer should be able to place and hang an average 24 linear ft. of wall cabinets per 8-hr. day at the following cost per linear ft.:

	Hours	Rate	Total	Rate	Total
Carpenter	0.33	—	—	$20.60	$ 6.80
Laborer	0.33	—	—	15.67	5.17
Cost per linear ft.	0.66		—		$11.97

Generally, two men are needed to install wall cabinets, one to align and hold and one to fasten.

To Install Ductwork Behind Soffit. Use segment of duct as template and scribe wall cutout. In outer wall, bore hole through center from inside. (If outside wall is masonry, use masonry drill). Cut exterior hole and insert duct cap. Connect interior ducting to duct cap.

For wood, to complete above, figure: ....6 hrs.
For masonry, to complete above, figure:............................8 hrs.

Labor To Set Cabinet Hardware

Unit	Hrs./Each
Surface bolts	.05
Offset bolts	.1
Catches	.1
Drawer pulls	.06
Knobs	.05
Rim Catches	.1
Mortise lock	.4

SETTING BASE CABINETS AND COUNTERTOPS

The standard height for base cabinets is 36". However, the trend is to lower this height to 30" when counters or peninsulas are used for meals or a member of the household is confined to a wheelchair. In fact, for the latter, it is becoming quite common to lower all base cabinets, including the sink and the range cabinets to facilitate meal preparation and minimize accidents which can be potentially serious, particularly around the range.

For materials cost see Chapter 4 for lumber and Chapter 4 for gypsum board.

To Install Base Cabinets. Locate relevant studs, draw plumb-lines. Check walls for flatness, eliminate high spots where possible. Mark where shimming is required. Check floor for level and mark where shimming is required. Chalk-line wall and floor for position.

A carpenter should be able to place and attach 24 linear ft. of base cabinets per 8-hour day at the following cost per linear ft.:

	Hours	Rate	Total	Rate	Total
Carpenter	.33	—	—	$20.60	$6.80
Cost per linear ft.			—		6.80

Courtesy Ashland Builders

Old wall with wood lath nailed to brick. Plaster was stripped and wall recovered, and new window installed.

To Install Countertops. Countertops come in a variety of surfaces, each having advantages and disadvantages. Formica® brand, plastic laminate, is still the most popular, since it won't fade or stain and is easy to maintain. Dollar-wise, it is one of the most economical. Sheet vinyl is the cheapest, also easy to clean, but it won't hold up and marks quite easily. The two with the longest life are stainless steel and tile. Although maintenance is easy the former is noisy and cold to the look and touch. With the latter, dishes break easily and joints loosen. Wood is difficult to clean and splinters. Although when it is covered with an acrylic coating, those problems are eliminated, the acrylic itself is susceptible to mars and cuts.

Still another counter top is Corion® by DuPont. This product is harder than marble, yet will not stain, smudge, etc.

In the example that follows the counter is U-shaped and the countertop is Formica.

Using standard section shapes, there will be two left corners (L) and two right corners (R) and no straight (S) sections. Mark the two (L) sections 1 and 3 and the two right (R) sections 2 and 4. When trimming sections to size, any fine-tooth or carbide saw can be used. To avoid ragged edges for cutting with either a circular or sabre saw, place decorative face down; when using a table saw or hand saw, place decorative face up. Laminate 1/32" thick can be cut with tin snips.

Cut 1/8 to 1/4" over size and trim after mounting. A special router bit, plane or file is used to trim and bevel corners. Start with sections 1 and 3. Apply contact bond cement on both the laminate and counter with a spreader, roller or brush following manufacturers instructions and specifications. Align front edges and top surface. Tighten joint fasteners front to back. Place sections on cabinet and fasten with wood screws from underneath.

Repeat procedure with sections 2 and 4.

A carpenter should be able to place and attach 5 linear ft. of countertops per hour at the following cost per linear ft.:

	Hours	Rate	Total	Rate	Total
Carpenter	.2	—	—	$20.60	$4.12
Cost per linear ft.			—		$4.12

Long tops, especially "L's" require 2 men on site.

Setting Factory Assembled and Finished Kitchen Cabinets.   When setting factory assembled and finished kitchen cabinets, such as used in the average apartment or residence, it will require about 0.1-hr. carpenter time for each sq. ft. of cabinet face area at the following labor cost per sq. ft.:

	Hours	Rate	Total	Rate	Total
Carpenter	0.1	—	—	$20.60	$2.06

First Grade Workmanship

In better class apartment and residences where a high class job of installation is required it will take about 1/6-hr. carpenter time for each sq. ft. of cabinet face area at the following labor cost per sq. ft.:

	Hours	Rate	Total	Rate	Total
Carpenter	0.16	—	—	$20.60	$3.30

Cutouts.   In making sink and range cutouts, use the sink trim ring and the range tub as templates. After marking, cover saw line with clear tape and drill ½" holes at opposite corners. Make cutout with fine-tooth saw, using fine tooth file from top to bottom to smooth edges. Figure a single carpenter one-hour per cutout.

However, countertops can be ordered with exact specifications including cut-outs from cabinet suppliers. Installation is simply position and fasten.

To Install Sink, Range (Gas or Electric) and Oven. Figure one man to do each installation at the following approximate flat-rate:

To place and connect sink $225.00
To place and connect range, Electric .... $ 60.00
                          Gas .... $ 75.00
To place and connect oven, Electric .... $ 60.00
                          Gas .... $ 75.00

SOFFITS, RANGE HOODS, DISPOSALS

To Make And Install Soffits. Soffits are generally made from 2" x 4" or 2" x 2" lumber. This estimate includes cutting, assembling, placing and finishing off with drywall or paneling. A carpenter should be able to accomplish the preceeding, installing 8 linear ft. per 1-hour at the following cost per linear ft.:

	Hours	Rate	Total	Rate	Total
Carpenter	.125	—	—	$20.60	$2.58
Cost per linear ft.		—	—		$2.58

Installing Range Hoods. This procedure describes installing a range hood which is exhausted through the wall cabinet and soffit using two men. The procedure for installing ductwork behind the soffit is described on Page 20. Position hood collar below bottom shelf of wall cabinet and mark shelf to show shape of duct cut out. Make appropriate cut-outs in shelves, soffit and ceiling, if duct is to go through roof. For roof vent, allow the following: Include placing vent cap, flashing where vent cap enters roof and replacing shingles for one-story vent, kitchen on second level or ranch. Connect electrical conduit to junction box, check operation of fan and light. Install and attach duct to collar and fasten hood to lower shelf. An electrician and carpenter should be able to accomplish the preceding in 7 hours at the following cost:

	Hours	Rate	Total	Rate	Total
Electrician	2.5	—	—	$22.51	$ 56.28
Carpenter	4.5	—	—	20.60	92.70
	7.0				$148.95

A popular consideration, especially in remodeling, is a ductless range hood. This unit filters the air through a grease filter and an activated charcoal filter, then back into the room. Figure installation will take 4.5 hrs. at the following cost:

	Hours	Rate	Total	Rate	Total
Electrician	2.5	—	—	$22.51	$56.28
Carpenter	2.0	—	—	20.60	41.20
	4.5				$97.48

Installing In-Sink Garbage Disposal. Since this represents a new installation and not a direct replacement, an outlet and wall switch should have been roughed-in prior to placing the cabinets and sink. For estimating installation of these items, see "Electrical" Chapter, pg. 185. For safety, wall on/off switch should be positioned 6 ft. from the sink center-line. Check disposal for vertical clearance. Apply plumbers putty around sink drain opening. Insert sink sleeve from above and mounting assembly from underneath. Secure with snap ring and tighten mounting screws evenly. Attach discharge tube and insert disposal into mounting assembly. Connect power and check operation. A plumber should be able to complete the preceeding installation in 1½ hrs. at the following labor cost:

	Hours	Rate	Total	Rate	Total
Plumber	1.5	—	—	$20.55	$30.83

Note: Obviously to remodel an entire kitchen entails considerably more work than has been covered in this Chapter. However, since such work as flooring could be replaced not only in kitchens, but in every room throughout the home, projects having such a broad application are covered in detail in the chapter covering that application or trade. For example, the reader should review the Chapter covering "Stairways and Floors" before estimating a flooring job. For specific installations consult the index.

Of all the rooms in the home, bathrooms are finally beginning to come into their own. They can range from the simple to the luxurious. Among the options are whirlpool baths, his and her lavatories, shampoo lavatories, bidets and starkly modern or nostalgically designed baths, toilets and lavatories.

When it comes to adding bathroom facilities, extra-small baths and half-baths can be installed in spaces as small as 4' x 4' which is room enough for a W.C. and lavatory.

Fixtures such as shower stalls are available in 32" x 32" or 36" x 36" in enameled steel and seamless plastic. Even tubs come in small sizes: 14" high by 42" long by 34" wide or 39" x 38" are just a couple of sizes which are readily available. There are also corner tubs, sunken tubs and raised tubs and tubs big enough for two, three or even four people.

Toilets also come in many different styles. There are low styles for invalids and new one-piece designs with integrated water tanks suitable for almost any size bath. Bidets, long a European tradition, are finding their way into American homes with increasing frequency. Not only do they come in a variety of colors and styles, they also come in sets so that the bidet and the toilet are compatible in style and color.

As for lavatories, the variety is practically unlimited. Again, the sizes vary. By checking around, a contractor can find one which will fit the decor and space of almost any type of bathroom design. Even such utilitarian items as bath cabinets are being designed to fit contemporary lifestyles. Equally important is the fact that they are being designed with the remodeling contractor in mind.

To that end, the trend is toward surface mounted cabinets. Behind this movement is the fact that for years there have been no standard wall openings, except for two general standards, defined geographically. In the East through the Midwest to Denver, the most common size is 14" x 18". From Denver West to the coast, 14" x 24". However, there are many variations in between. In addition, errors in size openings and location also occur with great frequency.

Changing construction techniques have also exerted an influence on the installation and style of bath cabinets. With most bathrooms being installed back-to-back, there just isn't room to recess the cabinets back-to-back.

Courtesy Monarch Metal Products

The new designs in surface mounted medicine cabinets are ideal for remodeling and require no cut-out. They also come with large mirror and storage areas.

And then there is the contractor's nemisis, "What's behind the wall?" Is it really worth cutting a hole in the wall for a $150.00 item only to discover that because of some wiring, plumbing or ductwork, it will take another $500.00 in labor and materials to complete the installation? Hardly.

Today's homeowner wants two things, the maximum amount of mirror and the maximum amount of storage. And surface mounted units provide both.

When it comes to style, swinging doors are the most popular, and wood, particulary oak, is the leader.

It is also interesting to note, that for every free-standing tub or lavatory a contractor removes to replace with built-ins, just as many built-ins are removed to be replaced with free-standing fixtures.

High style is making its mark everywhere, and bathrooms are no exception.

When doing bathroom remodeling, it is best to complete the bathtub installation first. Experts also suggest not putting the tub or shower against an outer wall, unless the wall and tub are properly insulated and have a vapor barrier. Make sure the fan is vented to the outside and not to the attic space. Otherwise, moisture will reach it's dew point and condense in the attic area, or water can condense on the outside of the tub or shower-wall and run down the wall cavity or seep into the flooring causing eventual deterioration.

BATHROOM FIXTURES/INSTALLATION DIMENSIONS.

Vanity Base Cabinet - Standard size: 30" high by 30" wide by 20" deep Back-saver model: 34½" high

Lavatories - Average vanity top should be 20" to 24" deep to accommodate standard lavatory bowl. However, lavatory bowls 16" deep are available for narrow spaces.

Double Lavatories - When double lavatories are installed, allow 30" from center to center between bowls. Allow 6" for end wall and side of lavatory.

Towel Racks - (Standard lengths) 18" for hand towels, 24" for bath towels.

Medicine Cabinets - 72" to 78" from floor. Allow 8" between cabinet bottom and vanity top.

Shower Heads - 60" for women; 66" for men.

Soap Dishes - Tubs 24" above floor; showers 54"

Safety Bars - Bath, 24" above floor; 56" to 60" for shower.

Shower Curtain Rods - 74" to 78" above floor.

Toilets - Tanks 1" to 3½" from wall, depending on make; 15" away from side walls on either side measured from center of bowl; 18" from front of toilet to facing wall. Water supply lines must be at least 6" from the center line of the bowl for two-piece units and 8½" for one-piece units. Wall installation must be 8" above floor for 2-piece and 2½" for one-piece.

TOILETS

To Remove Existing Toilet. Floor-mounted unit. As a rule, floor-mounted units can usually be removed by a single plumber. The procedure takes into consideration the following: draining toilet, disconnecting water supply lines, cutting or otherwise removing stubborn bowl mounting bolts, cleaning old setting compound from closet flange and floor and removing components from home for disposal. One man can accomplish the preceding in two hours.

Wall mounted unit. The procedure is basically the same, figure 2 hrs.

Shut-Off Valves. Many older homes lack shut-off valves and a new valve should be added before the new toilet is installed. Using flexible connector, figure ½ hr. for the installation and approximately $6.00 for the valve and the connector.

For wash basins, simply double the preceding.

To Install New Toilet. Floor-Mounted. When installing a floor-mounted unit to existing waste pipe and water supply, figure one plumber can complete the installation in 8 hours. To install a wall-mounted unit will require a helper. To the above, add 2 hrs. for helper time.

To Install A Bidet.   Not too long ago, such fixtures were usually found only in Europe. Today, however, they are becoming increasingly popular in the United States. The installation procedure is similar to that of floor-mounted toilets with the exception that it requires a hot water supply as well as cold and uses a smaller drain. However, the big cost in adding a bidet comes in installing a new waste pipe, cutting into the stack and new water supply lines. (See next paragraph.) Since bidets do not require water closets, figure one man can install and hook-up the bowl in 4 hours.

Roughing In.   Where new waste pipe and water lines, such as in the installation of the bidet above, are required or a bathroom appliance is to be moved to a different location and roughing in is required, see Chapter 9 "Plumbing" Pg. 173.

BATHTUBS

Removing Existing Tubs.   Free-Standing. Installations of this kind seldom pose any unusual problems with the exception that bathtubs because of their weight usually require two men for their removal. Allow 2 hrs. for a plumber and 2 hrs. for a helper to disconnect the existing fittings and pipes and remove the preceding.
Built-In Or Recess Tubs, add 2 hrs. to the preceding.

Roughing-In New Plumbing Connections.   Not infrequently older free-standing units are replaced with built-ins requiring new plumbing. In general, this would require a new elbow and strainer, stopper mechanism, overflow elbow and plate, waste pipe and hot and cold water lines. Allow one plumber 4 hrs. for this procedure.

Installing New Tub/Shower.   If new framing is required, add 2 hrs. for one carpenter to rough-in necessary studs and tub supports on three walls, if building code requires. Figure one plumber can do the necessary hook-ups including new fittings and installing the shower head in 1 hr. If removing or adding a tub or shower unit, make sure the opening is large enough for the unit to pass through! Add costs for removal of doors, opening of wall and door replacement if necessary.

CABINETS/VANITIES/WASH BASINS/ACCESSORIES

Wall Cabinets.   If an old wall cabinet exists, allow 1 hr. for its removal. If no cabinet exists, it will be necessary to cut and frame a recess for the new cabinet. Allow a minimum of 1½ hrs. for this procedure.

Lighted Cabinets.   Many of today's cabinets have self-contained lighting. Figure one electrician can complete the necessary hook-up from an existing 110-volt source at approximately $30.00 labor cost or 1½ hrs.

ILLUSTRATION

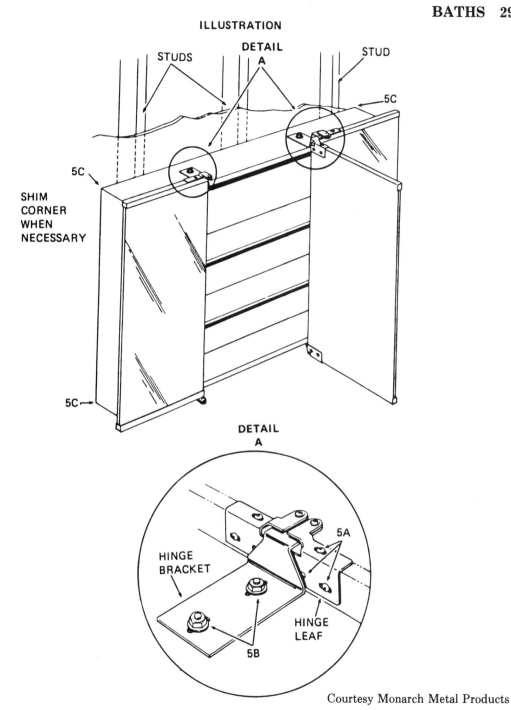

Courtesy Monarch Metal Products

Installation of surface mounted medicine cabinets is simple and quick. Doors can be made to open and close easily by adjusting screws at 5A and 5B. If walls are too irregular, shim at corners (5C) will usually correct the problem.

Fitting and Placing Closet Shelving.   A carpenter should fit and place 115 to 135 sq. ft. of closet shelving per 8-hr. day including setting of shelf cleats at the following labor cost per 100 sq. ft:

	Hours	Rate	Total	Rate	Total
Carpenter	6.4	—	—	$20.60	$131.84
Cost per sq. ft.			—		1.31

Installing Hanging Rods in Closets.   A carpenter should install about three hanging rods, including supports, per hr. at the following labor cost per rod:

	Hours	Rate	Total	Rate	Total
Carpenter	0.33	—	—	$20.60	$6.79

Setting Metal Medicine Cabinets.   A carpenter should set 10 to 12 average size medicine cabinets per 8-hr. day at the following labor cost per cabinet:

	Hours	Rate	Total	Rate	Total
Carpenter	0.75	—	—	$20.60	$14.83

Setting Bathroom Accessories.   In an 8-hr. day a carpenter should locate and set 30 to 34 bathroom accessories, such as towel bars, soap dishes, paper holders, etc. at the following labor cost per accessory:

	Hour	Rate	Total	Rate	Total
Carpenter	0.25	—	—	$20.60	$5.15

Removing Lavatory or Wash Basin.   To remove a wall-hung lavatory, figure 1 man can disconnect the waste and water lines and remove the fittings in 1 hr. (If new shut-off valves are required, see Page 27.)

Removing Vanities.   The removal of kitchen cabinets, vanities, and built-in cabinets is generally by the lin. ft. of facing. Figure 1/6 hr. carpenter time for each linear foot of vanity. Add for removal of debris and clean-up.

Installing Vanity.   Most vanities today come pre-assembled ready to install.
Figure a carpenter can install a standard 24" built-in vanity in 2 hrs.

Installing Wall Hung Lavatory.   Modern bathrooms dictate many configurations, including wall-hung lavatories.
Installing Lavatories Integrated with Countertops. 2 hrs.
Installing Lavatory From Above. Same
Installing Lavatory From Below. Same

VENTILATION

Ceiling Ventilators. Installing through-the-ceiling ventilators involves cutting an opening through the ceiling large enough for the ventilator housing, close to a joist. The housing is attached to the joist. The fan-motor assembly is screwed into the housing. A grid shield is attached to conceal the unit and the opening. Operation is by wall switch.

	Electrician	Rate	Total	Rate	Total
Open Ceiling	3.75 hrs.	—	—	$22.50	$ 84.37
Closed Ceiling	5.25 hrs.	—	—	22.50	118.12

Wall Ventilators. A typical through-the-wall ventilator consists of an outer sleeve inserted into the wall from outside the house, an inner sleeve forced into the outer sleeve from inside and a fan-motor assembly. Openings are cut through both inside and outside walls. The fan-motor assembly is attached to the inner sleeve. A concealment grid is placed on the inside and hinged door on the outside to prevent backdrafts. Operation is also by wall switch.

	Electrician	Rate	Total	Rate	Total
Open Wall....................................	4.75 hrs.	—	—	$22.50	$106.88
Closed Wall	6.25	—	—	22.50	140.63

If the exterior finish is stucco add 1 hr. to the preceding, 2 hrs. if brick.

AUXILIARY HEATERS

Ceiling Heaters. Most electrical ceiling heaters are flush-mounted to a mounting plate and secured to a junction box fastened to a ceiling joist. The unit is operated by wall switch.

	Electrician	Rate	Total	Rate	Total
Open Ceiling	3.75 hrs.	—	—	$22.50	$ 84.37
Closed Ceiling	5.25	—	—	22.50	118.12

Wall Heaters. Wall heaters are recessed into the wall and fastened to the nearest stud. Operation is by wall switch and electrical power is brought to the unit via conduit from an existing circuit.

	Electrician	Rate	Total	Rate	Total
Open Wall....................................	2.5	—	—	$22.50	$56.25
Closed Wall	4.0	—	—	22.50	90.00

Baseboard Heaters. Baseboard heaters are surface-mounted at the base of a wall. Like ceiling and wall heaters, a power source must be brought to the heater and activated by a wall switch.

	Electrician	Rate	Total	Rate	Total
Open Wall...............................	1.5 hrs.	—	—	$22.50	$33.75
Closed Wall	2.5	—	—	22.50	56.25

BATHROOMS

Combined Labor-Materials Cost   (Standard Grade)

Room size: 5' x 7'

Replace Plumbing fixtures
   Tub, lavatory and W.C. (White, Std. Grade) ....$ 950.00
                    (Color, Std. Grade).............................. 1025.00
   Tub, only (White, Std. Grade).. 575.00
   Lavatory only (White, Std. Grade)................................... 250.00
   Water Closet only (White, Std. Grade) 200.00
Shower Stall, 36" x 36" (Std. Grade, Metal)........................ 520.00
Vanity 24" with top (including plumbing, bowl and trim) 350.00
Medicine Cabinet
   Std. Grade/with flourescent..................................... 85.00
   Std. Grade/no lights.. 35.00
   Replace door only on wall-hung, recessed unit 120.00
Windows
   Double-hung window, same opening 125.00
   Change window to glass block (32" x 32" with
            16" x 16" vent) Brick Wall................................ 325.00
                    Frame Wall................................ 300.00
Walls
   "Prep" existing wall for new covering 100.00
   Install new water resistant drywall (walls only)............... 225.00
     (Add for ceilings done at same time)....................... 90.00
   Tape walls and ceilings 125.00
   Install ceramic tile (per sq. ft.) 4.50
Floors
   Install ⅝" C.D.X. Plywood 150.00
   Vinyl Tile.. 100.00
   Ceramic Tile (with wall-work per sq. ft.)................... 4.50
   Ceramic Tile (without wall-work, minimum)................... 175.00
Electric Ceiling Fixtures
   Replace with standard grade (same location)................. 30.00
   Replace with standard grade (new location)................. 60.00
Miscellaneous
   Shower enclosure on tub (Std. Grade)....................... 125.00
   Install soffit above tub...................................... 115.00
   Install bulkhead at end of tub 115.00
   Chrome accessories (3 towel rods, soap dish, glass
     holder, tissue dispenser, tub dish) 70.00

MATERIAL COSTS

VANITIES

Pre-assembled base complete with marble-
type top.
20" x 17"..............................$ 57.99
25" 97.95

Cutback to allow bathroom door to open.
37" x 19"..............................$159.95
Deluxe with 5 drawers

31" 117.95	43" x 19" 234.00
37" 161.95	49" x 19" 269.00
Corner Unit	Hardwood with oak front
22" x 22" 149.95	25" x 19" 173.00
	31" x 19" 197.00
	37" x 19" 244.00

FAUCETS
Tub and shower...................\$32.95 to \$56.95
Lavatory faucets
   (chrome)............................. 37.95 to 39.95
   (bronze) 48.95

MEDICINE CABINETS
Surface mounted (single door, unlighted) ....\$ 12.95 to \$24.55
Surface mounted (triple door, unlighted) 134.00
Recessed (with square framed mirror)... 59.95
Recessed (with round framed mirror).. 79.00
Recessed (with louvered door, unfinished wood) 44.95
Light fixture for above 49.95
Recessed (with beveled mirror).. 89.95

Tub Surrounds
Solid White \$73.00
Marble.. 89.00
Solid Colors................................. 83.00

Tub Enclosures
Satin finish (annodized aluminum frame, safety glass) ....\$ 64.95
Mirror door (annodized aluminum frame, safety glass).. 129.95

Tubs and Showers.
Porcelain-enamel, steel, recessed (60" x 30" x 15½ h.)

White	\$104.95
Color..	117.95
Black	135.95
Vinyl...	105.00–140.00

Shower Stall (vinyl) 185.00–225.00
Tub/Shower Combination...180.00–235.00

Lavatories
Wall-mounted, white (19" x 17") 32.95
Self-rimming bowl (17" x 20")

White	30.95
Color..	34.95

Toilets
Vitreous china, reverse trap (2-piece)

White	69.95
Color..	89.95
Black	117.95

WALL FINISHES

Paint. (Most economical). Flammable. Alkyd (solvent-thinned) will bond when applied over latex, bare wood and on wallpaper with proper surface preparation. Does not bond well to bare plaster, unprimed wall-board or bare masonry.

Latex. (Water-thinned). Non-flammable. Does not bond well to alkyd paint, wallpaper or new wood. Latex can be used over new plaster, cinder block and unprimed wallboard.

Urethanes and Epoxies. (Require special solvents for thinning and clean-up). Highly resistant to abrasion, moisture and household chemicals. Very durable. Urethanes adhere well to old paints including latex and alkyd and can be used on bare wood as primer sealer and finish. Epoxies are ideal for non-porous materials like tile and glass, even concrete. However, they do not adhere well to previously painted surfaces. For estimating interior painting see pgs. 142–165.

WALLPAPERS

Vinyls. Fabric-backed are best and easiest to work with. Next best are vinyl-coated paper or paper-backed vinyl. See Chapter 8 pg. 141.

Metallic Foils. Good, provided they are backed with fabric or paper. Somewhat difficult to work with compared to vinyl.

Prefinished Panels. Come in a variety of finishes, patterns and textures. Some even resemble ceramic tile in appearance and touch. Others come in rich wood grains protected with coatings to resist heat and humidity. The former are applied direct to smooth existing surfaces with adhesives. The later are nailed to studs or framing strips.

TILE

Ceramic is still the best finish for bathroom walls. Has a long-life and is easy to maintain. Tile wainscoting is still a practical and decorative favorite.

Bathroom floors and ceilings can be finished in a wide variety of materials as long as they are moisture resistant.

In fact, many of the materials used in other areas of the house are not only suitable for use in the bathroom, they are desirable because of the decorative options which they offer.

For floors, there are woods, strip flooring, parquet and plank, quarry and mosaic tile, carpeting, sheet vinyl and vinyl tile. For ceilings, ceiling tile and suspended ceilings are increasingly popular.

Ceramic Tile Bathroom Accessories. Numerous ceramic tile bathroom accessories are available in a variety of sizes and qualities. They may be

Courtesy Armstrong Floors

Fancy enough for any remodeled bath is this old-world Maltese cross design in pale blue "marble" from Armstrong's new Solarian Supreme collection of deluxe no-wax floors. See Chapter 6, "Flooring and Stairways."

recessed or surface mounted and they come in the full range of tile colors. Some of the more commonly used items are as follows:

Description	Price per Piece
Recessed soap holder	$12.00–14.00
Recessed glass holder	12.00–14.00
Roll paper holder	9.00
Robe hook	3.75
Double robe hook	4.25
Toothbrush holder	4.25
Tile bar brackets (pair)	8.48

Decorative Ceramic Wall Tiles. Glazed ceramic wall tile containing designs as an integral part of each piece of tile is also available. Normally supplied in 4¼"x4¼" and 6"x6" sizes, the price of this material will vary with the design selected and number of colors in the design. If the design is known, the estimator should obtain a firm price from a supplier. The general range is as follows:

One color	4¼"x4¼"	$1.50 per sq. ft.
	6 "x6 "	1.25 per sq. ft.
Two colors	4¼"x4¼"	1.75 per sq. ft.
	6 "x6 "	1.50 per sq. ft.
Three colors	4¼"x4¼"	2.00 per sq. ft.
	6 "x6 "	2.65 per sq. ft.

Ceramic Tile Adhesives and Accessory Materials

Item	Coverage	Price
Organic adhesive	40-50 sf/gal	$6.00/gal.
Dry-set mortar mix	35 lbs./100 sf	.30.lb.
Primer (for use in damp areas)....................................	125 sf/gal.	5.00/gal.
Plastic underlayment..	100 sf/unit*	6.00/unit
Wet tile grout..	15-20 sf/lb**	.15/lb.
Dry tile grout	12-15/sf/lb.**	.20/lb.

    *Unit consists of 1 gallon liquid & 34 lbs. aggregate.
    **When used with 4¼"x4¼" tile.

Cost of 100 sq. ft. of 4¼"x4¼" Glazed Ceramic Wall Tile using conventional mortar method of installation (unmounted tile).

	Hours	Rate	Total	Rate	Total
2 sacks portland cement........................	—	—		$ 5.66	$ 11.32
4 cu. ft. sand	—	—		.53	2.12
100 sq. ft. glazed wall tile	—	—		1.99	199.00
10 lbs. dry tile grout	—	—		—	9.99
Tile setter..	13.5	—		18.75	253.12
Cost per 100 sq. ft.	13.5	—			$475.55
Cost per sq. ft.		—			4.75

Cost of 100 sq. ft. of 4¼"x4¼" Glazed Ceramic Wall Tile using water resistant organic adhesive (unmounted tile).

	Hours	Rate	Total	Rate	Total
2.5 gallons adhesive...............................	—	—		$15.99	$ 39.98
100 sq. ft. glazed wall tile	—	—		1.99	199 .00
10 lbs. dry tile grout mix	—	—		—	9.90
Tile setter..	8.0	—		18.75	150.00
Cost per 100 sq. ft.	8.0	—			$398.97
Cost per sq. ft.		—			3.98

Cost of 100 sq. ft. of 4¼"x4¼" Glazed Ceramic Wall Tile using 'dry-set' portland cement mortar (unmounted tile).

	Hours	Rate	Total	Rate	Total
35 lbs. 'dry-set' mortar mix	—	—		$ .32	$ 11.20

	Hours	Rate	Total	Rate	Total
100 sq. ft. glazed wall tile		—	—	1.99	199.00
10 lbs. dry tile grout mix		—	—	—	9.99
Tile setter	10.0	—	—	18.75	187.50
Cost per 100 sq. ft.	10.0		—		$407.63
Cost per sq. ft.			—		4.07

Note: Add for plastering when specified.

Cost of 100 sq. ft. of 4¼"x4¼" Glazed Ceramic Wall Tile using conventional mortar method of installation (back-mounted tile).

	Hours	Rate	Total	Rate	Total
2 sacks portland cement		—	—	$ 5.66	$ 11.32
4 cu. ft. sand		—	—	.53	2.12
100 sq. ft. glazed wall tile		—	—	1.99	199.00
10 lbs. dry tile grout mix		—	—	—	9.99
Tile setter	12.0	—	—	18.75	225.00
Cost per 100 sq. ft.	12.0		—		$447.00
Cost per sq. ft.			—		4.47

Cost of 100 sq. ft. of 4¼"x4¼" Glazed Ceramic Wall Tile using water resistant organic adhesive (back-mounted tile).

	Hours	Rate	Total	Rate	Total
2.5 gallons adhesive		—	—	$15.99	$ 39.98
100 sq. ft. glazed wall tile		—	—	1.99	199.00
10 lb. dry tile grout mix		—	—	—	9.99
Tile setter	8.0	—	—	18.75	150.00
Cost per 100 sq. ft.	8.0		—		$398.97
Cost per sq. ft.			—		3.98

Cost of 100 sq. ft. of 4¼x4¼" Glazed Ceramic Wall Tile using 'dry-set' portland cement mortar (back-mounted tile).

	Hours	Rate	Total	Rate	Total
35 lbs. 'dry-set' mortar mix		—	—	$ .32	$ 11.20
100 sq. ft. glazed wall tile		—	—	1.99	199.00
10 lbs. dry tile grout mix		—	—	—	9.99
Tile setter	9.0	—	—	18.75	168.75
Cost per 100 sq. ft.	9.0		—		$388.94
Cost per sq. ft.			—		3.88

Note: Add for plastering when specified.

Cost of 100 sq. ft. 1"x1" Ceramic Mosaic Tile floors using conventional mortar method of installation (face-mounted tile).

	Hours	Rate	Total	Rate	Total
2 sacks portland cement		—	—	$ 5.66	$ 11.32
4 cu. ft. sand		—	—	.53	2.12
100 sq. ft. ceramic mosiac tile		—	—	1.69	169.00
25 lbs. dry tile grout mix		—	—	—	24.98
Tile setter	10.5	—	—	18.75	196.88
Cost per 100 sq. ft.	10.5		—		$404.30
Cost per sq. ft.			—		4.04

Cost of 100 sq. ft. of 1"x1" Ceramic Mosaic Tile floors using water resistant organic adhesive (face-mounted tile).

	Hours	Rate	Total	Rate	Total
2.5. gallons adhesive		—	—	$15.99	$ 39.98
100 sq. ft. ceramic mosaic tile		—	—	1.69	169.00
25 lbs. dry tile grout mix		—	—	—	24.98
Tile setter	8.0	—	—	18.75	150.00
Cost per 100 sq. ft.	8.0		—		$383.96
Cost per sq. ft.				—	3.83

Cost of 100 sq. ft. of 1"x1" Ceramic Mosaic Tile floors using 'dry-set' portland cement mortar (face-mounted tile).

	Hours	Rate	Total	Rate	Total
35 lbs. 'dry-set' mortar mix		—	—	$ .32	11.20
1 cu. ft. of sand	—	—			.53
100 sq. ft. ceramic mosaic tile		—	—	1.69	169.00
25 lbs. dry tile grout mix		—	—		24.98
Tile setter	9.0	—	—	18.75	168.75
Cost per 100 sq. ft.	9.0		—		$374.46
Cost per sq. ft				—	3.74

Note: Add for cement floor fill or plastic underlayment when required. See page 47.

Cost of 100 sq. ft. of 1"x1" Ceramic Mosaic Tile floors using conventional mortar method of installation (back-mounted tile).

	Hours	Rate	Total	Rate	Total
2 sacks portland cement		—	—	$ 5.69	$ 11.32
4 cu. ft. sand		—	—	.53	2.12
100 sq. ft. ceramic mosaic tile		—	—	1.69	169.00
25 lbs. dry tile grout mix		—	—	—	24.98
Tile setter	11.0	—	—	18.75	206.25
Cost per 100 sq. ft.	11.0		—		$413.67
Cost per sq. ft.				—	4.13

Cost of 100 sq. ft. of 1"x1" Ceramic Mosaic Tile floors using water resistant organic adhesive (back-mounted tile).

	Hours	Rate	Total	Rate	Total
2.5 gallons adhesive		—	—	$15.99	$ 39.98
100 sq. ft. ceramic mosaic tile		—	—	1.69	169.00
25 lbs. dry tile grout mix		—	—	—	24.98
Tile setter	8.0	—	—	18.75	150.00
Cost per 100 sq. ft.	8.0	—	—		$383.96
Cost per sq. ft				—	3.83

Cost of 100 sq. ft. of 1"x1" Ceramic Mosaic Tile floors using 'dry-set' portland cement mortar (back-mounted tile)

	Hours	Rate	Total	Rate	Total
35 lbs. 'dry-set' mortar mix	—	—	$ .32	$ 11.20
1 cu. ft. sand	—	—	—	.53

Courtesy Monarch Metal Products

Surface mounted medicine cabinet centered over double-bowl lavatory.

				Rate	Total
100 sq. ft. ceramic mosaic tile.............		—	—	1.69	169.00
25 lbs. dry tile grout mix		—	—	—	24.98
Tile setter...	9.5	—	—	18.75	178.12
Cost per 100 sq. ft...............................	9.5	—	—		$383.83
Cost per sq. ft......................................			—		3.83

Note: Add for cement floor fill or plastic underlayment when required.

Cost of 100 sq. ft. of 1"x1" Ceramic Mosaic Tile on walls using conventional mortar method of installation (face-mounted tile).

	Hours	Rate	Total	Rate	Total
2 sacks portland cement.......................		—	—	$ 5.66	$ 11.32
4 cu. ft. sand		—	—	.53	2.12
100 sq. ft. ceramic mosaic tile.............		—	—	1.69	169.00
25 lbs dry tile grout mix		—	—	—	24.98
Tile setter...	11.0	—	—	18.75	206.25

	Hours	Rate	Total	Rate	Total
Cost per 100 sq. ft.	11.0	—			$413.67
Cost per sq. ft.				—	4.13

Cost of 100 sq. ft. of 1"x1" Ceramic Mosaic Tile on walls using
water resistant organic adhesive (face-mounted tile).

	Hours	Rate	Total	Rate	Total
2.5 gallons adhesive	—		—	$15.99	$ 39.98
100 sq. ft. ceramic mosaic tile	—		—	1.69	169.00
25 lbs. dry tile grout mix	—		—		24.98
Tile setter	9.0	—		18.75	168.75
Cost per 100 sq. ft.	9.0			—	$402.68
Cost per sq. ft.				—	4.02

Cost of 100 sq. ft. of 1"x1" Ceramic Mosaic Tile on walls using
'dry-set' portland cement mortar (face-mounted tile).

	Hours	Rate	Total	Rate	Total
35 lbs. 'dry-set' mortar mix	—		—	$ .32	$ 11.20
1 cu. ft. sand	—		—	—	.53
100 sq. ft. ceramic mosaic tile	—		—	1.69	169.00
25 lbs. dry tile grout mix	—		—	—	24.98
Tile setter	9.0	—		18.75	168.75
Cost per 100 sq. ft.	9.0			—	$374.46
Cost per sq. ft.				—	3.74

Note: Add for plastering when specified.

Cost of 100 sq. ft. of 1"x1" Ceramic Tile on walls using
conventional mortar method of installation (back-mounted tile).

	Hours	Rate	Total	Rate	Total
2 sacks portland cement	—		—	$ 5.66	$ 11.32
4 cu. ft. sand	—		—	.53	2.12
100 sq. ft. ceramic mosaic tile	—		—	1.69	169.00
25 lbs. dry tile grout mix	—		—	—	24.98
Tile setter	10.5	—		18.75	196.88
Cost per 100 sq. ft.	10.5			—	$404.30
Cost per sq. ft.				—	4.04

Cost of 100 sq. ft. of 1"x1" Ceramic Mosaic Tile on walls using
water resistant organic adhesive (back-mounted tile).

	Hours	Rate	Total	Rate	Total
2.5 gallons adhesive	—		—	$15.99	$ 39.98
100 sq. ft. ceramic mosaic tile	—		—	1.69	169.00
25 lbs. dry tile grout mix	—		—	—	24.98
Tile setter	9.0	—		18.75	168.75
Cost per 100 sq. ft.	9.0			—	$402.68
Cost per sq. ft.				—	4.02

Cost of 100 sq. ft. of 1"x1" Ceramic Mosaic Tile on walls using
'dry-set' portland cement mortar (back-mounted tile).

	Hours	Rate	Total	Rate	Total
35 lbs. 'dry-set' mortar mix	—	—	$ .32	$ 11.20
1 cu. ft. sand	—	—	—	.53
100 sq. ft. ceramic mosaic tile.............	—	—	1.69	169.00
25 lbs. dry tile grout mix	—	—	—	24.98
Tile setter	9.0	—	—	18.75	168.75
Cost per 100 sq. ft................................	9.0		—		$374.46
Cost per sq. ft.....................................			—		3.74

Note: Add for plastering when specified.

Cost of 100 sq. ft. of 6"x6"x½" Quarry Tile floors using
conventional mortar method of installation

	Hours	Rate	Total	Rate	Total
2 sacks portland cement........................	—	—	$ 5.66	$ 11.32
6 cu. ft. sand	—	—	.53	3.18
100 sq. ft. quarry tile............................	—	—	1.56	156.00
35 lbs. portland cement grout.............	—	—	—	3.50
Tile setter	16.0	—	—	18.75	300.00
Cost per 100 sq. ft................................	16.0		—		$474.00
Cost per sq. ft.....................................			—		4.74

Cost of 100 sq. ft. of 6"x6"x½" Quarry Tile floors
using 'dry-set' portland cement mortar

	Hours	Rate	Total	Rate	Total
35 lbs. 'dry-set' mortar mix	—	—	$ .32	$ 11.20
2 cu. ft. of sand...................................	—	—	.53	1.06
100 sq. ft. quarry tile............................	—	—	1.56	156.00
35 lbs. portland cement grout.............	—	—	—	3.50
Tile setter	12.0	—	—	18.75	225.00
Cost per 100 sq. ft................................	12.0		—		$396.76
Cost per sq. ft.....................................			—		3.96

Placing Cement Floor Fill. Cement floor fill under ceramic tile floors is usually placed by tile setters and helpers, one tile setter and one or two helpers working together. The fill is placed one or two days in advance of the tile if the overall thickness from rough floor to finished tile surface is over 3". For 3" thickness and under, fill and setting bed may be placed in one operation. When such tile floors are to be placed over wood subfloors it is necessary to first place a layer of waterproof building paper and a layer of wire mesh reinforcing before placing the fill.

A tile setter and two helpers should place 450 to 500 sq. ft. of fill per 8-hour day in areas large enough to permit efficient operations, at the following cost per 100 sq. ft.

	Hours	Rate	Total	Rate	Total
6 bags portland cement........................	—	—	$ 5.66	$ 33.96
1 cu. yd. sand......................................	—	—	—	14.25
Tile setter	1.5	—	—	18.75	28.12

	Hours	Rate	Total	Rate	Total
Helper	3.0	—	—	15.72	47.16
Cost per 100 sq. ft...............................	4.5		—		$123.49
Cost per sq. ft.......................................			—		1.23

Labor Factors For Small Quantities

		Labor multiplier
Ceramic Mosaic Tile	Small rooms	1.75
	Countertops	3.00
Glazed Ceramic Wall Tile	Small rooms	1.50
	Mantel fronts	2.00
	Mantel front w/returns	1.90
Cove or Base	Small rooms	1.25
Cap	Small rooms	1.10

To estimate the cost of the smaller job, multiply the labor costs given in the applicable unit price development by the appropriate labor factor. Material costs do change.

CHAPTER 4

ROOM CONVERSIONS

Adding new rooms by converting existing, non-living space to living space represents one of the strongest growing marketing opportunities for the remodeling contractor.

Converting attics, garages and basements has already become a billion-dollar-plus segment of the remodeling market. As many contractors are learning, there are no geographical boundaries, it has become a national trend.

Before starting any such conversions, it is important that your local building codes be checked, since most cities require a building permit for any alteration to a home. There's also a trend taking place, which in a sense offers "add-on" profit opportunities. Today, many cities will not give out building permits when remodeling takes place, unless certain older services are brought up to current code standards. Included are plumbing, heating and electrical. So, although you may not have planned work in these areas, local codes may dictate otherwise.

It is also necessary that you plan the number of heating, plumbing and electrical outlets and add them to your estimate. Insulation is another area in which you should check the local building code, R-19 for walls and R-30 for ceilings may soon be the standard for all construction nationwide. And last, in attic conversions, you should recommend sound deadening to your customers. The room may be beautiful, but if all of the sounds from the room above penetrate the living space below, you won't have a happy client.

ATTICS

In many older homes, the attic represents the ideal place to add living space, since the area already exists. No exterior walls or roofing need to be considered. However, in newer homes where the roofing is of truss construction, such conversions may not be feasible.

Such additions can be as simple or as elaborate as a homeowner wishes, depending on their pocketbook and available space.

However, such things as adding stairways, additional heating, electrical and plumbing service are detailed in other chapters of this book. Therefore, if such options are being considered, you should review these chapters when making up an estimate.

Although many people add dormers for light, skylights are becoming increasingly popular. Louvers and other types of vents or fans should be added for proper ventilation.

Some homes may have sufficient head room while others will require dormers to provide sufficient head space. In still others, the attic can simply be left open and finished off for a cathedral ceiling effect. The possibilities are practically limitless.

The first thing to consider is the flooring. In many older homes the ceiling joists are 2 x 6's which are inadequate for supporting a floor in an area that is to be used for living space. Building codes usually require a live floor design capable of handling 30 lbs. per sq. in.

This problem can usually be remedied in two ways. One is to simply double existing joists. The other is to cut and install 2" x 4" solid bridging, 24" o.c. to distribute the load. The blocks should be staggered for easy nailing. See illustration.

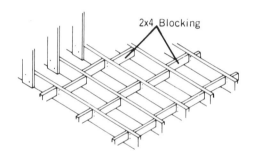

For extra support, add 2 x 4 blocks 24" o.c.

Figure one carpenter can cut and install 24 lin. ft. of blocks per hour at the following cost per linear foot:

	Hours	Rate	Total	Rate	Total
Carpenter...	.042	—	—	$20.60	$0.87
Cost per ln. ft.			—		$0.87

Ideally, the recommended sub-floor for attics is 4' x 8' x ¾" plywood panels. The panels should be laid across the joists, using 8 penny nails, nailed about every 6" along the outside edge and about every 8" along the joists. The butt end of all panels should meet exactly on the joist; however, the joints should be staggered so that the butt ends of all panels do not meet on the same joist. To estimate and finish flooring, see Chapter 6 "Flooring."

Installing New Windows. When installing new windows at gable ends, double 2 x 4's or 2 x 6's can be stood on an edge for the header, depending on the size of the opening.

For the sill, a 2 x 4 laid flat is adequate. Use 16 penny nails to nail through the studs into the header. Add additional 2 x 4 bracing below the window sill to support the additional weight of the new window. See illustration below. For additional information and estimating, see the Chapter on "Windows" page 289.

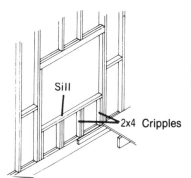

Sill

2x4 Cripples

Double 2 x 4's under windowsill for additional support.

Installing Skylights.   A popular skylight size is 32" x 32". To cut the opening for this size means cutting only one common rafter. Add braces to the rafter above and below the rafter being cut to support the roof. The shingles above the opening should be carefully removed to avoid damage to the roof and adjacent shingles. Cut hole in roof to accommodate the size of the skylight to be installed.

For a 32" x 32" skylight, frame the opening on the roof using 2 x 6's with the inside dimension of the framing measuring 30-⅜" x 30-⅜". Hold the frame square by nailing 1 x 3 blocks in each corner. Place the frame over the opening and mark a chalk line around the outside perimeter on the roof. Cut all shingles along the chalk line about 1-⅝" back from the edge of the opening. Temporarily loosen all shingles within 4" of the cut opening.

Cut and bend four strips of aluminum flashing to form the flange around the curb frame.

For a 32" x 32" skylight the flashing should be cut 9" x 39" and folded so that it covers the top and side of the frame and extends 3" onto the roof. The corners should be cut and bent as shown above. Apply roofing cement or sealant between the flashing, the roofing paper and the shingles. A layer of sealant between the flashing and the top of the curb also helps prevent leaks.

Toenail the frame on the inside into the rafters using 8 penny nails. Nail the flashing to the frame and the roof with 16 penny common nails. The skylight can now be fastened into position.

Figure one carpenter can complete the preceeding framing in 5 hours. To install the skylight itself, add 2 hours to the previous labor time.

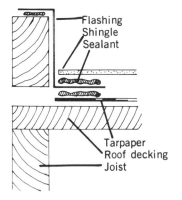

Caulk at key points with a good sealant to keep roof and skylight watertight.

Installing Walls, Partitions and Ceilings.   Before the partitions or ceilings are started, it is customary to frame the walls. Wall height can be 4' or 5' depending on the wishes of the homeowner.

A plumb bob is used to snap a chalk line from the rafter to the floor at the proper height to determine the position of the sole plate. Use a 2 x 4 for the sole plate and secure to the floor using 16 penny common nails. Nail 2 x 3 or 2 x 4 studs to each rafter and the sole plate at the desired room height. Check studs with a level to be sure they are plumb in all directions. To provide a nailing surface for the wall material, nail blocking between rafters at the top of the knee wall.

If the area behind the wall is to be used for storage, use a 2 x 4 for the header over the door opening which provides access to the storage area.

Ceiling joists can now be nailed to opposite rafters to frame the ceiling. These can be 7½' to 8' above the floor.

If a dividing wall is desired, it can be anchored to the ceiling joist and placed at any position in the attic. Similarly, a partition wall can also be placed in any position. Both are constructed by placing a sole plate in the proper location and framing out the wall by placing studs 16" o.c.

Figure one carpenter can frame 500 lin. ft. of wall and ceiling per day at the following cost per lin. ft.:

	Hours	Rate	Total	Rate	Total
Carpenter	.016	—	—	$20.60	$0.33
Cost per lin. ft.			—		$0.33

For wall and ceiling finishing, see Chapter 7, page 109.

To Add a Dormer.   Gabled Dormers: Gabled dormers are the most difficult to install since they involve the placement of valley rafters and constructed so that the pitch of the dormer roof is different than the main roof. Dormers with side walls should be positioned so that the side walls are located over roof rafters on both sides. These rafters are doubled to support the exterior studs and valley rafter.

The valley rafters are tied into a header which in turn is tied into the ridge with jack rafters. The dormer is then completed with conventional framing.

Care should be taken to provide proper flashing where the dormer walls intersect the roof.

Material Requirements To Add A Gabled Dormer

(Roofing, Siding, Painting and Interior Finishes Not Included)

Materials and Size		Width of Dormer				
		5'	6'	8'	10'	12'
Rafter Headers	2" x 6"	2–10'	2–12'	2–16'	4–10'	4–12'
Rafter Plates	2" x 6"	2–16'	2–16'	2–16'	2–16'	2–16'
Studs and Plates						
Side	2" x 4"	2–10'	2–10'	2–10'	2–10'	2–10'
Side	2" x 4"	2–12'	2–12'	2–12'	2–12'	2–12'
Front	2" x 4"	7–10'	8–10'	11–10'	13–10'	11–12'
Gable	2" x 4"	1–12'	1–12'	3–10'	2–10'	2–12'
Gable	2" x 4"	1–8'	1–8'	1–10'	1–14'	1–14'
Rafters	2" x 4"	6–8'	6–10'	6–12'	6–12'	6–14'
Ridge Boards	1" x 6"	1–10'	1–10'	1–10'	1–10'	1–10'
Framing						
Total BM		179BM	200BM	237BM	264BM	283BM
Sheathing	1" x 6"	60BM	70BM	70BM	85BM	80BM
Roof Boards	1" x 6"	60BM	72BM	86BM	100BM	120BM
Cornice Fascia	1" x 6"	22 lin. ft.	24 lin. ft.	26 lin. ft.	28 lin. ft	30 lin. ft.
Crown Mold	1" x 3"	22 " "	24 " "	26 " "	28 " "	30 " "
Nails		10 lb.	11 lb.	12 lb.	13 lb.	14 lb.
Flashing	12" wide	33 lin. ft.	35 lin. ft.	39 lin. ft.	42 lin. ft.	46 lin. ft.
Felt	30 lb.	1 Rl.	1 Rl.	1 Rl.	1 Rl.	2 Rl.
Window Frame	2/6x4/10	1	1	2	2	3
Window Sash	2/6x4/10	1	1	2	2	3
Labor to install		26 hrs.	27 hrs.	32 hrs.	36 hrs.	40 hrs.

Gabled Dormer Roof and Side Areas for ½ Pitch Roofs

	5' Width	6' Width	8' Width	10' Width	12' Width
Roof	60 sq. ft.	72 sq. ft.	86 sq. ft.	100 sq. ft.	120 sq. ft.
Wall	60 sq. ft.	70 sq. ft.	70 sq. ft.	85 sq. ft.	80 sq. ft.
Starter	10 lin. ft.	10 lin. ft.	10 lin. ft.	10 lin. ft.	10 lin. ft.
Ridge	12 lin. ft.	12 lin. ft.	12 lin. ft.	12 lin. ft.	12 lin. ft.

Shed Dormers. Shed dormers are much simpler to construct and are tied directly to the ridge. Side walls are also finished off using conventional framing procedures. The common rafters supporting the outer walls should be doubled the same as for gabled dormers.

To Estimate Shed Dormers: Figure two carpenters are required to complete the following:

Dormer Width	Labor	Cost Per Lin. Ft. (Including Materials)
10 ft.	4 days	$120.00 lin. ft.
16 ft.	6 days	100.00 lin. ft.
20 ft.	7 days	95.00 lin. ft.
24 ft.	8 days	90.00 lin. ft.

The above includes:
1. 2 x 4 studs, 16" o.c.
2. ½" gypsum sheathing
3. Aluminum siding
4. S.I.S. roofing
5. One window for each 10' of exterior linear wall.

For additional windows, add $75.00. (Includes window and labor.)

For insulated siding over 1" x 4" wood stripping over gypsum, add $75.00 per square to install furring strips.

To determine siding costs for the wall areas of dormers, use the following table: (Windows areas have already been deducted).

Side Wall Area for Dormers

		Type of Dormer	
Dormer Width	Lift Type	Gable Type	Hip Type
5'-0" (One Window)	88 sq. ft.	60	52
6'-0"	94	70	58
7'-0"	100	80	64
8'-0" (Two Windows)	88	70	52
9'-0"	94	75	58
10'-0"	100	85	64
11'-0"	106	90	70
12'-0" (Three Windows)	93	80	57

Add the net square feet of each elevation, gable and dormer together, add 8% for waste and figure to the nearest larger half or full square or nearest bundle of shingles for material costs.

Old siding may be stripped off before new is applied, or may be covered over either by applying an underlayment board or by applying wood stripping and felt over present siding. Underlayment board would figure the same quantity as siding. Wood stripping can be figured per square, depending on the exposure of existing siding, as follows:

Exposure in inches...........................	4"	4½"	5"	5½"	6"	6½"	8"
Lin. ft. of Stripping required	300	280	240	224	200	188	152

For corners, use full height for metal corners. For corner boards, figure one 4" and one 6" board for each corner. Add molding, flashing and caulking costs at doors and windows.

Labor Per Square, Shingles and Clapboards
Applied with Wood Stripping*

Size	Type	No. of Pcs./Sq.	Carpenter Hours
12" x 24"	Shingle	57	2.66
8" x 24"	Shingle	93	3.5
9½" x 8'	Clapboard	19	2.66

*See Chapter 12.

Basements. When it comes to converting basements into family or recreation rooms, the biggest problem you will probably run into is moisture. Sometimes a dehumidifier can reduce this problem; but, a waterproof seal is recommended before remodeling.

There are a number of waterproof coatings available which will help alleviate this problem with walls. The coverage rate of several different types are given in the Tables that follow. The rates were furnished by the various manufacturers. Note that some manufacturers specify one coat and some two. Regardless of the material used, sufficient material must be applied to completely seal the pores of the surface, otherwise results will be unsatisfactory.

Cost of 100 Sq. Ft. Liquid Water Repellents

Transparent liquids used for dampproofing brick, stone, stucco, concrete and cement surfaces without changing the color of the surface treated.

Name of Material	No. Coats	Sq. Ft. per Gal.	Gals. Reqd. 100 Sq. Ft.	Price per Gal.	Labor Hrs. Applying
Daracone	1	75-100	1¼	$11.00	1.6
Supertox	1	125-150	¾	9.80	0.8
Tremco 141 Invisible	2	75-100	1¼	9.25	1.6

Silicone Base Water Repellents. These water repellents permit the masonry to "breathe" while rendering the surface water repellent. They penetrate deeply into the cement or masonry surfaces, coating pores, cracks, and fissures with an insoluable, non-oxidizing film of silicone which effectively stops the capillary action by which the water is being absorbed.

The covering capacities and quantities in the following table were furnished by the manufacturers.

Cost of 100 Sq. Ft. Silicone Base, Transparent Liquid Water Repellents

Name of Material	No. Coats	Sq. Ft. per Gal.	Gals. Reqd. 100 Sq. Ft.	Labor Hrs. Applying
Dehydratine 22	1	75-100	1 1/4	0.8
Hydrocide Colorless SX	1	75-100	1	0.8
Sika Transparent	1	80-200	2/3	0.8
Tremco 147-3%	1	100-200	2/3	0.8
Tremco 147-5%	1	100-200	2/3	0.8
Devoe Super-Por-Seal	1	150	2/3	0.8

Labor Applying Transparent Liquid Waterproofing. When applying transparent liquid waterproofing by hand, a man should be able to cover 900 to 1100 sq. ft. per 8-hr. day at the following labor cost per sq. ft.:

	Hours	Rate	Total	Rate	Total
Applicator	.008	—	—	$15.67	$0.13
Cost per sq. ft.			—		$0.13

On the second and third coats, a man should apply 1000 to 1200 sq. ft. per 8-hr. day at the following labor cost per sq. ft.

	Hours	Rate	Total	Rate	Total
Applicator	.007	—	—	$15.67	$0.11
Cost per sq. ft.			—		$0.11

If the concrete slab floor is in good condition and dry, several different types of flooring, such as various tile or carpeting can be applied directly to the floor by following the manufacturer's recommended application procedure.

If the flooring is damp, then some type of dampproofing should be applied. A good vapor barrier is probably the best solution. One method is to follow the procedure for applying strip flooring over concrete outlined in Chapter 6, page 93. Another is to apply a mastic followed by a vapor barrier. Generally, treated plywood panels are laid over the sleepers for the subfloor and the finish flooring is applied according to manufacturer's recommendations.

Placing Wood Floor Sleepers. When placing 2 x 3 or 2 x 4 wood floor screeds or sleepers over concrete floors to receive finish flooring, a carpenter should place to 225 to 275 lin. ft. per 8-hr. day at the following labor cost per lin. ft.:

	Hours	Rate	Total	Rate	Total
Carpenter	.032	—	—	$20.60	$0.66
Labor	.008	—	—	15.67	0.13
Cost per lin. ft.			—		$0.79

For "first grade workmanship" 2 x 3 or 2 x 4 beveled floor sleepers are placed over the rough concrete floors and wedged or blocked up to provide a perfectly level surface to receive the finish flooring. The screeds are usually held in place by metal clips placed in the rough concrete or anchored with special concrete nails or fasteners.

For this type of work, a carpenter should be able to place, wedge and level 130 to 170 lin. ft. of sleepers per 8-hr. day at the following cost per lin. ft.:

	Hours	Rate	Total	Rate	Total
Carpenter	.053	—	—	$20.60	$1.09
Labor	.008	—	—	15.67	0.13
Cost per lin. ft.	.061		—		$1.22

Walls.   To finish walls, 2 x 2 furring strips are nailed to the wall 16" o.c. These are fastened at the bottom and top to 2 x 2 sole and top plates. If dampproofing was required, the 2 x 2's should be treated to prevent decay due to moisture. Nail, using standard masonry nails, 24" apart.

Another option is to build as a standard wall using 2" x 4" studs. This method provides space for wiring, plumbing and heating as desired. Also no nails or anchors are placed into the walls as the top plate is fastened to the floor joists and sole plate to the floor.

Placing Wood Furring Strips on Masonry Walls.   If the walls are straight and plumb, a carpenter should be able to place 500–550 lin. ft. of furring strips per 8-hr. day at the following cost per lin. ft.:

	Hours	Rate	Total	Rate	Total
Carpenter	.015	—	—	$20.60	$0.31
Cost per lin. ft.			—		$0.31

For "first grade workmanship" where it is necessary to plug the masonry wall and place all furring strips straight and plumb, a carpenter should place 200–250 lin. ft. of strips per 8-hr. day at the following cost per lin. ft.:

	Hours	Rate	Total	Rate	Total
Carpenter	.036	—	—	$20.60	$0.74
Cost per lin. ft.			—		$0.74

Insulation.   Fiber Glass or Rock Wool Batts. Insulation should be placed with the vapor barrier toward the warm side of the wall in winter. Faced insulation can be stapled by "Inset" or "Face" Stapling. A carpenter should be able to insulate 2500 sq. ft. of walls per 8-hr. day at the following labor cost per sq. ft.:

	Hours	Rate	Total	Rate	Total
Carpenter..	.0032	—	—	$20.60	$164.80
Cost per sq. ft.			—		$ 0.07

The walls are now ready for finishing. See Chapters 7 and 8. The most economical and efficient ceiling are those covered with ceiling tile or suspended ceilings using suspended ceiling grid metal. Not only are they attractive and simple to install, the allow easy access to electrical and plumbing lines if repairs are required. For ceiling treatments, see Chapter 7, page 123.

Studs

2" x 4" – 8' (economy grade, 92-⅝")...$	0.99 ea.
2" x 4" – 8' (top-quality, kiln-dried)...	1.49 ea.
2" x 4" – 7' (construction)	1.19 ea.

2 x 4 Construction

10' – 16' ($0.22 ft.)	330.00 M
18' – 20' (0.28 ft.)	420.00 M
22' – 24' (0.34 ft.)	510.00 M

2 x 6 Construction

8' – 16' ($0.33 ft.)	330.00 M
18' – 20' (0.42 ft.)	420.00 M
22' – 24' (0.51 ft.)	510.00 M

2 x 8 Construction

8' – 16' ($0.48 ft.)	360.00 M
18' – 20' (0.56 ft.)	420.00 M
22' – 24' (0.68 ft.)	510.00 M

2 x 10 Construction

8' – 16' ($0.65 ft.)	390.00 M
10' – 20' (0.70 ft.)	420.00 M
22' – 24' (0.85 ft.)	510.00 M

2 x 12 Construction

8' – 16' ($0.84 ft.)	420.00 M
18' – 20' (0.90 ft.)	450.00 M
22' – 24' ($1.20 ft.)	600.00 M

4 x 4 Construction

8' – 20' ($0.56 ft.)	420.00 M

Sanded Trim Boards (Select)

'D' Pine*		'D' Pine*		#1 + #2 Pine*	
1 x 2	$0.32	½ x 2	$0.43	5/4 x 2	$0.32
1 x 3	.47	½ x 3	.64	5/4 x 3	.48
1 x 4	.60	½ x 4	.85	5/4 x 4	.63
1 x 6	.90	½ x 6	1.28	5/4 x 6	.95
1 x 8	1.20	½ x 8	1.70	5/4 x 8	1.25
1 x 10	1.50	½ x 10	2.15	5/4 x 10	1.60
1 x 12	1.80	½ x 12	2.55	5/4 x 12	1.90

*per linear foot.

Plywood

Sanded Plywood

4' x 8' Sheets - Exterior Glue

Good One-Side	Ft.	Sheet
¼ AC/BC	$0.32	$10.24
⅜ AC/BC	.45	14.40
½ AC/BC	.52	16.64
¾ AC/BC	.67	21.44

Sheathing Plywood

4' x 8' Sheets - Exterior Glue

Rough Two-Sides	Ft.	Sheet
⅜ CDX	$0.27	$ 8.64
½ CDX (4-ply pine)	.30	9.60
⅝ CDX	.41	13.12
¾ CDX	.48	15.36

Hardboard Masonite

4' x 8' Sheets

Standard		Oil Treated	
⅛ "	$4.79 ea.	⅛ "	$5.99 ea.
¼ "	6.79 ea.	¼ "	7.99 ea.

Another option to gain more room is to convert an attached garage to living space. There are two things to check and correct that are usually found when converting garages. First, most garage floors are sloped to the door to provide for drainage. Consequently, when putting in the new floor, the sleepers should be shimmed up so that flooring is level throughout. This procedure is described on Page 51.

Second, usually there are no foundations under the door area. Since this area will probably be framed in and enclosed, it will have to be dug out and a new foundation and footings poured extending to the existing side foundations. See "Room Additions", next page, to estimate.

If building codes permit, the electrical service can be installed below the flooring, permitting the contractor to offer the homeowner a savings in labor and materials.

Since most slabs are on grade, they should be insulated around the perimeter and underneath the flooring. Insulation should also be installed in the walls and ceiling.

Perimeter Insulation. This can be accomplished by digging out around the foundation down to the depth of the footing. When used as recommended, expanded polystyrene qualifies for slab-on grade perimeter insulation. To meet HUD Minimum Property Standards, the following thicknesses of expanded polystyrene are recommended:

Unheated Slabs		Heated Slabs	
Winter degree days	EPS thickness	Winter degree days	EPS thickness
4000 or less	1"	2000 or less	1"
4001 to 8000	1½"	2001 to 3000	1¼"
8001 or more	2"	3001 to 5000	1½"
		5001 to 8000	2"
		8001 or more	2½"

To comply with FHA moisture protection requirements, use a vapor barrier rated at one perm or less. In most cases, since no attachment other than backfill is required, a man should be able to place approximately 3200 sq. ft. of expanded polystyrene board stock per 8-hr. day at the following labor cost per 100 sq. ft.:

	Hours	Rate	Total	Rate	Total
Carpenter..	.25	—	—	$20.60	$5.15
Cost per sq. ft..			—		0.05

Labor To Insulate Walls and Floors.   For most applications, fiber glass or mineral wool batts and blankets are used. They are supplied in three forms: foil-faced, kraft paper-faced and unfaced. Where the materials are faced, the facings act as a vapor barrier. Unfaced material requires a separate vapor barrier. For the actual perm rating of unfaced material check the manufacturer's literature. On faced material, the facing extends beyond the insulation to form a stapling flange. Unfaced material is friction fit. Both fiber glass and mineral wool are applied in the same manner. Mineral wool, because it is stiffer, takes a little bit longer to install. On slab floors, such as garages, the insulation is simply placed between the sleepers with the vapor barrier to the warm side. An experienced carpenter should be able to staple and fit 2000 to 3000 sq. ft. of insulation per 8-hr. day at the following labor cost per 100 sq. ft.:

	Hours	Rate	Total	Rate	Total
Carpenter..	.32	—	—	$20.60	$6.59
Cost per sq. ft..			—		0.06

To Insulate Ceilings.   An experienced carpenter should be able to staple and fit 1000 to 1800 sq. ft. of insulation per 8-hr. day at the following labor cost per sq. ft:

	Hours	Rate	Total	Rate	Total
Carpenter..	.006	—	—	$20.60	$0.12
Cost per sq. ft..			—		0.12

The doorway can be enclosed by using regular 2" x 4" studs. To figure see "Room Additions" in this chapter and Chapter 14 "Windows and Doors".

To install windows and doors and electrical service, see Chapters 14 and 10.

For additional information on insulating you may want to obtain a copy of Walker's "Insulating Estimator's Handbook".

Room Additions.   Room additions are basically new construction. The biggest problem occurs in matching the siding and roofing. Another problem in adding a room to either end of the house, is does sufficient property exist to permit the addition and still meet local zoning regulations?

For those reasons, more often than not, new rooms are added at right angles to the back of the house.

Placement of a new room, at either end or the center, etc., is frequently dictated by placement of the entry way. Two other things to consider are plumbing and electrical. How far away is the water supply for any new fixtures and how far away is the wastepipe into which it will drain. The same applies to electrical. Is there a box nearby or does a new one have to be installed? By carefully figuring these installations, a lot of headaches and costs can be avoided.

Courtesy Superior Fireplace Company

Fireplaces are popular with room additions. This innovative unit functions both as a conventional fireplace, or close the doors and adjust the dampers and it becomes a wood-burning stove.

Generally, most room additions are placed on concrete slabs. Whether footings are required will depend on local codes. Figure a 20' x 20' slab as follows: Generally, forming below grade for the foundation is not necessary. The foundation will require a trench 6" wide by 42" deep. Figure 1 laborer using a power trencher will dig 45-50 lin. ft. per hour.

	Hours	Rate	Total	Rate	Total
Laborer..	.021	—	—	$16.67	$0.35
Cost per lin. ft			—		0.35

In forming for the slab, figure 1 carpenter can set forms using stakes 3 ft. to 4 ft. apart at approximately 40 lin. ft. per hour:

	Hours	Rate	Total	Rate	Total
Carpenter..	.025	—	—	$20.60	$0.52
Cost per lin. ft			—		0.52

For fill below the slab, 1 laborer should be able to tamp and level 20' x 20' in one hour.

To place reinforcing, using 6" mesh, add ½-hr. to the above. To the above, add for dirt removal and trucking, if required.

For finishing reinforced concrete, the average will vary from 70 to 80 sq. ft. per hour or 560 to 640 sq. ft. per hour 8-hr-day at the following labor cost per 100 sq. ft.:

	Hours	Rate	Total	Rate	Total
Cement Mason..	1.3	—	—	$19.91	$25.88
Laborer..	1.3	—	—	16.67	21.67
Cost per 100 sq. ft................................			—		$47.55
Cost per sq. ft....................................			—		0.48

Labor To Frame Walls

Material	Size	b.f./lin. ft. per hr.
Partition Studs		50 b.f.
Partition Plates and Shoe.....		50 b.f.
Wall Backing...........................		50 b.f.
Grounds		85 lin.ft.
Knee Wall Plates....................	2"x4"	40 b.f.
	2"x6"	40 b.f.
Knee Wall Studs	2"x4"	40 b.f.
	2"x6"	50 b.f.
Outside Studs	2"x4"	40 b.f.
	2"x6"	50 b.f.

Outside Wall	2"x4"	40 b.f.
Plates and Shoe	2"x6"	50 b.f.
Headers .... {	2"x4"	40 b.f.
	2"x6"	50 b.f.
Gable-end Studs		50 b.f.
Fire Stops		50 b.f.
Corner Braces		50 b.f.

Labor To Apply Sheathing

Material	Size	Application Rate
Wood (horizontal application)	1"x6"	65 bd. ft./hr.
	1"x8"	70 bd. ft./hr.
	1"x10"	75 bd. ft./hr.
Gypsum Board	48"x96"	100 sq. ft/2.2 hrs.
Plywood	48"x96"	100 sq. ft/2.2 hrs.

Material And Labor To Install Ceiling Joists

Joist Size	b.f. Req'd 100 sq. ft.				Nails (lbs. per 1000 b.f.)	Labor b.f. per hr.
	12"o.c.	16"o.c.	20"o.c.	24"o.c.		
2"x4"	78	59	48	42	19	60
2"x6"	115	88	72	63	13	65
2"x8"	153	117	96	84	9	65
2"x10"	194	147	121	104	7	70
2"x12"	230	176	144	126	6	70

ESTIMATING LUMBER QUANTITIES

When estimating the quantity of lumber required for any job, the only safe method is to take off every piece of lumber required to complete that portion of the work. The following tables are given to simplify the work as much as possible and at the same time provide accurate material quantities:

Estimating Wood Joists. When estimating wood joists, always allow 4" to 6" on each end of the joist for bearing on the wall.

To obtain the number of joists required for any floor, take the length of the floor in feet, multiply the distance the joists are spaced and add 1 to allow for the extra joist required at end of span.

Example: If the floor is 28 ft. long and 15 ft. wide, it will require 16-ft. joists to allow for wall bearing at each end. Assuming the joists are spaced 16" on centers, one joist will be required every 16" or every 1 1/3 ft. In other words it will require 3/4 as many joists as the length of the span plus 1. To determine spacing factor divide 12 by the oc spacing. In this case 12/16=.75. Now, 28 times .75=21, plus 1 extra joist at end, makes 22 joists 16 ft. long for this span.

The following table gives the number of joists required for any spacing:

Number of Wood Floor Joists Required for any Spacing

Distance Joists are Placed on Centers	Multiply Length of Floor Span by	Add Joists	Distance Joists are Placed on Centers	Multiply Length of Floor Span by	Add Joists
12 inches	1	1	36 inches	1/3 or .33	1
16 inches	3/4 or .75	1	42 inches	2/7 or .29	1
20 inches	3/5 or .60	1	48 inches	1/4 or .25	1
24 inches	1/2 or .50	1	54 inches	2/9 or .22	1
30 inches	2/5 or .40	1	60 inches	1/5 or .20	1

Number of Feet of Lumber B.M. Required per 100 Sq. Ft. of Surface When Used for Studs, Joists, Rafters, Wall and Floor Furring Strips, etc.

The following table does not include any allowance for waste in cutting, doubling joists under partitions or around stair wells, extra joists at end of each span, top or bottom plates, etc. These items vary with each job. Add as required.

Size of Lumber	12-Inch Centers	16-Inch Centers	20-Inch Centers	24-Inch Centers
1"x2"	16⅔	12½	10	8⅓
2"x2"	33⅓	25	20	16⅔
2"x4"	66⅔	50	40	33⅓
2"x5"	83⅓	62½	50	41⅔
2"x6"	100	75	60	50
2"x8"	133⅓	100	80	66⅔
2"x10"	166⅔	125	100	83⅓
2"x12"	200	150	120	100
2"x14"	233⅓	175	140	116⅔
3"x6"	150	112½	90	75
3"x8"	200	133⅓	120	100
3"x10"	250	187½	150	125
3"x12"	300	225	180	150
3"x14"	350	262½	210	175

Number of Wood Joists Required for any Floor and Spacing

Length of Floor	Spacing of Joists									
	12"	16"	20"	24"	30"	36"	42"	48"	54"	60"
6	7	6	5	4	3	3	3	3	2	2
7	8	6	5	5	4	4	3	3	3	2
8	9	7	6	5	4	4	3	3	3	3

9	10	8	6	6	5	4	4	3	3	3
10	11	9	7	6	5	4	4	4	3	3
11	12	9	8	7	5	5	4	4	3	3
12	13	10	8	7	6	5	4	4	4	3
13	14	11	9	8	6	5	5	4	4	4
14	15	12	9	8	7	6	5	5	4	4
15	16	12	10	9	7	6	5	5	4	4
16	17	13	11	9	7	6	6	5	5	4
17	18	14	11	10	8	7	6	5	5	4
18	19	15	12	10	8	7	6	6	5	4
19	20	15	12	11	9	7	6	6	5	5
20	21	16	13	11	9	8	7	6	5	5
21	22	17	14	12	9	8	7	6	6	5
22	23	18	14	12	10	8	7	7	6	5
23	24	18	15	13	10	9	8	7	6	6
24	25	19	15	13	11	9	8	7	6	6
25	26	20	16	14	11	9	8	7	7	6
26	27	21	17	14	11	10	8	8	7	6
27	28	21	17	15	12	10	9	8	7	6
28	29	22	18	15	12	10	9	8	7	7
29	30	23	18	16	13	11	9	8	7	7
30	31	24	19	16	13	11	10	9	8	7
31	32	24	20	17	13	11	10	9	8	7
32	33	25	20	17	14	12	10	9	8	7
33	34	26	21	18	14	12	10	9	8	8
34	35	27	21	18	15	12	11	10	9	8
35	36	27	22	19	15	13	11	10	9	8
36	37	28	23	19	15	13	11	10	9	8
37	38	29	23	20	16	13	12	10	9	8
38	39	30	24	20	16	14	12	11	9	9
39	40	30	24	21	17	14	12	11	10	9
40	41	31	25	21	17	14	12	11	10	9

One joist has been added to each of the above quantities to take care of extra joist required at end of span.

Add for doubling joists under all partitions.

Estimating Quantity of Bridging. It is customary to place a double row of bridging between joists about 6'-0" to 8'-0" on centers. Joists 10'-0" to 12'-0" long will require one double row of bridging or 2 pcs. to each joists.

Joists 14'-0" to 20'-0" long will require 2 double rows of bridging or 4 pcs. to each joist.

Bridging is usually cut from 1"x3", 1"x4", 2"x2", or 2"x4" lumber.

The following table gives the approximate number of pcs. and the lin. ft. of bridging required per 100 sq. ft. of floor.

Joists Up to 12 Feet Long				Joists Up to 20 Feet Long			
12-Inch Centers		16-Inch Centers		12-Inch Centers		16-Inch Centers	
No. Pcs.	Lin. Ft.	No. Pcs.	Lin. Ft.	No. Pcs.	Lin. Ft.	No. Pcs.	Lin. Ft.
20	30	16	24	40	60	32	48

Estimating Number of Wood Studs. When estimating the number of wood partition studs, take the length of each partition and the total length of all partitions.

If a top and bottom plate is required, take the length of the wood partition and multiply by 2. The result will be the number of lin. ft. of plates required.

If a double plate consisting of 2 top members and a single bottom plate is used, multiply the length of the wood partitions by 3.

Example: Find the quantity of lumber required to build a stud partition 16'-0" long, 8'-0" high, with studs spaced 16" on centers and having single top and bottom plates. 16'-0"=192". 192" ÷ 16"=12 studs, plus 1 extra at the end equals 13 studs 8'-0" long. Two top and bottom plates 16'-0" long equal 32 lin. ft.

$$13 \text{ pcs. } 2x4 @ \ 8'\text{-}0 = 104$$
$$13 \text{ pcs. } 2x4 @ 16'\text{-}0 = \ \underline{\ 32}$$
$$\text{Total} = 136 \text{ lin. ft.}$$
$$136 \text{ lin. ft.} \times 2/3 = 90.67 \text{ bd. ft.}$$

After the total number of lin. ft. of lumber has been obtained, reduce to board measure, as above.

Feet of Lumber, B.M. Required for Wood Stud Partitions

2"x4" studs 16" on centers, with single top and bottom plates.

Length of Partition	Height of Partition				
	8'0"	8'-6"	9'-0"	10'-0"	12'-0"
3'-0"	20	22	22	24	28
4'-0"	27	29	29	32	37
5'-0"	33	37	37	40	47
6'-0"	40	44	44	48	56
7'-0"	41	45	45	49	57
8'-0"	48	53	53	57	67
9'-0"	55	60	60	65	76
10'-0"	61	67	67	73	85
11'-0"	63	69	69	75	87
12'-0"	69	76	76	83	96
13'-0"	76	83	83	91	105
14'-0"	83	91	91	99	115
15'-0"	84	92	92	100	116
16'-0"	91	99	99	108	125
17'-0"	97	107	107	116	135
18'-0"	104	114	114	124	144
19'-0"	105	115	115	125	145
20'-0"	112	123	123	133	155
21'-0"	119	130	130	141	164
22'-0"	125	137	137	149	173
23'-0"	127	139	139	151	175

Courtesy Rolscreen Corporation

This Sunroom addition provides extra living space and serves as a supplementary heat source due to passive solar design. This unit incorporates Pella aluminum-clad Casement windows for ventilation and the Pella Contemporary French Sliding Door for access to outdoors. The Pella Slimshade, a built-in narrow-slat blind, shown, blocks sun if desired.

Length of Partition	Height of Partition				
	8'0"	8'-6"	9'-0"	10'-0"	12'-0"
24'-0"	133	146	146	159	184
25'-0"	140	153	153	167	193
26'-0"	147	161	161	175	203
27'-0"	148	162	162	176	204
28'-0"	155	169	169	184	213
29'-0"	161	177	177	192	223
30'-0"	168	184	184	200	232
31'-0"	169	185	185	201	233
32'-0"	176	193	193	209	243
33'-0"	183	200	200	217	252
34'-0"	189	207	207	225	261
35'-0"	191	209	209	227	263
36'-0"	197	216	216	235	272
37'-0"	204	223	223	243	281
38'-0"	211	231	231	251	291
39'-0"	212	232	232	252	292
40'-0"	219	239	239	260	301

Add 2/3 ft. of lumber, b.m. for each lin. ft. of double top or bottom plate.

Number of Partition Studs Required for Any Spacing

Distance O.C. Spacing	Multiply Length of Partition by	Add Wood Studs
12 inches	1.0	1
16 inches	0.75	1
20 inches	0.60	1
24 inches	0.50	1

Add for top and bottom plates.

Number of Feet of Lumber Required Per Sq. Ft. of Wood Stud Partition Using 2"x4" Studs.

Studs spaced 16" on centers, with single top and bottom plates.

Length Partition In Feet	No. Studs Req'd	Ceiling Heights in Feet			
		8'-0"	9'-0"	10'-0"	12'-0"
2	3	1.25	1.167	1.13	1.13
3	3	0.833	.812	.80	.80
4	4	0.833	.812	.80	.80
5	5	0.833	.812	.80	.80
6	6	0.833	.812	.80	.80
7	6	0.833	.75	.75	.80
8	7	0.75	.75	.75	.70
9	8	0.75	.75	.75	.70
10	9	0.75	.75	.75	.70
11	9	0.75	.70	.70	.67
12	10	0.75	.70	.70	.67
13	11	0.75	.70	.70	.67
14	12	0.75	.70	.70	.67
15	12	0.70	.70	.70	.67

16	13	0.70	.70	.70	.67
17	14	0.70	.70	.70	.67
18	15	0.70	.70	.67	.67
19	15	0.70	.70	.67	.67
20	16	0.70	.70	.67	.67
For dbl. plate, add per sq. ft.		0.13	.11	.10	.083

For 2"x8" studs, double above quantities.

For 2"x6" studs, increase above quantities 50%.

Example: Find the number of feet of lumber, b.m. required for a stud partition 18'-0" long and 9'-0" high. This partition would contain 18x9=162 sq. ft.

The table gives 0.70 ft. of lumber, b.m. per sq. ft. of partition. Multiply 162 by 0.70 equals 113.4 ft. b.m.

Quantity of Plain End Softwood Flooring Required Per 100 Sq. Ft. of Floor

Measured Size Inches	Actual Size Inches	Add for Width	Ft. B.M. Req. per 100 Sq. Ft. Surface	Weight per 1000 Ft.
1x3	¾ x 2⅜	27%	132	1800
1x4	¾ x 3¼	23%	128	1900

The above quantities include 5% for end cutting and waste.

Quantity of End Matched Softwood Flooring Required Per 100 Sq. Ft. of Floor

Measured Size Inches	Actual Size Inches	Add for Width	Ft. B.M. Req. per 100 Sq. Ft. Surface	Weight per 1000 Ft.
1x3	13/16x2⅜	27%	130	1800
1x4	13/16x3¼	23%	126	1900

The above quantities include 3% for end cutting and waste.

Quantity of Square Edged (S4S) Boards Required Per 100 Sq. Ft. of Surface

Measured Size Inches	Actual Size Inches	Add for Width	Ft. B.M. Req. per 100 Sq. Ft. Surface	Weight per 1000 Ft.
1x 4	¾ x 3½	14%	119	2300
1x 6	¾ x 5½	9%	114	2300
1x 8	¾ x 7¼	10%	115	2300
1x10	¾ x 9¼	8%	113	2300
1x12	¾ x 11¼	7%	112	2400

The above quantities include 5% for end cutting and waste.

Lineal Foot Table of Board Measure
Number of Feet of Lumber, B.M., Per Lineal Foot of any Size.

2" x 4"=0.667	4"x 4"=1.333	8"x14"= 9.333
2" x 6"=1.	4"x 6"=2.	8"x16"=10.667
2" x 8"=1.333	4"x 8"=2.667	10"x10"= 8.333
2" x10"=1.667	4"x10"=3.333	10"x12"=10.
2" x12"=2.	4"x12"=4.	10"x14"=11.667
2" x14"=2.333	4"x14"=4.667	10"x16"=13.333
2" x16"=2.667	4"x16"=5.333	10"x18"=15.
2½"x12"=2.5	6"x 6"=3.	12"x12"=12.
2½"x14"=2.917	6"x 8"=4.	12"x14"=14.
2½"x16"=3.333	6"x10"=5.	12"x16"=16.
3" x 6"=1.5	6"x12"=6.	12"x18"=18.
3" x 8"=2.	6"x14"=7.	14"x14"=16.333
3" x10"=2.5	6"x16"=8.	14"x16"=18.667
3" x12"=3.	8"x 8"=5.333	14"x18"=21.
3" x14"=3.5	8"x10"=6.667	16"x16"=21.333
3" x16"=4.	8"x12"=8.	16"x18"=24.

Lengths of Common, Hip, and Valley Rafters Per 12 Inches of Run

1	2	3	4	5*	6†
Pitch of Roof	Rise and Run or Cut	Length in Inches Common Rafter per 12" of Run	Percent Increase in Length of Com. Rafter over Run		Length in Inches Hip or Valley Rafters
1/12	2 and 12	12.165	.014	1.014	17.088
1/8	3 and 12	12.369	.031	1.031	17.233
1/6	4 and 12	12.649	.054	1.054	17.433
5/24	5 and 12	13.000	.083	1.083	17.692
1/4	6 and 12	13.417	.118	1.118	18.000
7/24	7 and 12	13.892	.158	1.158	18.358
1/3	8 and 12	14.422	.202	1.202	18.762
3/8	9 and 12	15.000	.250	1.250	19.209
5/12	10 and 12	15.620	.302	1.302	19.698
11/24	11 and 12	16.279	.357	1.357	20.224
1/2	12 and 12	16.971	.413	1.413	20.785
13/24	13 and 12	17.692	.474	1.474	21.378
7/12	14 and 12	18.439	.537	1.537	22.000
5/8	15 and 12	19.210	.601	1.601	22.649
2/3	16 and 12	20.000	.667	1.667	23.324
17/24	17 and 12	20.809	.734	1.734	24.021
3/4	18 and 12	21.633	.803	1.803	24.739
19/24	19 and 12	22.500	.875	1.875	25.475
5/6	20 and 12	23.375	.948	1.948	26.230
7/8	21 and 12	24.125	1.010	2.010	27.000
11/24	22 and 12	25.000	1.083	2.083	27.785

| 11/12 | 23 and 12 | 26.000 | 1.167 | 2.167 | 28.583 |
| Full | 24 and 12 | 26.875 | 1.240 | 2.240 | 29.394 |

*Use figures in this column to obtain area of roof for any pitch. See explanation below.

†Figures in last column are length of hip and valley rafters in inches for each 12 inches of common rafter run.

To Obtain Area of Roofs For Any Pitch. To obtain the number of square feet of roof area for roofs of any pitch, take the entire flat or horizontal area of the roof and multiply by the figure given in the fifth column (*), and the result will be the area of the roof. Always bear in mind that the width of any overhanging cornice must be added to the building area to obtain the total area to be covered. Example: Find the area of a roof 26'-0"x42'-0", having a 12" or 1'-0" overhanging cornice. Roof having a ¼ pitch. To obtain roof area, 26'-0"+1'-0"+1'-0"=28'-0" width. 42'-0"+1'-0"+1'-0"=44'-0" length. 28 x 44=1232 or 1,232 sq. ft. of flat or horizontal area.

To obtain area at ¼ pitch: multiply 1,232 by 1.12*=1379.84 or 1,380 sq. ft. roof surface.

Add allowance for overhang on dormer roofs and sides.

*See column 5 above.

Table of Board Measure
Giving contents in Feet of Joists, Scantlings and Timbers

Size in Inches		Length in Feet										
		10	12	14	16	18	20	22	24	26	28	30
1	x 2	12/3	2	21/3	22/3	3	31/3	—	—	—	—	—
1	x 3	21/2	3	31/2	4	41/2	5	—	—	—	—	—
1	x 4	31/3	4	42/3	51/3	6	62/3	—	—	—	—	—
1	x 6	5	6	7	8	9	10	—	—	—	—	—
1	x 8	62/3	8	91/3	102/3	12	131/3	—	—	—	—	—
1	x10	81/3	10	112/3	131/3	15	162/3	—	—	—	—	—
1	x12	10	12	14	16	18	20	—	—	—	—	—
11/4x 4		41/6	5	55/6	62/3	71/2	81/3	—	—	—	—	—
11/4x 6		61/4	71/2	83/4	10	111/4	121/2	—	—	—	—	—
11/4x 8		81/3	10	112/3	131/3	15	162/3	—	—	—	—	—
11/4x10		105/12	121/2	147/12	162/3	183/4	205/6	—	—	—	—	—
11/4x12		121/2	15	171/2	20	221/2	25	—	—	—	—	—
11/2x 4		5	6	7	8	9	10	—	—	—	—	—
11/2x 6		71/2	9	101/2	12	131/2	15	—	—	—	—	—
11/2x 8		10	12	14	16	18	20	—	—	—	—	—
11/2x10		121/2	15	171/2	20	221/2	25	—	—	—	—	—
11/2x12		15	18	21	24	27	30	—	—	—	—	—
2	x 2	31/3	4	42/3	51/3	6	62/3	—	—	—	—	—
2	x 3	5	6	7	8	9	10	11	12	13	14	15
2	x 4	62/3	8	91/3	102/3	12	131/3	142/3	16	171/3	182/3	20
2	x 6	10	12	14	16	18	20	22	24	26	28	30
2	x 8	131/3	16	182/3	211/3	24	262/3	291/3	32	342/3	371/3	40

Size in Inches	10	12	14	16	18	20	22	24	26	28	30
					Length in Feet						
2 x10	16 2/3	20	23 1/3	26 2/3	30	33 1/3	36 2/3	40	43 1/3	46 2/3	50
2 x12	20	24	28	32	36	40	44	48	52	56	60
2 x14	23 1/3	28	32 2/3	37 1/3	42	46 2/3	51 1/3	56	60 2/3	65 1/3	70
3 x 4	10	12	14	16	18	20	22	24	26	28	30
3 x 6	15	18	21	24	27	30	33	36	39	42	65
3 x 8	20	24	28	32	36	40	44	48	52	56	60
3 x10	25	30	35	40	45	50	55	60	65	70	75
3 x12	30	36	42	48	54	60	66	72	78	84	90
3 x14	35	42	49	56	63	70	77	84	91	98	105

Table of Board Measure
Giving Contents in Feet of Joists, Scantlings and Timbers

Size in Inches	10	12	14	16	18	20	22	24	26	28	30
					Length in Feet						
4x 4	13	16	19	21	24	27	29	32	35	37	40
4x 6	20	24	28	32	36	40	44	48	52	56	60
4x 8	27	32	37	43	48	53	59	64	69	75	80
4x10	33	40	47	53	60	67	73	80	87	93	100
4x12	40	48	56	64	72	80	88	96	104	112	120
4x14	47	56	65	75	84	93	103	112	121	131	140
6x 6	30	36	42	48	54	60	66	72	78	84	90
6x 8	40	48	56	64	72	80	88	96	104	112	120
6x10	50	60	70	80	90	100	110	120	130	140	150
6x12	60	72	84	96	108	120	132	144	156	168	180
6x14	70	84	98	112	126	140	154	168	182	196	210
6x16	80	96	112	128	144	160	176	192	208	224	240
8x 8	53	64	75	85	96	107	117	128	139	149	160
8x10	67	80	93	107	120	133	147	160	173	187	200
8x12	80	96	112	128	144	160	176	192	208	224	240
8x14	93	112	131	149	168	187	205	224	243	261	280
8x16	107	128	149	171	192	213	235	256	277	298	320
10x10	83	100	117	133	150	167	183	200	217	233	250
10x12	100	120	140	160	180	200	220	240	260	280	300
10x14	117	140	163	187	210	233	257	280	303	327	350
10x16	133	160	187	218	240	267	293	320	347	373	400
12x12	120	144	168	192	216	240	264	288	312	336	360
12x14	140	168	196	224	252	280	308	336	364	392	420
12x16	160	192	224	256	288	320	352	384	416	448	480
14x14	163	196	229	261	294	327	359	392	425	457	490
14x16	187	224	261	299	336	373	411	448	485	523	560
14x18	210	252	294	336	378	420	462	504	546	588	630
14x20	233	280	327	373	420	467	513	560	607	653	700
16x16	213	256	299	341	384	427	469	512	555	597	640
16x18	240	288	336	384	432	480	528	576	624	672	720
16x20	267	320	373	425	480	533	587	640	693	747	800

Table of Board Measure
Giving Contents in Feet of Joists, Scantlings and Timbers

Size in Inches	Length in Feet										
	10	12	14	16	18	20	22	24	26	28	30
18x18	270	324	378	432	486	540	594	648	702	756	810
18x20	300	360	420	480	540	600	660	720	780	840	900
20x20	333	400	467	533	600	667	733	800	867	933	1000

NAILS REQUIRED FOR CARPENTER WORK

The following table gives the number of wire nails in pounds for the various kinds of lumber per 1,000 ft., board measure, or per 1,000 shingles and lath or per square (100 sq. ft.) of asphalt slate surfaced shingle, with the number of nails added for loss of material on account of lap or matching of shiplap, flooring, ceiling and siding of the various widths. The table gives the sizes generally used for certain purposes with the nailing space 16" on centers, and 1 or 2 nails per board for each nailing space.

Description of Material	Unit of Measure	Size and Kind of Nail	Number of Nails Required	Pounds of Nails Required
Wood Shingles	1,000'	3d Common	2,560	4 lbs.
Individual Asphalt Shingles	100 sq. ft.	7/8" Roofing	848	4 lbs.
Three in One Asphalt Shingles	100 sq. ft.	7/8" Roofing	320	1 lb.
Wood Lath	1,000'	3d Fine	4,000	6 lbs.
Wood Lath	1,000'	2d Fine	4,000	4 lbs.
Bevel or Lap Siding, 1/2"x4"	1,000'	6d Coated	2,250	*15 lbs.
Bevel or Lap Siding, 1/2"x6"	1,000'	6d Coated	1,500	*10 lbs.
Byrkit Lath, 1"x6"	1,000'	6d Common	2,400	15 lbs.
Drop Siding, 1"x6"	1,000'	8d Common	3,000	25 lbs.
3/8" Hardwood Flooring	1,000'	4d Common	9,300	16 lbs.
25/32" Hardwood Flooring	1,000'	8d Casing	9,300	64 lbs.
Subflooring, 1"x3"	1,000'	8d Casing	3,350	23 lbs.
Subflooring, 1"x4"	1,000'	8d Casing	2,500	17 lbs.
Subflooring, 1"x6"	1,000'	8d Casing	2,600	18 lbs.
Ceiling, 5/8"x4"	1,000'	6d Casing	2,250	10 lbs.
Sheathing Boards, 1"x4"	1,000'	8d Common	4,500	40 lbs.
Sheathing Boards, 1"x6"	1,000'	8d Common	3,000	25 lbs.
Sheathing Boards, 1"x8"	1,000'	8d Common	2,250	20 lbs.
Sheathing Boards, 1"x10"	1,000'	8d Common	1,800	15 lbs.
Sheathing Boards, 1"x12"	1,000'	8d Common	1,500	121/2 lbs.
Studding, 2"x4"	1,000'	16d Common	500	10 lbs.
Joist, 2"x6"	1,000'	16d Common	332	7 lbs.
Joist, 2"x8"	1,000'	16d Common	252	5 lbs.
Joist, 2"x10"	1,000'	16d Common	200	4 lbs.
Joist, 2"x12"	1,000'	16d Common	168	31/2 lbs.
Interior Trim, 5/8" thick	1,000'	6d Finish	2,250	7 lbs.
Interior Trim, 3/4" thick	1,000'	8d Finish	3,000	14 lbs.
5/8" Trim where nailed to jamb	1,000'	4d Finish	2,250	3 lbs.
1"x2" Furring or Bridging	1,000'	6d Common	2,400	15 lbs.
1"x1" Grounds	1,000'	6d Common	4,800	30 lbs.

*NOTE—Cement coated nails sold as two-thirds of pound equals 1 pound of common nails.

The following table gives the recommended nailing schedule for special (helically threaded) nails that are being used today throughout the building industry.

Nails Required for Subflooring.   On wood floors up to 4" wide, quantities are based on 8d flooring nails. For flooring 6" and wider, 10d nails have been figured.

The quantities given below are sufficient to lay 1,000 ft. of flooring, b.m.

Width Flooring	Joist Spacing 12" on Centers	Joist Spacing 16" on Centers
2"	40 lbs. 8d flg.	30 lbs. 8d flg.
3"	30 lbs. 8d flg.	23 lbs. 8d flg.
4"	22 lbs. 8d flg.	17 lbs. 8d flg.
6"	24 lbs. 10d com.	18 lbs. 10d com.
8"	17 lbs. 10d com.	13 lbs. 10d com.

Data on Common Wire Nails

Size of Nails	Length of Nails Inches	Gauge Number	Approximate Number to Pound	Approx. Price Per 100 lbs.
4d	1½	12½	316	$36.00
5d	1¾	12½	271	36.00
6d	2	11½	181	36.00
8d	2½	10¼	106	34.00
10d	3	9	69	34.00
12d	3¼	9	63	34.00
16d	3½	8	49	34.00
20d	4	6	31	34.00
30d	4½	5	24	34.00
40d	5	4	18	34.00
50d	5½	3	14	34.00
60d	6	2	11	34.00

ALUMINUM NAILS

Aluminum nails are excellent for use whenever the nailhead is exposed to the atmosphere or corrosive conditions. In other words, use aluminum nails wherever there is the possibility of rust or nail stain.

The manufacturers do not ordinarily recommend aluminum common nails for ordinary framing because there is no ecomomic advantage over steel wire nails for most common purposes and the bending resistance of aluminum nails is less than that of steel nails despite the larger diameter of the aluminum nails.

Aluminum nails weigh about one-third as much as steel wire nails but they are more expensive nail for nail—however they do save labor and painting where rust or nail stain is a factor.

Recommended Nailing Schedule for Common Applications in Building Construction

Application	Nailed into	Nail Size Inches	Nail Type	Head Diameter Type	Point Size	Point Type	Nailing	Spacing o.c.	Nails Per Joint
Mudsill, partition plate, 2"	Concrete	2 1/2-2 3/4x0.148 (3 1/4-)	Sc-1z	5/16" Checkered	Long	Dia.	Face	12"-24"	—
Ditto, in earthquake regions	Concrete	3 1/2x0.250	Sc-1z	9/16" Checkered	Med.	Ndl.	Face	24"-48"	—
Ditto, 3"	Concrete	4 1/2x0.250	Sc-1z	9/16" Checkered	Med.	Ndl.	Face	24"-48"	—
Furring strips	Concrete	1 1/2-1 3/4x0.148	Sc-1z	5/16" Checkered	Long	Dia.	Face	12"-24"	—
Mudsill	Mudsill	2 1/2x0.120	Sc-2	9/32" Flat	Med.	Dia.	Toe	—	2
Sleepers	Mudsill	2 1/2x0.120	Sc-2	9/32" Flat	Med.	Dia.	Toe	—	2
Joists	Mudsill	3 1/4x0.135	Sc-2	5/16" Flat	Med.	Dia.	Toe	—	2-3
Subflrg., 1" lumber, plywood	Mudsill, sleeper, joist	2 1/8x0.105	St-14	1/4" Flat, Csk.	Med.	Dia.	Face	6" & 12"	2(3)
Subflrg., 2" lumber, plywood	Mudsill, sleeper, joist	2 7/8x0.120	St-14	9/32" Flat, Csk.	Med.	Dia.	Face	6" & 12"	2(3)
Subflrg., 3/8"-1/2" plywood (dph.)	Mudsill, sleeper, joist	1 1/2x0.135	Hi-28	5/16" Flat, Csk.	Med.	Dia.	Face	6" & 12"	—
Subflrg., 5/8" plywood (dph.)	Mudsill, sleeper, joist	1 3/4x0.135	Hi-28	5/16" Flat, Csk.	Med.	Dia.	Face	6" & 12"	—
Subflrg., 3/4" plywd. (dph.), part bd.	Mudsill, sleeper, joist	2 x0.148	Hi-28	5/16" Flat, Csk.	Med.	Dia.	Face	6" & 12"	—
Subflrg., 1"-1 1/8" plywood (dph.) part. bd.	Mudsill, sleeper, joist	2 1/2x0.148	Hi-28	5/16" Flat, Csk.	Med.	Dia.	Face	6" & 12"	—
Underlayment, 1/4"-5/16" plywood	Subfloor	1 x0.083	St-16	3/16" Flat, Csk.	Med.	Dia.	Face	6" & 6"-12"	—
Underlayment, 3/8"-1/2" plywood	Subfloor	1 1/4x0.083	St-16	3/16" Flat, Csk.	Med.	Dia.	Face	6" & 6"-12"	—
Underlayment, 5/8" plywood	Subfloor	1 3/8x0.098	St-16	1/4" Flat, Csk.	Med.	Dia.	Face	6" & 6"-12"	—
Underlayment, 3/4" plywood	Subfloor	1 1/2x0.098	St-16	1/4" Flat, Csk.	Med.	Dia.	Face	6" & 6"-12"	—
Underlayment, 7/8" plywood	Subfloor	1 5/8x0.098	St-16	1/4" Flat, Csk.	Med.	Dia.	Face	6" & 6"-12"	—
Underlayment, 3/16"-5/8" hardboard	Subfloor	1-1 3/8x0.083	St-15	3/16" Flat, Csk.	Med.	Dia.	Face	6" & 12"	—
Flooring, T & G hardwood	Subfloor, joist, sleeper	2-2 1/2x0.115	Sc-4	13/64" Casing	Blunt	Dia.	Toe	10"-18"	—
Flooring, T & G softwood	Subfloor, joist, sleeper	2-2 1/2x0.115	Sc-4	13/64" Casing	Blunt	Dia.	Toe	10"-18"	—
Flooring, T & G hardwood, 3/8" and 1/2"	Subfloor, joist, sleeper	1-1 1/4x0.072	Sc-4	9/64" Casing	Blunt	Dia.	Toe	10"-18"	—
Flooring, T & G parquet	Subfloor	1 1/2x0.105	Sc-4	9/64" Casing	Blunt	Dia.	Face	—	—
Framing plates	Stud	3 1/4x0.135	Sc-2	5/16" Flat	Med.	Dia.	Face	16"-24"	2
Framing studs	Stud, cripple, lintel, sill	2 1/2x0.120	Sc-2	9/32" Flat	Med.	Dia.	Face	16"-24"	—
Framing studs	Plate, cripple, lintel, sill	2 1/2x0.120	Sc-2	9/32" Flat	Med.	Dia.	Toe	—	3
Framing sole plate	Mudsill	3 1/4x0.135	Sc-2	5/16" Flat	Med.	Dia.	Toe	16"	—
Framing top plate	Lower top plate	3 1/4x0.135	Sc-2	5/16" Flat	Med.	Dia.	Face	24"	—
Trussed rafter assembly		3 1/4x0.135	Sc-5	5/16" Flat	Med.	Dia.	Face	2 1/2"-3"	Given
Trussed rafter assembly		2 1/2x0.120	Sc-5	9/32" Flat	Med.	Dia.	Face	2 1/2"-3"	Given

See Notes, Key to Nail Types and Abbreviations on later page.

Application	Nailed Into	Nail Size Inches	Nail Type	Head Diameter Type	Point Size	Point Type	Nailing	Spacing o.c.	Nails Per Joint
Rafter, 4"	Top plate	3 1/4x0.135	Sc-2	5/16" Flat	Med.	Dia.	Toe	—	3
Rafter, 4"	Top plate	6 x0.177	St-34	7/16" Flat	Med.	Dia.	Face	—	2
Rafter, 4"	Top plate	7 x0.207	St-34	1/2" Flat	Med.	Dia.	Face	—	2
Rafter, 6", 8", 10"	Top plate	{ 4-6 x0.177 / 7-9 x0.203 }	St-34	7/16" Flat	Med.	Dia.	Toe	—	2-3
Sheathing, 1" lumber	Framing, rafter	2 x0.120	St-3	9/32" Flat	Med.	Dia.	Face	6" & 12"	2
Sheathing 3/8"-1/2" plywood	Framing, rafter	1 3/4x0.120	St-17	9/32" Flat	Med.	Dia.	Face	6" & 12"	—
Sheathing 5/16"-1/2" plywood (dph.)	Framing, rafter	1 1/2x0.135	Hi-17	5/16" Flat, Csk.	Med.	Dia.	Face	6" & 12"	—
Sheathing 5/8" plywood (dph)	Framing, rafter	1 3/4x0.135	Hi-17	5/16" Flat, Csk.	Med.	Dia.	Face	6" & 12"	—
Sheathing 3/4" plywood (dph.)	Framing, rafter	2 x0.148	Hi-17	5/16" Flat, Csk.	Med.	Dia.	Face	6" & 12"	—
Sheathing 1"-11/8" plywood (dph.)	Framing, rafter	2 1/2x0.148	Hi-17	5/16" Flat, Csk.	Med.	Dia.	Face	6" & 12"	—
Sheathing, insulation board, gypsumboard	Framing, rafter	1 1/2-2 x0.120	St-10g	3/8", 7/16" Flat	Blunt	Dia.	Face	3-4" & 6-8"	—
Sheathing, asbestosboard, 1/8"	Framing, rafter	1 1/4x0.083	St-6g	3/16" Flat, Csk.	Blunt	Dia.	Face	3-4" & 6-8"	—
Sheathing, asbestosboard, 1/4"	Framing, rafter	1 1/4x0.120	St-or / Sc-6g	5/16" Flat, Csk.	Blunt	Dia.	Face	3-4" & 6-8"	—
Sheathing, hardboard, 3/8"-5/8"	Framing, rafter	2 x0.115	Sc-7g	13/64" Flat, Csk.	Med.	Ndl.	Face	3-4" & 6-8"	—
Building paper	Sheathing	1/2-3/4x0.105	Sq-30	15/16" Square	Med.	Dia.	Face	6"-12"	—
Stripping, 3/8"x3 5/8"	Framing, joist, rafter	2 x0.120	St-3	9/32" Flat	Med.	Dia.	Face	—	2
Stripping, 1"x4"	Framing, joist, rafter	2 1/2x0.135	St-3	5/16" Flat	Med.	Dia.	Face	—	2
Stripping, 2"x3"	Framing, joist, rafter	3 1/2x0.165	St-3	5/8" Flat	Med.	Dia.	Face	—	2
Siding, wood, 1"	Sheathing and framing	2 1/8x0.101-0.115	St-14g	1/4" Flat, Csk.	Med.	Dia.	Face	—	1
Siding, wood, 1"	Sheathing and framing	2 x0.120	Dr-14	5/32" Flat, Csk.	Med.	Ndl.	Face	—	1
Siding, wood, 2"	Sheathing and framing	3 x0.135	Dr-14	5/32" Flat, Csk.	Med.	Ndl.	Face	—	1
Siding, plywood	Sheathing and framing	1 7/8x0.109	Dr-8	5/32" Casing	Med.	Ndl.	Face	6" & 12"	—
Siding, T & G wood	Sheathing and framing	1 3/4x0.105	Sc-8	5/32" Casing	Med.	Dia.	Toe	6" & 12"	—
Siding, asbestos shingle	Sheathing and framing	1 1/2-1 3/4x0.105	Dr-33	3/16" Flat Button	Med.	Dia.	Face	—	Given
Siding, asbestos shingle	Sheathing and framing	1 1/2-1 3/4x0.083	St-19t	3/16" Flat	Med.	Dia.	Face	—	Given
Siding, asbestos shingle	Sheathing and framing	1 1/2-1 3/4x0.076	St-20	3/16" Flat	Med.	Dia.	Face	—	Given
Siding, insulated brick, wood shingle	Sheathing and framing	1 3/4x0.095	St-18ge	3/16" Flat	Med.	Dia.	Face	8"-12"	2
Siding, wood shingle	Insulating sheathing	1 3/4-2 x0.083	St-18ge	5/32" Finishing	Blunt	Dia.	Face	—	2
Siding, wood shingle	Insulating sheathing	1 3/4-2 x0.105	Dr-18	5/32" Finishing	Blunt	Dia.	Face	—	2
Siding, wood shingle	Plywood	1 1/8x0.102	Dr-18	3/16" Flat	Med.	Dia.	Face	—	2
Siding, hardboard	Framing	2-2 1/2x0.115	Sc-7z	13/64" Casing	Long	Ndl.	Face	12"	
Siding, hardboard battenboard	Framing	1 1/2x0.083	Sc-7z	9/64" Casing	Long	Ndl.	Face	12"	—

See Notes, Key to Nail Types and Abbreviations on later page.

Application		Nail Size Inches	Nail Type	Head Diameter Type	Point Size	Point Type	Nailing	Spacing o.c.	Nails Per Joint
	Nailed Into								
Fascia, 1"	Framing, rafter	2 1/2-1 1/4x0.120	Sc-2g	9/32" Flat	Med.	Dia.	Face	—	2
Fascia, 2" lumber	Framing, rafter	3 1/4x0.135	Sc-2g	5/16" Flat	Med.	Dia.	Face	—	2
Roofing, built-up	Sheathing	3/4-1 1/4x0.105	Sq-30	15/16" Square	Med.	Dia.	Face	10"	—
Roofing, built-up	Poured gypsum	1 1/2-1 3/4x0.120	Sq-31	15/16" Square	Med.	Dia.	Face	10"	—
Roofing, asphalt shingle	Sheathing	3/4-2 x0.120	St-10g	3/8" Flat	Blunt	Dia.	Face	—	2-3
Roofing, asphalt shingle	Sheathing	3/4-2x.120-.135	Dr-10	3/8" Flat	Blunt	Dia.	Face	—	2-3
Roofing, wood shingle	Sheathing	3/4-2x.105-.120	Dr-18	3/16" Flat	Blunt	Dia.	Face	—	2
Roofing, wood shingle	Sheathing	1 3/4-2 x0.083	St-18g	1/8" Flat, Csk.	Blunt	Dia.	Face	—	—
Roofing, asbestos shingle	Sheathing	As for siding							
Roofing, aluminum (corr. and flat)	Rafter, purlin	1 1/2-1 3/4x0.145	Dr-10	13/32" Flat ★	Long	Dia.	Face	12"	—
Roofing, sheet metal (corr. and flat)	Rafter, purlin	1-3 x0.135	St-or	7/16" Flat ★	Long	Dia.	Face	12"	—
Roofing, glass fiber (corr. and flat)	Rafter, purlin	1 1/2-3 x0.135	Sc-9g	7/16" Flat ★	Long	Dia.	Face	12"	—
Roofing, glass fiber (corr. and flat)	Rafter, purlin	1 1/2-3 x0.148	Dr-9 or 10	7/16" Flat ★	Long	Dia.	Face	12"	—
				★=With Neoprene washer attached					
Lath, expanded metal, K-lath	Framing, joist	1 1/2x0.148	St-22g	L-Shaped	Med.	Dia.	Face	6" & 12"	—
Lath, gypsum plasterboard	Framing, joist	1 1/4x0.101	St-23b	19/64" Flat, Csk.	Long	Dia.	Face	5"	—
Gypsumboard, 3/8"	Framing, joist	1 1/4x0.098	St-24	1/4"-19/64" Flat, Csk.	Long	Dia.	Face	5"-8"	—
Gypsumboard, 1/2" 5/8"	Framing, joist	1 3/8x0.098	St-24	1/4"-19/64" Flat, Csk.	Long	Dia.	Face	5"-8"	—
Gypsumboard, prefinished	Framing, joist	1 3/8x0.083	K-32e	3/16" Flat, Csk.	Long	Dia.	Face	5"-8"	—
Paneling, trim		1-1 1/4x0.054	K-32e	3/32" Casing	Blunt	Dia.	Face	—	—
Paneling, trim, exterior		1-1 1/2x0.072	St-13	3/32" Casing	Blunt	Dia.	Face	—	—
Paneling, trim, exterior		1 x0.065	St-12	3/32" Casing	Blunt	Dia.	Face	—	—
Paneling, trim, exterior		1 x0.076	Sc-12	3/32" Oval	Blunt	Dia.	Face	—	—
Paneling, trim		1 x0.072	Sc-11	3/32" Casing	Blunt	Dia.	Face	—	—
Paneling, trim		1 1/2-1 3/4x0.083	Sc-11	1/8" Casing	Blunt	Dia.	Face	—	—
Paneling, trim		2 1/2x0.105	Sc-11	9/64" Casing	Blunt	Dia.	Face	—	—
Acoustic tile		1-1 3/4x0.062	St-25z	—	Blunt	Dia.	Face	—	—
Electric conduit	Wood	1 1/2-2 x0.162	St-26z	1" Hook	Blunt	Ndl.	Face	—	—
Electric conduit	Masonry	1 1/2-2 x0.162	St-27z	1" Hook	Blunt	Ndl.	Face	—	—
Fencing wire	Softwood (treated)	1 1/2x0.148	St-22g	L-Shaped	Med.	Dia.	Face	—	—
Fencing wire	Hardwood	1 1/2x0.148	St-21g	L-Shaped	Med.	Dia.	Face	—	—

See Notes, Key to Nail Types and Abbreviations on next page.

Key to Nail Types

Sc-iz	Screw-Tite Masonry Nail, hardened HCS, zinc plated
Sc-2	Screw-Tite Framing Nail, hardened HCS
Sc-2g	Screw-Tite Framing Nail, hardened HCS, galvanized
Sc-3	Screw-Tite Framing Nail, bright LCS
Sc-3g	Screw-Tite Framing Nail, bright LCS, galvanized
Sc-4	Screw-Tite Flooring Nail, hardened HCS
Sc-5	Screw-Tite Trussed Rafter Nail, hardened HCS
Sc-6g	Screw-Tite Asbestosboard Nail, hardened HCS, galvanized
Sc-7g	Screw-Tite Exterior Hardboard Nail, hardened HCS, galvanized
Sc-7z	Screw-Tite Exterior Hardboard Nail, hardened HCS, zinc plated
Sc-8	Screw-Tite Casing Nail, silver bronze
Sc-9g	Screw-Tite Roofing Nail, hardened HCS, galvanized
Sc-10g	Screw-Tite Roofing Nail, bright LCS, galvanized
Sc-11	Screw-Tite Finishing Nail, bright LCS,
Sc-12	Screw-Tite Finishing Nail, stainless steel
St-3	Stronghold Framing Nail, bright LCS
St-4	Stronghold Parquet Flooring Nail, hardened HCS
St-6g	Stronghold Asbestosboard Nail, hardened HCS, galvanized
St-9g	Stronghold Roofing Nail, hardened HCS, galvanized
St-10g	Stronghold Roofing Nail, bright LCS, galvanized
St-12	Stronghold Finishing Nail, stainless steel
St-13	Stronghold Finishing Nail, monel metal
St-14	Stronghold Sinker Nail, bright LCS
St-14g	Stronghold Sinker Nail, bright LCS, galvanized
St-15	Stronghold Underlay Nail, Hardened HCS
St-16	Stronghold Underlay Nail, bright LCS
St-17	Stronghold Sheathing Nail, bright LCS
St-18g	Stronghold Shingle Nail, bright LCS, galvanized
St-18ge	Stronghold Shingle Nail, bright LCS, galvanized and enameled
St-19t	Stronghold Shingle Nail, bronze, tin plated
St-20	Stronghold Shingle Nail, stainless steel
St-21g	Stronghold Fence Staple, hardened HCS, galvanized
St-22g	Stronghold Fence Staple, bright LCS, galvanized
St-22z	Stronghold Fence Staple, bright LCS, zinc plated
St-23b	Stronghold Lath Nail, bright LCS, blued
St-24	Stronghold Drywall Nail, bright LCS
St-25z	Stronghold Kollarnail, hardened HCS, zinc plated
St-26z	Stronghold Conduit Staple, bright LCS, zinc plated
St-27z	Stronghold Knurled Conduit Staple, hardened HCS, zinc plated
St-34	Stronghold Spike, hardened HCS
Hi-28	"Hi-Load" Shear-Resistant Nail bright LCS
Hi-17	"Hi-Load" Sheathing Nail, bright LCS
Sq-30	Squarehed Annular Thread Cap Nail, bright LCS
Sq-31	Squarehed Spiral Thread Can Nail bright LCS
K-32e	Annular Thread Kolorpin, bright LCS, enameled
Dr-8	Drive-Rite Spiral Thread Casing Nail, aluminum
Dr-9	Drive-Rite Screw Thread Roofing Nail aluminum
Dr-10	Drive-Rite Spiral Thread Roofing Nail aluminum
Dr-14	Drive-Rite Spiral Thread Sinker Nail, aluminum
Dr-18	Drive-Rite Screw Thread Shingle Nail, aluminum
Dr-20	Drive-Rite Spiral Thread Shingle Nail, aluminum
Dr-33	Drive-Rite Knurled Asbestos-Cement Shingle Face, aluminum

NOTES: For fastening redwood, use only aluminum or stainless steel nails.

Local conditions, customs and popular usage may dictate minor variations in length and gauge of nails. Consult the Technical Service Department of Independent Nail & Packing Company, Bridgewater, Mass.

The above chart is based on a table appearing in Bulletin No. 38 (Revised Edition). "Better Utilization of Wood Through Assembly with Improved Fasteners," a study undertaken at Wood Research Laboratory, Virginia Polytechnic Institute, under the sponsorship of Independent Nail & Packing Company. Bridgewater, Mass. manufacturers of Stronghold® Annular Thread and Screw-Tite® Spiral Thread Nails and other improved fasteners.

ABBREVIATIONS USED IN THIS TABLE:
Corr.—Corrugated
Dph.—Diaphragm
Part. bd—Particle board
LCS—Low Carbon Steel
HCS—High Carbon Steel
Plywd.—Plywood   Med.—Medium
Csk.—Countersunk   Dia.—Diamond
Flrg.—Flooring   Ndl.—Needle
Shgl.—Shingle

STRONGHOLD ® ANNULAR THREAD NAIL

SCREW-TITE ® SPIRAL THREAD NAIL

STRONGHOLD ® SCREW THREAD NAIL

SCREW-TITE ® KNURLED MASONRY NAIL

Common 3d to 20d nails will run $2.30 per lb., 30d to 60d around $2.05 per lb.

HARDWARE ACCESSORIES USED FOR WOOD FRAMING

The following items may be used to advantage in all types of wood construction. Developed primarily to provide better joints between wood framing members, in many cases their use has resulted in lower overall costs—the additional material cost being more than offset by increased labor efficiency.

Steel Joist Hangers.   Used for framing joists to beams and around openings for stair wells, chimneys, hearths, ducts, etc. Made of galv. steel, varying from 12 ga. to 3/16" in thickness, with square supporting arms, holes punched for nails and with bearing surfaces proportioned to size of lumber. Approximate prices for sizes most commonly used are as follows:

Joist Size	Gauge	Depth of seat	Opening in Hanger	Price Each
2"x 6"	12	2"	15/8"x5"	$0.70
2"x 8"	12	2"	15/8"x5"	.78
2"x10"	12	2"	15/8"x81/2"	.81
2"x12"	10	21/2"	15/8"x81/2"	1.00
4"x 8"	11	2"	35/8"x51/4 "	.94
4"x10"	9	2"	35/8"x51/4 "	1.12
4"x12"	3/16	21/2"	35/8"x81/2"	1.73

Teco* Framing Accessories.   Used in light wood construction to provide facenailed connections for framing members. Adaptable to most framing connections, they eliminate the uncertainties and weaknesses of toenailing. Manufactured of zinc-coated, sheet steel in various gauges and styles. Framing accessories are designed to provide nailing on various surfaces. Special nails, approximately equal to 8d common nails, but only 1¼" long, to prevent complete penetration of standard nominal 2" lumber, are furnished with anchors. Approximate prices are as follows:

Type	Price Per 100	Type	Price Per 100
Trip-L-Grips	$25.00	Post Caps	$66.00
Du-Al-Clip	20.00	H Clips	4.00
Truss Plates	30.00	Angles	45.00

---

*Timber Engineering Company, Inc., Washington, D.C.

QUICK REFERENCE CHART #1

Labor Factors for Rough Framing

Item Description	Unit	Factor	
Sills & Plates - Bolted	BF	.02000	
Studs	BF	.02500	
Floor Joists			
2" x 6"	BF	.02200	
2" x 8"	BF	.02200	
2" x 10"	BF	.02000	
2" x 12"	BF	.02000	
Girders - Built up	BF	.02000	
Rafters - Gable			
2" x 4"	BF	.03300	
2" x 6"	BF	.03000	
2" x 8"	BF	.03000	
2" x 10"	BF	.03000	
2" x 12"	BF	.03000	
Rafters - Hip			
2" x 4"	BF	.03600	
2" x 6"	BF	.03300	
2" x 8"	BF	.03000	
2" x 10"	BF	.03000	
2" x 12"	BF	.03300	
Rafters - Flat			
2" x 6"	BF	.02800	
2" x 8"	BF	.02600	
2" x 10"	BF	.02400	
2" x 12"	BF	.02400	
Dormers	BF	.04000	
Beams/Girders - Heavy	BF	.03000	
Trusses	BF	.06000	
Bridging	BF	.08000	
Furring			
On Masonry	LF	.04000	
On Wood Studs	LF	.03000	
Grounds			
On Wood Studs	LF	.04000	
On Masonry	LF	.06000	
Wall Sheathing		Diagonal	Horizontal
1" x 6"	BF	.02000	.01600
1" x 8"	BF		.01600
5/16" Plywood	BF		.01400
25/32" Insulated	BF		.01400
Subfloor		Diagonal	Horizontal
1" x 4"	BF	.02000	.01800
1" x 6"	BF	.01700	.01500
1" x 8"	BF	.01600	.01400
5/8" Plywood	BF		.01200

Labor Factors For Rough Framing—Cont'd.

Item Description	Unit	Factor
Roof Sheathing - Gable		
1" x 6"	BF	.02000
1" x 8"	BF	.01800
5/16" Plywood	BF	.01400
Open Roof Boards	BF	.02000
Roof Sheathing - Hip		
1" x 6"	BF	.02200
1" x 8"	BF	.02000
5/16" Plywood	BF	.01800
Roof Sheathing - Flat		
1" x 6"	BF	.01600
1" x 8"	BF	.01400
5/16" Plywood	BF	.01200
1" x 8" Horizontal	BF	.02717
1/2" Plywood	BF	.02046
5/8" Plywood	BF	.02132
3/4" Plywood	BF	.02217
Columns		
8" x 8"	BF	.06250
10" x 10"	BF	.04167
Scaffolding		
Wood to 18'	BF	.01316
	SF	.01389
	LF	.25000
Steel Tubular	SF	.03000

SECTION II/Interiors

CHAPTER 6

STAIRWAYS AND FLOORING

Except for custom stairs, most stairs in present as well as older homes will fall under one of six categories. These are the straight run, wide U, Narrow U, Wide L, Double L and Long L. These are called the "principal" stairs and are designed to provide access to other floors in the main areas of living.

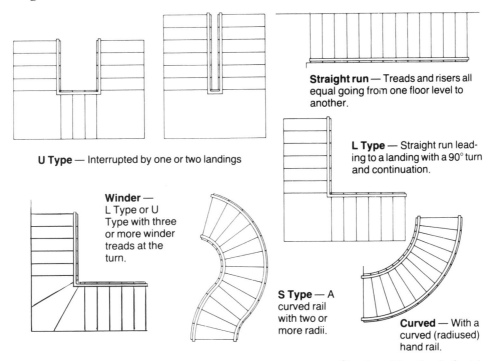

Straight run — Treads and risers all equal going from one floor level to another.

U Type — Interrupted by one or two landings

L Type — Straight run leading to a landing with a 90° turn and continuation.

Winder — L Type or U Type with three or more winder treads at the turn.

S Type — A curved rail with two or more radii.

Curved — With a curved (radiused) hand rail.

Courtesy Mansion Industries, Inc.

Today's design considerations and homeowners demand that they be as pleasing to the eye as they are functional. Newels and balusters must fit the decor. Staircases must be wide enough to permit two people to pass comfortably and furniture to be carried up and down. The best width is 3 to 3½ ft. They should also have a proper rise and run. If the rise is too steep, the steps are tiring going up, dangerous coming down. If the run is too long, the foot may kick the riser at each step and the attempt to space steps is tiring and awkward.

Although there are a number of rules to determine rise and run, it is generally accepted that the riser be 7-7½" high and the tread 10-11" wide. Another way to state it is that the sum of one riser and one tread should total between 17 to 18". For example: a riser of 7½" plus a tread of 10" totals 17½".

Headroom is also important. Even though the FHA minimum is 6'8" studies indicate this may not be sufficient. A more functional dimension if space is available, is 7'7" which provides more room for furniture and other household items to be moved upstairs and down with greater convenience. Stairs labeled "service" stairs generally lead to the basement or attic. They are usually steeper and made of less expensive materials.

Removing Existing Staircases. To remove an existing staircase, allow 3 to 5 hours, depending upon the method of construction. When a railing is attached, it must be removed first; likewise, any carpet must be lifted. If treads and risers are not dadoed into the stringers, one tread can be pried loose, and the remainder removed from beneath. If the staircase is open and treads and risers not dadoed, the entire stair can be removed after the ends of the stringers are loosened.

Where the stringers are part of an existing wall, that is to be left intact, each stair must be cut in the middle so that the ends of the tread and riser can be pulled from the stringer. If the staircase was pre-built, stringers will most likely be damaged as the stairs are removed; the stringers must be repaired before the stair can be rebuilt: allow about 2 hours for the repair work.

	Hours	Rate	Total	Rate	Total
Carpenter	4	—	—	$20.60	$82.40

Framing and Installing Wood Stairs/Unassembled. To frame and erect ordinary wood stairs having closed stringers where the treads and risers are not housed, it will require 3-4 hrs. to lay out the job, cut-out for stringers and risers and place stringers for a single flight of ordinary wood stairs up to 4'-0" wide and 11'0" story height at the following labor cost:

	Hours	Rate	Total	Rate	Total
Carpenter	3.5	—	—	$20.60	$72.10

Placing Treads and Risers. To place treads and risers, figure 2-3 hrs. at the following labor cost per flight (does not include nosing, newels, balusters or handrail):

	Hours	Rate	Total	Rate	Total
Carpenter	2.5	—	—	$20.60	$51.50

Placing Rails. To place 4" x 4" newels, 2" x 4" rails and 1" x 2" balusters

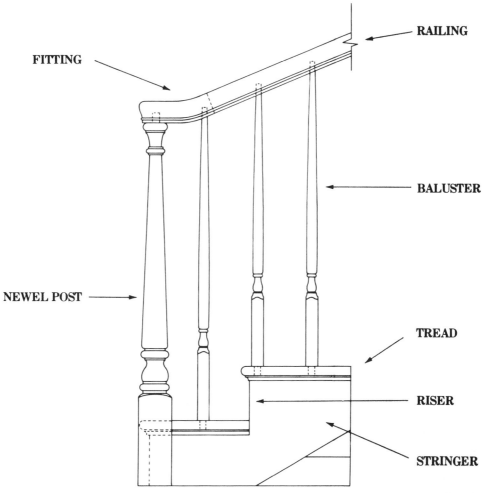

RAILING

FITTING

BALUSTER

NEWEL POST

TREAD

RISER

STRINGER

Courtesy Mansion Industries, Inc.

for the above type of stairs, allow 2-3 hrs. time at the following cost per flight:

	Hours	Rate	Total	Rate	Total
Carpenter	2.5	—	—	$20.60	$51.50

Erect Complete Staircase With Handrails Only. To lay out and erect a complete stair case, including plain wall handrail secured by brackets, figure 6-8 hrs. time at the following labor cost per flight:

	Hours	Rate	Total	Rate	Total
Carpenter	7	—	—	$20.60	$144.20

To complete the above including newels, handrail and balusters, one side, figure 7-10 hrs. time, at the following labor cost per flight:

	Hours	Rate	Total	Rate	Total
Carpenter...	8.5	—	—	$20.60	$175.10

SHOP-MADE STAIRS (Wood)

Placing Shop-made Stairs. To place shop-made stairs with stringers housed out to receive risers and treads, figure 6-8 hrs. stair-builders time to lay out the work, set stringers, treads and risers (wall rail attached to brackets) at the following labor cost per flight:

	Hours	Rate	Total	Rate	Total
Stair-builder..	7	—	—	$20.60	$144.20

Placing Short Flights. Stairs having two short flights with an intermediate landing will require 10-12 hrs. stair-builder's time to lay out work, place stringers treads and risers and install plain handrail at the following labor cost.

	Hours	Rate	Total	Rate	Total
Stair-builder..	11	—	—	$20.60	$226.60

Plain Box Stairs. To install a plain box stair (3' to 4' wide and 9' to 10' story height) using open stringers will require 6-8 hrs. stair-builder's time to lay out work, place stringers, treads and risers (not including balustrade or handrail) at the following labor cost for a single flight:

	Hours	Rate	Total	Rate	Total
Stair-builder	7	—	—	$20.60	$144.20

Plain Box Stairs/Two Flights. Plain box stairs consisting of two short flights having an intermediate landing between stories will require 10-12 hrs. of stair-builder's time to lay out the work, place stringers, treads and risers for each short flight of stairs at the following labor cost per flight:

	Hours	Rate	Total	Rate	Total
Stair-builder..	11	—	—	$20.60	$226.60

Short Flights/Complete. The complete labor cost for two short flights of stairs, including newels, handrails and balusters per story height should be approximately as follows:

	Hours	Rate	Total	Rate	Total
Stair-builder..	16	—	—	$20.60	$329.60

WOOD STAIR/OPEN STRINGERS

Open Stringer (Return Nosing).   Wood stairs of the open stringer type having treads with a return nosing projecting out beyond the face of the stringer, will require about 12-14 hrs. of stair-builder's time to lay out the work, place stringers, treads and risers for one flight of stairs containing 16-18 risers at the following labor cost per flight:

	Hours	Rate	Total	Rate	Total
Stair-builder	13	—	—	$20.60	$267.80

If required to place newels, handrail and balusters add approximately 8-9 hrs. stair-builder's time to the above at the following labor cost per flight:

	Hours	Rate	Total	Rate	Total
Stair-builder	8.5	—	—	$20.60	$175.10

Framing Intermediate Landings.   A carpenter should be able to lay out, cut and place a 4' x 8' landing in about 4 to 6 hrs. at the following labor cost per sq. ft.:

	Hours	Rate	Total	Rate	Total
Carpenter	.16	—	—	$20.60	$3.30
Cost per sq. ft				—	3.30

Placing Wood Handrail (On Brackets).   The recommended height for handrails is 34" on landings and 30" on stairs. A carpenter should set brackets and install about 130-140 lin. ft. of wall hung wood rail per 8-hr. day at the following labor cost per 100 lin. ft.:

	Hours	Rate	Total	Rate	Total
Carpenter	5.9	—	—	$20.60	$121.54
Cost per lin. ft				—	1.22

Placing Wood Handrail (On Metal Balusters).   A carpenter should place about 90-110 lin. ft. of wood handrail on metal balusters per 8-hr. day at the following labor cost per 100 lin. ft."

	Hours	Rate	Total	Rate	Total
Carpenter	8	—	—	$20.60	$164.80
Cost per lin. ft				—	1.65

Stairs/Labor Only

Work Unit	Labor/Hours
Cut new well (not including plaster)	8 hrs.
Exterior rear stairs, including rail (limit 16 risers)	16 hrs.

Work Unit	Labor/Hours
Add for each additional riser	1 hr.
Add for each winder	1 hr.
Exterior Front Stairs, including rail (limit 7 risers)	8 hrs.
Replace steps, per tread, including riser, but not stringers	1 hr.
Landings 4' x 7' (add for columns and piers)	4 hrs.
Interior strips - carpenter made per run, plus well	20 hrs.
Stair Repair	
Tread only	½ hr.
Winders	1 hr.
Replace carriage on existing stairs	
Straight runs, per riser	½ hr.
Winders, per riser	1 hr.
Minimum charge for carriages	4 hrs.

Inside Stair Material

Starting Steps

Quarter circle	Red Oak	4' long	$32.00
Half circle	Red Oak	4'-6" long	40.00
Bull nose	Red Oak	4'-6" long	36.00
Scroll end	Red Oak	4'-6" long	40.00

Stringers (not housed)

3/4"x11¼" x 8'-0" long	Red Oak	$26.00
x 10'-0" long	Red Oak	32.00
x 12'-0" long	Red Oak	48.00
x 14'-0" long	Red Oak	54.00
x 16'-0" long	Red Oak	62.00

Treads (not returned; for returns add $1.75)

11/16"x10½" x 3'-0" long	Red Oak	$10.00
x 3'-6" long	Red Oak	11.00
x 4'-0" long	Red Oak	13.00
11/16"x11½" x 3'-0" long	Red Oak	13.00
x 3'-6" long	Red Oak	15.00
x 4'-0" long	Red Oak	17.50
x 5'-0" long	Red Oak	22.00
x 6'-0" long	Red Oak	27.00

Return Nosing

1⅛"x1¾"x1'-2" with 2" return	Red Oak	$ 4.50

Tread Nosing

1⅛"x1¾"x1'-2" long	Red Oak	1.50
11/16"x1⅛"x1'-2" long	Red Oak	1.65

Landing Tread Nosing

11/16"x3½"x3'-0" long	Red Oak	2.40
x3'-6" long	Red Oak	2.70
x4'-0" long	Red Oak	3.00

Tread Brackets

12"x7¾"x¼" 3 ply	Nat. Birch	1.75

Newel Posts

	Birch	Red Oak
3¼"x3¼"x3'- 2" tapered starting—	$14.00	$13.00
x3'-10" tapered, starting—	16.00	16.00
x5'- 3" tapered, landing—	22.00	20.00
x7'- 0" tapered, angle—	26.00	24.00

A custom-built stairway that is both functional and beautiful.

Balusters		**Birch**	**Red Oak**
15/16" round	30" L..	$ 2.15	$ 1.90
or square	33"...	2.25	2.00
	36"..	2.35	2.10
	39" or 42"..	2.65	2.40
Railings—Natural birch, random length			
13/4"x15/8"..		$ 1.70	
13/4"x111/16"...		1.95	
25/8"x111/16"...		2.10	
21/4"x23/8"..		4.25	
Rail Bolts and Plug..		.35	

CUSTOM/SPIRAL/DISAPPEARING STAIRS

Installing Custom Stairs.   When the remodeling project involves a touch of elegance, it may be advisable to include a custom staircase. These units are available in a range of styles, at prices starting at about $1500.00.

If custom stairs are purchased pre-assembled, the installation is greatly simplified. After the opening is boxed in, or the upper level reinforced as necessary, the stair can be set in place. Because of their size and weight, three people are usually required to complete the job. Once in place, all that is needed is to secure the stringers.

	Hours	Rate	Total	Rate	Total
Stair-builder..	2	—	—	$20.60	$41.20
Two helpers...	1	—	—	15.45	30.90
					$72.10

Pre-cut custom stairs are also available, and can be installed by a stair-builder working alone. Stringers must be placed and secured, then treads and risers attached. Allow 6 to 8 hours to complete the installation.

	Hours	Rate	Total	Rate	Total
Stair-builder..	7	—	—	$20.60	$144.20

The installation of pre-assembled or pre-cut custom stairs complete when newels, balusters and rail are placed; a wall railing can also be used if necessary. Figure 2-3 hours for these items.

	Hours	Rate	Total	Rate	Total
Stair-builder..	2.5	—	—	$20.60	$51.50

"Deluxe" - All Wood Spiral Stairways

Red Oak	4'-0" Diameter...................................$3173.00
13 Risers	4'-6" Diameter...................................$3192.00

Carpet Grade Treads }

5'-0" Diameter $3336.00
5'-6" Diameter $3395.00
6'-0" Diameter $3554.58

Above prices include standard 1¾" square baluster with ¼" chamfered edge, 12 carpet grade treads, center support post, platform for carpet wrap, circular rail, landing rail across one side of platform and all necessary hardware for installation. Hardware on spiral stair comes exposed, with an option for hidden hardware at additional cost.

Prices are for knocked down parts for self installation.

Landing Rail: $45.00 per foot. (Rail needed to enclose stair opening includes rail, balusters, trim and hardware.)

Additional:
Newel Post: $45.00 each.
Turned Newel Post: Add $19.00 Per Post.
Turned Balusters: Add $13.00 per baluster.
Additional Risers: Add $263.00 each.
Solid Oak Treads: Add $9.50 each.
Solid Oak Platform: Add $92.00.
Hidden Hardware: Add $103.00.

"Standard" - All Wood Spiral Stairways

Red Oak
13 Risers
Carpet Grade Treads }

4'-0" Diameter $2438.00
4'-6" Diameter $2458.00
5'-0" Diameter $2600.00
5'-6" Diameter $2661.00
6'-0" Diameter $2819.00

Above prices include standard 1-¾" square baluster with ¼" chamfered edge, 12 carpet grade treads, center support post, platform for carpet wrap, circular rail, landing rail across one side of platform and all necessary hardware for installation. Hardware on spiral stair comes exposed, with an option for hidden hardware at additional cost. (Prices for additions are same as in "Deluxe" stairway). Prices are for knocked down parts for self installation.

Landing Rail: $45.00 per foot, includes rail.
Additional:
　Hemlock Tread Stock
　　36".. $ 7.29 ea.
　　42"..　 8.49 ea.
　　48'..　 10.55 ea.
Hidden Hardware:　Add $103.00

Spiral Metal Stairs.　These stairs are finding increasing kinds of use from cottages to luxury homes. Construction is standardized to meet most code and design requirements. To the basic steel structure can be added various types of treads, handrails and railings. The stairs are shipped knocked down and assembly and installation is simple. No welding is required. Figure a stair-builder can assemble and place one flight of spiral metal stairs in 12 hrs. at the following labor cost per flight:

	Hours	Rate	Total	Rate	Total
Stair-builder..	12	—	—	$20.60	$247.00

Installing Disappearing Stairs. Disappearing stairs are primarily used for attics where space for a regular stair is not available. The units come factory assembled ready to install. The standard size disappearing stair opening is 22" x 54", 25" x 54" and figure a carpenter can cut and frame the necessary opening in 2-3 hrs. at the following cost per opening:

	Hours	Rate	Total	Rate	Total
Carpenter..	2.5	—	—	$20.60	$51.50

Since the stair units are quite heavy, 100-150 lbs., installation of the stair requires two carpenters. Allow 2-3 hrs. and two carpenters to install the unit properly at the following cost per installation:

	Hours	Rate	Total	Rate	Total
Carpenter..	5	—	—	$20.60	$103.00

Disappearing Stairways. (Opening 22' x 54", 25" x 54")

7'10" to 10'...$54.95
10'...$57.95

Spiral Wood Stairs. Wood stairs come in 3'6", 4', 4'6" and 5' diameters with heights made to fit the job conditions. The balusters and center column are steel, but the treads, platforms and railings can be wood. Since the stairs are factory finished and assembled, two carpenters should be able to install the unit in one day at the following cost:

	Hours	Rate	Total	Rate	Total
Carpenter..	16	—	—	$20.60	$329.60

FLOORING

Hardwood Floors. Hardwood strip flooring is still one of the most beautiful, longwearing floors a home can have. It comes in a wide variety of woods, the most common being oak, maple, beech, birch and pecan. The flooring is cut in narrow widths of varying thicknesses. The thinner strips are used primarily for remodeling when the floor is laid over an existing floor in order not to reduce room height. This is a benefit for the remodeler since thinner strips cost less than thicker strips, and consequently he can offer the homeowner the beauty of wood at less cost. Oak is the most common and is used in almost 80% of the homes having hardwood flooring. Sizes vary from 1" to 3 1/2" in width, from 5/16" to 33/32" in thickness. In tongue and groove flooring the most commonly used is 25/32" which comes in 1½", 2", 2¼" and 3¼", with 2¼" being the width most frequently installed.

For square-edge oak, the thickness is 5/16" in the following: 1", 1⅛", 1½" and 2" widths. Maple, beech, birch and pecan come in 25/32" and 33/32" with 2½" and 3½" widths in each thickness.

GRADING/ALL WOODS

Pecan. Manufactured in six standard grades, two specifying heartwood and one bright sapwood. Otherwise color variation is not considered.

Maple, Beech, Birch. The grading of maple, beech and birch is almost identical. Neither sapwood or varying colors are considered a defect in standard grades. These grades are first, second and third, with first being the best grade. Each of these grades comes in special color grades, selected for uniformity of color "Selected First Grade Light Northern Hard Maple" and "Selected First Grade Amber Northern Hard Maple".

Oak. *(Quarter Sawed)*

Clear. The face shall be practically clear, admitting an average of ⅜" of bright sap. The question of color shall not be considered. Bundles shall be 2' and up. Average length 4¼'.

Select. The face may contain sap, small streaks, pin worm holes, burls, slight imperfections in working, and small tight knots which do not average more than one to every 3 feet. Bundles to be 2' and up. Average length 3¾'.

Oak. *(Plain Sawed)*

Clear. The face shall be practically clear, admitting an average of ⅜" of bright sap. Color shall not be considered. Bundles to be 2' and up. Average length 4¼'.

Select. The face may contain sap, small streaks, pin worm holes, burls, slight imperfections in working, and small tight knots which do not average more than one to every 3 feet. Bundled, 2' and up. Average length 3¾'.

No. 1 Common. Shall be of such nature that will lay a good residential floor and may contain varying wood characteristics, such as flags, heavy streaks and checks, worm holes, knots and minor imperfections in working. Bundles are 2' and up. Average length 2½'.

No. 2 Common. May contain sound natural variations and manufacturing imperfections. The purpose of this grade is to make available an economical flooring for homes, general utility use or where character and natural imperfections for appearance are desired. Bundles are 1¼' and up. Average length 2½'.

1¼ **Shorts.** Pieces 9-18" long. Pieces graded No. 1 Common, Select and Clear, bundled together and designated as such. Pieces graded No. 2 Common are bundled and labeled separately. Although pieces 6" under or only 3" over the nominal length of the bundle may be included, pieces must average 1¼' long.

Standard Thicknesses And Widths

(Tonque and Groove)		(Square Edge)	
Width	Thickness	Width	Thickness
25/32	1½", 2"		
	2¼", 3¼"		7/8", 1", 11/8"
3/8"	1½", 2"	5/6"	11/4", 11/3", 11/4"
1/2"	1½", 2"		and 2"

REMOVALS

To Remove Old Hardwood Strip Flooring. Figure one carpenter and one helper can remove 100 sq. ft. of flooring per hour at the following cost per sq. ft.:

	Hours	Rate	Total	Rate	Total
Carpenter	1	—	—	$20.60	$20.60
Helper	1	—	—	17.10	17.10
Cost per 100 sq. ft.			—		37.70
Cost per sq. ft.			—		.38

To the above add .75 hrs. for removal of debris.

Removal of Wood Subflooring. Where existing subfloors are badly worn and must be removed, figure one carpenter and one helper can remove 100 sq. ft. per hour at the following cost:

	Hours	Rate	Total	Rate	Total
Carpenter	1	—	—	$20.60	$20.60
Helper	1	—	—	17.10	17.10
Cost per 100 sq. ft.			—		37.70
Cost per sq. ft.			—		.38

To the above add .5 hrs. for removal of debris.

Replacing Wood Subflooring. In small cut-up areas a carpenter should be able to lay between 700-800 ft. b.m. of 1" x 6" or 1" x 8" at the following labor cost per 100 b.f.:

	Hours	Rate	Total	Rate	Total
Carpenter	1	—	—	$20.60	$20.60
Helper	.75	—	—	17.10	12.85
Cost per 100 b.f.	1.75		—		33.45

To Add Plywood Over Existing Subfloors. Labor for 100 sq. ft. of plywood added over existing subfloor would be as follows:

	Hours	Rate	Total	Rate	Total
Carpenter	1	—	—	$22.60	$22.60
Helper	.50	—	—	17.10	8.55
Cost per 100 sq. ft.			—		31.15
Cost per sq. ft.			—		.31

Estimating Material By Board Size

Flooring Size Inches	Bd. Ft. Per 100 Sq. Ft.	1000 Bd. Ft. Will Lay Sq. Ft.
25/32 x 1 1/2"	155.0	645.0
25/32 x 2"	142.5	701.8
25/32 x 2 1/4"	138.3	723.0
25/32 x 3 1/4"	129.0	775.2
3/8 x 1 1/2"	138.3	723.0
3/8 x 2"	130.0	769.0
1/2 x 1 1/2"	138.3	723.0
1/2 x 2"	130.0	769.0

Nails Per 100 Sq. Ft.

Flooring	Nails	Spacing	Approx. Lbs. Per 100 Sq. Ft.
25/32 x 1 1/2" T&G	7d, 8d cut or screw or 2" barbed	10-12"	3.7
25/32 x 2 1/4" T&G	7d, 8d cut or screw or 2" barbed	10-12"	3.0
25/32 x 3 1/4" T&G	7d, 8d cut or screw or 2" barbed	10-12"	2.3
1/2 x 2" T&G	5d cut or screw	8-10"	3.0
3/8 x 1 1/2" T&G	4d cut or screw	8"	3.7
Installing On Wooden Subfloor			
3/8 x 2" T&G	4d wire, cut or screw or 1 1/4" barbed	6-8"	3.0
3/8 x 1 1/2" T&G	4d cut or screw	8"	3.7

Underlayment Prices

Plywood underlayment (Smooth one-side, "C" Cross Band)

Sq. Edge (⅝ P & TS)	0.43 ft.	13.768	4'x8'
T&G (¾)	0.50 ft.	15.99	4'x8'

Particle board (under layment)

4' x 8'-⅜"	6.59 ea.
4' x 8'-½"	7.19 ea.
4' x 8'-⅝"	7.79 ea.
4' x 8'-¾"	10.55 ea.

Labor Laying 1000 ft. B.M. Soft and Hardwood Flooring

Flooring/Location	Ordinary Workmanship		
	Ft. B.M. Laid Per 8 Hr. Day	Installer Hrs.	Labor Hrs.
25/32" x 31/4" face softwood floors for porches, kitchens, etc.	500–600	14.5	4
25/32" x 21/4" face oak flooring	350–400	21.0	4
Same as above laid by experienced floorlayer	400–450	19.0	4
25/32" x 11/2" face oak flooring	250–280	30.0	5
Same as above laid by experienced floorlayer	350–400	21.0	5
First Grade Workmanship			
25/32" x 21/4" face oak flooring	275–300	28.0	4
Same as above laid by experienced floorlayer	325–375	23.0	4
25/32" x 11/2" face oak flooring	175–225	39.0	5
Same as above laid by experienced floorlayer	275–300	28.0	5

Estimating Quantities Of Wood Flooring*

Measured Size/Inches	Inches	Bundle	Waste/%	For Quantity of Flooring Required Multiply Area By	No. of Ft. of Flooring Required For 100 sq. ft.
1 x 2	3/8 x 11/2	24	331/3	11/3 or 1.33	133
1 x 21/2	3/8 x 2	24	25	11/4 or 1.25	125
1 x 21/4	25/32 x 11/2	12	501/3	11/2 or 1.50	150
1 x 23/4	25/32 x 2	12	371/2	13/8 or 1.375	1371/2
1 x 3	25/32 x 21/4	12	331/3	11/3 or 1.33	133
1 x 4	25/32 x 31/4	8	25	11/4 or 1.25	125

*When estimating the quantity of wood flooring required for any job, take the actual number of sq. ft. in space to be floored and add allowances as shown above.

Laying Wood Floors.   In larger cities, workmanship is apt to be categorized in three classes. The first is generally a carpenter who does nothing but lay flooring. In the second are floorlayers who also do nothing but lay floors, but because of their proficiency can generally lay more flooring, more efficiently than a carpenter/floorer. The last category refers to a floorlayer who is not only proficient in laying floors but offers a quality of workmanship required in high class buildings and residences. First grade workmanship means all flooring closely driven up, laid free of hammer marks, with all nails set.

Labor Laying 100 Sq. Ft. of Hardwood Floors

Description of Work	Sq. Ft. Laid 8 hr. day	Installer Hrs.	Labor Hrs.
(Ordinary Workmanship)			
25/32 x 3¼" Softwood for porches, kitchens, etc.	400–500	1.8	0.6
25/32 x 2¼" Face Oak	250–300	2.9	0.6
Experienced floorlayer for above	300–350	2.5	0.6
25/32 x 1½" Face Oak	150–200	4.5	0.8
Experienced floorlayer for above	225–275	3.2	0.8
(First Grade Workmanship)			
25/32 x 2¼" Face Oak	200–225	3.8	0.6
25/32 x 1½" Face Oak	120–150	6.0	0.8

Laying Strip Flooring Over Concrete. Many homes today are built on concrete slabs because of the savings that can be achieved. In such dwellings, however, the slab serves as the subflooring. A fast, economical way to provide nailing for strip wood flooring over concrete subfloors is to lay sleepers in mastic.

Clean the slab and prime the surface. Snap a chalk line at right angles to the direction the flooring will run and cover the lines with adhesive according to the manufacturer's recommendations. Bottom sleepers treated with a wood preservative, are placed in the adhesive, and nailed at intervals of 24". The bottom sleepers are covered with polyethylene film 0.004 thick which is joined by lapping the edges over the sleepers. A second course of 1 x 2's (untreated) is laid over the bottom course of sleepers and nailed through the polyethylene film into the bottom sleeper, spacing nails 18-24" apart. Using appropriate flooring nails, the flooring is blind nailed at right angles to the sleepers. A minimum of ½" to 1" clearance between flooring and wall should be left to allow for expansion.

Under ordinary circumstances an installer should prime concrete, spread mastic, place sleepers and film at a rate of 50 sq. ft. per hour. Labor for placing the strip wood flooring is the same as for wood subflooring.

FINISHING HARDWOOD FLOORS

Although most unfinished hardwood flooring comes smoothly surfaced from the factory, scratches, nicks and blemishes generally occur when it is laid. Consequently sanding is usually required. The work should usually be let out to a specialist.

The floors are first sanded with a floor sanding machine with the edges being finished by a disc-type edging sander which is capable of sanding up

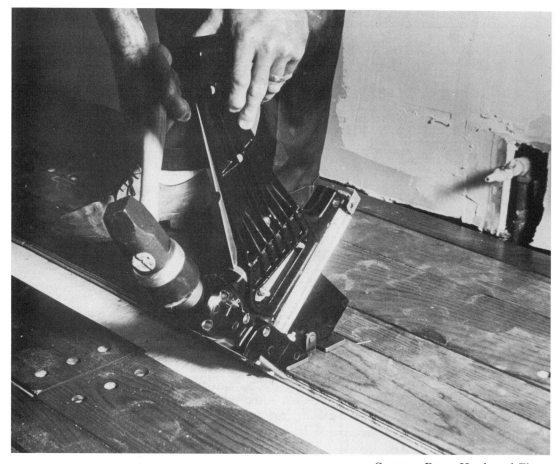

Courtesy Bruce Hardwood Floors

Proper nailing equipment aids efficient installation of hardwood floors.

to the base shoe or quarter round. For a high quality job, most manufacturers recommend at least four sandings, starting with No. 2 grit, going down to No. ½, No. 0 and last No. 00. However, the grits used will vary with the condition of the floor.

Sanding/Ordinary Grade Workmanship. The class of workmanship or number of operations governs production and cost but where an ordinary grade of workmanship is required in average size rooms, a good machine and operator should finish and edge 800-900 sq. ft. per 8-hr. day at the following cost per 100 sq. ft.:

	Hours	Rate	Total	Rate	Total
Machine Expense	1	—	—	$ 5.00	$ 5.00
Sand Paper		—	—	1.00	1.00
Operator	1	—	—	17.00	17.00
Cost per 100 sq. ft.			—		23.00
Cost per sq. ft.			—		0.23

Sanding/First Grade Workmanship. In residences where first grade workmanship is required to eliminate all irregularities and waves, nicks and scratches, about four cuts are required. First with No. 1½ or No. 2 grit, then No. ½ or No. 1 grit and the last two cuts with No. 0 grit. On work of this kind an experienced operator should finish and edge 400-500 sq. ft. of floor per 8 hr. day at the following cost per 100 sq. ft.:

	Hours	Rate	Total	Rate	Total
Machine Expense	1.75	—	—	$ 5.00	$ 8.25
Sand Paper		—	—	2.00	2.00
Operator	1.75	—	—	17.00	29.75
Cost per 100 sq. ft.		—	—		40.50
Cost per sq. ft			—		0.41

Resurfacing Old Floors/First Grade Workmanship. There is little difference between resurfacing an old floor and surfacing a new floor except that under normal conditions one extra cut with a special open-faced abrasive is necessary to remove old varnish or paint. First grade workmanship generally requires four cuts. The amount of sq. ft. finished in one day will vary with the condition of the floor, with the spread running from 300 to 1000 sq. ft. per 8 hr. day. The following is an approximation of the cost per sq. ft. of finish flooring in old floors:

	Hours	Rate	Total	Rate	Total
Machine expense	1	—	—	$ 5.00	$ 5.00
Sand Paper		—	—	2.00	2.00
Operator	1	—	—	17.00	17.00
Cost per hour			—		24.00

Cost per sq. ft. (300 sq. ft. per 8-hr. day)	$0.64
” (500 ”)	0.38
” (750 ”)	0.26
” (1000 ”)	0.19

STAINING/SEALING

Staining. The first coat of stain or other finish should be applied the same day as the last sanding, otherwise, the wood grain can rise and the subsequent finish will be slightly rough. If stain is used, it should be applied before the wood filler and any other finishes. A painter should be able to apply 1200-1600 sq. ft. of stain per 8-hr. day at the following cost per 100 sq. ft.:

	Hours	Rate	Total	Rate	Total
Stain		—	—		$2.50
Painter	0.7	—	—	$17.50	12.25
Cost per 100 sq. ft..................................			—		$14.75

The cost of good stain runs from $8.00 to $15.00 per gallon. A gallon will cover about 800 sq. ft.

Wood Filler.   Paste wood filler is customarily used to fill the crevices and large pores usually found in hardwoods. For residential oak flooring, it is always recommended. It is usually applied after floor stains and seals, but always before other finished materials. IT SHOULD BE ALLOWED TO DRY 24-HRS. BEFORE THE NEXT OPERATION IS BEGUN. Paste wood filler comes in 3 lb. cans with prices running from $7.00 to $8.00. A 1-lb. can will normally cover about 100 sq. ft. A painter can usually apply about 1300-1400 sq. ft. of filler per 8-hr. day at the following cost per 100 sq. ft.:

	Hours	Rate	Total	Rate	Total
Filler		—	—		$ 2.50
Painter	0.6	—	—	$17.50	10.50
Cost per 100 sq. ft..................................			—		$13.00

Sealing.   Today's homeowner wants a floor surface that's attractive, durable, easy to maintain and can be retouched in worn areas without creating a patchy appearance. The three types of finish preferred are floor seal, varnish and shellac. Floor seal has the advantage in that it penetrates the fibers and cells of the wood, sealing the pores in such a way that they are highly resistant to dirt, water and stains, and wears only as the wood wears down. Floor seal comes in a variety of decorator type colors, averaging $15.00 per gallon with coverage ranging from 400-450 sq. ft. per gallon for the first coat, 650-750 for the second. An experienced painter can finish about 1000 sq. ft. of natural finish floor per 8-hr. day at the following cost per 100 sq. ft. (Color seals take more time as the excess pigment must be wiped by hand):

	Hours	Rate	Total	Rate	Total
Sealer (first coat)...................................		—	—		$ 3.75
Painter	0.8	—	—	$17.50	14.00
Cost per 100 sq. ft..................................			—		17.75
Cost per sq. ft					0.18

Varnish averages $14.00 per gallon with coverage being 350-400 sq. ft. for the first coat and 450-500 for the second.

Plank Flooring/Prefinished. Oak is preferred for plank floors. However, they can be obtained in other woods as well as various veneers. The most popular oak comes in ¾" thickness in widths of 3-8" with random lengths. Generally, the pieces are tongue and grooved, with square or matched ends. They are also produced with square edges or matched ends. Special distressed finishes and pegging are also available. Plain flooring in mixed widths will run about $4.00 per sq. ft.

Courtesy Bruce Hardwood Floors

Modern hardwood planking with "pegs" for an authentic appearance.

Premium finishes will add as much as $2.00 per sq. ft. One carpenter should lay at least 150 sq. ft. per 8-hr. day.

	Hours	Rate	Total	Rate	Total
Carpenter..................................	8	—	—	$20.60	$164.80
Oak Planking		—	—		600.00
Nails		—	—		5.00
Cost per 150 sq. ft............................			—		$769.80
Cost per sq. ft...........................			—		5.13

PARQUET FLOORING

Wood parquet is available in many designs and woods, including mahogany, oak, walnut, teak, cherry and maple and more. Patterns are available in "prime grade", "character marked", squared and beveled edges. Sizes run from 9" x 9", to 12" x 12", 16" x 16" up to 36" x 36". Standard thickness is 5/16", with custom orders going 11/16" and 13/16". Prices range from $3.00 per sq. ft. for standard quality to $6.00 per sq. ft. for premium quality. Parquet flooring may be nailed over wood subfloors, or old finish floors or laid in mastic over concrete. It can also be laid in mastic over subfloors and existing wood floors. Where installation is over square edge board subflooring, one layer of 15 lb. asphalt saturated felt should be laid

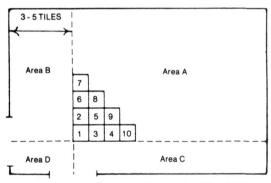

Courtesy Kentucky Wood Floors

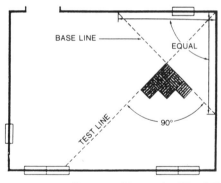

Courtesy Kentucky Wood Floors

Layout For Parquet—Use a chalk line to lay out working lines, as above. Walls are seldom square, so be sure lines are at right angles to each other. One test for this is to measure from the intersection 3 ft. down one line and 4 ft. down the other. The distance between these two points should be 5 ft. Lines should be placed 3 to 5 tiles distance from each wall or centered on physical features of the room, e.g. doors, bay windows and fireplaces. Measuring with actual tiles will save unnecessary cutting at these two walls. Small areas such as entry foyers or halls may not require working lines.

Alternate Layout—An alternate method is to lay the parquet squares in a diagonal pattern. Although slightly more difficult, the change in appearance can be dramatic. Measure equal distances from one corner of a room along both walls, and snap a chalk-line between these points to form the base line as shown above. This pattern need not be at a precise 45° angle to walls in order to appear perfect. A test line should again intersect the center of the base line at exactly 90°.

in standard linoleum paste to keep the mastic from seeping through joints. Expansion joints must be left around all perimeters of rooms according to manufacturers specifications. Cost Per Sq. Ft. 9" x 9" Parquet Flooring Installed With Mastic:

	Hours	Rate	Total	Rate	Total
100 sq. ft. Oak Parquet		—	—	—	$350.00
3½ lbs. nails		—	—		$ 3.15
Floorlayer	5.0	—	—	$22.00	110.00
Helper	5.0	—	—	16.50	82.50
Cost per 100 sq. ft				—	545.65
Cost per sq. ft				—	5.46

For 8" x 8" parquet figure labor for 100 sq. ft. at approximately 6.5 hrs. for nailing and 3.5 hrs. for adhesive.

Laminated Oak Blocks. Laminated oak blocks are fabricated from 3-ply all oak plywood and come factory finished in 9" x 9" x ½" squares. A 27 sq. ft. carton (48 pieces) will cost about $94.50. Installation is generally the same as for parquet flooring and the cost per sq. ft. installed would be the same as above taking into account the difference in cost between the two products.

TILE AND SHEET FLOORING

Resilient flooring includes asphalt tile, vinyl asbestos tile, rubber tile, cork and linoleum. Since each product has various performance characteristics, it should be selected more for its performance than its cost, and manufacturers recommendations should be carefully checked before installation.

For example, if it is to be installed on or below grade, linoleum, cork and certain vinyls should not be used. If grease is a problem, rubber, cork and asphalt tile should not be used. If resilience and quietness are desired, cork and rubber should be considered, but leave vinyl out. One of the advantages of sheet goods is that it does not shrink. On the other hand, some tiles will shrink and as a result, separate.

Asphalt Tile. Asphalt tiles are usually furnished 12" x 12" in various colors and patterns. It is one of several types that can be used on concrete and below grade, such as basement floors, as it is not susceptible to the moisture and alkali always present in concrete in contact with the ground. Asphalt tiles are used in residences where a low-cost flooring is desired. Prices per tile are approximately $0.20-0.65 for 12" x 12" tile.

When applying resilient flooring over wood subfloors, the floor should be smooth and level and covered with a layer of lining felt bonded to the wood with an approved mastic (such as Armstrong S235 which averages $5.50 per gallon and covers approximately 133 sq. ft.) 15 lb. Lining felt comes in rolls 36" wide by 50 yds. long (or 432 sq. ft.) costing about $12.50 per roll or $.82 per sq. yd. Figure one man can lay 250 to 300 sq. ft. per hour.

In some cases, resilient flooring requires an underlayment of plywood or particle board. The boards should be staggered at the joints and separated by about 1/32" to allow for expansion. Underlayment boards come in 4' x 8' x 3/8" and average $5.30 per board. One man can lay 320 sq. ft. of boards in 8 hours.

When estimating the quantity of resilient flooring to be installed, always figure a percentage for waste. The allowable percentages are shown below:

Approximate Percentages For Allowable Waste

Up to 50 sq. ft.	14%
50 to 100 sq. ft.	10%
100 to 200 sq. ft.	7% to 9%
200 to 300 sq. ft.	6% to 7%
500 to 1000 sq. ft.	4% to 5%
1000 to 5000 sq. ft.	4%
5000 to 10,000 sq. ft.	3% to 4%
10,000 and up	1½% to 3%

Primer and Asphalt Cement Required.   When priming concrete floors, one gallon of primer sealer should cover 275 to 325 sq. ft. depending upon the porosity of the surface. Primer costs about $15.00 gal. One gallon of asphalt mastic cement should lay about 175 to 225 sq. ft. of tile depending on the condition of the subfloor. One gallon costs about $18.00. One gallon of asphalt emulsion used to install asphalt tile over lining felt on wood floors will cost about $7.50 and will cover about 130 to 150 sq. ft.

Labor Laying Asphalt Tile.   An experienced tile setter should be able to lay the following quantity of tile per 8-hr. day.

Tile Size	Sq. Ft. Per 8-Hr. Day	Hours Per 100 Sq. Ft.
9" x 9"	400-425	2.0
12" x 12" (½')	650-700	1.2

Sq. Ft. Prices/Asphalt Tile
Price Per Tile*

Size

12" x 12"	25-65¢ (+ 10¢ per tile for self-adhesive)

   *Depends on color

Courtesy Kentucky Wood Floors

Parquet designs are almost as limitless as a kaliedoscope. This is Burl Walnut Citation with Oak Bands and is ¾" x 36" x 36".

Cost of Laying 100 Sq. Ft. Asphalt Tile
Over Concrete Floors

	Hours	Rate	Total	Rate	Total
0.6 Gal. Asphalt Primer		—	—		$ 9.00
105 Sq. Ft. Tile (12" x 12")...................		—	—		47.25
0.5 Gal. Asphalt Cement......................		—	—		9.00
Tile-Setter	1.6	—	—	$18.75	30.00
Cost per 100 sq. ft.............................			—		$95.25
Cost per sq. ft...................................			—		0.95

If concrete primer is not required, deduct asphalt primer, asphalt cement, 0.4 hr. labor and add 0.75 gal. of asphalt emulsion.

Cost of Laying 100 Sq. Ft. Asphalt Tile
Over Wood Subfloor

	Hours	Rate	Total	Rate	Total
0.75 Gal. Emulsion Adhesive...............		—	—		$ 6.00
12 Sq. Yds. Lining Felt.........................		—	—		6.00
105 Sq. Ft. Tile....................................		—	—		47.25
0.75 Gal. Asphalt Emulsion.................		—	—		13.50
Tile-Setter	1.2	—	—	$18.75	22.50
Cost per 100 Sq. Ft............................			—		$95.25
Cost per Sq. Ft.			—		0.95

VINYL TILE

Asbestos. Vinyl asbestos tiles are relatively inexpensive and can be used anywhere, above or below grade. They come in a wide variety of colors and designs and are one of the most widely used floor coverings today. They have good durability and low maintenance cost. They are generally available in 9" x 9" and 12" x 12" squares in thicknesses of 1/16", 3/32" and 1/8". Costs are about $.50 to $.75 per sq. ft. Installation costs are approximately the same as those for asphalt tile. Figure approximately the following:

Tile Size	Sq. Ft. Per 8-Hr. Day	Hours Per 100 Sq. Ft.
9" x 9"	360-390	2.4

Plastic. Vinyl plastic tile is a more expensive resilient flooring material. However, it is very stable, will not shrink or expand and is highly resistant to oils, fats, greases, acids, alkalis, detergents, soaps and most solvents. Subfloor requirements are the same as for other resilient floorings. It can also be laid over concrete floors, on grade or below grade using special adhesives. Sizes available include: 9" x 9" and 12" x 12" tile.

Material costs vary according to pattern, ranging from $1.05 sq. ft. for 1/16" embossed patterns to $8.00 per sq. ft. for 1/8" clear patterns. Comes in

1/16", 3/32", & 1/8" thicknesses. Installation rates are about the same as those for asphalt tile. However, you can figure a tile setter can lay 100 sq. ft. of 9" x 9" tile in approximately 2.4 hrs. For 100 sq. ft. of tile figure 1.35 gals. of mastic.

Estimating Floor Tile Quantities

Sq. Ft.	Tiles Required			
	6" x 6"	9" x 9"	12" x 12"	9" x 18"
20	80	36	20	18
40	160	72	40	36
60	240	107	60	54
80	320	143	80	72
100	400	178	100	90
200	800	356	200	178

Vinyl Parquet and Plank. New on the market is an elastomeric floor covering which looks like wood and has a grain you can actually feel. It is being marketed for both new construction and remodeling.

The interlocking parquet pieces come in two patterns and both the parquet and plank come in five different simulated woods of varying colors to fit a wide variety of decors. Both have a polymer coating giving them excellent resistance to abrasion stains and cigarette burns.

The interlocking parquet modules come in two sizes, approximately 19¾" x 19" x ¾" for the larger and 16¾" x 13⅜" for the smaller. The approximate laying area for the former is 33 sq. ft. per case and the latter 35 sq. ft. per case. All planks are approximately 60" long and come in three face widths: approximately 4.4", 6.4" and 8.4".

Installation can be made over most sound substrates which are smooth, clean and free from hydrostatic water or moisture problems. It is set in mastic with a special adhesive supplied by the manufacturer. A gallon of adhesive will cost approximately $30.00 and cover 150-200 sq. ft.

Approximate prices for each product are:

19¾"x19¾" Tile (unfinished)	$1.29 sq. ft.
16¾"x13¾" " "	1.29 sq. ft.
Oak Strip Flooring	
¾"x2¼" (unfinished)	1.79 sq. ft.
¾"x2¼" (finished)	2.69 sq. ft.
Oak Plank	
¾"x4.4" (unfinished)	5.00 sq. ft.
¾"x6.4" "	5.00 sq. ft.
¾"x8.4" "	5.00 sq. ft.
Kentile, Briarwood	
12"x12"x⅛"	5.12 sq. ft.
4"x36"x⅛"	3.86 sq. ft.
Kentile, Parquet	
12"x12"x⅛"	3.75 sq. ft.

Courtesy Armstrong Floors

Random Plank in light woodtone is one of 12 offerings in Armstrong's new Woodstock collection of durable vinyl floors that look like wood. There is also another plank, plus four parquet squares whose designs were inspired by the ornate wood floors in historic American houses.

An experienced floor layer should be able to install about 100 sq. ft. of parquet or plank per 8-hr. day at the following cost per sq. ft.:

	Hours	Rate	Total	Rate	Total
Installer	8	—	—	$18.75	$150.00
Tile		—	—		794.85
Adhesive	0.5 gal.	—	—		5.50
Cost per 100 sq. ft			—		$950.35
Cost per sq. ft			—		9.50

SHEET FLOORING

Vinyl. Vinyl sheet flooring is presently one of the most popular floor coverings for modern residential use. There's a color and pattern to suit almost any decor. What's more, research and technology have all but eliminated the few drawbacks exhibited when vinyl was first introduced.

Today's products have exceptional stain and abrasion resistance. Installation can be at all grade levels. New backings resist alkali moisture and hydrostatic pressure. Some even inhibit the growth of mildew. New surface coatings up to 25-mills thick minimize wear and upkeep.

Installation time and costs have been reduced with the addition of 12' widths to complement the standard 6' width. And under certain conditions a number of vinyls can be loose-laid without adhesive.

When applying vinyl sheet, many installers install a new subfloor over the old surface before putting the new covering down. Not only does this eliminate the irregularities of old flooring, but the composition of some of the new subfloor materials help provide a better bond and surface for the new flooring. One of the newer products for this purpose is Armstrong "Tempboard"®. It comes in two sizes, 3' x 4' and 4' x 4', both ¼" thick.

Figure an experienced installer can place about 270 sq. ft. of Tempboard in 4-hrs. at the following cost per 100 sq. ft.:

	Hours	Rate	Total	Rate	Total
Installer	1.48	—	—	$22.50	$ 33.30
Tempboard		—	—		240.00
Cost per 100 sq. ft.			—		$273.30
Cost per sq. ft.			—		2.73

Labor to Install 175 Gauge Vinyl Sheet Flooring. A recommended adhesive for vinyl sheeting is S235 costing approximately $17.00 per gallon. Coverage is about 150-175 sq. ft. per gallon. An experienced installer of sheet vinyl should place about 450 sq. ft. of flooring in 4-hrs. at the following cost per 100 sq. ft.:

	Hours	Rate	Total	Rate	Total
Installer	.89	—	—	$22.50	$20.03
Adhesive	3 gal.	—	—		51.00
Cost per 100 sq. ft.			—		$71.03
Cost per sq. ft.			—		0.71

For loose-laying and stapling, figure about 150 sq. ft. per hr. at a cost of approximately $0.15 per sq. ft.

Courtesy Armstrong Floors

No-wax floors like this fleur-de-lis on white design from Armstrong's new Solarian Supreme collection, are now turning up in elegant family rooms, baths and foyers, as well as kitchens.

QUICK REFERENCE CHART #2

Labor Factors For Installing Stairs

Item Description	Unit	Factor			
Balusters		30" SW	30" HW	42" SW	42" HW
Minimum	EA	.2857	.2857	.2963	.2963
Maximum	EA	.3077	.3077	.3200	.3200
Newels		Starting		Landing	
Minimum	EA	1.1429		1.6000	
Maximum	EA	1.3333		2.0000	
Railings		Minimum		Maximum	
Built up HW	LF	.1333		.1455	
Subrail	LF	.0727			
Risers		Softwood		Hardwood	
1 x 8	LF	.1212		.1250	
Skirt board					
1 x 10	LF	.1455			
1 x 12	LF	.1538			
Treads	Length	3'-0"	4'-0"	5'-0"	6'-0"
5/4 x 10 Oak	EA	.4444	.4706		
5/4 x 12 Oak	EA	.4444			.5714
2" Maple	EA	.4444		.5000	
2 1/4 Maple	EA	.4444		.5333	
Box Stairs	Height	2'-0"	4'-0"	6'-0"	8'-0"
Prefabricated					
3'-0" Wide	FLIGHT	2.7200	3.4000	3.8857	4.5333
3'-6" Wide	FLIGHT	3.2000	4.0000	4.5714	5.3333
4'-0" Wide	FLIGHT	3.5200	4.4000	5.0285	5.8667
Prefab rail					
W/Balusters	RISER	.26667			
Basement Prefab 3' Wide					
W/Open Riser	FLIGHT	4.0000			
Open Stairs		2'-0"	4'-0"	6'-0"	8'-0"
Prefab RSC no rail					
3'-6" Wide	FLIGHT	3.2000	4.0000	4.5714	5.3333
Prefab RSC w/rail					
3'-6" Wide	FLIGHT	4.2667	5.1429	5.8014	6.6667
3/6 x 3/6 Landing	EA		4.0000		
Curved Stairs-Oak			9'-0"	10'-0"	
Open 1 Side w/rail					
3'-3" Wide	FLIGHT		22.8571	22.8571	
Open 2 Side					
3'-3" Wide	FLIGHT		32.0000	32.0000	
Residential-Oak					
Prefab	FLIGHT	10.6667			
Built in place	FLIGHT	36.3636			
Spiral-Oak w/rail					
Prefab					
4'-6" Dia	FLIGHT	10.6667			

CHAPTER 7

DRYWALL, PANELING AND CEILING TILE

Walls and Ceilings. When it comes to walls, women look for the right colors and aesthetic qualities while men want to know the material options and the advantages of each.

On the whole, however, color has become the big marketing tool. The trend is to softer and lighter colors. Light colors give rooms a more spacious feeling, and permit rooms to be better lighted with less fixtures. The use of fewer lights and smaller living spaces have been dictated by energy. Wall coverings are reflecting these changes in life-style.

In paneling for example, there is a trend to light-colored woodgrains such as birch or light pecan. The oaks, pines, maples and walnuts remain as strongly established woods. And paneling is no longer limited to family rooms or dens, it's being used in every room in the house.

The message here is that remodeling contractors should keep abreast of decorator trends even though they tend to originate in new construction. Today's homeowners want their homes to reflect contemporary styling even though they may be remodeling only one room.

However, in the older home, it isn't paneling or other types of wall treatments the remodeling contractor has to deal with initially; frequently, it's plaster. Often they are asked what caused cracks in walls and ceilings and whether to repair, replace or reface them. Many cracks are not due to workmanship, but faults in the material to which they are applied. These can be lumber shrinkage; foundation settlement, inadequate bracing and expansion and contraction.

However, because of poor workmanship, plaster can spall, crack and disintegrate. A common condition occurs when the white coat is applied over a base coat that has been allowed to dry out too much. When the white coat is applied, the base coats soaks the moisture from the finish coat and a spidery pattern of cracking occurs. If the surface of the plaster seems soft, the plaster has probably been oversanded. If cracks occur at random on the white coat, the coat was probably too thin.

Unless major defects are involved, structural cracks reach an equilibrium and can be successfully patched if the plaster on each side is not loose.

If the crack is less than ½" wide, dig out an inverted "v" joint, moisten the adjacent areas to reduce suction and fill with prepared patching compound in two stages.

For larger cracks, the crack should be made large enough to accommodate a piece of metal lath. The resulting channel can then be filled with a three-coat application. For small patch jobs, figure a minimum of $75.00 for labor and materials.

Stripping Walls. To strip a masonry wall of plaster and leave ready to relath and replaster, figure one laborer will strip 60 to 70 sq. ft. per hour.

	Hours	Rate	Total	Rate	Total
Laborer	1.54	—	—	16.67	25.67
Cost per sq. ft:			—		0.26

Replastering Stripped Walls. To replaster a stripped masonry wall with 2-coat gypsum cement plaster figure the cost per sq. yd. as follows:

	Hours	Rate	Total	Rate	Total
1100 lbs. gypsum plaster	—	—	—		$ 58.30
33 cu. ft. sand			—		17.81
340 lbs. hydrated lime		—	—		23.80
170 lbs. of gauging plaster		—	—		12.75
Plasterer	17	—	—	20.45	347.65
Laborer	10	—	—	17.38	173.80
Cost per 100 sq. yds.			—		634.11
Cost per sq.yd.			—		6.34

Three coat work will run around $9.34 a square yard. Work involving small areas with corner beads, etc. will run considerably more.

Relath and Replaster Stripped Walls. To add ⅜" gypsum lath and 2-coat gypsum cement plaster on stripped wood studs, figure the cost per sq. yd. as follows:

	Hours	Rate	Total	Rate	Total
900 sq. ft. ⅜" gypsum lath	—	—	—		118.90
7 lbs. nails		—	—		5.95
Lather	8	—	—	21.17	169.36
1000 lbs. gypsum plaster		—	—		53.00
25 cu. ft. sand		—	—		15.00
510 lbs. fin. hydrated lime		—	—		34.60
Plasterer	16	—	—	20.45	372.20
Laborer	9	—	—	17.38	156.42
Cost per 100 sq. yds.			—		925.43
Cost per sq. yd.			—		9.25

Beads and moldings should be figured separately. If wired or stapled to lath, figure 2½ hrs. per 100 lin. ft; if nailed to masonry figure 3 hrs. per 100 lin. ft. Where door and window casing beads are involved, figure 1 hour for each opening. Corner reinforcing at inside angles can be figured at about 500 lin. ft. per 8-hr. day.

PLASTERING

Combined Labor And Materials Costs*

Price Per Yd. on Rooms 8' to 10' High
(No Allowance For Openings)

Charge One Yard For Each Linear Ft. Of Wall Area

30 yards or under	$ 15.00 per yd.
32 yards to 100 yards	14.00 per yd.
Over 100 yards	12.00 per yd.
Over Stairways	20.00 per yd.

ADD FOR:
Patching Around Windows

Single	$ 20.00 per window
Mullion	30.00 per window
Triple	40.00 per window

Arches

3 ft.	$100.00 per arch
4' to 5'	135.00 per arch
6' to 8'	150.00 per arch
Corner Bead/Outside Corners	.40 per lin. ft.
Close Window Openings With Plaster	30.00 per single opening

*Based on Chicago area costs. Figures will vary according to geographical area.

DRYWALL

Drywall basically refers to sheet material which does not require the use of water for its application. Included are plywood, wood, hardboard, fiberboard and gypsum paneling.

Their benefit is that they require few tools for application and that when correctly applied thay can cover any imperfections of the previous wall.

Required Thicknesses For Various Framing

Panel Thickness		Plywood	Fiberboard	Paneling	Gypsum	Framing
"	"	1/4"	1/2"	3/8"	3/8"	16"
"	"	3/8"	3/4"	1/2"	. . .	20"
"	"	3/8"	3/4"	5/16"	1/2"	24"

Plywood Paneling. Before application, panels should be stored in the room in which they are to be applied, or stored in an area having a similar room temperature. During storage, they should be stored flat with scraps of wood separating each panel so that they can breathe and absorb room moisture, and be covered. The number of panels required for an 8 ft. ceiling room can be determined by measuring the perimeter of the room and using the table shown below.

Estimating The Number Of 4x8 Panels Required
Based On Perimeter Of Room

Room Perimeter	Panels Required	Room Perimeter	Panels Required
36'	9	60'	15
40'	10	64'	16
44'	11	68'	17
48'	12	72'	18
52'	13	76'	20
56'	14	92'	23

1. For example, if the room measures 14' x 20' by 20, the total perimeter is 68' which would require 17 panels.

2. For openings such as doors and windows, use the following deductions: Doors deduct ⅓ panel; windows deduct ¼ panel and fireplaces deduct ½ panel.

3. Always use the next higher number of panels when the total perimeter is between the ranges shown in the table.

Approximate Prices/Paneling

Georgia Pacific
Deluxe Hardwood (4' x 8', ¼")
Barnboard (gray, white, brown) ....$18.55 ea.
Bridgeport (port side pine) .... 19.95 ea.
Old World (cedar) .... 20.55 ea.
    "   "   (birch) .... 16.55 ea.
Firelite (cedar) .... 18.95 ea.

Paneling

Old Savannah ....$16.33 ea.
Blue Pine .... 16.77 ea.

Chestnut Creek - Russet
4' x 8' 1/4" (can be used below grade) .... 7.77 ea.

Bungalow Paneling
4' x 8', 5/32" Mushroom, Tanbark .... 4.49 ea.

Deluxe Print Panels
4' x 8', 5/32" (three patterns, 4 colors) .... 11.95 ea.

Mill Plank, wood veneers
4' x 8', 5/32" (three patterns) .... 12.55 ea.

Weyerhauser
First quality prints on lauan (4' x 8', 5/32")

Romain	$12.77 ea.	Planked Pecan	$ 7.99 ea.
Country Road Autumn	13.55 ea.	Pocono	11.95 ea.
Block house pecan	12.95 ea.	Misty Blue	11.95 ea.
Driftwood	11.55 ea.	Lodi	10.95 ea.
Seashore	12.95 ea.	Wild Life	12.95 ea.
Edgemont	6.77 ea.	Union Oak	12.55 ea.
Alpine	6.77 ea.	New England Scene (1/4")	18.95 ea.

Abitibi
Hardboard Panels
Chesapeake Cherry (4' x 8' - 1/4")..$13.55 ea.
Burnished Cypress   "   "   .... 14.55 ea.

Paneling

Masonite
Louisiana
Walnut   (4' x 8' - 1/4")   ....$ 9.66 ea.
Delaware
Walnut   "   "   .... 9.66 ea.
Tan Brick   "   "   .... 18.22 ea.
Hazelnut   "   "   .... 13.55 ea.
Barnstable
Whites   "   "   .... 14.95 ea.

PPI Plywood Panels
Winter Birch   (4' x 8')   11.55 ea.
Wisconsin Birch   "   11.55 ea.
Michigan Walnut   "   11.55 ea.
Canadian Maple   "   11.55 ea.
Kentucky Oak   "   11.55 ea.
Southern Pecan   "   11.55 ea.
Maple Strip   "   12.55 ea.
Crossover Oak   "   12.55 ea.

Decorator Board (Wallpaper type)
Rigid vinyl covering (4' x 8' - 1/4") 13.77 ea.

Bath and Kitchen Panels (Marlite type)
For high-moisture areas (4' x 8' - 1/8") 13.22 ea.

Adhesives
Tubes....................................$1.99   Quarts ....$ 5.15
Qt. tubes .... 4.19   Gallons.................................... 10.99
Putty Sticks (all colors) $.99 each

Ceilings

Suspended Ceiling Panels
Decorator .... $ 2.39 to $3.39 ea.
Vinyl Coated ....   3.44 ea.
Fire-rated Acoustical......................................   2.77 to 5.66 ea.

Ceiling Grid Metal
Wall Molding (10 ft.)....................................   2.29 ea.
Main Runners (12 ft.)....................................   4.49 ea.
Cross Tees (2 ft.) $0.84 ea. (4 ft.)....................   1.55 ea.
Hanger Wire (6 ft.) ....   .29 ea.
Hanger Hooks ....   1.29 doz.

Luminous Panels
Milk or Clear.................................... $ 3.79 to 8.49 ea.
Scenic ....   6.49 ea.
Colored ....   5.95 to 10.95 ea.

Ceiling Tiles (12" x 12")

Decorator Tiles	$ 0.29 to 0.68 ea.
Vinyl Coated Tiles	0.45 to 0.50 ea.
Acoustical Tiles	0.44 to 0.51 ea.

Accessories

Furring strips (1" x 3")	$ 0.08 lin. ft.
Tile Cement (Qts., $5.29) .... Gal.	14.95
Staples (1000 per box)	2.15

WALL PREPARATION

Existing Walls.   If the existing wall is in good condition the paneling can be applied directly to it. In closed wall applications all studs are located and marked with a chalk line, which should be extended 2" to 3" onto the floor and ceiling. A level on a 2 x 4 should be used to get all markings plumb and straight. All ceiling and floor moldings, window and door moldings, light fixtures and wall plates should be removed. BE SURE ELECTRICITY IS TURNED OFF AT MAIN CONTROL BOX. Tape all exposed wire ends or use wire nuts.

Open Stud Walls.   Be sure all studs are plumb and evenly spaced. This application generally requires a header at the top and bottom between studs and blocking in the center which helps prevent twisting and gives added wall support. Both should be nailed flush with the stud face. Note: On perimeter walls, insulation batts and a vapor barrier should be installed before the paneling is applied. This is priced separately.

If the studs are not wide enough to form nailing pieces for the panels, a strip of wood, usually 1" x 1" is nailed to either side of the stud along its entire length and flush with the face of the stud. With studs spaced 16" on center, a carpenter should cut and place 225 to 275 lin. ft. per 8-hr. day at the following labor cost per 100 lin. ft.

	Hours	Rate	Total	Rate	Total
Carpenter	3.2	—	—	20.60	65.920
Cost per lin. ft.			—		0.66

Concrete and Plaster.   On masonry and concrete walls, furring strips should be applied every 16" horizontally, allowing ¼" between the ceiling and floor of the top and bottom strips. Vertical strips are inserted every 48" to support the panel edges. To obtain a level surface, the furring should be shimmed with wood shims and nailed through the furring strip to hold them in place. With studs 16" on center, a carpenter should cut

It is important all walls be plumb and straight before applying any kind of drywall or paneling.

and place 300 to 350 lin. ft. of furring strips per 8-hr. day at the following labor cost per 100 lin. ft.:

	Hours	Rate	Total	Rate	Total
Carpenter..	2.5	—	—	20.60	51.50
Cost per lin. ft.		—	—		0.52

Installing Panels.   Since the shade and texture of the panels vary somewhat, it's best to simply stand the panels in position against the wall before installation. Rearrange them to achieve the most attractive sequence of color texture.

Before installation, each panel should be cut ¼" shorter than actual ceiling height. Measure floor to ceiling height in several locations to detect any variations. If height varies no more than ¼", take the shortest height, subtract ¼" and cut all panels to that size. If height varies more than ¼" each panel must be cut separately. Ceiling and floor moldings will cover height variations of up to 2".

Place the first panel in the corner against the adjacent wall. Be sure it is perfectly plumb and the right edge is centered over the stud. If not, cut the other edge of the panel so it will. Many times, the corner will be irregular where you are to begin. To allow for such irregularities, place the panel in a plumb position and scribe a line, using a compass, from top to bottom. Cut the scribe line with a coping saw. With the first panel in position, the remainder of the panels should also fall on stud centers

When nailing to studs, use 4d finishing nails spaced 6" on panel edges and 12" in grooves. When nailing to furring, use 2d nails, 8" apart along edges and 16" apart elsewhere. Use matching color head nails or countersink and fill with matching color putty.

The actual cost of placing paneling will vary with the size and shape of the room, whether full size sheets are used or considerable cutting and fitting is necessary. On straight work in large rooms, a carpenter should be able to fit and place approximately 100 sq. ft. or three 4' x 7' or 4' x 8' panels in approximately 1.6 hrs. at the following cost per sq. ft.:

	Hours	Rate	Total	Rate	Total
Carpenter..	1.6	—	—	20.60	32.96
Cost per sq. ft.		—	—		0.33

Gypsum Drywall.   Gypsum drywall is sheet material made of gypsum faced on both sides with heavy grade protective paper. It is used for walls and ceilings in all types of buildings and takes all kinds of decorating including paint and wallpaper.

Sizes And Thicknesses Of Gypsum Wallboard

Thickness	Width	Length
¼"	48"	6 to 12 ft.
⅜"	48"	6 to 12 ft.
½"	48"	6 to 14 ft.
⅝"	48"	6 to 14 ft.

Quarter-inch gypsum wallboard is used as a lightweight, low-cost, utility wallboard. It is also used for curved surfaces or to cover existing wall surfaces. Three-eighths is used principally for repair or remodeling work or in double-wall construction. Half-inch is used in new construction, and ⅝" Type "X" is used where a one-hour fire-rating is required or framing space is in excess of ½" wallboard limitation.

The edges along the length are tapered, and on some types, the ends are also tapered. This permits taping and filling the joint. Gypsum wallboard joints reinforced with tape and cement make a joint as strong as the wallboard itself.

Installing Gypsum Board.   Gypsum board can be installed horizontally or vertically with nails, screws or adhesives. It is best to apply the panels horizontally using full sheets as this keeps the number of joints to a minimum. Any joints necessary should be made at windows and doors. If this is not possible, the joints should be staggered. For ⅜" material use a 4d (1 ⅜" long) nail. If ring shank nails are used, a nail about ⅛" shorter will provide adequate holding power.

The following are nail recommendations with respect to size and spacings, courtesy of the Gypsum Association:

Nails	Wallboard Thickness	Nail	Spacing Walls	Ceilings
GWB-54 Annular	3/8"	11/4 GWB-54	8"	7"
Ring Nails—1/4" head—	1/2"	13/8 GWB-54	8"	7"
.098 gauge—ASTM	5/8"	13/8 GWB-54	8"	7"
C380-60T	1/2" Type "X"	5d Cooler	7"	6"
11/4" long	5/8" Type "X"	6d Cooler	7"	6"
	3/8" Backer Bd.	11/4" GWB-54	8"	7"
13/8" long	1/2" Backer Bd.	13/8" GWB-54	8"	7"*
Cooler Type Nails	1/4"	1" penetration	8"	7"
4d—13/8" long—				
7/32 head—14 ga.				
5d—15/8" long—				
15/64 head—131/2 ga.				
6d—17/8" long—				
1/4 head—13 ga.		*5" on framing spaced 24" o.c.		

Nails should be spaced 6-8" with a minimum edge distance of ⅜". Nail spacing is the same for horizontal and vertical application. If screws are used, the spacing is not more than 12" apart when the studs are 24" o.c. and 16" apart when the studs are 16" o.c. Nails should always be driven so that they dimple the panel.

"Nail pops", in which the head begins to come out causing a bubble, are caused by several reasons. Drying out of the framing is one and this can be reduced if the moisture content of the framing is less than 15% when the panel is applied. Another, is movement of the panel itself. This can be minimized by one of two options. The first is special screws. The second is by "double nailing". The latter consists of nailing the panel to each stud 12" o.c. The top and bottom are fastened with one nail at each stud. Spacing around the perimeter is 7" o.c. The last step is to place a second nail 2" from each nail on the inner surface.

Labor Placing Gypsum Wallboard. When placing ⅜" gypsum wallboard in average size rooms, two professional drywallers should place about 2000-2200 sq. ft. of wallboard per 8-hr. day at the following labor cost per 100 sq. ft.:

	Hours	Rate	Total	Rate	Total
Drywaller	.76	—	—	$19.05	$14.48
Cost per sq. ft.			—		0.14

For a carpenter to do patch work utilizing the same material, cut the preceding installation rate in half.

When placing ⅜" or ½" wallboard in small rooms or spaces requiring considerable fitting and cutting in proportion to the number of sq. ft. of board placed, 2 drywallers should be able to place 800 to 1000 sq. ft. per 8-hr. day at the following labor cost per sq. ft.:

	Hours	Rate	Total	Rate	Total
Drywaller	1.78	—	—	$19.05	$33.91
Cost per sq. ft.			—		0.34

Where fire resistant ⅝" material is specified, 2 drywallers should place around 1600 sq. ft. per 8-hr. day on straight wall and ceiling construction at the following labor cost per sq. ft.:

	Hours	Rate	Total	Rate	Total
Drywallers	1.0	—	—	$19.05	$19.05
Cost per sq. ft.			—		.19

Drywall Material Prices

4 x 8-⅜ "..................................$3.49	4 x 10-½ "..................................$ 4.66 ea.
4 x 8-½ ".................................. 3.69	4 x 12-½ ".................................. 5.66 ea.
Rock Lath (32 sq. ft. bundles,16" x 48" pcs.) .... 3.99 bdl.	
Moisture Resistant Drywall (4 x 8-½ ") .... 5.79 ea.	
Fire Shield Drywall (4 x 8-⅝ ") .... 5.49 ea.	

Drywall Accessories

Ready Mixed Joint Compound	1 gal............................	3.88
	5 gal............................	11.55
Joint Compound (add water)	5 lb............................	2.49
	25 lb............................	6.19
Joint Tape	60' roll	.97
	250' roll	1.66
Drywall Corner Bead (8' lgth)	....	1.15 ea.

Plaster Supplies

Gypsolite (80 lbs.).............................	5.49
Finish Lime (50 lb.)...........................	3.79
Slo-Set (100 lb.)...............................	8.55
Wood Fiber (50 lb.)	3.19
Retarder (1-½ lb.)	1.09
Plaster Patch (5 lb.)	2.59
Mason's Sand (80 lb.)........................	2.29

Taping Joints.   After the wallboard has been installed, joints and corners have to be finished. Tape is supplied in perforated fiber strips 2 1/16" wide by 250 ft. long with sufficient compound included for installation. For patchwork it also comes in boxes containing 60 ft. of tape and compound sufficient to cover 150 sq. ft. of wall.

It is applied in four steps. First the tapered channel is filled with compound. Tape is immediately pressed into the compound squeezing excess out from under the edges. When thoroughly dry, at least 24 hours, a second coat is applied over the tape and feathered several inches beyond. For best results, a third coat is applied after the second has dried. This is also feathered out beyond the second coat so that the total width of the seam is 12-14". Joints should be sanded after they dry to ensure a smooth, inconspicuous joint. Nail heads are not taped; however, they should also be filled with compound and brought flush with the surface of the board. Two to three coats are desirable.

On an average job, an experienced taper should apply and finish 200 to 225 lin. ft. per 8-hr. day at the following labor cost per lin. ft.:

	Hours	Rate	Total	Rate	Total
Taper...................................	8	—	—	19.05	152.40
Cost per lin. ft.			—		0.76

Taping By Machine.   Most professional drywall joint finishers use a taping machine for applying perforated tape to the joints. An average operator using a taping machine can apply tape up to five times faster than by hand, resulting in an overall labor saving of 15 to 20 percent.

Some contractors set a minimum cost of approximately $50.00 for taping when patching during remodeling work. Average material costs in the Chicago area work out to $0.35 to $0.40 per lin. ft. for small jobs and $0.25 to $0.35 per lin. ft. for large jobs. This does not include labor.

CERAMIC TILE

Ceramic tile provides a durable, colorful surface that is virtually maintenance free. Its applications include interior and exterior finishes as well as countertops for functional and decorative purposes. Special uses include acid resistant and electrically conductive installations. Ceramic tile is available in many sizes and shapes.

Among the most commonly used ceramic tile are:

Glazed Ceramic Wall Tile.   Tile having an impervious surface fused onto the body of the tile. Comes in many colors.

Ceramic Mosaic Tile.   Either glazed or unglazed having a facial area of less than six square inches and usually mounted on sheets approximately 1' x 2' facilitate setting.

Quarry Tile.   A rugged tile used primarily as a finish flooring (interior and exterior) where a long-wearing, easily-cleanable surface is desired.

Developments in the ceramic tile industry make it necessary to stress the importance of relating tile costs to each individual job specification. Glazed ceramic wall tile, for example, can be backmounted or unmounted, and can be installed using conventional portland cement mortar; various types of adhesives or by "dry-set" portland cement. All of these variations can affect costs, both material and labor, and, the estimator should review his job requirements carefully prior to making the estimate.

However, the estimator's job has been simplified in recent years. Virtually the entire ceramic tile industry has adopted a "simplified practice" prepared under the auspices of the Tile Council of America which has reduced the number of sizes and shapes and established generally recognized standards for the industry.

Estimating Quantities.   Ceramic tile is estimated by the sq. ft. with trim pieces such as base, cap, etc. being estimated by the linear ft. The estima-

tor should deduct door and window openings, but the trim pieces necessary to finish such openings must be added. The quantities should be related to the type and size of material, since these items will affect the cost of the ceramic tile when priced. The finished estimate should include:
1. Cost of tile delivered to job site.
2. Cost of accessory materials such as wire mesh, sand and cement for floor fill under ceramic tile.
3. Cost of mixing and placing floor fill.
4. Direct labor cost of laying and cleaning the tile.
5. Tile contractor's overhead.

When ceramic tile is to be applied to a plaster base, the question arises as to who will do the plastering, the tile contractor or the plasterer. The estimator should check the building trade jurisdictional agreements in his area. If no information is available, assume that the tile contractor will plaster bathrooms, vestibules and small halls in private residences and that all other plasterwork will be done by a plastering contractor. For information on plastering see the beginning of this chapter.

The three methods for setting ceramic tile most commonly used and accepted are:

Conventional Portland Cement Mortar Method.   By this method the tile is bonded with a layer of pure portland cement paste to a portland cement setting bed. This is done while the setting bed is still plastic. Wall tile must be soaked in water so that the water needed for curing is not absorbed from the paste. Although this is the traditionally accepted method, it is also the most costly.

Dry-Set Portland Cement Mortar Method.   This method utilizes a dry curing portland cement mortar (accomplished through the use of water retaining additives) and has made ceramic tile installation cheaper and simpler. "Dry-set" is ideally suited for use with concrete masonry, brick poured concrete and portland cement plaster. It should not be used over wood or gypsum plaster. Labor costs are appreciably reduced when this method is used.

Water-Resistant Organic Adhesive.   Organic adhesives can be used over smooth base materials, such as wallboards, plywood and metal. It should not be used, however, in wet areas over surfaces that are subject to moisture penetration. Labor productivity is comparable to that of "dry-set" mortar.

For large jobs or standard jobs the labor to set a specific amount of tile can be estimated using the table shown below.

Labor Productivity*

(sq. ft. per team day; team is 1 tile setter and 1 helper)

	Description	Face-mounted	Back-mounted	Unmounted
Conventional Mortar	Glazed wall tile	....	75-90 SF	55-65 SF
	Ceramic mosaic			
	tile—walls	45-50 SF	55-65 SF	....
	floors	100-125 SF	100-125 SF	....
	Quarry tile floors	....	....	100-125 SF
'Dry-Set' Mortar	Glazed wall tile	....	125-150 SF	100-125 SF
	Ceramic mosaic			
	tile—walls	100-125 SF	120-140 SF	....
	floors	125-150 SF	125-150 SF	....
	Quarry tile floors	....	....	125-150 SF
Organic Adhesive	Glazed wall tile	....	150-175 SF	120-140 SF
	Ceramic mosaic			
	tile—walls	120-140 SF	125-150 SF	....
	floors	150-175 SF	175-200 SF	....
	Quarry tile floors	....	....	....
	Cove Or Base	65-75 lin. ft.		
	Cap	80-90 lin ft.		

*For specific estimating tables, see pages 36–41.

For smaller jobs, such as those frequently encountered in remodeling, the labor can be estimated by using the "Labor Factor" from the table below and multiplying it times the labor cost per sq. ft. of a standard job.

For example, to determine the cost of setting 10 sq. ft. of 1" x 1" ceramic mosaic tile in a small room using adhesive and one tile setter. Figure one man can set approximately 100 sq. ft. per 8-hr.day. Using a labor figure of $20.00 per hour, it will cost $160.00 per day to set 100 sq. ft. or $1.60 per sq. ft. To find the cost of the 10 sq. ft. multiply the $1.60 times the labor factor 1.75 which equals $2.80 per sq. ft., or $28.00 for 10 sq. ft.

Labor Factors For Small Quantities

		Labor Factor
Ceramic Mosaic Tile	Small Rooms	1.75
	Countertops	3.00
Glazed Ceramic Wall Tile	Small rooms	1.50
	Mantel fronts	2.00
	Mantel front w/returns	1.90
Cove or Base	Small rooms	1.25
Cap	Small rooms	1.10

To estimate the cost of the smaller job, multiply the labor costs given in the applicable unit price development by the appropriate labor factor. Material cost does not change.

Plastic Wall Tile. Plastic wall tile made of styron, polystyrene and other similar plastics, is usually furnished in 4¼" x 4¼" and 9" x 9" tiles, in many colors, plain, granite tone, and marbleized. It can be used as wainscoting in bathrooms, kitchens, laundries and any place where other kinds of wall tile are used.

A smooth base must be provided, such as plaster, gypsum wallboard or other smooth, hard-surfaced materials. It should never be applied over porous insulation board. It can be cut with a cutter similar to that used for shingles. One hundred sq. ft. will require about 2½ gallons of adhesive. After the base has been applied, an experienced man should be able to apply about 100 sq. ft. of tile per 8-hr. day at the following labor cost per sq. ft.:

	Hours	Rate	Total	Rate	Total
Tiler	8	—	—	18.75	150.00
Cost per sq. ft.			—		$ 1.50

Metal Wall Tile. Wall tile of aluminum, having a baked enamel finish in various colors, or tile of copper or stainless steel are used for the same purposes as plastic wall tile. They require the same type of base; are applied with adhesive and a man will apply about the same number of sq. ft. per day as plastic tile.

CEILINGS

Ceiling tile and suspended ceilings offer excellent alternatives to gypsum drywall and plaster for the remodeling contractor. Made from natural wood or cane fibers, ceiling tile has excellent accoustic and insulating properties and come in a variety of sizes, styles and colors. Since they are factory finished, they don't require painting or additional decoration and upkeep is minimal for the homeowner.

Installation also poses no particular problems. The tiles can be applied directly to old plaster, providing the surface is level and in good condition; to gypsum drywall; over lath; lath over open beams or suspended, using suspended ceiling grid metal. If it is cemented to gypsum wallboard the wallboard should be at least ⅜" thick and nailed on 16" centers.

The most frequently used sizes are 12" x 12" and 12" x 24" in ½" thickness with interlocking tongue and groove joints. It also comes in two other sizes which are less frequently used, 16" x 16" and 16" x 32" in ½" or ¾" thickness.

Removing Old Ceilings. To remove plaster from ceiling joists, figure one man will clear about 50 sq. ft. per hour. If the ceiling is suspended and the hangers are also to be removed, figure about 30 sq. ft. per hour.

To strip a plastered ceiling of acoustical tile, figure one man can clear 75 sq. ft. per hour.

Figure approximately $16.67 per hour to clean up and remove debris for the preceding.

To add new plaster to ceilings will run approximately the same as for walls, the extra labor in the ceilings being offset by the fact that there are few if any openings. Thus, ⅜" gypsum lath and 2-coat gypsum plaster will run around $9.52 per sq. yd. in fairly large areas.

To Install New Ceiling Tile Over Plaster.   The first step is to measure the length and width of the room to determine whether or not the tile size being used will fit without cutting. Generally, however, it will have to be cut. This can occur when either the length, width or both work out to an odd size. In order to get the best appearance, the border tiles on adjacent walls should be the same width.

To figure the size of the border tiles for either the length or width of a room, use the following formula: (using 12" x 12" tiles.) Assume the room is 15 ft. 6 in. long. This leaves an odd dimension of 6 inches. Add 12 inches to the 6 inches making 18 inches and divide by 2, giving 9 inches. Thus, to get an even border on each side, you will need 14 full length tiles and two 9 inch tiles, one at each end. (16" x 16" tiles) Convert the length or width of the ceiling to inches and divide by 16. Repeat the previous procedure but add 16 inches to the extra inches instead of 12 and again divide by 2. Bear in mind that the end border should never be less than 6 inches.

When applying the first tile directly to an existing ceiling, it should be placed in the center of the room. However, the position of the first tile will vary, depending on the width of the border tiles. Follow the manufacturer's instructions for positioning the first tile.

Adhesive is placed in each corner and the middle of the underside of the tile. When pressing the tile in place it should be slid back and forth slightly to insure a good bond. Succeeding tiles should be slid together firmly to engage the tongue and groove, but without pressure. All border tile should be cut with a reverse bevel so that the exposed face fits flush against the wall.

To tile an existing plaster ceiling with 12" x 12" tile, figure two men working together on a scaffolding of horses and planks can install 800 tiles per 8-hr. day at the following cost per 100 sq. ft.:

	Hours	Rate	Total	Rate	Total
100 sq. ft. tile		—	—	29.00	29.00
1.75 gal. adhesive		—	—	14.90	26.08
Installers	16	—	—	18.75	300.00
Cost per 100 sq. ft.			—		355.08
Cost per sq. ft.			—		3.55

Installing Tile On Furring Strips.   When installing tile on furring strips the placement of the first two furring strips is important in order to provide a properly spaced nailing surface for the border tiles.

Using 1" x 3" or 1" x 4" furring strips, nail the first flush against the wall at right angles to the joists. The second should parallel the first, at a distance equal to the width of the border tile plus ½" for the nailing flange.

Taking the previous example, the border tile figured out to 9". Adding the ½" for the nailing flange, the position of the second furring strip would be 9½" from the wall. Succeeding furring strips should be nailed 12" o.c. which would place the next to the last strip 9½" from the opposite wall. The last strip should be nailed flush to the wall.

For larger tile the same procedure is used, with the furring strips being attached at a distance equivalent to the dimensions of the larger tile.

The labor to attach furring strips for tile is approximately the same as attaching furring strips for wall panel. (see page 114.)

The tiles are installed starting in the corner and working diagonally across the room. Each is fastened with 1⅛" blue nails or 9/16" staples. Figure one man can fasten 35–40 tiles per hour at the following labor cost per 100 sq. ft.:

	Hours	Rate	Total	Rate	Total
Installer	2.5	—	—	$18.75	$46.88
Cost per sq. ft.			—		$ 0.47

Suspended Ceilings.   Suspended ceilings are quickly and easily installed. One of their big advantages is that they can be adjusted to fit any ceiling height. They also reduce sound from the floor above, provide insulating value and space for ceiling lights. There are a number of different types of grid metal by which the ceiling is hung, however, the labor rates to install each is approximately the same.

The grid should fall 2-2½" below the joists or ceiling in order to allow enough room to insert the panels.

The principal elements of the grid are the main runners, cross tees and wall angles. The main runners, usually 12' long, are placed at right angles to the joists. They are spaced 2' or 4' on center, depending on the panel size. Cross tees are also spaced 2' or 4' apart, depending on the panel size.

The wire used to hang the runners and tees is spaced 4' along the main runner and on each side of any splices. A chalk line around the room perimeter at the ceiling height is used to determine the position of the wall angle.

Figure amount of material to order by measuring the long and short walls and rounding the numbers up until the dimensions can be divided by two. Thus, a room 12' 4" wide by 16' 6" is rounded up to 14' x 18'. Multiply the two dimensions to determine the number of sq. ft. of material required. In this case, 252 sq. ft. Figure one man can hang 200 sq. ft. of grid an 8-hr. day at the following cost per sq. ft.:

	Hours	Rate	Total	Rate	Total
				$18.75	$150.00
Installer	8	—	—	$18.75	$150.00
Cost per sq. ft.				—	1.50

INTERIOR MOULDING

When estimating the labor cost of interior mouldings, the grade of workmanship should be taken into consideration since the amount of work performed will vary considerably. The following costs are broken down into Ordinary Workmanship and First Class Workmanship. Ordinary Workmanship is the most common and is usually found in medium price residences, cottages, etc. First Class Workmanship is usually required in higher priced homes.

Removing Existing Wood Base.   A carpenter and helper working together should remove a one-member wood base at the rate of 100 lin. ft. per hour.

	Hours	Rate	Total	Rate	Total
Carpenter	1	—	—	$20.60	$20.60
Labor	1	—	—	16.67	16.67
Cost per 100 lin. ft.				—	37.27
Cost per lin. ft.				—	0.37

Placing Wood Base.   This cost will vary with the size of the rooms and whether a single member or 2 or 3-member base is specified.

Where there are 55 to 60 lin. ft. of 2 member base in each room without an unusually large amount of cutting and fitting, a carpenter should place 125 to 150 lin. ft. per 8-hr. day, at the following labor cost per 100 lin. ft.:

	Hours	Rate	Total	Rate	Total
Carpenter	5.8	—	—	$20.60	$119.48
Labor	1.0	—	—	15.45	15.45
Cost per 100 lin. ft.	6.8			—	134.93
Cost per lin. ft.				—	1.35

If there are an unusually large number of miters to make, such as required in closets and other small rooms, increase the above costs accordingly.

A carpenter should place almost as many lin. ft. of 3-member base (consisting of 2 base members and a carpet strip), as 2-member base (consisting of one member and carpet strip), as it is much easier to fit a small top member against the plastered wall than it is to nail a wide piece of base so that it will fit snug against the wall and follow the irregularities in the plaster.

Where there are 50 to 60 lin. ft. of base in a room, a carpenter should place 110 to 130 lin. ft. per 8-hr. day, at the following labor cost per 100 lin. ft.:

	Hours	Rate	Total	Rate	Total
Carpenter	6.7	—	—	$20.60	$138.02
Labor	1.0	—	—	15.45	15.45
Cost per 100 lin. ft.	7.7				153.47
Cost per lin. ft.				—	1.53

FIRST GRADE WORKMANSHIP

In average size rooms, a carpenter should place 100 to 115 lin. ft. of 2-member hardwood base per 8-hr. day, at the following labor cost per 100 lin. ft.:

	Hours	Rate	Total	Rate	Total
Carpenter	7.4	—	—	$20.60	$152.44
Labor	1.0	—	—	15.45	15.45
Cost per 100 lin. ft.	8.4				167.89
Cost per lin. ft.					1.68

Where 3-member hardwood base is used in average size rooms, a carpenter should place 85 to 100 lin. ft. (2 ordinary rooms) per 8-hr. day, at the following labor cost per 100 lin. ft.:

	Hours	Rate	Total	Rate	Total
Carpenter	8.7	—	—	$20.60	$179.22
Labor	1.0	—	—	15.45	15.45
Cost per 100 lin. ft.	9.7			—	$194.67
Cost per lin. ft.					1.95

On work of this class, the wood grounds should be straight, so that it will not be necessary to "force" the wood base to make it fit tight against the finished plaster wall.

Where a single 1 x 4 pine base is to be fitted to straight runs, a carpenter should set around 200' per day.

	Hours	Rate	Total	Rate	Total
Carpenter	4	—	—	$20.60	$82.40
Cost per lin. ft.				—	0.82

Placing Wood Picture Moulding. Where just an ordinary grade of workmanship is required, a carpenter should place picture moulding in 5 or 6 average sized rooms per 8-hr. day. This is equivalent to 250 to 275 lin. ft. at the following labor cost per 100 lin. ft.:

	Hours	Rate	Total	Rate	Total
Carpenter	3.0	—	—	$20.60	$61.80
Labor	.5	—	—	15.45	7.73
Cost per 100 lin. ft.	3.5	—	—		$69.53
Cost per lin. ft.					.69

FIRST GRADE WORKMANSHIP

Where the wood picture moulding must fit close to the plastered walls with perfect fitting miters, a carpenter should place moulding in 4 to 5 ordinary sized rooms per 8-hr. day. This is equivalent to 175 to 200 lin. ft., at the following labor cost per 100 lin. ft.:

	Hours	Rate	Total	Rate	Total
Carpenter	4.4	—	—	$20.60	$90.64
Labor	0.5	—	—	15.45	7.73
Cost per 100 lin. ft.	4.9	—	—		$98.37
Cost per lin. ft.					.98

If the picture moulding is placed in fireproof buildings having tile or brick partitions, it will be necessary to place wood grounds for nailing the picture moulding but in non-fireproof buildings, the nails may be driven into the plaster, as the nails will obtain a bearing in the wood studs or wall furring.

Placing Wood Chair or Dado Rail. In large rooms, long, straight corridors, etc., a carpenter should fit and place 275 to 300 lin. ft. of wood chair rail per 8-hr. day, at the following labor cost per 100 lin. ft.:

	Hours	Rate	Total	Rate	Total
Carpenter	2.8	—	—	$20.60	$57.68
Labor	0.5	—	—	15.45	7.73
Cost per 100 lin. ft.	3.3	—	—		$65.41
Cost per lin. ft.					.65

In small kitchens, pantries, closets, bathrooms, etc., a carpenter will place only 160-180 lin. ft. of chair rail per 8-hr. day at the following labor cost per 100 lin. ft.:

	Hours	Rate	Total	Rate	Total
Carpenter	4.7	—	—	$20.60	$ 96.82
Labor	0.5	—	—	15.45	7.73
Cost per 100 lin. ft.	5.2	—	—		$104.55
Cost per lin. ft.					1.05

FIRST GRADE WORKMANSHIP

Where first grade workmanship is required, a carpenter should place 200–225 lin. ft. of chair rail per 8-hr. day, at the following labor cost per 100 lin. ft.:

	Hours	Rate	Total	Rate	Total
Carpenter	3.8	—	—	$20.60	$78.28
Labor	0.5	—	—	15.45	7.73
Cost per 100 lin. ft.	4.3		—		$86.01
Cost per lin. ft.					.86

In small rooms, such as kitchens, pantries, bathrooms, etc., requiring considerable cutting and fitting around medicine cabinets, wardrobes, kitchen cases, etc., a carpenter should place 120 to 135 lin. ft. of chair rail per 8-hr. day, at the following labor cost per 100 lin. ft.:

	Hours	Rate	Total	Rate	Total
Carpenter	6.3	—	—	$20.60	$129.78
Labor	0.5	—	—	15.45	7.73
Cost per 100 lin. ft.	6.8		—		$137.51
Cost per lin. ft.					1.38

Placing Wood Cornices. Where 3 or 4-member wood cornices are placed in living rooms, reception rooms, dining rooms, etc., a carpenter should place cornice in one average sized room per 8-hr. day, which is equivalent to 50 to 60 lin. ft., and the labor cost per 100 lin. ft. would be as follows:

	Hours	Rate	Total	Rate	Total
Carpenter	14.5	—	—	$20.60	$298.70
Labor	2.0	—	—		30.90
Cost per 100 lin. ft.	16.5		—		$329.60
Cost per lin. ft.					3.30

FIRST GRADE WORKMANSHIP

Where it is necessary that the wood members fit the plastered walls and ceilings closely, with all miters true and even, two carpenters working together should complete one to one and a quarter rooms per day.

This is at the rate of 35 to 40 lin. ft. per 8-hr. day for one carpenter at the following labor cost per 100 lin. ft.:

	Hours	Rate	Total	Rate	Total
Carpenter	21	—	—	$20.60	$432.60
Labor	2	—	—	15.45	30.90
Cost per 100 lin. ft.	23		—		$463.50
Cost per lin. ft.					4.63

Placing Vertical Wood Panel Strips. When vertical wood panel strips or "battens" are nailed to plastered walls to produce a paneled effect, a carpenter should place 22 to 28 pcs. (175 to 225 lin. ft.) per 8-hr. day, at the following labor cost per 100 lin. ft.:

	Hours	Rate	Total	Rate	Total
Carpenter..	4.0	—	—	20.60	82.40
Labor..	0.5	—	—	15.45	7.73
Cost per 100 lin. ft.	4.5	—	—		90.13
Cost per lin. ft.					.90

Placing Wood Strip Paneling. Where panels are formed of wood molding 1½" to 2½" wide, making it necessary to cut and miter both ends of each panel strip, the lin. ft. cost will vary with the size of the panels and the amount of cutting and fitting necessary, as there is almost as much labor required on a panel 2'-0" x 3'-0" as one 3'-0" x 6'-0", although there are only half as many lin. ft. in the former as in the latter.

On small sized panels up to 2'-0" x 4'-0", requiring 12 lin. ft. of molding, a carpenter should complete 9 to 11 panels, containing 110 to 135 lin. ft. of molding per 8-hr. day, at the following labor cost per 100 lin. ft.:

	Hours	Rate	Total	Rate	Total
Carpenter..	6.5	—	—	20.60	133.90
Labor..	0.5	—	—	15.45	7.73
Cost per 100 lin. ft.	7.0	—	—		141.63
Cost per lin. ft.					1.41

On larger panels 3'-0" x 5'-0" to 4'-0" x 6'-0" in size, where each panel contains 16 to 20 lin. ft. of molding, a carpenter should complete 7 to 9 panels, containing 140 to 180 lin. ft. of molding per 8-hr. day, at the following labor cost per 100 lin. ft.:

	Hours	Rate	Total	Rate	Total
Carpenter..	5.0	—	—	20.60	103.00
Labor..	0.5	—	—	15.45	7.73
Cost per 100 lin. ft.	5.5	—	—		110.73
Cost per lin. ft.					1.11

FIRST GRADE WORKMANSHIP

Where wood panel moldings are used over canvassed or burlap walls, with all strips plumb and level, fitting closely to the plastered walls with perfect fitting miters, a carpenter should complete 7 to 9 small panels, requiring 90 to 115 lin. ft. of molding per 8-hr. day, at the following labor cost per 100 lin. ft.:

	Hours	Rate	Total	Rate	Total
Carpenter..	7.8	—	—	20.60	160.68
Labor..	0.5	—	—	15.45	7.73
Cost per 100 lin. ft.	8.3	—	—		168.41
Cost per lin. ft.					1.68

On larger panels 3'-0" x 5'-0" to 4'-0" x 6'-0" in size, where each panel contains 16 to 20 lin. ft. of panel molding, a carpenter should complete about 6 to 8 panels, containing 120 to 150 lin. ft. of molding per 8-hr. day, at the following labor cost per 100 lin. ft.:

	Hours	Rate	Total	Rate	Total
Carpenter	6.0	—	—	20.60	123.60
Labor	0.5	—	—	15.45	7.73
Cost per 100 lin. ft.	6.5	—			131.33
Cost per lin. ft.			—		1.31

FIRST GRADE WORKMANSHIP

Where wood panel moldings are used over canvassed or burlap walls, with all strips plumb and level, fitting closely to the plastered walls with perfect fitting miters, a carpenter should complete 7 to 9 small panels, requiring 90 to 115 lin. ft. of molding per 8-hr. day, at the following labor cost per 100 lin. ft.:

	Hours	Rate	Total	Rate	Total
Carpenter	7.8	—	—	$20.60	$160.68
Labor	0.5	—	—	15.45	7.73
Cost per 100 lin. ft.	8.3	—			$168.41
Cost per lin. ft.			—		1.68

On larger panels 3'-0"x5'-0" to 4'-0"x6'-0" in size, where each panel contains 16 to 20 lin. ft. of panel molding, a carpenter should complete about 6 to 8 panels, containing 120 to 150 lin. ft. of molding per 8-hr. day, at the following labor cost per 100 lin. ft.:

	Hours	Rate	Total	Rate	Total
Carpenter	6.0	—	—	$20.60	$123.60
Labor	0.5	—	—	15.45	7.73
Cost per 100 lin. ft.	6.5	—			$131.33
Cost per lin. ft.			—		1.31

Placing Wood Ceiling Beams.   In buildings where built-up ceiling beams are used, the labor costs will vary according to the number of intersections of beams in each room and the length of the beams, as it is just as easy to erect a 12'-0" built-up beam as an 8'-0" one.

On average work, a carpenter should place 35 to 45 lin. ft. of built-up wood beams per 8-hr. day, at the following labor cost per 100 lin. ft.:

	Hours	Rate	Total	Rate	Total
Carpenter	20	—	—	$20.60	$412.00
Labor	3	—	—	15.45	46.35
Cost per 100 lin. ft.	23	—			$458.35
Cost per lin. ft.			—		4.58

FIRST GRADE WORKMANSHIP

In the better class of buildings using wood ceiling beams, a carpenter should place 30 to 35 lin. ft. per 8-hr. day, at the following labor cost per 100 lin. ft.:

	Hours	Rate	Total	Rate	Total
Carpenter	25	—	—	$20.60	$515.00
Labor	3	—	—	15.45	46.35
Cost per 100 lin. ft.	28	—	—		$561.35
Cost per lin. ft.			—		45.61

MOULDINGS

Divider (8')	$1.59 each
Cap (8')	1.59 each
Inside Corner (8')	1.59 each
Outside Corner (8')	1.59 each
Bathboard moulding (8')	1.89 each
Decorator Board moulding (8', vinyl wrapped)	$2.95 each

White Pine (unfinished)

21/4" SL casing	$0.43 lin. ft.	31/4" cove	.60 lin. ft.
21/4" oval casing	.45 lin. ft.	21/4" cove	.43 lin. ft.
21/4" OG casing	.45 lin. ft.	11/2" cove	.36 lin. ft.
2" comb. casing and base	.20 lin. ft.	3/4" cove	.19 lin. ft.
3" SL base	.45 lin. ft.	3/8" 1/4rd.	.10 lin. ft.
31/4" OG base	.49 lin. ft.	1/2" "	.14 lin. ft.
Comb. base and shoe	.40 lin. ft.		

White Pine (unfinished)

13/8" SL stop	.18 lin. ft.	3/4" 1/4 rd.	.22 lin. ft.
11/4" OG stop	.24 lin. ft.	11/16" 1/4 rd.	.41 lin. ft.
3/4" cap mold	.24 lin. ft.	1/2" x 3/4" base shoe	.16 lin. ft.
Stool	.64 lin. ft.	Flat screen mold	.14 lin. ft.
3/4" corner bead	.21 lin. ft.	Brick mold	.47 lin. ft.
11/8" corner bead	.44 lin. ft.	Drip cap	.27 lin. ft.
15/16" corner bead	.55 lin. ft.	11/16" full rd.	.39 lin. ft.
3/4" Parting stop	.15 lin. ft.	15/16" full rd.	.45 lin. ft.
11/8" lattice	.14 lin. ft.	2" modern rail	.59 lin. ft.
13/8" "	.17 lin. ft.	21/4" chair rail	.44 lin. ft.
13/4" "	.21 lin. ft.	13/8" panel mold	.21 lin. ft.
Colonial Band	.44 lin. ft.	11/4" Bed mold	.25 lin. ft.
15/8" Econ. base	.39 lin. ft.	15/8" Bed mold	.33 lin. ft.
31/4" Crown	.54 lin. ft.	3/4" x 3/4" Baluster	.18 lin. ft.
35/8" Crown	.79 lin. ft.	Steel Closet Rod	.55 lin. ft.

Cellular

Corners (8')	$2.19 each
Cap (8')	2.19 each
Casing (7')	2.19 each
Cove (8')	2.19 each
Stop (8')	2.19 each
Base (8')	2.59 each

Colonial

Corners (8')	2.99 ea.
Cap (8')	2.99 ea.
Stop (8')	2.99 ea.
Base (8')	3.55 ea.
Casing (8')	3.55 ea.
Crown 48')	3.55 ea.

QUICK REFERENCE CHART #3

Labor Factors For Plastering

Item Description	Unit	Factor
Cornices		
Mitre	LF	1.50000
Running	SF	.16000
Ornaments		
2"	LF	.08000
3"	LF	.09500
4"	LF	.12000
Beam		
Arrises	LF	.06000
Soffits	SF	.03500
Cement Base		
With Cove	LF	.11000
Beveled Top	LF	.14000
W/O Cove	LF	.06000
Beveled Top	LF	.09000
Marking For Tile Effect		
Squares	SF	.01444
Broken Joint	SF	.01667
Sand Finish		
Interior		
Floated	SF	.00444
Troweled	SF	.00667
Coffered Ceiling		
10 SF Coffer	SF	.17500
15 SF Coffer	SF	.16000
20 SF Coffer	SF	.14500
Over	SF	.13000
Acoustical Plaster		
1/4"		
2 Coat	SF	.03000
Vaulted Ceiling		
1 Radius	SF	.02000
Groined Ceiling		
2 Radii		
Internal	SF	.04000
External	SF	.06667
Textured Finish		
Sand		
Fine	SF	.01667
Course	SF	.01500
Texture		
Light	SF	.01333
Course	SF	.01667
Putty		
Texture		
Light	SF	.01333
Course	SF	.01667

Labor Factors For Plastering—Cont'd.

Item Description	Unit	Factor
Portland Cement Mortar		
On Cork		
3 Coat	SF	.05778
Arrises	LF	.10000
Drywall		
Standard	SF	.00361
Cut Up	SF	.00691

QUICK REFERENCE CHART # 4
Labor Factors for Interior and Exterior Trim

Item Description	Unit	Factor	
Baseboard		Softwood	Hardwood
1 Member	LF	.06000	
2 Member	LF	.07000	
3 Member	LF	.08000	.10000
Chair Rail	LF	.05000	.06000
Plate Rail			
2 Member	LF		.12000
3 Member	LF		.16000
Picture Mould	LF	.05000	
Ceiling Mould	LF	.06000	
7/8" Panel Strips	LF	.08000	
Water table	LF	.04000	
Drip cap	LF	.04000	
Corner boards	LF	.05000	
Verge boards	LF	.04000	
Closed Cornice-			
2 member	LF		.08000
Boxed Cornice-			
3 member	LF		.12000
Wood Gutters	LF		.10000

Labor Factors For Interior Millwork

Item Description	Unit	Factor						
MOULDINGS		Softwood		Hardwood				
Apron								
2"	LF	.0320						
31/2"	LF	.0364						
Astragal								
13/4"	LF	.0314						
23/16"	LF	.0333						
Band								
11/8"	LF	.0296						
13/4"	LF	.0320						
Baluster								
11/16"	LF	.0333						
15/8"	LF	.0364						
Base								
31/2"	LF	.0333						
41/2"	LF	.0400						
Bed								
13/4"	LF	.0296						
2"	LF	.0333						
Casing								
21/2"	LF	.0333						
31/2"	LF	.0372						
Chair Rail								
21/2"	LF	.0296						
31/2"	LF	.0333						
Closet Pole								
11/8"	LF	.0400						
15/8"	LF	.0400						
Cornice Moulding								
13/4"	LF	.0242						
21/4"	LF	.0267						
Cornice Boards		2"	4"	6"	8"	10"	12"	
1"	LF	.0242	.0320	.0400	.0400	.0444	.0444	
3 Member	LF	Minimum		Maximum				
		.1000		.1231				
Cove								
13/4"	LF	.0296						
23/4"	LF	.0314						
Crown								
35/8"	LF	.0320						
45/8"	LF	.0364						
Casing-Door	SET							
11/8" Plain		.4706						
11/8" Detailed		.4706						

Labor Factors For Interior Millwork—Cont'd.

Item Description	Unit	Factor	
MOULDINGS-cont'd.		Softwood	Hardwood
Cased Opening			
2 1/2" Trim	EA	1.3559	
4 1/2" Trim	EA	1.5094	
Glass Bead			
11/16"	LF	.0281	
1/2"	LF	.0291	
7/8"	LF	.0296	
Half Round			
1/2"	LF	.0296	
1"	LF	.0314	
Handrail			
1 3/4"	LF	.1000	
2 1/2"	LF	.1053	
Lattice			
1 1/8"	LF	.0296	
1 3/4"	LF	.0320	
Milled Moulding			
1"	LF	.0296	.0333
3"	LF	.0333	.0372
Parting Stop			
3/8" x 3/4"	LF	.0291	
1/2" x 3/4"	LF	.0314	
Quarter Round			
1/4"	LF	.0291	
3/4"	LF	.0314	
Stool			
11/16" x 3 1/4"	LF	.0400	
1 1/8" x 3 1/4"	LF	.0533	
Threshold			
Inside	EA		.2500
Outside	EA		.5000
Wainscot			
Minimum	LF	.1053	
Maximum	LF	.1231	
Full Bound w/stool			
Minimum	SET	.6154	
Average	SET	.8000	
Maximum	SET	1.3333	
PANELING		1/8"	1/4"
Temp Hardboard	SF	.0320	.0320
Temp Pegboard	SF	.0320	.0320
Mouldings			
Minimum	LF	.0320	
Maximum	LF	.0376	

Labor Factors For Interior Millwork—Cont'd.

Item Description	Unit	Factor	
PANELING-Cont'd.			
Plywood		1/8"	1/4"
Birch			
Minimum	SF		.0320
Average	SF		.0381
Maximum	SF		.0457
Mahogany			
African	SF		.0400
Philippine	SF		.0320
Oak/Cherry			
Minimum	SF		.0320
Maximum	SF		.0400
Rosewood	SF		.0500
Teak	SF		.0400
Chestnut	SF		.0427
Pecan	SF		.0400
Walnut			
Minimum	SF		.0320
Maximum	SF		.0400

CHAPTER 8

PAINTING AND WALLPAPER

There are a variety of paints which can be used on interior walls. However, the paint selected and applied depends to a great extent on the room in which it is to be used; the surface to which it is to be applied and to some extent the wear-and-tear that a particular room experiences.

Primers, undercoats and sealers not only improve the appearance of finish coats, but because they reduce the penetration of succeeding coats, they reduce the amount of paint needed.

The best all-purpose wall paint is flat alkyd paint, because it will cover plaster, wood, wallboard, metal and wallpaper. Furthermore, it works well with one-coat application, goes on easy and is washable and odorless. Latex is another because it is easy to apply, dries quickly and brushes can be easily cleaned with water.

Some paints, although they may be labeled washable, may not be suitable for rooms where there is apt to be considerable moisture, such as bathrooms, laundry rooms and even kitchens. Some flat, no-sheen paints, whose color pigments lie near the surface, will hold moisture. If a housewife attempts to scrub away spots or stains, some of the pigment can come off leaving an undesirable streak.

Among the different types of undercoats which are suggested for use in various rooms and for various surfaces are as follows: On wood floors, a primer followed by a floor seal, then floor or deck enamel. Wood paneling and trim should have a primer or undercoat and can be finished with latex, flat oil paint, semi-gloss paint, wood seal or varnish. Kitchen and bathroom walls also require a primer or undercoat and are best finished with semi-gloss paint.

Drywalls and plaster can be finished with latex or flat oil paint after they have been primed with a good primer or undercoat.

Dark and bright colors are harder to keep clean than pastels or whites because scrub marks and scratches, waterspots and streaks show up more on the former than they do on the latter.

For medium or dark tone walls, choose a paint having a certain amount of gloss. High gloss is the most durable and moisture resistant. However, high-gloss paints tend to reflect glare spots of light which many people find annoying. Thus many people find flat and semi-gloss paints are easier to live with.

Wood not only deserves, but requires special consideration. Woods are divided in open-grained and close-grained. For a smooth surface, open-grained woods require a paste filler before the wood can be finished. Birch, maple, gum and cherry require only a liquid filler. Close grained woods don't require a filler; however, they should be treated with a surface filler.

CLOSE-GRAINED WOODS

Fir, Gum, Pine, Basswood, Redwood, Cedar, Cottonwood, Cyprus, Poplar, Apple, Birch, Boxweed, Cherry, Ebony, Maple, Pear and Satinwood.

OPEN-GRAINED WOOD

Ash, Beech, Butternut, Chestnut, Elm, Mahogany, Oak and Walnut.

Paste fillers come ready-mixed from paint stores or building materials suppliers and consist of silica, linseed oil, turpentine, driers and dyes. Tints can be added to achieve various colors. Liquid fillers can also be purchased ready-mixed or made by thinning paste fillers with turpentine.

Paste fillers are applied with a stiff brush, brushing both ways, with the grain and across the grain. The excess is brushed away with a piece of coarse cloth or burlap, then allowed to dry for 24-hrs.

The wood is then sealed with shellac or sealer made by thinning some of the top coat. A glazing coat is applied before the final top coat, if an antique finish is desired.

The top coat is brushed on in two coats, allowing appropriate drying time between coats. Sanding between coats with a 220 grit paper will insure a smooth surface.

Estimating Dimensions Of Interior Woodwork, Walls and Ceilings to be Painted.   Since in many cases you will be dealing with more than two dimensions in painting, certain surfaces and materials have to be factored in order to obtain the total dimension of the surface being painted.

The following rules will provide more precise dimensions.

Picture Mold and Chair Rail.   On picture mold, chair rail, etc., less than 6" wide, obtain the number of lin. ft. to be painted or varnished and figure ¾ sq. ft. per lin. ft.

Wood and Metal Base.   Wood or metal base 6" to 1'-0" high should be figured as 1'-0" high; under 6", figure at .5 sq. ft. per lin. ft.

Wood Panel Strips, Cornices, Etc.   When estimating quantities of wood panel strips, wainscot rail and ceiling cornices, measure the girth of the member and if less than 1'-0" wide, figure as 1'-0".

If over 1'-0" wide, multiply the actual girth by the length, viz., 1'-3"x200'-0"=250 sq. ft. (1.25 times 200)

Refer to rule for exterior cornices.

Interior Doors, Jambs and Casing. When estimating quantities for interior doors, jambs and casing, add 2'-0" to the width and 1'-0" to the height of the opening. This allows for painting or varnishing the edges of the door, the door jambs which are usually 6" wide, and the casing on each side of the door which average from 4" to 6" wide. Example: on a 3'-0"x7'-0" door opening, add 2'-0" to the width and 1'-0" to the height, which gives an opening 5'-0"x8'-0", containing 40 sq. ft. on each side. Some painters figure all single doors at 40 sq. ft. per side, or 80 sq. ft. for both sides, while others figure them at 50 sq. ft. per side or 100 sq. ft. for both sides. Do not deduct for glass in doors.

If a sash door, containing small lights of glass, add 2 sq. ft. for each additional light. A 4-lt. door would contain 8 sq. ft. additional; a 12-lt. door 24 sq. ft. additional, etc.

Interior Windows, Jamb Linings, Sash and Casings. When estimating painting quantities for windows and window trim, add 2'-0" to the sides and length to allow for jamb linings, casing at the top and sides, and window stool and apron at the bottom. Example: If the window opening is 3'-0"x6'-0", adding 2'-0" to both the width and length gives a window 5'-0"x8'-0", containing 40 sq. ft. of surface.

If sash contain more than one light each, such as casement sash, etc., add 2 sq. ft. for each additional light. A 6-lt. window would contain 12 sq. ft. additional; a 12 lt. window, 24 sq. ft. additional, etc.

Stairs. When estimating quantities of paint or varnish for wood stairs, add 2'-0" to the length of treads and risers to allow for stair stringers on each side of the stair. A stair tread is 10" to 12" wide, riser is about 7" high, and the average cove and underside of a stair tread 2" in girth, so each tread should be figured 2'-0" wide. Multiply the width by the length to obtain the number of sq. ft. of paint or varnish required for each step. Multiply the area of each step by the number of treads in the stair, and the result will be the number of sq. ft. of finish. Example: A flight of stairs containing 20 treads, 4'-0" long. Adding 2'-0" to the length of the treads to allow for the stringers, gives 6 lin. ft. in each tread, which, multiplied by the girth of 2'-0" gives 12 sq. ft. of surface in each step. Since there are 20 treads in the stairs, 12x20=240 sq. ft.

For painting the soffits of stairs, use same rules of measurement as given above.

Balustrades and Handrails with Balusters. When estimating balustrades around well holes or stair handrail and balusters, measure the distance from the top of the treads to the top of the handrail and add 6" for painting or varnishing the handrail. Multiply the height of the balustrade by the length and the result will be the number of sq. ft. of balustrade. An easy method for computing the length of the stairs is to allow 1 lin. ft. in length for each tread in the stairs. Example: If the handrail is 2'-6" above the treads and the stairs contain 20 treads, add 6" to the height of 2'-6" to take care of the extra work on the handrail proper, making a total height of 3'-0". 3x20=160 sq. ft. of surface for one side of the balustrade or 320 sq. ft. if balustrade is on both sides.

The balustrade around the stair well hole is easily estimated by multiplying the height by the length.

On fancy balustrades having square or turned spindles which require considerable additional labor, use actual measurements as given above and multiply by 4 to allow for extra labor.

Wood Ceilings. When estimating quantities for wood ceilings, multiply the length by the width. Do not deduct for openings less than 10'-0"x10'-0".

Wainscoting. Plain wainscoting, obtain actual area. Paneled wainscoting, obtain actual area and multiply by 2.

Floors. To compute the quantities of floors to be finished, multiply the length of each room by the width, and the result will be the number of sq. ft. of floor to be finished.

Plastered Walls and Ceilings. To obtain the area of any ceiling, multiply the length by the breadth and the result will be the number of sq. ft. of ceiling.

When estimating walls, measure the entire distance around the room and multiply by the room height. The result will be the number of sq. ft. of wall to be decorated. For instance, a 12'-0"x15'-0" room has two sides 12'-0" long and two sides 15'-0" long, giving a total of 54 lin. ft. If the ceilings are 9'-0" high, 54x9=486 sq. ft. the area of the walls.

Do not deduct for door and window openings.

Cases, Cupboards, Bookcases, Etc. When estimating surfaces of cupboards, wardrobes, bookcases, closets, etc., to be painted or varnished, obtain the area of the front and multiply by 3 if the cases do not have doors.

If the cases have doors, obtain the area of the front and multiply by 5.

This takes care of painting or varnishing doors inside and out, shelves 2 sides, cabinet ends and backs.

Radiators. For each front foot, multiply the face area by 7.

Sanding and Puttying Interior Trim. Sanding and puttying on high grade interior trim should be figured as one coat of paint or varnish; on medium grade trim, figure at 50 percent of one coat of paint or varnish.

COVERING CAPACITY OF PAINTS

It is difficult to say how many sq. ft. of surface one gallon of paint will cover, as there are several items that influence the covering capacity. By brushing the paint out very thin it will cover more surface than when applied thick. Dark paint will hide the surface better than light paint, and for that reason it can be brushed out thinner than the lighter colors. Also, a rough surface will require considerably more paint than a smooth surface.

Soft and porous wood will absorb more oil and require more paint than close grained lumber.

Another thing that must be considered are the ingredients entering into the paint. Different brands of paint vary in covering capacity or hiding power.

Painting Interior Wood. New interior wood should receive three coats of paint, a priming coat, a second coat and a final or finish coat.

Paint coverage for interior wood surfaces will vary with the type of work, such as doors and windows, running trim, paneling, etc., in accordance with the standard method of measuring the quantities.

For doors and windows, coverage per gallon should be: first coat, 575 to 600 sq. ft.; second coat, 475 to 500 sq. ft.; third coat, 500 to 550 sq. ft.

For running trim up to 6" wide, coverage per gallon should be: first coat, 1,100 to 1,200 lin. ft; second and third coats, 800 to 900 lin. ft.

For ordinary flat wood paneling, coverage per gallon should be: first coat, 500 to 550 sq. ft.; second and third coats, 450 to 500 sq. ft.

When painting interior woodwork that has been previously painted and is in good condition, one gallon of paint should cover approximately the same as given for the second and third coats on new wood.

Painting Interior Walls. When painting interior walls, the covering capacity of the paint will depend upon the surface to be painted, whether smooth or sand finished plaster, porous or hard finished wallboard, etc.

Three coats are recommended for interior plaster which has never been painted—a priming coat, a second or body coat, and a third or finishing coat.

However, if a two coat job on unpainted plaster is desired, use a good wall primer or sealer for the first coat, followed by the second or finishing coat. To make two coats hide better, tint the first to nearly the same color as the second coat.

If the surface has been painted before and the old paint is still in good condition, two coats are sufficient, no priming coat being required.

On smooth plaster or hard finished wallboard, one gallon of good wall primer or sealer should cover 575 to 625 sq. ft. for the priming coat. For the second coat, figure 500 to 550 sq. ft. per gallon and for the third coat, 575 to 625 sq. ft. gallon.

On rough, porous sand finished plaster, one gallon of wall primer or sealer may cover only 275 to 300 sq. ft. while on very porous wallboard it may be only 150 to 200 sq. ft. per gallon.

For the second and third coats on rough surfaced plaster or wallboard, figure 400 to 475 sq. ft. per gallon.

One Coat Wall Finishes. There are any number of "one-coat" wall finishes on the market, but when applied to new plastered surfaces or over surfaces that have been previously unpainted, it is advisable to use a primer or wall seal coat, which seals the pores in the plaster or other surface and provides a base suitable to receive the one coat finish. Fully described above.

Latex Base Paints. There are any number of latex base paints on the market that are compatible to most surfaces.

When used over smooth plastered surfaces, one gallon should cover 450 to 500 sq. ft. first coat and 550 to 650 sq. ft. second coat.

When applied over rough sand finish plaster one gallon should cover 325 to 350 sq. ft. per coat.

Covering Capacity of Wall Size. The covering capacity of wall size will vary greatly with the material used.

Water size consisting of ground or flake glue and water will cover 600 to 700 sq. ft. of surface per gallon.

Varnish size consisting of varnish, benzine or turpentine and a little paint, will cover 450 to 550 sq. ft. per gallon.

Hard oil or gloss oil size consisting of rosin and benzine will cover 450 to 500 sq. ft. per gallon.

Covering Capacity of Wood Fillers. Liquid filler is usually used with close grained woods, such as pine, birch, etc., and one gallon should cover 500 to 550 sq. ft.

It is necessary to use a paste filler to fill the pores of all open grained wood, such as oak, ash, walnut, mahogany, etc.

If paste filler is used on oak, one gallon of filler should cover about 450 sq. ft. of surface.

Covering Capacity of Shellac. The covering capacity of shellac will vary with its purity but one gallon of good shellac should cover 550 to 750 sq. ft. of surface, depending upon whether first, second or third coat.

Covering Capacity of Varnish. One gallon of good varnish should cover 400 to 450 sq. ft. of softwood floors with one coat; 200 to 225 sq. ft. with 2 coats and 135 to 150 sq. ft. with 3 coats.

When applied to hardwood floors, one gallon of good varnish should cover 500 to 550 sq. ft. with one coat; 250 to 275 sq. ft. with 2 coats and 170 to 185 sq. ft. with 3 coats.

When applied to softwood interior finish, one gallon of good spar finishing varnish should cover 400 to 425 sq. ft. with one coat; 200 to 215 sq. ft. with 2 coats and 135 to 145 sq. ft. with 3 coats.

When applied to hardwood interior finish, one gallon of good spar varnish should cover 425 to 450 sq. ft. with one coat; 210 to 225 sq. ft. with 2 coats and 140 to 150 sq. ft. with 3 coats.

Covering Capacity of Wax. One gallon of good liquid wax should cover 1,050 to 1,075 sq. ft. of surface.

Covering Capacity of Varnish Remover. The amount of varnish remover required to remove old varnish from floors and interior finish will depend upon the condition of the old work, but one gallon of good varnish remover should be sufficient for 150 to 180 sq. ft. of surface.

Enamel Finish. Where interior woodwork is to receive an enamel finish, at least three coats are required, as follows: first coat, oil base paint primer and sealer; second coat, prepared enamel undercoat; third coat, enamel finish coat. If a four-coat job is specified, the third coat may be a mixture of ½ undercoat and ½ enamel, followed by the enamel finish coat.

For flat work, figure material coverages per gallon as follows: paint primer and sealer, 575 to 600 sq. ft.; undercoat, 375 to 400 sq. ft.; enamel finish, 475 to 500 sq. ft.

For running trim, one gallon of material should cover as follows: paint primer and sealer, 1,100 to 1,200 lin. ft.; undercoat, 775 to 800 lin. ft.; enamel finish, 775 to 800 lin. ft.

Glazed Finish. One gallon of good glazing liquid, colored with oil colors, should cover 500 to 550 sq. ft. of surface.

For glazed finish on interior running trim, not over 6" wide, one gallon should cover 1,050 to 1,100 lin. ft.

ESTIMATING LABOR COSTS

Perhaps in no other trade will labor costs vary to a greater extent than in painting and decorating. On some classes of work the material costs are almost negligible, while the labor costs may make it one of the most expensive kinds of work.

Cost of 100 Sq. Ft. (1 Sq.) 2-Coat Flat Finish Paint Applied to Smooth Plaster

	Hours	Rate	Total	Rate	Total
First Coat					
0.19 gal. paint		—	—	$14.50	$ 2.76
Painter	0.22	—	—	17.52	3.85
Second Coat					
0.19 gal. paint		—	—	14.50	2.76
Painter	.24	—	—	17.52	4.20
Cost 100 sq. ft.	0.46		—		$13.57

Cost of 100 Sq. Ft. (1 Sq.) 2-Coat Flat Finish Paint Applied to Sand Finish Plaster

	Hours	Rate	Total	Rate	Total
First Coat					
0.21 gal. paint		—	—	$14.50	$ 3.05
Painter	0.27	—	—	17.52	4.73
Second Coat					
0.24 gal. paint		—	—	14.50	3.48
Painter	.30	—	—	17.52	5.26
Cost 100 sq. ft.	0.57		—		$16.51

Cost of 100 Sq. Ft. (1 Sq.) 3-Coat Industrial Enamel Applied to Smooth Plaster

	Hours	Rate	Total	Rate	Total
First Coat					
0.19 gal. primer		—	—	$17.50	$ 3.33
Painter	0.22	—	—	17.52	3.85
Second Coat					
0.24 gal. undercoat		—	—	14.50	3.48
Painter	.25	—	—	17.52	4.38
Third Coat					
0.21 gal. enamel		—	—	18.80	3.95
Painter	.28	—	—	17.52	4.91
Cost 100 sq. ft.	0.75		—		$23.89

Cost of 100 Sq. Ft. (1 Sq.) Exterior Painting Applied From a Swing Scaffold

	Hours	Rate	Total	Rate	Total
0.17 gal. paint		—	—	$17.60	$ 2.99
Painter	1.6	—	—	17.52	28.03
Cost 100 sq. ft.	1.6		—		$31.02

Add same as given above for second and third coats.

Cost of 100 Sq. Ft. (1 Sq.) 2-Coat Oil Painted Applied to Smooth Metal Surfaces

	Hours	Rate	Total	Rate	Total
First Coat					
0.19 gal. paint		—	—	$18.80	$ 3.57

	Hours	Rate	Total	Rate	Total
Painter	0.43	—	—	17.52	7.53
Second Coat					
0.18 gal. paint		—	—	18.80	3.38
Painter	0.38	—	—	17.52	6.66
Cost of 100 sq. ft...................................	0.81		—		$21.15

Cost of 100 Sq. Ft. (1 Sq.) 3-Coat Oil Paint Applied To New Steel Factory Sash
For old work, add 10 to 20 percent to prepare surfaces.

	Hours	Rate	Total	Rate	Total
First Coat					
0.10 gal. paint		—	—	$18.80	$ 1.88
Painter	1.18	—	—	17.52	20.67
Second Coat					
0.10 gal. paint		—	—	18.80	16.64
Painter	0.95	—	—	17.52	18.52
Third Coat					
0.08 gal. paint		—	—	18.80	1.50
Painter	0.77	—	—	17.52	13.49
Cost 100 sq. ft.......................................	2.90		—		$56.07

Refer to "Methods of Measuring . . ." at beginning of this section.

Paint costs vary according to quality used, color and local material prices. Add for surface preparation.

Cost of Sanding and Preparing 100 Sq. Ft. (1 Sq.) Interior Trim Before First Coat

	Hours	Rate	Total	Rate	Total
Painter	0.35	—	—	$17.52	$ 6.13

Cost of Sanding and Puttying 100 Sq. Ft. (1 Sq.) Interior Enamel Trim Between Coats

	Hours	Rate	Total	Rate	Total
Painter	0.80	—	—	$17.52	$14.02

Cost of Light Sanding 100 Sq. Ft. (1 Sq.) Interior Enamel Trim Between Coats

	Hours	Rate	Total	Rate	Total
Painter	0.72	—	—	$17.52	$12.61

Cost of 100 Sq. Ft. (1 Sq.) 4-Coat Enamel Applied to Interior Doors, Windows, Cases, Etc.

	Hours	Rate	Total	Rate	Total
First Coat					
0.17 gal. primer...............................		—	—	$17.50	$ 2.98
Painter	0.70	—	—	17.52	12.26
Second Coat					
0.26 gal. undercoater...........................		—	—	17.50	4.55
Painter	1.10	—	—	17.52	19.27
Third Coat					
0.11 gal. undercoater...........................		—	—	17.50	1.93
Painter	1.10	—	—	17.52	19.27

Fourth Coat	Hours	Rate	Total	Rate	Total
0.21 gal. enamel		—	—	18.80	3.95
Painter	1.00	—	—	17.52	17.52
Cost 100 sq. ft.....................................	3.90		—		$81.73

For preparatory work and sanding between coats, add as given above.
For three coat work, omit cost of third coat.
For each additional coat, add same as fourth coat.

Cost of 100 Lin. Ft. 4-Coat Enamel Applied to Base, Chair Rail
and Other Trim Less Than 6 Inches in Width

First Coat	Hours	Rate	Total	Rate	Total
0.09 gal. primer.....................................		—	—	$17.50	$ 1.58
Painter	0.40	—	—	17.52	7.01
Second Coat					
0.13 gal. undercoater............................		—	—	17.50	2.28
Painter	.67	—	—	17.52	11.74
Carried Forward	1.07		—		$22.60

FINISHING INTERIOR WOODWORK

The greatest variations in costs will be found in interior finishing, as this is principally a labor proposition. For instance, where two, three or four coats of paint, enamel or varnish are specified, some painters will apply the entire number of coats without sanding between coats, regardless of specifications. This saves time but produces an inferior job.

To produce a first class finish on interior woodwork it is necessary to sand or rub down between coats to produce a smooth surface to receive the following coats. The finish coat will then be smooth and without rough spots, dust marks, etc. It is practically impossible to obtain this finish without sanding between coats.

The costs given on the following pages cover a customary, good residential job but if an exceptionally high grade of workmanship is required, increase labor costs accordingly.

Cost of Sanding 100 Sq. Ft. (1 Sq.) Interior Trim Before First Coat

	Hours	Rate	Total	Rate	Total
Painter	0.35	—	—	$17.52	$6.13

Paint costs vary according to quality used, color and local material prices. Add for surface preparation.

Cost of Sanding and Puttying 100 Sq. Ft. (1 Sq.) Interior Trim
Between Coats

	Hours	Rate	Total	Rate	Total
Painter	0.50	—	—	$17.52	$8.76

Cost of 100 Sq. Ft. (1 Sq.) Light Sanding Interior Trim Between Coats

	Hours	Rate	Total	Rate	Total
Painter	0.30	—	—	$17.52	$5.26

Cost of Backpriming 100 Lin. Ft. of Interior Trim Up to 6 Inches Wide

	Hours	Rate	Total	Rate	Total
0.09 gal. primer		—	—	$17.50	$1.58
Painter	0.21	—	—	17.52	3.68
Cost 100 lin. ft.	0.21		—		$5.26

Cost of 100 Sq. Ft. (1 Sq.) 3-Coat Oil Paint Applied to Interior Doors, Windows, Cases, etc.

Priming Coat	Hours	Rate	Total	Rate	Total
0.17 gal. paint		—	—	$17.50	$ 2.98
Painter	0.70	—	—	17.52	12.26
Second Coat					
0.21 gal. paint		—	—	18.80	3.95
Painter	.85	—	—	17.52	14.89
Third Coat					
0.19 gal. paint		—	—	18.80	3.57
Painter	.85	—	—	17.52	14.89
Cost 100 sq. ft.	2.40		—		$52.54

For two coat work, deduct cost of third coat.
For each additional coat of paint, add same as third coat.
Add for sanding and puttying as given on previous pages.

Cost of 100 Lin. Ft. 3-Coat Oil Paint Applied to Base, Chair Rail and Other Trim Less Than 6 Inches Wide

First Coat	Hours	Rate	Total	Rate	Total
0.19 gal. paint		—	—	$17.50	$ 1.57
Painter	0.40	—	—	17.52	7.01
Second Coat					
0.12 gal. paint		—	—	18.80	2.26
Painter	.60	—	—	17.52	10.51
Third Coat					
0.12 gal. paint		—	—	18.80	2.26
Painter	.70	—	—	17.52	12.26
Cost 100 lin. ft.	1.70		—		$35.87

For two-coat work, deduct cost of third coat.

For each additional coat of paint, add same as third coat.
Add for sanding and puttying as given on previous pages.

Cost of 100 Sq. Ft. (1 Sq.) Spirit Stain Applied to Interior Woodwork

	Hours	Rate	Total	Rate	Total
0.25 gal. spirit stain................................		—	—	$16.75	$ 4.19
Painter	0.5	—	—	17.52	8.76
Cost 100 Sq. Ft......................................	0.5		—		$12.95

Cost of 100 Sq. Ft. (1 Sq.) Penetrating Oil Stain Applied to Interior Woodwork

	Hours	Rate	Total	Rate	Total
0.15 gal. oil stain		—	—	$16.75	$ 2.51
Painter	0.5	—	—	17.52	8.76
Cost 100 sq. ft.......................................	0.5		—		$11.27

Cost of 100 Sq. Ft. (1 Sq.) Stain, Filler and Sealer, Wipe Off

	Hours	Rate	Total	Rate	Total
0.25 gal. paste filler		—	—	$ 6.00	$ 1.50
Painter	1.5	—	—	17.52	26.28
Cost 100 sq. ft.......................................	1.5		—		$27.78

Paint costs vary according to quality used, color and local material prices. Add for surface preparation.

Cost of 100 Sq. Ft. (1 Sq.) Shellac Applied to Interior Woodwork

	Hours	Rate	Total	Rate	Total
0.15 gal. pure shellac.............................		—	—	$12.00	$1.80
Painter	0.45	—	—	17.52	7.88
Cost 100 sq. ft.......................................	0.45		—		$9.68

For sanding and puttying between coats, add as given on previous pages.

Cost of 100 Sq. Ft. (1 Sq.) One Coat Gloss Varnish Applied to Interior Woodwork

	Hours	Rate	Total	Rate	Total
0.23 gal. varnish....................................		—	—	$15.00	$ 3.45
Painter	0.6	—	—	17.52	10.51
Cost 100 sq. ft.......................................	0.6		—		$13.96

For sanding and puttying between coats, add as given on previous pages.

Cost of 100 Sq. Ft. (1 Sq.) Flat Varnish Applied to Interior Woodwork

	Hours	Rate	Total	Rate	Total
0.16 gal. varnish	—	—		$15.00	$ 2.40
Painter	0.6	—	—	17.52	10.51
Cost 100 sq. ft.	0.6	—	—		$12.91

For sanding and puttying between coats, add as given on previous pages.

Cost of 100 Sq. Ft. (1 Sq.) Wax and Polish Applied to Interior Woodwork

	Hours	Rate	Total	Rate	Total
0.18 gal. liquid wax	—	—		$ 9.00	$ 1.62
Painter	0.95	—	—	17.52	16.64
Cost 100 sq. ft.	0.95	—	—		$18.26

For sanding and puttying between coats, add as given on previous pages.

Paint costs vary according to quality used, color and local material prices. Add for surface preparation.

Cost of Rubbing 100 Sq. Ft. (1 Sq.) Varnish Finish to Dull Rubbed Finish

	Hours	Rate	Total	Rate	Total
0.33 lb. powd. pumice stone		—	—	$ 0.25	$ .08
0.13 gal. rubbing oil		—	—	1.50	.20
1 lb. cotton waste		—	—	.75	.75
Painter	2.25	—	—	17.52	39.42
Cost 100 sq. ft.	2.25	—	—		$40.45

Cost of 100 Sq. Ft. (1 Sq.) Interior Finish Consisting of 1-Coat Shellac and 1-Coat Varnish

First Coat	Hours	Rate	Total	Rate	Total
0.15 gal. pure shellac		—	—	$12.00	$ 1.80
Painter	0.45	—	—	17.52	7.88
Second Coat					
0.23 gal. varnish		—	—	15.00	3.45
Painter	.60	—	—	17.52	10.51
Cost 100 sq. ft.	1.05	—	—		$23.65

For each additional coat of varnish, add same as second coat.

For sanding and puttying between coats, add as given on previous pages.

Cost of 100 Sq. Ft. (1 Sq.) Interior Finish Consisting of 1-Coat
Oil Stain, 1-Coat Shellac and 2-Coats Varnish

First Coat	Hours	Rate	Total	Rate	Total
0.15 gal. oil stain		—	—	$16.75	$ 2.51
Painter	0.50	—	—	17.52	8.76
Second Coat					
0.15 gal. pure shellac............................		—	—	12.00	1.80
Painter	0.45	—	—	17.52	7.88
Third Coat					
0.23 gal. varnish....................................		—	—	15.00	3.45
Painter	0.60	—	—	17.52	10.51
Fourth Coat					
0.23 gal. varnish....................................		—	—	15.00	3.45
Painter	0.60	—	—	17.52	10.51
Cost 100 sq. ft....................................	2.15	—			$48.88

For each additional coat of varnish, add same as fourth coat.

For sanding and puttying between coats, add as given on previous pages.

If last coat of varnish is rubbed to a dull rubbed finish, add as given on previous pages.

Cost of 100 Sq. Ft. (1 Sq.) 2-Coat Synthetic Resin Finish
Applied to Standing Trim

	Hours	Rate	Total	Rate	Total
First Coat					
0.17 gal. resin finish.............................		—	—	$17.45	$ 2.97
Painter	0.50	—	—	17.52	8.76
Second Coat					
0.16 gal. resin finish.............................		—	—	17.45	2.79
Painter	.47	—	—	17.52	8.23
Cost 100 sq. ft....................................	0.97	—			$22.75

Finishing Hardwood Floors

Cost of 100 Sq. Ft. (1 Sq.) 2-Coat Paint Applied to Wood Floors

	Hours	Rate	Total	Rate	Total
First Coat					
0.19 gal. paint		—	—	$15.55	$ 2.95
Painter	0.35	—	—	17.52	6.13
Second Coat					
0.23 gal. paint		—	—	15.55	3.58
Painter	.38	—	—	17.52	6.66
Cost 100 sq. ft....................................	0.73	—			$19.32

Cost of 100 Sq. Ft. (1 Sq.) Paste Filler Applied to Hardwood
Floors

	Hours	Rate	Total	Rate	Total
0.19 gal. paste filler		—	—	$ 6.00	$ 1.14
Painter	0.57	—	—	17.52	9.99
Cost 100 sq. ft.	0.57		—		$11.13

Cost of 100 Sq. Ft. (1 Sq.) Varnish Applied to Hardwood Floors

	Hours	Rate	Total	Rate	Total
0.19 gal. varnish		—	—	$15.00	$ 2.85
Painter	0.33	—	—	17.52	5.78
Cost 100 sq. ft.	0.33		—		$ 8.63

PAINTING AND DECORATING WALLS AND CEILINGS

Cost of Taping, Filling Joints and Sanding 100 Sq. Ft. (1 Sq.) Gypsum Wallboard

Based on approximately 1 lin. ft. of joint to 3 sq. ft. of sheetrock.

	Hours	Rate	Total	Rate	Total
33 lin. ft. tape-cement		—	—	$ 0.04	$ 1.32
Painter	1	—	—	17.52	17.52
Cost 100 sq. ft.	1		—		$18.84

Cost of 100 Sq. Ft. (1 Sq.) Sizing Applied to New Smooth Finish Walls

	Hours	Rate	Total	Rate	Total
0.16 gal. size		—	—	$ 6.00	$ .96
Painter	0.27	—	—	17.52	4.73
Cost 100 sq. ft.	0.27		—		$ 5.69

Cost of 100 Sq. Ft. (1 Sq.) Prepared Wall Primer or Sealer Applied to Smooth Plaster or Dense Wallboard

	Hours	Rate	Total	Rate	Total
0.17 gal. sealer		—	—	$ 5.50	$ .94
Painter	0.45	—	—	17.52	7.88
Cost 100 sq. ft.	0.45		—		$ 8.82

If applied over porous insulating or fiber wallboard, figure 0.5 gal. of primer per 100 sq. ft.

Cost of 100 Sq. Ft. (1 Sq.) Prepared Wall Primer or Sealer to Sand Finish Plaster

	Hours	Rate	Total	Rate	Total
0.35 gal. sealer		—	—	$ 5.50	$ 1.93
Painter	0.80	—	—	17.52	14.02
Cost 100 sq. ft.	0.80		—		$15.95

Cost of 100 Sq. Ft. (1 Sq.) 1-Coat Sealer, 2-Coats Flat Wall Paint, Stippled, Applied to Smooth Plaster

First Coat	Hours	Rate	Total	Rate	Total
0.17 gal. sealer...............................		—	—	$ 5.50	$ .94
Painter	0.45	—	—	17.52	7.88
Second Coat					
0.19 gal. paint		—	—	14.50	2.76
Painter	.60	—	—	17.52	10.51
Third Coat					
0.17 gal. paint		—	—	14.50	2.47
Painter	.55	—	—	17.52	9.64
Stippling					
Painter	.52	—	—	17.52	9.11
Cost 100 Sq. ft................................	2.12		—		$43.30

For 2-coat work, deduct cost of third coat.

Cost of 100 Sq. Ft. (1 Sq.) 1-Coat Sealer, 2-Coats Flat Wall Paint Applied to Sand Finish Plaster

First Coat	Hours	Rate	Total	Rate	Total
0.35 gal. sealer...............................		—	—	$ 5.50	$ 1.93
Painter	0.80	—	—	17.52	14.02
Second Coat					
0.24 gal. paint		—	—	14.50	3.48
Painter	.70	—	—	17.52	12.26
Third Coat					
0.22 gal. paint		—	—	14.50	3.19
Painter	.80	—	—	17.52	14.02
Cost 100 sq. ft................................	2.30		—		$48.89

For 2-coat work, deduct cost of third coat.

Cost of 100 Sq. Ft. (1 Sq.) 1-Coat Sealer, 2-Coats Gloss or Semi-Gloss Oil Paint Applied to Smooth Plaster

First Coat	Hours	Rate	Total	Rate	Total
0.17 gal. sealer...............................		—	—	$ 5.50	$ .94
Painter	0.45	—	—	17.52	7.88
Second Coat					
0.19 gal. paint		—	—	18.80	3.57
Painter	.57	—	—	17.52	9.99
Third Coat					
0.19 gal. paint		—	—	18.80	3.57
Painter	.70	—	—	17.52	12.26
Stippling					
Painter	1.10	—	—	17.52	19.27
Cost 100 sq. ft................................	2.82		—		$57.49

For 2-coat work, deduct cost of third coat.

Cost of 100 Sq. Ft. (1 Sq.) 1-Coat Sealer, 2-Coats Gloss or Semi-Gloss Oil Paint Applied to Sand Finish Plaster

First Coat	Hours	Rate	Total	Rate	Total
0.35 gal. sealer...........................		—	—	$ 5.50	$ 1.93
Painter	0.80	—	—	17.52	14.02
Second Coat					
0.26 gal. paint		—	—	18.80	4.89
Painter	.83	—	—	17.52	14.54
Third Coat					
0.24 gal. paint		—	—	18.80	4.51
Painter	.80	—	—	17.52	14.02
Cost 100 sq. ft............................	2.43	—			$53.90

Cost of 100 Sq. Ft. (1 Sq.) Glazing and Mottling Over Smooth Plaster

	Hours	Rate	Total	Rate	Total
0.10 gal. glazing liquid...........................		—	—	$ 6.50	$ .65
Painter	1.15	—	—	17.52	20.15
Cost 100 sq. ft...	1.15	—			$20.80

Cost of 100 Sq. Ft. (1 Sq.) Glazing and Mottling Over Sand Finish Plaster

	Hours	Rate	Total	Rate	Total
0.12 gal. glazing liquid...........................		—	—	$ 6.60	$ .79
Painter	1.60	—	—	17.52	28.03
Cost 100 sq. ft...	1.60	—			$28.82

Cost of 100 Sq. Ft. (1 Sq.) Glazing and Highlighting Textured Plaster

	Hours	Rate	Total	Rate	Total
0.12 gal. glazing liquid...........................		—	—	$ 6.50	$ .78
Painter	1.15	—	—	17.52	20.15
Cost 100 sq. ft...	1.15	—			$20.93

Cost of 100 Sq. Ft. (1 Sq.) 1-Coat Latex Base Paint Applied to Smooth Plaster

	Hours	Rate	Total	Rate	Total
0.31 gal. latex paint...............................		—	—	$14.50	$ 4.50
Painter	0.67	—	—	17.52	11.74
Cost 100 sq. ft...	0.67	—			$16.23

Cost of 100 Sq. Ft. (1 Sq.) 1-Coat Latex Base Paint Applied to Sand Finish Plaster

	Hours	Rate	Total	Rate	Total
0.37 gal. latex paint...............................		—	—	$14.50	$ 5.37
Painter	0.83	—	—	17.52	14.54
Cost 100 sq. ft...	0.83	—			$19.91

Cost of 100 Sq. Ft. (1 Sq.)Starch and Brush Stipple over
Painted Glazed Surfaces

	Hours	Rate	Total	Rate	Total
Painter	0.83	—	—	$17.52	$14.54

Colors in Oil

Colors ground fine in pure linseed oil. One-half pint cans.

Blacks	Price		Green	Price
Drop Black	$0.80		Palco Green..	$1.75
Lamp Black...	.70		Chrome Green, L.	1.05
			Chrome Green, M.	1.05
Blue			Chrome Green, D.	1.05
Palco Blue	1.60			
Prussian Blue...	1.30		**Red**	
Cobalt Blue	1.30		Vermilion..	1.35
Ultramarine Blue...................................	1.30		Rose Lake..	1.10
			Venetian Red...	.90
Brown				
Raw Turkey Umber	.59		**Yellow**	
Burnt Turkey Umber	.59		Chrome Yellow, L..................................	1.60
Raw Italian Sienna................................	.66		Chrome Yellow, M.................................	1.60
Burnt Italian Sienna.............................	.66		Chrome Yellow, O.................................	1.60
Vandyke Brown......................................	.59		Ochre..	1.60

Shellac and Varnish

Kind of Material	Per Gal.
Shellac, White, 4-lb. Cut...	$ 9.00–$11.00
Shellac, Orange, 4-lb. Cut...	8.00– 10.00
Cabinet Finish Varnish	10.00– 12.00
Floor Varnish	10.00– 12.00
Flat Varnish	10.00– 12.00
Spar Varnish	12.00– 14.00
Varnish Remover, Liquid..	8.00– 12.00
Varnish Remover, Paste..	10.00– 14.00
Wallpaper Lacquer..	6.00– 7.00
Wallpaper Lacquer Thinner	4.00– 5.00
Lacquer	10.00– 12.00
Lacquer Thinner	5.00– 6.00

Paints

Wall and ceiling...	$14.95 gal.
Interior and Exterior Enamel..	18.77 gal.
House Paint	17.55 gal.
Primer (regular)..	16.45 gal.
Primer (1st quality)	17.45 gal.
Overcoat/acrylic latex (to cover old paint, hardboard or metal)...................	17.45 gal.
Floor and deck..	15.50 gal.
Stains and Wood Preservatives (siding, fences, decks)	
Clear Preservative	14.99 gal.

Labor and Material Required for Interior Painting and Finishing

Finishing Interior Trim—Residential Description of Work	Painter No. Sq. Ft. per Hr.	Painter Hours 100 Sq. Ft.	Material Coverage Sq. Ft. per Gal.
Preparatory Work for Painting..................Sanding	290-300	0.35	....
Sanding and Puttying	190-200	0.50	....
Light Sanding	340-350	0.30	....
Back Priming Interior Trim Up to 6" Wide..........Lin. Ft.*	475-500*	0.21*	1,100-1,200*
Doors and Windows, Painting Interior..............First Coat	140-150	0.70	575-600
Second Coat	115-125	0.85	475-500
Third Coat	115-125	0.85	500-550
Oiling or Priming Wood Sash..................No. of Sash	9-10	0.10	600-700
Base, Chair Rail, Picture Mold, and Other Trim Up to 6" Wide. All Quantities are in Lineal Feet.......First Coat	250-260*	0.40*	1,100-1,200*
Second Coat	165-175*	0.60*	800-900*
Third Coat	140-150*	0.70*	800-900*
Preparatory Work for Enamel Finishes...........Sanding	290-300	0.35	....
Sanding and Puttying	120-130	0.80	....
Light Sanding	135-145	0.72	....
Doors and Windows, Enamel Finish..........Paint First Coat	140-150	0.70	575-600
Undercoat Second Coat	90-100	1.10	375-400
Enamel Third Coat	100-110	1.00	475-500
Four Coat Work. Add ½ Underc. ½ Enamel.........Add'l Coat	90-100	1.10	425-450
Base, Chair Rail, Picture Mold, and Other Trim Up to 6" Wide. All Quantities are in Lineal Feet.......First Coat	250-260*	0.40*	1,100-1,200*
Second Coat	145-155*	0.67*	775-800*
Third Coat	125-135*	0.77*	775-800*
Four Coat Work, Add ½ Underc. ½ Enamel.........Add'l Coat	135-145*	0.72*	775-800*
Stain Interior Woodwork..................One Coat	215-225*	0.45	700-725
Stain and Fill Interior Woodwork, Wipe Off..........One Coat	65-70	1.50	400-450
Shellac Interior Woodwork..................One Coat	215-225	0.45	700-725
Varnish, Gloss, Interior Woodwork..............One Coat	165-175	0.60	425-450
Varnish, Flat, Interior Woodwork..............One Coat	170-180	0.57	600-625
Wax and Polish—Standing Trim..............One Coat	100-110	0.95	600-625
Penetrating Stainwax—Standing Trim...........First Coat	170-180	0.57	550-600
Second Coat	190-200	0.51	525-550
Polishing Second Coat	190-200	0.51	600-625

*Lineal Feet

Labor and Material Required For Interior Painting and Finishing—Con't.

Finishing Interior Trim—Residential Description of Work	Painter No. Sq. Ft. per Hr.	Painter Hours 100 Sq. Ft.	Material Coverage Sq. Ft. per Gal.
Sanding for Extra Fine Varnish Finish..........................Sanding	40-45	2.25	....
Synthetic Resin Finish, Requires Wiping....................First Coat	190-200	0.50	550-600
Second Coat	210-220	0.47	625-675
Spackling or Swedish Putty over Flat Trim.....................One Coat	60-65	1.60	140-150*
Glazing and Wiping over Enamel Trim.............................One Coat	60-65	1.60	1,050-1,100
Brush Stippling Interior Trim, Painted................................	85-90	1.15	....
Flat Varnishing and Brush Stippling over Glazed Trim.......Varnish	170-180	0.57	600-625
Stipple	240-250	0.42	....
Old Work			
Washing Average Enamel Finish......................................Washing	85-90	1.15	....
Washing Better Grade Enamel Finish.............................Washing	60-65	1.60	....
Polishing Better Grade Enamel Finish.................................Polish	170-180	0.57	1,700-1,800
Removing Varnish with Liquid Remover......................Flat Surfaces	30-35	3.00	150-180
Wash, Touch Up, One Coat Varnish.........................Wash-Touch Up	165-175	0.60	....
Varnish	100-110	0.95	575-600
Wash, Touch Up, One Coat Enamel.........................Wash-Touch Up	140-150	0.70	....
Enamel	70-75	1.40	375-400
Wash, Touch Up, One Coat Undercoat and...............Wash-Touch Up	140-150	0.70	....
One Coat Enamel...Undercoat	75-85	1.25	475-500
Enamel	75-85	1.25	475-500
Burning Off Interior Trim..	20-25	4.00	....
Burning Off Plain Surfaces..	30-35	3.00	....

On most commercial and industrial work, a painter will perform 10 to 15 percent more work than given in the above table.

*Per Lb.

Labor and Material Required For Interior Floors

Description of Work	Painter No. Sq. Ft. per Hr.	Painter Hours 100 Sq. Ft.	Material Coverage Sq. Ft. per Gal.
Painting Wood Floors..................First Coat	290-300	0.35	525-550
Second Coat	260-270	0.38	425-450
Filling Wood Floors, Wiping............Fill-Wipe	170-180	0.57	425-450
Penetrating Stainwax—Hardwood Floors....First Coat	390-400	0.25	525-550
Second Coat	480-490	0.21	600-625
Floor Seal...............................First Coat	490-500	0.20	600-625
Second Coat	590-600	0.17	1,200-1,250
Shellac................................First Coat	390-400	0.25	500-550
Second Coat	475-500	0.21	650-675
Stainfill, 1 Shellac, 1 Varnish.........Stainfill	260-270	0.38	475-500
Shellac	390-400	0.25	650-675
Varnish	300-310	0.33	500-550
Stainfill, 1 Shellac, Wax and Polish....Stainfill	260-270	0.38	475-500
Shellac	390-400	0.25	650-675
Wax-Polish	200-210	0.50	1,050-1,075
Varnish, each Coat over Shellac..........Varnish	300-310	0.33	500-550
Buffing Floors—by Machine.................Buffing	390-400	0.25	
Waxing over 2 Coats of Seal and Polish..Wax-Polish	200-210	0.50	1,050-1,075
Waxing Linoleum—Same as Above			
Linoleum—Varnishing......................Varnish	300-310	0.33	500-550
Old Work			
Removing Varnish with Liquid Remover....Flat Surfaces	40-45	2.20	170-180
Clean, Touch Up and Varnish...........Clean-Touch Up	125-135	0.77	
Varnish	300-310	0.33	525-550
Clean, Touch Up, Wax and Polish.......Clean-Touch Up	125-135	0.77	
Wax-Polish	200-210	0.50	1,050-1,075

Labor and Material Required For Painting Interior Walls

Description of Work		Painter No. Sq. Ft. per Hr.	Painter Hours 100 Sq. Ft.	Material Coverage Sq. Ft. per Gal.
Taping, Beading, Spotting Nail Heads and Sanding Gypsum Wallboard	One Coat	90-110	1.00	....
Texture Over Gypsum Wallboard	One Coat	250-270	0.39	8-10*
Casein or Resin Emulsion over Textured Gypsum Wallboard	Sizing	300-320	0.32	325-350
Sizing New Smooth Finish Walls	Sealer	350-400	0.27	600-700
Wall Sealer or Primer on Smooth Walls	Sealer	200-225	0.45	575-625
Wall Sealer or Primer on Sand Finish Walls	Sealer	125-135	0.80	575-300
Smooth Finish Plaster—Flat Finish	Second Coat	200-225	0.45	575-625
	Third Coat	165-175	0.60	500-550
	Stippling	175-185	0.55	575-625
Sand Finish Plaster, Flat Finish	Sealer	190-200	0.52	....
	Second Coat	125-135	0.80	275-300
	Third Coat	135-145	0.70	400-450
Smooth Finish Plaster, Gloss or Semi-Gloss	Sealer	125-135	0.80	425-475
	Second Coat	200-225	0.45	575-625
	Third Coat	170-180	0.57	500-550
	Stippling	140-150	0.70	500-550
Sand Finish Plaster, Gloss or Semi-Gloss	Sealer	85-95	1.10	....
	Second Coat	125-135	0.80	275-300
	Third Coat	115-125	0.83	375-400
Texture Plaster, Average, Semi-Gloss	Sealer	125-135	0.80	400-450
	Second Coat	100-110	0.95	250-275
	Third Coat	115-125	0.83	325-350
Smooth Finish Plaster—Latex Rubber Paints	First Coat	125-135	0.80	375-400
	Second Coat	140-160	0.67	300-350
Sand Finish or Average Texture Plaster—Latex Rubber Paints	First Coat	140-160	0.67	300-350
	Second Coat	110-130	0.83	250-300
Glazing and Mottling over Smooth Finish Plaster		110-130	0.83	250-300
Glazing and Mottling over Sand Finish Plaster		80-90	1.15	1,050-1,075
Glazing and Highlighting Textured Plaster		60-65	1.60	875-900
Starch and Brush Stipple over Painted-Glazed Surface		80-90	1.15	825-850
		115-125	0.83	....

* Per Lb.

Labor and Material Required For Painting Interior Walls—Con't.

Description of Work	Painter No. Sq. Ft. per Hr.	Painter Hours 100 Sq. Ft.	Material Coverage Sq. Ft. per Gal.
Flat Varnish and Brush Stipple over Painted-Glazed Surface..........	105-115	0.90	500-550
Texture Oil Paint over Smooth Finish Plaster..........Size	215-225	0.45	675-725
Texture	40-45	2.30	125-150
Water Texture over Smooth Finish Plaster..........Size	215-225	0.45	700-725
Texture	50-55	1.90	85-95
Latex Base Paint, New Smooth Plaster..........First Coat	190-200	0.50	500-550
Second Coat	210-220	0.47	650-700
On Rough Sand Finish Plaster..........One Coat	150-160	0.65	325-350
On Cement Blocks..........One Coat	135-145	0.70	300-325
On Acoustical Surfaces..........One Coat	135-145	0.70	200-225
Casein Paint, over Smooth Finish Plaster..........First Coat	270-280	0.37	500-550
Second Coat	300-310	0.33	500-550
Over Rough Sand Finish Plaster..........One Coat	250-260	0.40	325-350
Over Cement Blocks..........One Coat	165-175	0.60	300-325
Over Acoustical Surfaces..........One Coat	165-175	0.60	200-225
Over Cinder Concrete Blocks..........One Coat	125-135	0.77	125-150.

When applying paint to walls and ceilings using a roller applicator, increase above quantities 10 to 15 percent and reduce painter time by the same amount.

Labor and Material Required For Painting Interior Walls

Old Work Description of Work	Painter No. Sq. Ft. per Hr.	Painter Hours 100 Sq. Ft.	Material Coverage Sq. Ft. per Gal.
Washing off Calcimine—Average Surfaces..................	115-125	0.83	....
Washing Smooth Finish Plaster Walls—Average.................	145-155	0.67	....
Washing Sand Finish Plaster Walls—Average.................	100-110	1.00	....
Washing Starched Surfaces and Restarching, Smooth Surfaces..............Washing	145-155	0.67	....
Restarching	130-140	0.75	....
Removing Old Wall Paper—Not Over 3 Layers.................	65-75	1.45	....
Washing Off Glue After Removing Paper (including Fixing Average Cracks and Sizing)..........	125-135	0.77	....
Cutting Hard Oil or Varnish Size Walls (including Fixing Average Cracks).............	125-135	0.77	....
Cutting Gloss Painted Walls (including Fixing Cracks............	125-135	0.77	....
Washing, Touch Up, One Coat Gloss Paint to Smooth Plaster Surfaces.......... Wash-Touch Up	125-135	0.77	....
One Coat	125-135	0.77	450-500
Synthetic-Resin Emulsion Paint over Old Painted Walls.......... One Coat	190-200	0.50	400-425
Wallpaper, Canvas, Coated Fabrics, Paper Hanging, Wood Veneer			
Canvas Sheeting.................	50-60	1.82	....
Coated Fabrics.................	2-2½		
Wallpaper—One Edge Work............. Single Roll	3½-4		
Wire Edge Work............ Single Roll	2½-3		
Butt Work............ Single Roll	2¼-2¾		
Scenic Paper 40"x60"............ Single Roll	1-1¼		
Wood Veneer.......... Sq. Ft.	12-13		
Lacquer Finish Over Wood Veneer.......... First Coat	300-310	0.33	275-325
Second Coat	300-310	0.33	450-500
Penetrating Wax or Synthetic Resin Application over Wood Veneer.......... First Coat	550-575	0.18	550-600
Second Coat	600-625	0.1	650-675

Green Preservative..16.99 gal.
Semi-transparent..17.99 gal.
Solid colors...18.99 gal.

WALLPAPER

Wallpaper is estimated by the roll containing 36 sq. ft. Most rolls are 18" or 20½" wide and contain 36 sq. ft. or 4 sq. yds. of paper. The double roll contains just twice as much as the single roll, viz.: 72 sq. ft. or 8 sq. yds. of paper.

Estimating the Quantity of Wallpaper Required for any Room.   When estimating the quantity of wallpaper required for any room, measure the entire distance around the room in lin. ft. and multiply by the height of the walls or the distance from the floor to the ceiling. The result will be the number of sq. ft. of surface area.

Make deductions in full for the area of all openings such as windows, doors, consoles, mantels, built-in bookcases, etc. The difference between the area of the walls and the area of the openings will be the actual number of sq. ft. of surface to be papered.

When adding for waste in matching, cutting, fitting, etc., paper hangers use different methods and allow different percentages, contingent upon the height of the ceiling, the design of the paper, and the size of the pattern or figure, but an allowance of 15 to 20 per cent will prove sufficient in nearly all cases.

When estimating the quantity of paper required for walls, bear in mind it is not necessary to run the side wallpaper more than one or two inches above the border, when a border is used. The height of the wood base should also be deducted from the total height of the wall.

In rooms having drop ceilings, the depth of the drop should be deducted from the height of the wall, which will decrease the area of side wallpaper in the same amount as it increases the quantity of ceiling paper.

If a border is required, measure the distance around the room and the result will be the number of lin. ft. of border. Dividing by 3, gives the number of yards of border required.

When estimating the quantity of wallpaper required for ceilings, multiply the width of the room by the length, and the result will be the number of sq. ft. of ceiling to be papered.

In rooms having a drop ceiling, add the depth of the drop or the distance the ceiling paper extends down the side walls to the length and breadth of the room and multiply as described above.

After the side walls and ceiling area have been computed in sq. ft. divide by 36, and the result will be the number of single rolls of paper required; or by dividing by 72 gives the number of double rolls of paper required.

Paste Required Hanging Wallpaper. The quantity of paste required for hanging wallpaper will vary with the weight of the paper and the surface to which it is applied.

Where light or medium weight wallpaper is used, one gallon of paste should hang 12 single rolls of paper.

If heavy or rough texture paper is used, it will often be necessary to give it two or three applications of paste to obtain satisfactory results. On work of this kind one gallon of paste should hang 4 to 6 single rolls of paper.

There are prepared pastes on the market which require only the addition of cold water to make them ready for use.

One pound of prepared cold water dry paste should make 1½ to 2 gallons of ready to use paste.

Sufficiently prepared cold water dry paste to make 3 gallons of ready to use paste should cost as follows:

	Hours	Rate	Total	Rate	Total
2-lbs. dry paste		—	—	$ 0.25	$0.50
Labor	0.25	—	—	18.33	4.58
Total cost 3 gals. paste	0.25		—		5.08
Cost per gal.			—		1.69
Cost per roll lgt. wt. paper			—		.14
Cost per roll hvy. wt. paper			—		.32

Labor Hanging Wallpaper. Different methods of hanging wallpaper are used in different sections of the country. In some localities a paper hanger and helper work together, one man trimming the paper and pasting while the other man hangs the paper, while in many cities the work is performed by one man, who cuts, trims, fits, pastes and hangs the paper.

The quantities and costs given on the following pages are based on the performance of one man but will prove a fair average for use in any locality.

Hanging Wallpaper on Walls and Ceilings, One Edge Work. When hanging light or medium weight paper on ceilings and drops, a paper hanger should hang 28 to 32 single rolls of paper per 8-hr. day, at the following labor cost per roll:

	Hours	Rate	Total	Rate	Total
Paper hanger	0.27	—	—	$18.33	$4.95

Hanging Wallpaper on Walls, Butt Work. Where light or medium weight paper is used for bedrooms, halls, etc., and where a good grade of workmanship is required with all paper trimmed on both edges and hung with butt joints, a paper hanger should trim, fit and hang 20 to 24 single rolls of paper per 8-hr. day, at the following labor cost per roll:

	Hours	Rate	Total	Rate	Total
Paper hanger	0.36	—	—	$18.33	$6.60

Another thing that will slow up the work is where new paper is applied over old rough textured wallpaper, such as oatmeal designs, etc.

Hanging Wallpaper, First Grade Workmanship. Where a good grade of medium or heavy weight wallpaper is used, with all paper hung with butt joints, a paper hanger should trim, fit and hang 16 to 20 single rolls of paper per 8-hr. day, at the following labor cost per roll:

	Hours	Rate	Total	Rate	Total
Paper hanger	0.44	—	—	$18.33	$8.07

Labor Hanging Scenic Paper. Where scenic paper or paper having mural designs are used over the wall or up stairways, a paper hanger will hang only 8 to 10 single rolls per 8-hr. day, at the following labor cost per roll:

	Hours	Rate	Total	Rate	Total
Paper hanger	0.9	—	—	$18.33	$16.50

Placing Wallpaper Borders. Wallpaper borders are usually estimated by the lin. ft. or yd. and as the width varies from 3" to 18" there is never over one width required.

The average size room requires 50 to 60 lin. ft. or 17 to 20 yds. of border.

A paper hanger should place border in a room of this size in 30 to 40 minutes, which is at the rate of 100 to 125 lin. ft. an hr.

The labor cost per 100 lin. ft. (33⅓ yds.) should run as follows:

	Hours	Rate	Total	Rate	Total
Paper hanger	0.9	—	—	$18.33	$16.50
Cost per 100 lin. ft.	0.9		—		16.50
per lin. ft.			—		.17
Cost per yd.			—		.50

Hanging Coated Fabrics. Where coated fabrics, such as Walltex, Sanitas, etc., are used, a paper hanger should hang 16 to 20 single rolls per 8-hr. day, at the following labor cost per roll:

	Hours	Rate	Total	Rate	Total
Paper hanger	0.44	—	—	$18.33	$8.07

Canvassing Plastered Walls. When applying canvas to plastered walls, an average mechanic should apply 50 to 60 sq. ft. an hour.

Cost of 100 Sq. Ft. Canvassed Walls

	Hours	Rate	Total	Rate	Total
12 sq. yds. canvas	—	—	—	$ 2.00	$24.00
4 lbs. dry paste	—	—	—	.25	1.00
Paper hanger	1.82	—	—	18.33	33.36
Cost 100 sq. ft.	1.82	—	—		$58.36
Cost per sq. ft.	—			—	.58

Flexwood.* Flexwood is a genuine wood veneer cut to 1/85 of an inch, glued under heat and hydraulic pressure to cotton sheeting with a waterproof adhesive. A patented flexing operation breaks the cellular unity of the wood to produce a limp, pliable sheet which may be applied by hand to any smooth surface, flat or curved. Waterproof Flexwood 710 Adhesive, which makes a permanent bond, is used to apply Flexwood. Standard sizes of stock material are 18-in. and 24-in. widths and 8-ft. to 12-ft. lengths.

The mechanics of installing Flexwood are as follows: the background is sized with Flexwood cement. Another coating of cement is brushed on the Flexwood which is then hung in the manner of any sheet wall covering. A stiff, broad knife used with considerable pressure, smooths out the Flexwood, removes air spaces and furnishes the necessary contact.

Some of the wood available in Flexwood are mahogany, walnut, oak, prima vera, knotty pine, orientalwood, satinwood, zebrawood, rosewood, English oak, maple, lacewood, etc. The cost of the material varies from $1.10 to $3.00 per sq. ft. depending upon the kind of wood. The majority of woods run from $1.25 to $1.50. Adhesive runs $7.50 per gallon.

It requires a skilled and thoroughly competent paper hanger to apply this material and the labor costs vary considerably with the design to be obtained.

Considerable time is usually required to lay out any room to obtain the desired effect, spacing of strips, etc. This is especially true where certain designs must be obtained on columns, walls and pilasters and where narrow strips of contrasting woods are used to obtain inlay effects.

On plain walls without inlays, a paper hanger experienced in this class of work should apply 95 to 105 sq. ft. of Flexwood per 8-hr. day, at the following labor cost per 100 sq. ft.:

	Hours	Rate	Total	Rate	Total
Paper hanger	8	—	—	$18.33	$146.64
Cost per sq. ft.	—			—	1.47

---

*U.S. Plywood, Louisville, Ky.

On pilasters, columns and walls inlaid with narrow strips of contrasting woods, the work is considerably slower, due to the additional cutting and fitting required. On work of this kind, a paper hanger, experienced in this class of work should apply 50 sq. ft. per 8-hr. day, at the following labor cost per 100 sq. ft.:

	Hours	Rate	Total	Rate	Total
Paper hanger	16	—	—	18.33	$293.28
Cost per sq. ft.			—		2.93

Additional time for paper hanger or foreman will be required laying out the work into patterns, marking off strips, etc. This will vary with the size of the job.

Add for overhead expense and profit.

After the Flexwood is applied, the joints should be sanded lightly to remove any imperfections in the joints.

Finishing Flexwood. Flexwood will take any wood finish but where the natural color of the wood is desired, the Flexwood is given one coat of lacquer sealer, sanded lightly between coats and then given one coat of lacquer for a finish coat.

One gallon of lacquer sealer will cover about 300 sq. ft. of surface, one coat.

After the sealer has been applied, one gallon of lacquer should cover 450 to 550 sq. ft.

An experienced painter should apply lacquer sealer, sand lightly between coats and apply one coat of lacquer to 90 to 110 sq. ft. of surface an hr. at the following labor cost per 100 sq. ft.:

	Hours	Rate	Total	Rate	Total
Painter	1	—	—	$18.33	$18.33
Cost per sq. ft.			—		.18

Vinyl Wall Covering. Vinyl wall covering is composed of a woven cotton fabric to which a compound of vinyl resin, pigment and plasticizer is electronically fused to one side. It comes 54" wide in 30 yard rolls in three weights: heavy (36 oz. per lineal yard); medium (24-33 oz. per lineal yard); and light (22-24 oz. per lineal yard). It is available in over 1000 color pattern combinations.

Some of the patterns available simulate linens, silks, moires, grasses, tweeds, Honduras mahogany, travertine, damasks and burlaps. Costs range from 20¢ to 50¢ per square foot.

Vinyl fabric is hung using regular wallpaper hanging procedures for hanging fabric baked wallcoverings. A broad knife is used to smooth out any wrinkles, air pockets and insures a good contact. Wash off any excess paste that remains on the surface of the material: No further finishing is necessary.

A competent paper hanger can apply approximately 400 sq. ft. per 8 hr. day at the following costs per 100 sq. ft.

	Hours	Rate	Total	Rate	Total
Paper hanger..	2	—	—	$18.33	$36.66
Cost per sq. ft.					.37

One gallon of paste covers approximately 10 lineal yards of 54" width material.

To the above add overhead expenses and profit.

If excessive cutting and fitting is required the above figures should be increased to allow for the above conditions.

To prepare an accurate detailed estimate on plumbing and sewerage requires a working knowledge of the trade as all work must be laid out on paper and the number of lineal feet of each kind of pipe estimated separately, such as tile or cast iron sewers, soil and vent pipe, water pipe, gas pipe, drains, valves, pipe fittings, etc. Inasmuch as very few, if any, general building contractors or estimators possess this knowledge, it makes it doubly difficult for them to prepare more than an approximate estimate on the various kinds of plumbing work.

Budget figures for average plumbing installations can be estimated in one of two ways; as a percentage of the total cost of a project; or, as the grand total of a predetermined cost allowance for the installation of each fixture.

Plumbing estimates as a percentage of the total job will vary from a minimum of 3% on up to 12% depending on the number and type of fixtures required and on their disposition within the building. Percentage estimates would be valid for general plumbing only; process and other special condition piping would of course have to be entered as a separate item.

When figuring plumbing work where jobs are less than 4 hrs., multiply all hourly rates by 1.9 for service work and 1.8 for remodeling work.

The private residence is difficult to peg. Where kitchens and baths can be back to back, the percentage is on the low side. But, in a large, rambling house with a central powder room area with kitchens, family and master bedrooms all in separate wings and with hose bibs and lawn sprinkling systems on all fours sides and sunken bathtubs, shellshaped lavatories and gold plated fixtures, even 12% may be too low.

The allowance per fixture estimate is generally more accurate. An experienced plumber can acquire very accurate prices on this although he will have to use some judgment on how much to add for bringing in the main waste and supply lines, depending on how spread out the project may be.

The per fixture price will be the cost of the fixture itself plus the cost of the immediate piping connections and installation within the room. Some per fixture costs have added to them a prorated cost of the central piping system. It would be more accurate to add this, together with the cost of bringing waste and supply lines from the street to the building and permit costs and overhead and profit, each as separate items, as some buildings as we have noted above require a much more extensive central system to supply fewer fixtures than others. Per fixture allowances are discussed later in this chapter.

PLUMBING SYSTEMS

Estimating Quantities and Costs of Sewer Work. Sewerage is estimated by the lineal foot, obtained by measuring the number of lineal feet of each size sewer pipe required, such as 4", 6", 8" and 12" pipe, and all fittings should also be listed in detail, giving the number of ells, Y's., T's, etc.

Cast iron sewer pipe is estimated in the same manner as tile sewer pipe.

Most plumbers estimate their sewer work at a certain price per lineal foot, including excavating, sewer pipe and labor. This is all right on ordinary jobs that do not require more than the usual amount of deep excavation, but if there is an exceptionally large amount of deep excavation, (from 7 to 15 feet deep), then the excavating, shoring and bracing should be estimated separately.

Undoubtedly, the best method is to estimate the number of cubic yards of excavating required for sewers, based on a trench 1'-6" wider than the pipe diameter by the required depth.

Where 4 to 6-inch sewer pipe is used, an experienced sewer layer should lay 12 to 15 lineal feet of pipe an hour or 100 to 125 lineal feet per 8 hour day.

Add for excavating and additional time for setting catch basins, gravel basins, triple basins, etc.

As an example of the method used, the cost of excavating a trench 3 feet deep and placing 100 lineal feet of 6-inch tile sewer pipe, should be estimated as follows:

	Hours	Rate	Total	Rate	Total
Labor excavating	39.0	—	—	$16.67	$650.13
Labor backfilling	10.5	—	—	16.67	175.00
100 lin. ft. 6" pipe		—	—	5.25	525.00
Pipe layer	7.0	—	—	20.55	143.36
Total cost 100 lin. ft	56.5	—			$1493.36
Average per lin. ft		—			14.94

Estimating Quantities of Cast Iron Soil Pipe, Downspouts, Stacks and Vents. When estimating soil pipe, stacks, vents, etc., note the number of stacks and length of each, listing the number of lineal feet of each size pipe; the number of pieces, size, and kind of fittings required, and price them at current market prices. The labor cost of placing cast iron pipe is given on the following pages.

Estimating Quantity of Pipe and Fittings.   When estimating the quantity of black or galvanized pipe, list the number of lineal feet of each size pipe required, such as ½", ¾", 1", 1-¼", 1-½", 2", 2-½", 3", etc., and estimate at the current market price.

After the cost of the pipe has been computed, take 60 to 75 percent of the cost of the pipe to cover the cost of all fittings required.

Brass or copper pipe and fittings should be estimated in the same manner as galvanized pipe.

Estimating the Quantity and Prices of Valves.   All valves of the different sizes should be listed on the estimate separately, stating the number of each size required, and pricing them at the current market price.

Estimating the Quantity of Fixtures.   Each type of fixture such as sinks, lavatories, laundry trays, water closets, bathtubs, drinking fountains, shower baths, hot water tanks and heaters, house pumps, bilge pumps, etc., should be listed separately and priced at the current market prices.

Labor Roughing in for Plumbing.   The usual practice among plumbers is to allow a certain percentage of the cost of the roughing materials to cover the labor cost of installing them. This will vary with the type of building and grade of work.

The total cost of the roughing in materials, such as cast iron soil pipe, downspouts, stacks, vents, and fittings; also all black and galvanized pipe and fittings, all valves, increasers, tees, Ys, ⅛ bends; nipples; in fact, all pipe required to rough in the job is computed. Then the labor cost is estimated at a certain percentage of the cost of the pipe.

In medium price one and two story residences, the labor cost of roughing in the job will vary from 75 to 85 percent of the cost of the roughing materials, with 80 percent a fair average.

In apartment buildings of non-firepoof construction, the labor cost of roughing in will average about 90 to 100 percent of the cost of the roughing in materials, while on high grade fireproof construction, the labor cost roughing in will run from 100 to 120 percent of the cost of the roughing in materials.

Sewer work is estimated separately from roughing in.

Labor Handling and Placing Plumbing Fixtures.   The labor cost handling and placing all kinds of fixtures, such as laundry tubs, kitchen sinks, lavatories, bathtubs, shower baths, water closets, drinking fountains, etc., is usually estimated at 25 to 30 percent of the cost of the fixtures.

Plumbing Contractor's Overhead Expense and Profit.   Plumbing contractors like to add 10 percent to the cost of their work for overhead expense, and an additional 10 percent for profit, but most frequently the jobs are let on the basis of a straight 10 percent or less, depending upon the competition and how badly the contractor needs the work.

PREPARING DETAILED PLUMBING ESTIMATES

When preparing detailed estimates on plumbing, it is necessary to list the quantity of each class of work separately, such as the number of lineal feet of 4", 6" and 8" sewers, and fittings; number of lineal feet of each size soil pipe, vents and fittings, number of lineal feet of water pipe and fittings of different materials and sizes; number of valves of the various kinds and sizes; number of each type of fixture required, such as hot water heaters, laundry trays, kitchen sinks, slop sinks, bathtubs, lavatories, water closets, shower baths, etc., together with a list of fittings and supplies required for each.

The following is a list of items the plumbing contractor should include in his estimate:

1. Sewerage, including double sewer system.
2. House tanks, foundations, etc.
3. Compression tanks, foundations, etc.
4. Sewer ejector and bilge pump and basins.
5. Iron, gravel, catch and other basins.
6. Water filters, foundations.
7. Water meter.
8. Soil and vent pipe and fittings.
9. Roof flashings.
10. Shower and urinal traps.
11. Closet bends.
12. Drum traps.
13. Lead, solder, sundries.
14. Inside downspouts.
15. Outside downspouts.
16. Downspout heads.
17. Iron sewer and fittings.
18. Floor drains.
19. Back water gates.
20. Service pipe to building.
21. Mason hydrant.
22. Stop cock and box.
23. Galvanized pipe and fittings.
24. Brass or copper pipe and fittings.
25. Valves, check valves.
26. Pet cocks, sill cocks, hose bibbs.
27. Hot water tank and heater.
28. Pipe covering, tank covering, heater covering, filter covering, painting.
29. Gas fitting, mains, ranges, heaters, etc.
30. Manholes and covers.
31. Catch basins and covers.
32. Surface drain basins and covers.
33. Fire system, incl. pumps, hose, Siamese connection, meter, etc.
34. Roughing in material.
35. Fixtures, such as water

closets, lavatories, bathtubs, shower baths, sinks, laundry tubs, drinking fountains, N.P. fittings.

36. Permits, insurance, trucking, freight, telephone, watchman, etc.

37. Overhead expense.

38. Profit.

PIPE AND PIPE FITTINGS

Approximate Lineal Foot Prices of Cast Iron Soil Pipe

All prices on all types of pipe and pipe fittings and supplies should be checked from a supplier at the time of the job as they are subject to continual change.

Size	Single Hub		Double Hub	
	Service	Extra Heavy	Service	Extra Heavy
2"	$ 2.00	$ 3.00	$ 2.60	$ 4.00
3"	2.50	3.75	3.25	5.00
4"	3.40	5.10	4.40	6.80
5"	4.30	6.50	5.60	8.60
6"	5.20	7.80	6.75	10.40
8"	8.75	13.15	11.40	17.50
10"	13.75	20.50	17.90	27.50
12"	19.25	28.75	25.00	38.50

Prices of Cast Iron Soil Pipe Fittings

Description of Fitting	Sizes in Inches					
	2"	3"	4"	5"	6"	8"
Quarter bends, service	$ 2.30	$ 4.50	$ 6.70	$ 7.75	$ 10.90	$ 35.00
Extra heavy	2.50	6.00	8.90	11.25	14.20	36.00
Eighth bends, service	1.80	3.35	5.30	7.00	8.25	25.00
Eighth bends Extra heavy	$ 2.05	$ 4.75	$ 6.90	$ 8.25	$ 11.25	$ 29.00
Sanitary T & Y branches Extra heavy	6.20	10.75	13.90	18.50	23.00	50.00

Description of Fitting	Size in Inches					
	2"	3"	4"	5"	6"	8"
Plain Traps S P or ¾ Service	5.25	6.50	10.50	21.00	30.00	80.00
T cleanout Extra heavy	18.00	23.00	36.00	70.00	105.00	130.00
Comb. Y & eighth bends Extra heavy	7.00	8.25	12.00	24.00	32.00	80.00

Closet bends slip collar type—4"x4"x12"—$12.00; 4"x4"x18"—$15.00

Lineal Foot Prices of Buttweld Steel Pipe

Size	Standard Weight		Extra Heavy	
	Black	Galvanized	Black	Galvanized
¼ "	$0.30	$0.45	$0.45	$0.60
"	.40	.50	.55	.65
½ "	.42	.52	.57	.68
¾ "	.60	.70	.75	.90
1 "	.90	1.10	1.15	1.30
1¼ "	1.05	1.40	1.45	1.70
1½ "	1.35	1.65	1.75	2.05
2 "	1.80	2.20	2.35	2.75
2½ "	2.60	3.25	3.65	4.25
3 "	3.40	4.25	4.80	5.60
3½ "	4.20	5.20	5.95	7.00
4 "	5.00	6.10	7.10	8.25

Prices on Standard Malleable Iron Fittings

Type of Fitting	Size								
	½ "	¾ "	1"	1¼ "	1½ "	2"	3"	4"	6"
Tee - Black	$.55	$ .80	$1.40	$2.30	$2.80	$4.15	$10.50	$21.50	$60.00
Galv.	.80	1.15	1.85	3.30	4.00	5.35	14.50	30.00	85.00
90° El Black	.45	.50	.95	1.50	2.00	2.85	9.50	16.00	48.00
Galv.	.65	.70	1.35	2.10	2.80	4.00	13.00	22.50	65.00
45 El Black	.65	.85	1.10	1.80	2.20	3.00	10.50	17.00	55.00
Galv.	.95	1.20	1.55	2.20	3.00	3.20	14.50	23.70	75.00

Lineal Foot Prices of Copper Water Tubing

	Normal Size									
	¼ "	⅜ "	½ "	⅝ "	¾ "	1"	1¼ "	1½ "	2"	3"
Light Type M	$.35	$.40	$.60	$ .70	$ .85	$1.15	$1.60	$2.10	$2.30	$6.00
Medium Type L	.37	.50	.75	.90	1.10	1.50	1.95	2.50	3.75	7.25
Heavy Type K	.40	.65	.85	1.00	1.40	1.80	2.25	2.90	4.35	8.50

Prices of Wrought Copper Soldered Joint Fittings

Type	Nominal Size							
	½ "	¾ "	1"	1¼ "	1½ "	2"	3"	4"
Tee	$.20	$.50	$1.50	$2.35	$3.00	$4.80	$15.70	$32.00
90° Elbow	.15	.30	.70	1.10	1.50	2.65	8.00	18.00
45° Elbow	.25	.45	.75	1.30	1.70	2.50	9.75	20.00

PIPING SPECIALTIES

Cast Iron Drum Traps

Drum trap with cover and gasket, 4"x8", 2 inlets $6.25
Drum trap with cover and gasket, 4"x8", 3 inlets 6.50

Roof Drains

	3"	4"	5"	6"	8"
Cast Iron	$115.00	$120.00	$175.00	$190.00	$300.00
Galv.	195.00	200.00	250.00	270.00	380.00

Floor Drains

	Size		
	3"	4"	5"
Type	outlet	outlet	outlet
Flat round top cast iron	$ 35.00	$ 40.00	$ 75.00
Flat square top cast iron	50.00	50.00	85.00
Funnel type brass	70.00	70.00	
Drain with bucket cast iron	100.00	100.00	105.00
Trench drain 10"x24"	115.00	135.00	

Septic Sewage Disposal Tanks

Septic tanks are used in rural or suburban districts where running water is available but no sewers, and are used for homes, hotels, summer resorts, etc.

The capacity of a septic tank should be at least equal to the maximum daily flow of sewage. This is normally estimated at 50 gallons per person per day. For part time service in factories, churches, schools, etc., 25 gallons per person per day is generally satisfactory for estimating tank capacities. In some localities, health authorities require at least a 500 gallon tank for residential installation.

They are commonly furnished in 12 and 14 gauge copper bearing steel, electrically welded and covered with a thick coating of asphalt to protect the tanks against corrosive action.

Size of Tank	Capacity Gallons	Size Tile Connection	Weight Pounds	Capacity Home Use No. Persons	Price Each
46" dia. x 48"	300	4"–6"	275	5– 6	$ 67.50
52" " x 60"	500	4"–6"	380	6– 7	102.00
46" " x 120"	750	6"	575	7–12	140.00
48" " x 144"	1000	6"	980	12–15	195.00

Prices of Brass Valves

	Size in Inches							
Kind of Valve	½"	¾"	1"	1¼"	1½"	2"	2½"	3"
Gate valve, 100 lbs. pressure	$ 8.00	$10.00	$13.00	$16.50	$19.25	$30.00	—	—
Gate valve, 125 lbs. pressure	11.00	13.75	17.00	22.00	28.00	40.00	80.00	120.00
Globe valve, 100 lbs. pressure	9.50	12.50	17.00	22.00	29.00	43.00	—	—

Size in Inches

Globe valve, 125 lbs. pressure............................	10.00	13.50	18.00	25.00	32.00	48.00	80.00	125.00
Check valve, horizontal, 125 lbs.	15.00	20.00	28.00	36.00	45.00	74.00	100.00	140.00
Check valve, 125 lb. swing.............................	12.00	14.00	18.00	23.00	27.00	39.00	70.00	100.00

Angle valves, same price as Globe valves.

Gas Heaters

Capacity Gals.	Over-all Dia.	Over-all Ht.	Approx. Wt.	Prices 5 Year	10 Year
20	14½"	61"	144 Lbs.	$100.00	$120.00
30	16¼"	64"	174	120.00	170.00
40	18½"	65"	195	150.00	185.00
50	20¼"	65"	274	190.00	240.00

Electric Heaters

Capacity Gals.	Over-all Dia.	Over-all Ht.	Approx. Wt.	Prices 10 Yr.
40	20	50	160	$170.00
52	23	50	181	200.00
66	23	62	227	220.00
82	25	63	270	250.00
110	28	69	430	290.00

PLUMBING FIXTURES AND TRIM

Residential kitchens and bathrooms have tended to go full circle. When plumbing first moved indoors it was generally installed in a full sized room and was arranged about the walls as so much "furniture". Later sanitary concerns became paramount and kitchens and baths were designed as machines — all chrome and tile and porcelain enamel and reduced to minimum dimensions to facilitate cleaning.

A few years ago, with the realization that maids were a thing of the past, the kitchen emerged as an entertainment center where family and friends could gather. Today it is often difficult to tell where the family room ends and the kitchen begins. All this has had its effect on the materials used with appliances and fixtures made as inconspicuous as possible.

The bathroom now seems to be following suit, especially the bathing area which is often in a separate room together with built in equipment for exercise and relaxation and sometimes even a sauna, greenhouse and fireplace! Often the contractor will be called in to convert a spare bedroom into a bath and dressing room suite.

The following discussion of fixtures and their prices give figures which include the fittings. Also are included averages for the piping hook-ups to the main risers and stacks that might be added to arrive at per fixture installed budget figures.

Bathtubs. The least expensive, standard, recessed tub is made of enamelled steel. This will cost around $300–$325 for the 4'6" length and $350–$400 for the 5' lengths. Units made of cast iron will run $450–$475 in those sizes in white, add $100 for color. If these units are to be recessed into the floor, add another $20. Square recessed tubs 42" x 48" will run $390 in cast iron.

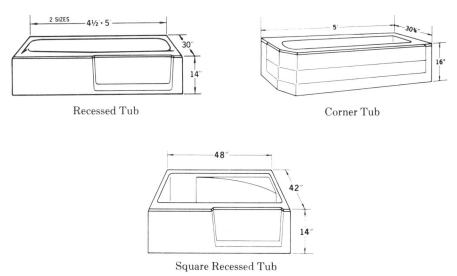

Recessed Tub

Corner Tub

Square Recessed Tub

Courtesy Eljer Plumbing Ware Division Wallace Murray Corp.

Units complete with three enclosing walls can be had in fiberglass for around $275.

A plumber with a helper should set a tub with shower in about two hours.

To arrive at a per-fixture installed budget figure add around $210.

Shower Stalls. These can range from simple baked enamel on steel units costing around $100 to custom marble enclosures costing six times that. Prefabricated fiberglass units are very poplular and can be had with built-in seats and grab bars for the elderly. A 3' x 3' unit will run $235 complete.

Often the plumber will find his work limited to furnishing the receptor and mixing valve and outlet with other trades providing finished walls. A precast receptor pan in terrazzo together with chrome fittings will cost $90 in 3' x 3' size and $110 in 3' x 4'. One man can install this in half a day.

Lavatories. Wall hung lavatories are available in porcelain enamelled cast iron or vitreous china. A 19" x 17" unit will run $125.00 in white, cast iron, $175.00 colored; $100 china white, $120 china colored. A 22" long unit will run $140 cast iron white, $155.00 cast iron colored and $170 china white and $180.00 china colored.

Allow two men one hour to install. Add $230 to arrive at a per fixture installed price.

Drop-in, counter top units are mainly self-rimming today. They come in cast iron, china, steel, stainless and molded plastic. An 18" round unit in cast iron of vitreous will run around $65 in white, $75 in color, in stainless, $120 and in enamelled steel, $50. A 20" by 18" unit will cost some $10 more. Two men will take an hour and a half to set a unit.

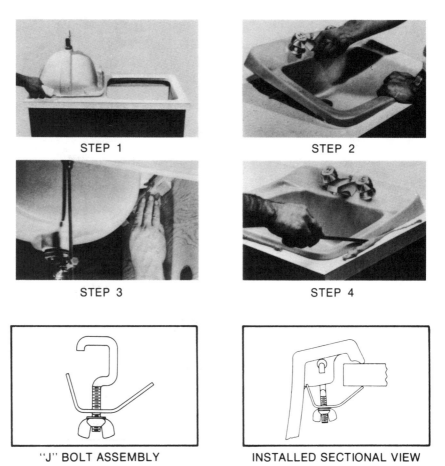

STEP 1 STEP 2

STEP 3 STEP 4

"J" BOLT ASSEMBLY INSTALLED SECTIONAL VIEW

Courtesy Eljer Plumbingware Division Wallace Murray Corp.

Allow approximately two hours plumber time to install a self-rimming lavatory.

Also available for vanity units are precast, one piece, bowl and countertops in a variety of marbleized colors and patterns. These are generally locally manufactured and prices should be checked but a 2' long top and bowl should run around $75 and take two men an hour and a half to set and a six foot top with double bowl should cost around $175 and take three hours to set.

Water Closets.   Water closets can be either wall hung or floor mounted, have a tank or flush valve water supply and the tank can be a separate piece or the unit can be cast in one piece with the tank dropped behind the seat.

A floor mounted one piece will cost $240 in white, $285 in color. A floor mounted two piece unit will cost $110 in white, $135 in color. For areas where water supply is a problem units designed to flush with as little as two quarts can be had, but will cost around $400.

Floor mounted units will take two men one and one half hours to set. For a per fixture installed budget figure, add $180.

Bidets.   For the ultimate touch in the luxury bath, install a bidet. It will cost about $250 in white, $290 in color and take two men two hours to set.

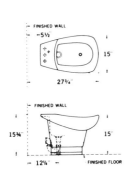

Floor Mounted Bidet

Courtesy Eljer Plumbingware Division Wallace Murray Corp.

Sinks.   Kitchen sinks are usually self-rimming and set into a cabinet top of plastic or tile. With electric dishwashers many are single bowl. Even in luxury kitchens a single bowl may be set where the dishes are washed with a second bowl near the refrigerator for washing vegetables and a third near the ice making machine for making drinks.

A single bowl 24" x 21" will cost $75 in enamelled steel, $112.50 in white cast iron, $137.50 in colored cast iron and $156.25 in stainless. Figure two men three hours to set. Add $375 for a per fixture installed price.

A double unit 42" x 21" will cost $156.25 in steel, $205.00 in cast iron white, $225.00 in cast iron color and $250 in stainless. Two men will take three and a half hours to set such a unit.

Cast iron sink tops with drain board will run $225 for single bowl 42" unit, $260 for double bowl 60" unit.

Enamelled steel sink and drain board tops will run $150 for a 42" length, $200 for a double bowl 60" length.

Laundry sinks in enamelled cast iron will cost $150 for a single compartment, $225 for a double; in cast stone, $75 and $115; in fiberglass, $60 and $90; in stainless steel, $150 and $250. Two men will set a single unit in one and one half hours; a double in two hours.

Electric Dishwashers.   Many modern homes and apartments are now being equipped with electric dishwashers. These dishwashers may be installed as separate units or they may form a part of a complete sink.

The various units may be purchased at the following prices:
Dishwasher unit only with floor cabinet but without top and backsplasher, where used under a continuous countertop. Size 24" x 25" and 34½" high. Price. . .$400.00.

Dishwasher unit with porcelain enamel top and backsplasher. Cabinets made of electrically welded rust-resistant steel with baked on enamel finish. Size 23" x 27" and 39" high. Price. $430.00

Add installation charges to all of the above prices.

Garbage Disposal Units.   The disposal does away with the kitchen garbage can. It is a self-contained unit attached to the kitchen sink to form an enlarged drain into which all kitchen food wastes can be placed.

The unit consists of a housing in which is contained a propeller and shredding mechanism. A ¼ h.p. motor is directly connected to the propeller and shredding mechanism and supplies the power for operating the waste unit.

Waste material can be accumulated in the upper receptacle of the unit until a normal charge is collected or it may be operated to dispose of the material immediately. The capacity of the waste receptacle is 1 qt.

Waste material passed through a series of shredders where they are reduced to a fine pulp. This pulp then passes into a revolving strainer disc through which it is forced centrifugally into a chamber below and around the flywheel. Fins on the flywheel centrifugally force the pulp into the outlet passage connected to the drainline which carries the waste to the sewer. Cold water from the faucet flowing through the unit during the grinding operation thoroughly flushes the waste down the drain.

The price of this unit averages about $135.00.

Add installation charge to the above price. See "Kitchens".

Perhaps the most universal aspect of any major remodeling job is the need to provide electrical service. Contemporary life styles have made electricity even more necessary than in the past, making it essential that it be considered no matter what area of the house is involved. A home is not complete unless there is access to an outlet in every room and hallway from attic to basement. And it's doubly true in the kitchen. Before any remodeling job is begun, it's wise to consider whether the electrical service will be involved . . . usually it will be. In older homes, for instance, it may be necessary to replace the entire service because it has become unsafe. Where wiring has become worn, or major portions of the system have sustained damage, strong consideration should be given to replacement, starting at the service entrance.

In some areas, a building permit will not be issued unless older wiring is brought up to present day codes.

Convenience is another good reason for including electrical service in the job. Many homes, even homes of relatively recent vintage, do not have an adequate number of outlets and fixtures in places where they are wanted. Whenever remodeling work is done in any room, the time is probably right to add more convenient service. The job is simpler and less expensive then, too. In some areas, the code calls for an outlet every 12' in remodeling and new construction.

When major appliances are added, or central air conditioning, there will often be a need to provide additional power. Again, the need is more likely to occur in older homes where the service originally provided was adequate at the time, but no longer is. It is not unusual to find that the original service is rated at 60 amps, 115 volts. Unless the home is unusually small, a more realistic service for today's needs will be 100–120 amps, 230 volts. Many large appliances, ranges and air conditioners in particular, require 230 volts and cannot be installed unless the proper wiring is added.

Whenever a remodeling project includes the addition of a complete room or other new construction, the need for including electrical service is self-evident. Provision for power will be part of the basic plans, and will ordinarily be shown on construction drawings if they are prepared. If extensive drawings are not part of the project, be ready to suggest to the customer where service ought to be provided to satisfy any present or

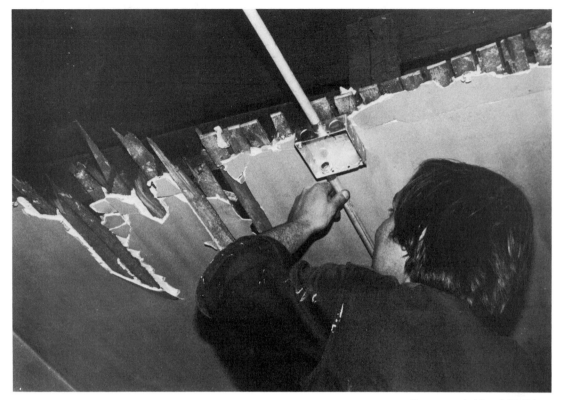

Courtesy Ashland Builders

Removal of wiring and fittings can be complex, especially if they are a distance from the service entrance or wiring is inaccessible.

future need. New construction presents a unique opportunity to add all the convenience desired, at a time when the wiring can be done very easily as part of the total job.

Another opportunity exists when the project is remodeling or finishing a previously unfinished area, such as a basement or an attic. As walls are roughed in, but before any finishing work is begun, whatever wiring may be needed can be done in a minimum of time, without having to disturb existing construction. It's also a good time to suggest further improvements to the customer, making the end result of the project even more pleasing and convenient.

Finally, there is the question of codes. Every locality has construction codes that include electrical service. These are, of course, designed to insure that safe wiring is provided and that the homeowner gets what he pays for. Since a building permit is frequently required for major remodeling jobs, the work will be inspected. It's important that electrical service be brought up to date, in accordance with local codes, so that the inspection will be successful. It's also important that you consult local codes at the time a job is being planned and estimated so that nothing is overlooked.

Special Problems To Consider.   Electrical service in remodeling generally requires opening or removing portions of walls, ceilings and even floors so that the wiring can be done.

Furthermore, it is often necessary to remove old wiring. This is especially true when rigid conduit was used originally, and the plans call for using some or all of what is there. If wiring must be upgraded, the old wires must be removed, unless the conduit is of adequate size to accommodate the new along with the old. The job may be as simple as disconnecting the old and trimming the ends, or as complicated as pulling out every length of existing wire for reasons of safety, space or to meet code requirements.

Use the following to determine the capacity of standard sizes of conduit.

CHART A

Size Of Conduit

Size Of Wires	Number Of Wires				
	2	3	4	5	6
TW					
14	½"	½"	½"	½"	½"
12	½"	½"	½"	½"	½"
10	½"	½"	½"	½"	¾"
8	½"	¾"	¾"	1"	1"
THW					
14	½"	½"	½"	½"	½"
12	½"	½"	½"	¾"	¾"
10	½"	½"	½"	¾"	¾"
8	¾"	¾"	1"	1"	1¼"
TW and THW					
6	¾"	1"	1"	1¼"	1¼"
4	1"	1"	1¼"	1¼"	1½"
2	1"	1¼"	1¼"	1½"	2"
1/0	1¼"	1½"	2"	2"	2½"
2/0	1½"	1½"	2"	2"	2½"
4/0	2"	2"	2½"	2½"	3"

As mentioned earlier, if a remodeling job adds a significant number of new circuits, or appliances with heavy power demands, the present service will probably not be adequate. Consequently, the service should be upgraded. Also provided in this chapter are guidelines for estimating change-over of the service entrance, and total power requirements.

Removing Existing Equipment.   Three parts of the system should be considered in the estimate: the service entrance; permanently mounted fixtures; and present wiring and fittings.

Updating the service entrance always involves a direct replacement of present equipment. Ideally, this should be done as a single operation to avoid lengthy interruption of power. In some instances, the present box can be converted to a subpanel, rather than removing it. In the section of this chapter entitled "Service Entrance Installation" there are estimating guidelines for this part of the job.

The labor to remove existing fixtures can vary widely, depending upon room location and type of fixture.

Removal:

Ceiling/wall lamps and fixtures	15 min. each
Base plugs/receptacles (115V.)	10 min. each
Appliance receptacles (230V.)	15 min. each
Switches/dimmer controls	10 min. each

Removing existing wiring and fittings can become a complex operation, especially if the remodeling work is distant from the service entrance or the wiring is inaccessible. It may be that existing wires need not be removed, depending upon whether they will interfere with new work and the local code requirements.

If the present wiring is metallic or non-metallic flexible cable, it can probably be cut off after the fixture is removed, and no further time must be spent in removing it. If rigid conduit was used previously, its condition should be checked. When there are obvious leaks, or fire damage, it should not be used for new wiring. If it is in good condition, and placed appropriately for the remodeling work, it can usually be used for new wiring, or the existing wiring used if it is of adequate size. Where conduit is large enough, new wires can be pulled, and old ones cut off; if this isn't possible, then the old wiring will have to be removed before new wires are pulled. Unless rigid conduit is in the way it can be left in even if it will not be reused.

Figure the following to remove wire from conduit:

	Less than 25' from jct. box	More than 25' from jct. box
Open wall, ceiling or floor adjacent	15 min. per box (switch, plug, etc.)	30 min. per box (switch, plug, etc.)
No open area adjacent	30 min. per box	45 min. per box

Careful planning for this part of the job can save time and work later on. Consider whether portions of the present wiring can be reused.

Courtesy Ashland Builders

It is important that electrical service be brought up to date in accordance with local codes.

Planning Guides
Determining Total Power Needs

When a remodeling project is planned, the total electrical load must be calculated in order to determine whether the service is adequate. The National Electrical Code suggests the following method:
(1) Using outside dimensions, multiply the number of square feet of living space by 3 watts.
(2) Add 1500 watts for each 20-amp small appliance circuit.
(3) Add the actual requirement for each major appliance.
(4) Subtract 10,000 watts from the total, and multiply the difference by 40%; add the 10,000 watts for a subtotal.
(5) Add the actual requirement for air conditioning or heating—whichever is larger.
(6) Convert load to current by dividing the final total by 240 volts.
NOTE: The service entrance panel must have a rating higher than the number of amps calculated.

For a service rating less than 100 amps, proceed as follows:
(1) Follow steps 1 and 2 above.
(2) To the first 3000 watts, add 35% of the amount over 3000 watts.
(3) To the subtotal, add the actual requirements for all major appliances.

(4) Convert to current by dividing the total by 120 volts or 240 volts, depending upon existing service. For 100-amp service or higher, you can construct a simple chart:

_____ sq. ft. living space x 3 watts		_____ watts
_____ 20-amp circuits x 1500 watts		_____ watts
Laundry circuit (1500 watts)		_____ watts
Major appliances: water heater		_____ watts
clothes dryer		_____ watts
dishwasher		_____ watts
disposal		_____ watts
range		_____ watts
other		_____ watts
	TOTAL	_____ watts
		- 10,000 watts
	difference	_____
	x 0.40	_____
		+ 10,000 watts
	Subtotal	_____ watts
Air conditioner or heater		_____ watts
	Total Load	_____ watts
	÷ 240 volts	_____ amps

If the present service is less than the total number of amps when new circuits are included, the service entrance will have to be updated to accommodate the increased load.

CHART B

Ampacity Of Insulated Copper Conductors

Wire Size	Insulation Type	Ampacity
14	TW, THW, THWN	15
12	TW, THW, THWN	20
10	TW, THW, THWN	30
8	TW	40
8	THW, THWN	45
6	TW	55
6	THW, THWN	65
4	TW	70
4	THW*, THWN*	85
2	TW	95
2	THW*, THWN	115
1	THW, THWN	130
2/0	THW*, THWN	175

*Exception - when used as service entrance conductor:

4	THW, THWN	100
2	THW, THWN	125
1	THW, THWN	150
2/0	THW, THWN	200

Number Of Conductors Per Box

Type Of Box	Size	Number Of Conductors*			
		#14	#12	#10	#8
Octagonal	4"x11/4"	6	5	5	4
	4"x11/2"	7	6	6	5
	4"x21/8"	10	9	8	7
Square	4"x11/4"	9	8	7	6
	4"x11/2"	10	9	8	7
	4"x21/8"	15	13	12	10
	411/16"x11/4"	12	11	10	8
	411/16"x11/2"	14	13	11	9
Switch	3"x2"x21/4"	5	4	4	3
	3"x2"x21/2"	6	5	5	4
	3"x2"x23/4"	7	6	5	4
	3"x2"x31/2"	9	8	7	6

*Count all grounding wires in a box as one conductor.
Count each device as one conductor.
Count each wire entering and leaving the box without splice as one conductor.
Pigtails are not counted at all.

Basic Installations. If the service entrance panel is to be replaced, calculating the total power requirements will determine the size equipment needed. Remember, include the cost of the service riser (pipe) or underground conduit riser in the total cost of equipment. See check list, page 204 for typical costs.

Check with the utility company to determine where wires will be brought to the riser, and installation starts there. For underground service, it may be necessary to provide a trench and conduit to the utility pole or property line. Or the utility may bring the trench to a junction box (pull box) a specified distance from the house. Estimate according to the distance you'll have to take the pipe and cable. Additional estimating information for service entrance equipment is included in "Service Entrance Installation", page 193.

To estimate the remaining electrical work, draw up a wiring plan. This will determine where circuits are needed, how long each run must be, and the size and type of conduit and fittings. It will also help in deciding whether the circuits should be wired directly to the service entrance panel, or to a subpanel served by a large branch line. It's also possible to convert the existing service entrance to a subpanel if the existing circuits will remain in place and the service entrance must be upgraded.

If the number of circuits must be increased, as is often the case, the estimate must include the necessary circuit breaker, conduit and cable or shielded cable, and the fittings to be used in the circuit. Calculate the length of circuits and the number of each type of fitting, then the size and length of wire or cable to determine the total material cost. Be sure to add 2' of cable for each box and 6' for connection to a panel or subpanel.

Labor Per Circuit With One Connection

(Average 20')

	Open Wall	Closed Wall
Rigid Conduit	$16.90	$28.15
Romex or BX..................................	16.50	22.50

Also important in estimating electrical work is whether the walls will be open. In new construction, or rooms where wall coverings have not been installed, wiring can be done more quickly. This also permits use of rigid conduit, generally considered the safest method. If local code permits, metallic cable is equally safe when properly installed. Non-metallic cable can be installed more quickly, but it is often prohibited by the code.

If walls and ceilings are closed, installation becomes more complicated. Metallic cable is the recommended method; however, check local codes. Wiring plans should take into consideration the direction of joists, and whether the cable can run along the joists or must run through them.

Labor Per Circuit Through Studs

(Average 20')

	Open Wall	Closed Wall
Rigid Conduit	$24.40	$46.90
Romex or BX..................................	22.50	39.95

Boxes and necessary fittings must also be included in the estimate of material. The wiring plan will help determine the number and types of items needed — see the check list for typical costs. Each new circuit will involve: (1) Running conduit if walls are open and code requires it, or cut holes for boxes if not, with additional openings at corners or behind baseboard if necessary to install wiring; (2) Pulling wires through conduit or running required cable to boxes; (3) Installing and wiring switches, receptacles or other hardware at each box; (4) Connecting wires or cable at panel or junction box. Use the following to estimate labor.

CHART C

Estimating Table for Basic Circuit Installation

(Minutes/Dollars)

	Indoors		Outdoors	
	open wall	closed wall	frame wall	masonry wall
For each 10' - 115V				
Rigid conduit & wire:	15 $5.60	45 $16.80	15 $5.60	15* $5.60
Shielded cable with ground:	15 $7.50	30 $11.25	—	—

For Each 10' - 230V

Rigid conduit & wire:	$\dfrac{20}{\$7.50}$	$\dfrac{50}{\$18.75}$	$\dfrac{20}{\$7.50}$	$\dfrac{20*}{\$7.50}$
Shielded cable with ground:	$\dfrac{15}{\$5.60}$	$\dfrac{30}{\$11.25}$	—	—

When wiring must go through studs, estimate as follows for each 10'

	open wall	closed wall
Rigid conduit	$\dfrac{20}{\$7.50}$	$\dfrac{50}{\$18.75}$
Shielded cable...	$\dfrac{15}{\$5.60}$	$\dfrac{45}{\$16.80}$
	115V	**230V**
For connections at each junction box or outlet box, add:..................................	$\dfrac{15**}{\$5.60}$	$\dfrac{20}{\$7.50}$
For connecting each circuit at service entrance or subpanel, add:	$\dfrac{10}{\$3.75}$	$\dfrac{15}{\$5.60}$

*   Add 15 minutes for masonry anchors.
** Add 5 minutes for 3-way switch.

After estimating all circuits, add all installation time and multiply total time by the hourly rate:

	Hours	Rate	Total	Rate	Total
Electrician	10	—	—	$22.50	$225.00

When existing conduit will be left in place, and wiring upgraded, figure 5 min. ($1.90) for each 10' of hot and neutral wire to be pulled, and an additional 5 min. ($1.90) for each box in the circuit.

When cable is installed across open joists in basements and attics, it may be necessary to provide wooden raceways — local code will specify what is required. Figure 10 min. ($3.75) for each 10' of raceway installed.

Where wiring must be installed in existing walls, surface raceway is also a possibility. It is not recommended for residential use because it is generally considered unattractive. However, it can be used in a garage or utility room, or other areas where appearance is not a major concern. See the check sheet for typical material costs: figure installation at 15 min. ($5.60) for each 10' of surface raceway, plus 15 min. ($5.60) for installation of each box.

Service Entrance Installation.   When additional power is needed, include the service entrance material shown on the check list and the electrician's labor to install it in the estimate. Whether the wiring is overhead or underground from the utility lines, allow approximately one full day (eight hours) for the changeover.

To install a new service entrance include the following: (1) Disconnect service entrance cables from utility lines; (2) Disconnect house circuits from panel; (3) Remove conduit or cable connectors from one box, and pull wires from box; (4) Pull existing service entrance cable from mast or underground riser; (5) Remove existing mast or riser and install replacement*; (6) Remove service entrance panel and install replacement; (7) Pull new cable through mast or riser; (8) Connect cable to meter socket and/or main disconnect; (9) Reconnect existing house circuits.

It will be necessary to coordinate the work with the local utility, since their personnel must cut power to the cable before it is disconnected. Likewise, the panel must be inspected before service is reconnected, which will usually involve additional time. Another variable to consider is where the utility will bring the wires, especially for underground installation. Length of the trench, conduit and cable must be figured accordingly. Figure one electrician can complete the preceding in 8 hrs.

	Hours	Rate	Total	Rate	Total
Electrician	8	—	—	$22.50	$180.00

* If existing mast or riser can be left in place, deduct two hours from time required to install new service entrance.

If the service from the utility company is adequate to the needs of additional circuits, but the existing service entrance panel will not accommodate the circuits, it may be necessary to install only a new panel. This may also be the case if the existing panel is damaged or outdated. If only a panel is needed, the following work must be estimated: (1) Disconnect service entrance cables from main circuit breaker; (2) Disconnect house circuits from panel; (3) Remove conduit or cable connectors from box, and pull wires from box; (4) Remove panel and install replacement; (5) Connect cable to meter socket and/or main disconnect; (6) Reconnect existing house circuits.

Again, power from the utility lines must be shut off before the new panel can be connected and time must be allowed for the panel to be inspected. Allow one electrician 4 hours.

	Hours	Rate	Total	Rate	Total
Electrician	4	—	—	$22.50	$90.00

When only a few additional circuits are needed, or a single appliance circuit is added, both the power service and the present panel may be adequate. It's often necessary to add circuit breakers to the panel to accommodate the additional wiring. In most panels of recent manufacture, it is relatively simple to add them, then simply wire the new circuits in. When estimating, allow 15 min. ($5.60) for each circuit breaker to be added to the existing panel.

Another possibility is that the power and the service entrance panel are adequate, but there is no space remaining in the panel for additional circuit breakers. In this case, a subpanel can be added, either next to the main panel or near the appliance the subpanel will serve. Branch circuits can be run from the subpanel as needed.

Figure the following: (1) Install subpanel box; (2) Connect conduit and pull cable -or- run heavy cable as provided in local code; (3) Connect cable at subpanel box; (4) Turn off power and connect cable at service entrance panel.

	Hours	Rate	Total	Rate	Total
Electrician	2	—	—	$22.50	$45.00

Another practical solution may be to convert the existing panel to a subpanel. This leaves circuits intact that are already connected, while providing for whatever increased service is needed. It may also prevent having to turn off power until most of the rewiring is done, and the service is ready to be moved to the new panel. Figure the installation of the new service entrance panel as shown before, and the conversion as follows: (1) Disconnect original service entrance cable, and remove wires or fold and tape them out of the way; (2) Remove grounding conductor and bonding screw; (3) Remove branch circuit grounding wires (if any) and connect them to new panel; (4) Run conduit and/or subfeed cable to new panel; (5) Connect subfeed cable at existing panel and at new service entrance panel.

	Hours	Rate	Total	Rate	Total
Electrician	3	—	—	$22.50	$67.50

A final word about installing a new service entrance: This is the best time to change the location of power lines if it's desirable to do so. Be sure to consider whether the present entrance is the best place, or whether new construction or the design of the home dictate a new location for the service entrance. If so, it's best to make all the changes at the same time so that it won't be necessary to do the work a second time at some later date. Careful planning of the job will help to determine whether a change of location should be recommended.

Distribution.   After you've determined service entrance installation, the next consideration is how the power will be distributed to needed areas.

Local codes and the particulars of the job will usually determine the type of conductor to be used. A room addition, for instance, where the walls are open, IMC or EMT conduit is sometimes required. Many areas will permit metallic cable to be used if walls are open; most areas permit its use where walls are not open. Non metallic cable is the simplest to work with, but codes vary widely on where it can be used. Common sense dictates that it shouldn't be used where the wiring is exposed if there is any danger of damage to the wiring, or people coming in contact with it. See page 204 for typical costs of each type conductor; be sure to calculate cost of conduit *and* wires when IMC or EMT are used.

Planning the wiring is the next step. Basically, there are three ways to go: Through the basement, the attic or existing walls. Labor costs will depend upon which of these routes is available. Since it's a fairly simple job to run cable along joists, or through holes in them, in a basement or attic, less time will be needed than for working in areas where access is limited.

In planning each circuit, check to see whether the wiring can run between the studs where it must run behind a finished wall. If not, extra time must be allowed for opening the wall and making holes through the studs. A safe and practical short-cut to look for is back-to-back boxes. If a new box can be connected into another where the wiring is already in place, much less time is required for the installation. Remember, too, that if strips and other access openings are made in the wall or ceiling, it's *not* usually the electrician's job to repair them. See the chapter on installing and repairing wall coverings.

Wiring size will depend on the type of circuit. Later in this chapter are recommended amperage ratings for circuits most likely found in the home. The type of wire will also vary depending on code requirements, whether the circuit is for an appliance or other heavy-duty use. See the check sheet for typical costs of wire usually designated for homes.

Outdoor wiring presents some special considerations in estimating. When installing an air conditioner, hot tub or other outdoor appliance, it is often most practical to run the circuit from the service entrance along the outside of the house. This type installation will generally require rigid conduit or IMC, and a small subpanel with circuit breakers. Check local code requirements and be sure to include any special equipment needed when preparing the estimate.

TYPICAL REMODELING WORK

The following sections will provide recommendations for planning and estimating work typically done in remodeling a home.

Living Room, Dining Room & Hallways.   Unless there are special needs that must be figured separately, work in these rooms will usually involve simple 115 volt circuits for ceiling and wall lighting fixtures; base plugs or other receptacles; and switches. 15 amp circuits, with grounded receptacles, are recommended, with a 20 amp circuit for the dining room to allow for use of a coffee maker or other food service appliance requiring fairly large amounts of current. (Light fixtures should not be connected to the 20 amp circuit.)

In the living rooms or hallways, at least one receptacle should be wired to a switch for convenience in turning a lamp on or off from the entrance. This can be a split receptacle, with only one of the plugs controlled from the switch.

These circuits and all those that follow can be figured as shown in "Basic Installations"; see chart "C" for estimating guidelines. Add 15 minutes for each split receptacle. Or use the following guides to estimate simple circuits.

For wiring only, average hallway, including ceiling fixture, switch and receptacle:

	Electrician	Rate	Total	Rate	Total
Open Wall...	2.5 hrs.	—	—	$22.50	$56.25
Closed Wall	4	—	—	22.50	90.00

(Add ½ hr. for each 10' of circuit that runs through joists)

For wiring only, average living or dining room, including switch and four receptacles (one split) in living room or switch, ceiling fixture, two receptacles and one 20-amp receptacle in dining room:

	Electrician	Rate	Total	Rate	Total
Open Wall:...	4.5	—	—	$22.50	$101.25
Closed Wall:	7.5	—	—	22.50	168.75

(Add ½ hr. for each 10' of circuit that runs through joists)

Bedrooms.   Ceiling and wall lighting fixtures, receptacles and switches constitute the usual requirements for a bedroom, and 115 volt, 15 amp grounded circuits are recommended. If extensive wiring is planned for the master bedroom, a central control unit can be used to switch lamps and appliances on and off in other parts of the house. These usually range in cost from $60.00 to $100.00.

For convenience, at least one outlet per bedroom should be controlled by a switch near the door. Special consideration should also be given to out-of-ordinary requirements such as lights in closets, with switches outside the closet; lighting or convenience outlets near beds; or any other needs indicated by the customer's lifestyle.

For wiring only, average bedroom, including switch and four receptacles:

	Electrician	Rate	Total	Rate	Total
Open Wall:...	4 hrs.	—	—	$22.50	$ 90.00
Closed Wall:	7	—	—	22.50	157.50

(Add ½ hr. for each 10' of circuit that runs through joists)

Bathrooms.   Because the modern bathroom tends to be much more elaborate than it was in the past, it merits some careful planning. 115 volt,

15 amp circuits are recommended for ceiling and wall lighting fixtures and convenience outlets. Multiple boxes should be planned for dramatic lighting over tubs or vanities; for exhaust fans; for sunlamps and auxiliary lighting over counters or in powder room areas.

When remodeling the bath, the customer may wish to add a whirlpool, a sauna, or both. If so, it may be necessary to include a 230 volt, 40-50 amp circuit for heaters. The plan must include the necessary switches for whatever equipment is installed, as well as the placement of the switches. Be sure to calculate total current needs carefully so that adequate circuits can be provided. (See page 190).

Costs of individual fixtures will vary depending upon the unit—check with the supplier before preparing the estimate. Some typical items are:

Whirlpool	$1000 to $2000
Sauna Unit	1200 to 3000
Sun Lamp/Heat Lamp	40 to 60
Radiant Heat Panel	40 to 100
Exhaust Fan	20 to 50

For quick estimates, use the following tables:
For wiring only, average bathroom circuit including ceiling or wall fixture, switch and receptacle:

	Electrician	Rate	Total	Rate	Total
Open Wall:	2.25 hrs.	—	—	$22.50	$50.65
Closed Wall:	4.25	—	—	22.50	95.65

For a 230-volt circuit, add:

Open Wall	1.25	—	—		28.15
Closed Wall	2.5	—	—		56.25

Add ½ hr. for each 10' of circuit that runs through joists.

Kitchens. Perhaps more than any other room in the house, planning for electrical needs in the kitchen is an absolute necessity. Not simply for reasons of safety, although that's important; but because the kitchen often becomes a focal-point of family living and entertaining. (See chapter on kitchen remodeling.) Circuits designed for the kitchen should all be 115 volt, 20 amp; or 230 volt, 20 to 50 amp, depending upon the appliances. A 15 amp circuit can be included for lamps only.

Another reason planning is so important is that the kitchen presents a number of specialized requirements that must be taken into account when estimating. The basics are there, of course: Ceiling and wall lighting fixtures, base plugs and receptacles for counter-top use, and the usual switches. A range hood or ventilating fan has become standard, and if the range is electric, then a separate high-amperage circuit must be provided for it.

Courtesy Ashland Builders

Setting junction box flush with old ceiling in 30–40 year old kitchen. New ceiling will be dropped by using tiles and ceiling grid metal.

Likewise, separate 20 amp circuits should be provided for the dishwasher and for the garbage disposal. Check code requirements for placement of the switch controlling the disposal; usually it must be a minimum distance from the appliance for safety. If the refrigerator/freezer is a large unit, it may even be advisable to provide a separate circuit for that.

While the kitchen is in the planning stages, consider also that other popular items may be added, such as a trash compactor or a food processor built into the counter top. And it's not unusual for a microwave oven to require 10 amps or more, which requires that the circuits be adequate to the load.

All of these needs can and should be provided for when figuring the electrical work in the kitchen. Figure each circuit according to the guidelines in "Basic Installations", using chart "C" for estimating. Also see the check sheet for any special fitting and receptacle needs.

For wiring only, average kitchen, including ceiling fixture, switch and three receptacles:

	Electrician	Rate	Total	Rate	Total
Open Wall:	2.5 hrs.	—	—	$22.50	$90.00
Closed Wall:	4	—	—	22.50	56.25

For stove or other 230-volt circuit, add:

Open Wall:	1.25	—	—	$22.50	$28.13
Closed Wall:	2.5	—	—	22.50	56.25

Add ½ hr. for each 10' of circuit that runs through joists.

Utility Room.   Because of the appliances found here, this room is likely to need circuits somewhat out of proportion to the size of the room. Wall outlets, for instance, should be 115 volt, 20 amp grounded circuits to accommodate the usual clothes washer and gas dryer.

Separate 230 volt circuits will be needed for the dryer or the hot water heater, if either is electric; usually the dryer will require 20 to 30 amps, and the heater 50 amps. A circuit for central air conditioning is another frequent addition to utility room service. It will also require 230 volts, 40 amps, and most codes require a circuit breaker in a box with a cut-off switch within a few feet of the compressor unit.

Be sure to allow for a switchbox connection adjacent to the furnace. Although it doesn't usually require high amperage, the furnace circuit and switch are often spelled out very specifically in electrical codes. Allow an additional 15 minutes for the air conditioning circuit if it must go through a wooden frame wall, or an additional 30 minutes if the wall is cement block or masonry. Or use the following guidelines:

For wiring only, average utility room, including ceiling fixture, switch and two receptacles:

	Elecrician	Rate	Total	Rate	Total
Open Wall:	3 hrs.	—	—	$22.50	$ 67.50
Closed Wall:	5	—	—	22.50	112.50

For each 230-volt circuit, add:

Open Wall:	1 hrs.	—	—	$22.50	$22.50
Closed Wall:	2	—	—	22.50	45.00

Add ½ hr. for each 10' of circuit that runs through joists.

Family Room/Den.   Ever since the American household abandoned the formal parlor, the family room has gained in importance as a gathering point for activities and entertainment. Convenience is once again the key word in planning for electrical needs.

Circuits will be needed for ceiling fixtures—especially if the room is on a previously unfinished lower level—and wall lighting; wall outlets and switches. Receptacles may be required for special areas such as a fireplace, a bar, or in an area where an electronic game or jukebox will be placed.

For the most part, circuits to this type of room can be 115 volt, 15 amp grounded. If a refrigerator or other heavy appliances are a possibility, then a 20 amp circuit should be included. At least one wall receptacle controlled by a switch is also a good idea.

For wiring only, average family room, including ceiling fixture, switch and four receptacles:

	Electrician	Rate	Total	Rate	Total
Open Wall..	4.5 hrs.	—	—	$22.50	$101.25
Closed Wall...	7.5	—	—	22.50	168.74

(Add ½ hr. for each 10' of circuit that runs through joists)

For stereo or TV wiring, figure the labor as comparable to installing a standard 115 volt circuit. Consult the manufacturer or retailer for the proper wiring and receptacles to be used.

Garage / Outdoors. Adding or updating circuits in the garage will often be a simpler task than elsewhere for two reasons:

(1) It's usually the location, or near the location, of the service entrance; and (2) walls are often open, simplifying the wiring job. Circuits will usually be needed for ceiling fixtures, especially in a "workshop" area; 115 volt, 15 amp service is adequate for that purpose. Three-way switches are desirable so that lights can be controlled from the door into the house as well as near the garage door itself

Other receptacles in the garage should be 115 volt, 20 amp circuits to allow for use of tools and appliances. It may also be necessary to include a 230 volt circuit with a special plug to meet the customer's particular need; amperage will depend upon the intended use. When the wiring will be left exposed, it's wise to specify IMC or metallic cable even if the local code doesn't require it.

Frequently, special wiring needs are present in a garage, such as including an electric door opener or even a doorbell transformer. These can usually be connected to existing boxes for light fixures, but must be included in the estimate if additional work will be necessary.

Outdoor receptacles should also be part of the plans. If fixtures are to be mounted near the garage doors, or floodlights on the soffits, circuits will have to be provided. Standard wiring and boxes will usually be adequate, since the fixtures will protect them from weather. Weatherproof receptacles should also be provided for convenience outside the garage, on a patio, or elsewhere as needed. See the checklist for suggested special hardware that will be required for them.

Figure the work for garage and outdoor circuits according to the guidelines in "Basic Installations"; chart "C" provides estimating assistance. If an outdoor receptacle is mounted on a frame wall, add 15 minutes for each box; if on a masonry wall, add 30 minutes for each box. The following chart can be used for simple circuits:

For wiring only, average garage, including ceiling fixture, switch and two receptacles:

	Electrician	Rate	Total	Rate	Total
Open Wall:	3 hrs.	—	—	$22.50	$ 67.50
Closed Wall:	5	—	—	22.50	112.50

For 230-volt appliance circuit, add:

	Electrician	Rate	Total	Rate	Total
Open Wall:	2 hrs.	—	—	$22.50	$ 45.00
Closed Wall:	3	—	—	22.50	67.50

(Add ½ hr. for each 10' of circuit that runs through joists)

Special Projects. There are many possible wiring jobs that don't relate specifically to one room in the house, or are not ordinarily part of a remodeling project. For this type of work, some additional planning will be necessary. Even where the customer doesn't request these installations, it may be wise to suggest one or more of them for the improvement of the house.

Ceiling Fans (typical cost: $60.00 to $300.00)—since energy savings has become more important than ever, these can be a valuable addition to the home. In many cases, they can be added to an existing circuit that served a ceiling lamp fixture. If not, a 115 volt, 15 amp grounded circuit with a switch is all that is required — a fairly simple addition if other electrical work is being done in the room.

Intercom / Stereo (typical cost: $200.00 to $400.00)—an installation that doesn't usually require an electrician, but that can be done along with other electrical work. Since heavy current loads are not involved, the wiring is usually light duty; check the manufacturer's recommendations. If extensive remodeling is being done, or a somewhat isolated room is being added, the stereo or intercom may be a welcome extra. Figure the wiring as similar to installing a 115 volt line not requiring conduit, and estimate it accordingly.

Alarms/Remote Controls (typical cost: $50.00 to $200)—for these projects, the work will vary with the complexity of the system. Consult the local electrical code for requirements relating to smoke, fire and burglar alarms. The work will be similar to installing 115 volt lines, and one of those will often be necessary to furnish power to the alarm system. Remote controls may involve wiring into each circuit to be controlled from the master station. If so, figure the length of each run and estimate as you would for other circuits, taking into account the type of wiring needed and the number of connections.

Auxiliary Heating Units (typical cost: $30.00 to $100.00)—especially useful in rooms that have been added to the house, or in attics and basements. These units will usually require an additional 230 volt, 40 amp isolated circuit. If the heater is gas-fired with an electric fan, the circuit rating can be less; 115 volt, 15 amp service will be adequate.

Electronic Air Cleaners (typical cost; $175.00 to $250.00)—an important "luxury" in a home that must remain closed most of the time for heating and air conditioning. Since these are most frequently mounted on the furnace, they can be connected to an existing circuit in the utility room or basement, or to the circuit that serves the furnace itself.

Low-voltage Lighting (typical cost: $75.00 to $125.00)—an excellent idea for accenting decorative planting and lighting walkways. A transformer must be mounted outside the house, and a suitable UF cable must be run to the lights. Check manufacturers' specifications for required wiring, and figure the work as similar to other circuits; be sure to allow for trenching or burying the cable to the various location of the lamps.

Outdoor Fixtures (typical cost: $10.00 to $75.00)—ranging from spotlights mounted on the house, to post lamps, garden lighting, or convenience outlets for any purpose. The major difference in estimating outdoor wiring is in figuring the type of materials to be used. Rigid steel or PVC conduit is usually required, and if plastic is used, ground wires must be provided. Driptight or watertight panels, switchboxes and receptacles will also be needed.

Electrical codes now require that new outside receptacles be protected with a GFCI. Wiring these and other outdoor circuits can be figured using the guidelines in "Basic Installations"; the estimate may also have to include time for running underground wiring when necessary. If the circuit will connect to an existing box, add 15 minutes for adding an extender ring. If power will be brought from a box inside the house, add 15 minutes to bring wiring through a frame wall, or 30 minutes for a masonry wall. The following guidelines can also be used:

For each 10' of circuit:

	Electrician	Rate	Total	Rate	Total
Open Wall:	1 hr.	—	—	$22.50	$ 22.50
Closed Wall:	1.5	—	—	22.50	33.75
Average air-conditioner circuit: 5 hrs. @$22.50					112.50

Add ½ hr. for each 10' of circuit that runs through joists.

Basements/Attics.   Usually the installation in these areas will be similar to new construction—the walls are open and existing circuitry is reasonably accessible. Depending upon appliances to be used, either 115 volt or 230 volt circuits will be needed. 15-20 amp circuits should be included for general purposes, and heavier circuits as needed for large appliances.

When an attic is remodeled, usually it will be converted to a bedroom or other living space. The plan should include circuits for lighting, receptacles and possibly a ventilator. If auxiliary heating is needed, a separate circuit of the proper size must also be figured.

For basement remodeling, 115 volt, 15 or 20 amp circuits will be needed for lighting and receptacles. 230 volt, 20 to 50 amp circuits will be needed if the utility room is part of the project. Kitchens and bathroom type installations are also frequently part of a basement project, and must be planned for. Whether basement or attic, the circuit plan is essential in estimating the work involved.

For wiring only, average basement and attic, including ceiling fixture, switch and four outlets:

	Electrician	Rate	Total	Rate	Total
Basement:	4 hrs.	—	—	$22.50	$ 90.00
Attic:	7	—	—	22.50	157.50

For 230-volt air-conditioning or appliance circuit, add:

Basement:	2 hrs.	—	—	22.50	45.00
Attic:	3.5	—	—	22.50	78.75

Add ½ hr. for each 10' of circuit that runs through joists

Grounding and GFCI's.   A final word about grounded circuits: They are highly recommended. In most instances, electrical codes require that circuits be grounded and that grounded outlets be provided. Even when they are not required, they are advisable for the safety of your clients.

Protection afforded by ground fault circuit interrupters is also recommended. Required for many outdoor installations, they are a good idea for any circuit where a hand-held appliance will be used. For the small amount that they will increase the cost of the job, they are valuable protection that your customer will appreciate. Typical costs run $35.00 to $50.00

Estimating Check Sheet.   Once the job has been planned, use a check sheet to tally the needed supplies before attempting to estimate the job. The sample check sheet below includes the items that are most likely to be used in a residential remodeling project.

Service Entrance   **Cost**
(200 AMP Ser. 2" Pipe)
Service Entrance Head Mast (Service Riser) .... 15.34 ea.
Underground Meter Socket .... 80.00 ea.
Roof Tie... 3.50 ea.
Hub... 1.85 ea.
2 Hole Pipe Straps - .... 20.00 ea.
½" Ground Clamp (42 CKT 200 AMP Main Breaker)... 5.00 ea.
Service Entrance Panel ....150.00 ea.
                          2-Pole .... 10.00 ea.
Circuit Breakers .... 20.00 ea.

Wire Connectors 73B.. $4.00 ea.
Locknuts .... .50 ea.
Bushings .... .60 ea.

Single Conductors   **Cost**
Low Voltage #18 MTW... 55.00 M
Standard 12 TW... 60.00 M
Heavy Duty (3/0)...1425.00 M

Multi-conductor Cable   **Cost**
14–2 Type NM (Non-Metallic Sheath) ....125.00 M
14–2 Type UF (Underground Feeder) ....166.00 M
8/3 Type SE (Service Entr.)..876.00 M

Conduit ½"   **Cost**
½ Intermediate Metal (IMC) .... 47.00 C
½" Couplings (Threaded) .... 45.00 C
½" No Thread Compression Connectors..125.00 C
Thinwall Metal (EMT) .... 19.00 C
½ Couplings (Set Screw) .... 25.00 C
½ Couplings (Compression) .... 40.00 C
½ Connectors (Set Screw).. 20.00 C
½ Connectors (Compression) .... 32.00 C
⅜" Flexible Metal Conduit... 20.00 C
(BX) Connector - Angle Flex .... 44.00 C
Takeall Connector Adaptors... 20.00 C

Boxes and Accessories   **Cost**
(4x4) Extender Ring ....1.25 ea.
(4x4) Switch Box W/Bracket...1.25 ea.
(2x4) Gem Box - Removable Sides..1.00 ea.
(2x4) Switch Cover... .30 ea.
(2x4) Duplex Cover.. .30 ea.
Outlet Box:
    Octagonal.. .80 ea.
        Plain Cover... .40 ea.
    Square Box ....1.00 ea.
        Plaster Rings .... .50 ea.
        Raised Covers .... .80 ea.
Junction Box:
    Octagonal/Cover .... .30 ea.
    Square/Cover... .40 ea.
Special Boxes:
    Weatherproof ....3.00 ea.
    Switch Cover ....2.75 ea.
    Receptacle Cover ....2.50 ea.
    "Handy" Box .... .85 ea.
    Covers.. .30 ea.
    Gem Box (For Drywall)..1.00 ea.

Switches   **Cost**
Single Pole...1.50 ea.
Three-way...2.50 ea.
Four-way...8.25 ea.
Dimmer Incandescent...6.50 ea.

Receptacles	**Cost**
Duplex - Grounded	1.25 ea.
Recessed (Clock)	1.75 ea.
Special:	
Air Conditioner	
or	
Clothes Dryer	4.00 ea.
Kitchen Range	4.00 ea.

Circuit Breakers	**Cost**
Slide-in	4.50 ea.
Receptacle (GFCI)	40.00 ea.

Miscellaneous	**Cost**
Conduit Straps	.05 ea.
Staples	.01 ea.
Wire Connectors (T&B)	4.00 ea.

In recent years, much improvement has been made in the methods of heating and cooling buildings, especially in residential work, largely due to the research programs conducted by heating and air conditioning associations, engineering societies, equipment manufacturers and research departments of various universities.

Types of Conventional Heating Systems. There are four basic types of conventional heating systems—warm air, hot water, steam and electric, including both resistance types and heat pumps, each of which may be used separately or in combination. Solar heating is still in the experimental stage although in certain areas of the country there are enough installations and research that soon reliable information should be available.

For small to medium size residences, stores, churches, etc., of similar size and construction, warm air systems are most widely used. For medium size to large residences and non-residential structures of comparable size, hot water systems are usually selected. For large scale installations, steam systems are generally required. Inasmuch as there are no definite rules stating just when to select one system in preference to another, there is much overlapping in their application. An owner's preference for a particular system may be governed by initial cost of installation; operation cost; convenience of operation; adaptability of system to other uses, such as summer cooling using ducts of a warm air system, snow melting using hot water piping connected to a hot water system; fuel availability, and aesthetics.

Panel Heating Systems. Panel heating systems are used in residential work and for some non-residential structures as well. These systems use large areas of room surfaces, heated to relatively low temperatures (80° to 100° F.), as radiant panels. Panels usually are heated by warm water piping, warm air ducts or low temperature electrical resistance elements embedded in, or located behind, ceiling, wall or floor surfaces.

At the present time, the warm water piping method is most frequently used, with the piping embedded in concrete floors or plastered ceilings—in some cases, both floors and ceilings are used as radiant panels. Piping in floors is usually welded joint black wrought iron pipe, steel pipe or copper tubing. For installations in plastered ceilings copper tubing is usually used.

Estimating the Cost of Heating Systems.   There is no fast, easy, "rule of thumb" method for estimating the cost of a heating system. This requires expert knowledge, as most jobs must be designed and laid out before they can be estimated. In residential and small commercial work, architects seldom give more information than merely specifying the type of system desired, the performance expected, and the kinds of material to use. It is then up to the heating contractor to figure the heating loads and design a system to fit the conditions before estimating the job. On larger work, the heating system is usually designed and laid out diagrammatically, but the heating contractor must work out details for piping equipment connections, controls, etc., which all influence the cost.

To acquire the necessary technical knowledge for this purpose requires everyday participation in this line of work plus constant study to keep up to date. Heating and air conditioning is too complex a subject to treat in a volume of this kind, however, much useful data and information can be gained from manuals published by the North American Heating & Air Conditioning Wholesalers Assn., 1200 W 50th Ave., Columbus, Ohio 43212 and the "Handbook of Air Conditioning, Heating and Ventilating."

Anything appearing in this volume on this involved subject is only the most elementary and approximate—for "roughing" or approximate estimates only.

Boilers are now designed for burning special fuels, such as hard coal, soft coal, oil, gas, etc., the costs varying with boiler sizes and accessories, such as domestic hot water heaters, thermostatic controls, etc.

The ordinary cast iron radiators standing in the room are practically a thing of the past in modern heating systems and concealed convection type radiators of baseboard radiation are now used. These are all items that affect costs.

Copper piping is now used for both heating and plumbing. The cost of this work depends to a large extent upon the experience of the contractor installing same. Mechanics familiar with sweating joints and installing copper piping can install this work rapidly, while those who are not accustomed to its use, will spend considerable time on it.

For the above reasons, the estimator should be familiar with the requirements of the trade in order to prepare intelligent estimates.

Determining Heating Loads.   The first step in designing and estimating heating work is to determine the maximum heating load. For most residential work, the maximum heating load is the total heat loss of the structure figured at design temperatures. For commercial and industrial structures, special purpose heating loads and pick-up loads may be required which must be added to the total building heat loss to obtain maximum heating load.

Heating loads and heat losses are invariably expressed in Btu per hour. A Btu (British thermal unit) is the quantity of heat required to raise the temperature of 1 lb. of water 1 degree F.

Building heat losses vary considerably depending upon climatic location of job, design temperatures, exposure, building size, architectural design, purpose of structure, construction materials used, quality of construction workmanship and other factors.

Heat losses should be figured separately for each room so that the proper amount of radiation may be provided for comfort in all areas. Space limitations in this volume do not permit giving detailed information and data on figuring building heat losses and anything less would be misleading. Complete information and data on this subject are contained in the manuals and guide previously mentioned.

FORCED WARM AIR HEATING SYSTEMS

Forced warm air heating is the most widely used residential heating method in use at the present time. Generally speaking, the forced warm air heating method differs from the old gravity type by using blower equipment to circulate the air in the system.

It is practically impossible for the average general estimator to compute the cost of a modern forced warm air heating system, unless he has a working knowledge of this subject and is able to calculate building heat losses and design systems which will satisfy heating requirements under design conditions. In addition, the subject has become so complex it cannot be covered in a volume of this kind so as to provide adequate information for the preparation of a cost estimate, other than a rough approximation to be used for preliminary purposes only. Always obtain firm quotations from reputable warm air heating contractors before submitting bids on jobs containing this work.

Winter Air Conditioning Systems. Forced warm air heating systems which are equipped with automatic humidifying devices and air filters are popularly known as Winter Air Conditioning Systems. Most forced air installations are of this type.

Each system consists of a direct fired heating unit, a blower, a system of warm air ducts and return air duct system. Air filters are located in the return air duct system just ahead of the blower—humidifying equipment is placed in the warm air plenum chamber over the furnace unit. Air cooling equipment may be added to make this a year 'round system.

The unit may be gas, oil or coal fired. Gas or oil fired units designed for that particular fuel operate at high efficiency; although satisfactory, if less efficient results may be obtained through the use of conversion burners installed in units primarily designed for solid fuel.

Thermostatic control of the heating unit is highly desirable and invariably used. Automatic controls vary the supply of heat in accordance with demand set up by a thermostat located in the living portion of the home. Actuated by limit controls, the blower commences operation automatically when the heated air in the generating unit has reached a pre-determined temperature and cuts out after the source of heat has been shut down and the temperature in the bonnet dropped to a pre-determined point.

Design of air conveying systems of this kind presents an engineering problem which can only be solved with a reasonable degree of accuracy by a competent designer. The heat loss of the building, room by room, is established and the volume of heated and conditioned air required for indoor comfort establishes data from which a duct system can be designed with due regard for velocities, static pressures and delivery temperatures.

Items to be Included in the Estimate.   Costs vary considerably and methods of estimating also differ, but every estimate for a winter air conditioning system should include the following items:
1. Cartage of material and equipment from shop to job.
2. Winter air conditioning unit, complete with humidifier, air filters, and controls.
3. Labor assembling and setting up unit.
4. Oil storage tank installation, including fill and vent piping, oil booster pump if required, oil gauge, piping to unit, oil filter, etc., for oil fired units or—piping for gas fired units.
5. Installation of smoke pipe, fittings and accessories.
6. Warm air and return air plenum chambers.
7. Warm air and return air duct systems.
8. Diffusers, registers, intakes, grilles, etc.
9. Special insulation.
10. Electrical work.
11. Labor starting plant in operation and balancing system.
12. Service allowance.
13. Miscellaneous costs.
14. Overhead and profit.

Cartage.   The cost of trucking material and equipment from shop to job will vary depending upon size of job and distance from shop. An allowance of $60.00 to $120.00 should cover this item on most small jobs.

Cost of Winter Air Conditioning Units.   Sizes, capacities and prices of units vary with the different manufacturers, but the following listings are representative of models available for residential use.

Approximate Net Prices of Winter Air Conditioning Units
Complete with Automatic Controls, Humidifier and Air Filters

Bonnet Rating Btu per Hr.	Register Rating Btu per Hr.	Heating Only	Net Price	With Cooling
	Gas Fired Units			
60,000	48,000	$280.00	24 MBH	$1100.00
76,000	60,800	310.00	29 MBH	1350.00
90,000	72,000	330.00	36 MBH	1450.00
108,000	86,400	400.00	47 MBH	1750.00
120,000	96,000	480.00	47 MBH	1850.00
150,000	120,000	625.00	58 MBH	2300.00
180,000	144,000	700.00	—	—
	Oil Fired Units			
84,000	71,400	525.00	36 MBH	1450.00
112,000	95,200	600.00	42 MBH	1750.00
140,000	119,000	700.00	47 MBH	2000.00
175,000	148,750	800.00	—	—
210,000	178,500	900.00	—	—

Assembling and Setting up Unit.   Most gas fired units can be assembled and set up by a sheet metal worker and a helper in 3 to 4 hours. For an oil fired unit, figure 4 to 5 hours for this work.

Oil Storage Tanks.   Common practice for oil storage tanks in the use of one or two inside storage tanks with a capacity of 275 gals. each. Occasionally outside buried tanks of 550 or 1,000 gallon capacity are used. On a contract basis, these tanks installed, including all piping, cost as follows:

1–275 gallon inside tank $200.00
2–275 gallon inside tanks 390.00
1–550 gallon outside tank... 300.00
1–1,000 gallon outside tank.. 500.00

In the use of an outside tank a basement wall type pump costing from $60.00 to $80.00, must be used with some types of burner equipment.

Gas Piping.   For average installations, an allowance of $100.00 to $150.00 should cover cost of material and labor for connecting gas to unit within the heating room.

Smoke Pipe.   Material and labor for smoke pipe connection from unit to flue should cost $40.00 to $60.00 for gas fired and oil fired units.

Plenum Chambers.   Plenum chambers must be fabricated to order in the shop and are usually made from light gauge galvanized steel. They are mounted on top of the furnace and serve to connect the warm air and return air duct systems to the unit. Two plenum chambers are required for each installation.

Plenums will run $4.50/sq. ft in 18 ga., $5.50 in 16 ga., $6.00 in 14 ga.

Warm Air and Return Air Duct Systems.   The cost of duct work will vary with the size of job and type of distribution.

Under ordinary conditions, the warm air heating contractor will measure and list each type and size of duct, fitting and accessory. These quantities are priced for material and then an estimate is made of labor required for installation. This is a lengthy operation and requires an experienced heating man.

When pressed for time, the duct system cost may be approximated on an outlet basis, using a unit price which covers both material and labor. For ordinary installations, the following costs per outlet are about average where sheet metal workers' wages are from $15.00 to $16.00 per hr.:

Type of System	Cost per Outlet
Conventional system—warm air outlets located on inside walls.	
1st floor outlets	$ 70.00 to $ 80.00
2nd floor outlets	95.00 to 105.00
Capped stacks	27.00 to 33.00
Radial perimeter system in small 1-sty. buildings with basement or crawl space.	
Low velocity—6" to 8" dia. ducts	$ 70.00 to $ 80.00
High velocity—4" and 5" dia. ducts	65.00 to 70.00
Large central return air duct	87.00 to 95.00
Radial perimeter system in small 1-sty. basementless buildings.	
Galv. steel sheet metal pipe and fittings	$ 88.00 to $ 93.00
Fiber duct with galv. steel fittings	88.00 to 93.00
Cement asbestos pipe and fittings	105.00 to 115.00
Trunk and branch perimeter system in medium-size, 1 sty. buildings with basement or crawl space.	
Std., galv. steel, rectangular ducts	$100.00 to $110.00

Add for diffusers, registers, intakes, special insulation, etc. Excavation, backfill and concrete encasement where required, not included.

Diffusers, Registers and Intakes.   Diffusers and registers generally used are of pressed steel construction, with prime coat finish, are fully adjustable and are available in floor, baseboard or wall types. Return air intakes are of same construction and finish, but are non-adjustable.

Floor type diffusers cost $11.00 to $14.00 for sizes commonly used. Baseboard type diffusers cost $10.00 for 2'0" lengths and $14.00 for 4'-0" lengths. Wall type registers cost $5.00 to $10.00. Wall type intake grilles cost $6.00 to $12.00.

Special Insulation. Ducts in unexcavated spaces or in unheated attic spaces, both supply and return, should be insulated with not less than ½" of adequate insulating material. This material is furnished in flexible form and averages $1.00 to $1.25 per sq. ft. applied.

Electrical Work. Custom varies with respect to the supply and installation of electrical circuit from meter to fused safety switch adjacent to unit. Likewise for the connection of blower motor to 110 volt controls and also for the 22 volt wiring to thermostat when used. Most often the job electrician runs the 110 volt service to the safety switch adjacent to unit. From this point it is handled as a subcontract under the heating contractor and represents a cost from $60.00 to $150.00 for complete wiring installation of all controls and motors.

Labor Starting and Balancing Systems. It is customary for the heating contractor to start the plant in operation, test all controls and balance the air distribution system. For jobs completed during summer months, this means a come back call at the beginning of the heating season.

Labor costs for this work will run $75.00 to $125.00 depending upon size of job.

Service Allowance. Most jobs carry a 1-year free service warranty and an allowance should be included in the estimate to cover this contingency. Average costs for service during the first year of operation are $65.00 for gas fired and $90.00 for oil fired systems.

Miscellaneous Costs. Under miscellaneous costs are classified such items as federal tax, sales tax, permits for oil burner or for installation, if required.

Overhead and Profit. Most heating contractors would like to add 10 percent for overhead and 10 percent for profit to their estimates but, in the present competitive market, the majority of jobs are being quoted with a straight 10 percent mark-up.

Approximate Cost of a Complete System Installed. Based on installations in residences of ordinary construction, located in the larger cities, the cost of average winter air conditioning systems ranges as follows for gas fired units. For oil fired units, add 10 to 15 percent.

Floor Area Sq. Ft.	Heat Loss Btu per Hr.	Price for Complete Gas Fired Installation
Conventional Systems, 1-Sty. Buildings with Basements or Crawl Space.		
1,000	65,000	$1500.00 to $2000.00
1,500	80,000	2000.00 to 2300.00
2,000	100,000	2300.00 to 2500.00
Conventional Systems, 2-Sty. Buildings with Basements.		
1,500	75,000	$2000.00 to $2300.00
2,000	90,000	2500.00 to 3000.00
Perimeter Systems, 1-Sty. Buildings with Basements or Crawl Space.		
1,000	65,000	$1500.00 to $2000.00
1,500	80,000	2000.00 to 2300.00
2,000	100,000	2500.00 to 2800.00
Perimeter Systems, 1-Sty. Basementless Buildings.		
1,000	65,000	$1500.00 to $2000.00
1,500	80,000	2000.00 to 2300.00

The above prices are for individual jobs. For multiple housing projects, where large numbers of similar dwelling units are involved, much better prices may be obtained.

As previously mentioned, in this industry, equipment, design and practices, vary greatly even in localized areas. No safe guide may be set down for general use. So much depends upon correct design, proven equipment and experienced installation that it behooves the buyer to carefully investigate all of these items before awarding a contract for this important part of the building.

SUMMER AIR CONDITIONING

Residential summer air conditioning is now available to the general public at a price the average home owner can afford. This applies to both existing homes and new homes under construction and is especially true where forced warm air heating is used, as the same air distribution duct system can be utilized for both heating and cooling. Various warm air heating equipment manufacturers make cooling units for this purpose and installation work is usually done by heating contractors.

The function of summer air conditioning equipment is the reverse of winter air conditioning—circulating air is cooled and de-humidified—but design problems are similar, although more complex. A basic requirement for designing a cooling system is calculating the total cooling load or total heat which must be removed from the structure to achieve a pre-determined inside temperature and humidity under design conditions. Heat gain calculations are much more involved than those for heat losses as many additional factors must be considered, such as sun effect on roof, wall and glass areas; internal heat gains from human occupancy, cooking, lighting, appliances, etc. and latent heat energy involved in dehumidification.

Heat gain calculations are always expressed in Btu per hour. Cooling equipment capacities are usually stated per ton of refrigeration. A ton of refrigeration will remove heat at the rate of 12,000 Btu per hr. In a 24-hr. period, this is equivalent to the heat required to melt a ton of ice. With water-cooled compression refrigeration equipment, one horsepower usually equals about one ton of cooling capacity.

Types of Cooling Equipment for Residential Use. There are several types of cooling units available and in popular use for residential summer air conditioning. In general, equipment may be classified as water-cooled or air-cooled, with each type available for several methods of application.

One method employs a remotely located condensing unit, with refrigerant lines connected to a cooling coil installed in the warm air plenum chamber of a forced warm air heating system. This method uses the heating system blower and ducts for air distribution.

Another method uses a self-contained unit, with the condenser, cooling coil and blower combined in one cabinet. This type may be cut in to the heating ducts, or may have its own duct system where hot water or steam heat is used.

Net Prices of Remote System Cooling Units. Approximate prices are for units factory assembled with heating and cooling thermostat included. No pipe, duct materials or blower assembly included.

Capacity Tons	Rating Btu per Hr.	Net Price Air-cooled	Labor To Install
2	24,000	$ 600.00	8 hr
3	36,000	850.00	14 hr
5	60,000	1800.00	30 hr

Where a complete air circulation duct system is required, figure same as previously given for winter air conditioning systems.

Approximate Cost of Complete Cooling Unit Installation. Based on conditions of average difficulty, complete residential cooling unit installations should cost approximately as follows:

Capacity Tons	Rating Btu per Hr. Remote, Water-cooled System	Price for Complete Installation
2	24,000	$2200.00 to $2500.00
3	36,000	2500.00 to 2800.00

Table Giving Cubical Contents of Various Size Rooms

Size of Rooms in Feet (Use Nearest Size)

3x16½	4x18¾	5x20	6x21	7x21½	8x22	9x22	10x22½	11x23	12x23	13x23	14x23	15x23	16x23½	17x23½
4x12½	5x15	6x16½	7x18	8x18¾	9x19½	10x20	11x20½	12x21	13x21	14x21½	15x22	16x22	17x22	18x22
5x10	6x12½	7x14½	8x15½	9x16½	10x17½	11x18	12x18¾	13x19	14x20	15x20	16x20	17x20½	18x21½	19x21½
6x 8½	7x10½	8x12½	9x14	10x15	11x16	12x16½	13x17¼	14x18	15x18	16x18½	17x19½	18x19½	19x20½	20x20
7x 7	8x 9½	9x11	10x12½	11x13½	12x14½	13x15½	14x16	15x16½	16x17½	17x17½	18x18	19x18	20x19	21x19
8x 6½	9x 8½	10x10	11x11½	12x12½	13x13½	14x14¼	15x15	16x15	17x16	18x16	19x17	20x17	21x18	22x18

Air Space in Rooms in Cubic Feet

Height of Ceilings															
8	400	600	800	1000	1200	1400	1600	1800	2000	2200	2400	2600	2800	3000	3200
8½	425	640	850	1060	1275	1490	1700	1910	2125	2340	2550	2760	2975	3190	3400
9	450	675	900	1125	1350	1575	1800	2020	2250	2480	2700	2920	3150	3370	3600
9½	475	715	950	1190	1425	1660	1900	2140	2375	2610	2850	3090	3325	3560	3800
10	500	750	1000	1250	1500	1750	2000	2250	2500	2750	3000	3250	3500	3750	4000
10½	525	790	1050	1310	1575	1840	2100	2360	2625	2890	3150	3420	3675	3940	4200
11	550	825	1100	1375	1650	1925	2200	2480	2750	3030	3300	3580	3850	4130	4400
11½	575	860	1150	1440	1725	2010	2300	2600	2875	3170	3450	3740	4025	4310	4600
12	600	900	1200	1500	1800	2100	2400	2700	3000	3300	3600	3900	4200	4500	4800
12½	625	940	1250	1560	1875	2190	2500	2820	3125	3440	3750	4070	4375	4690	5000
13	650	980	1300	1625	1950	2280	2600	2930	3250	3580	3900	4240	4550	4880	5200
13½	675	1010	1350	1690	2025	2360	2700	3040	3375	3720	4050	4400	4725	5060	5400
14	700	1050	1400	1750	2100	2450	2800	3160	3500	3860	4200	4550	4900	5250	5600
14½	725	1085	1450	1810	2175	2540	2900	3260	3625	4000	4350	4700	5075	5440	5800
15	750	1125	1500	1880	2250	2620	3000	3380	3750	4140	4500	4880	5250	5625	6000

Courtesy American Radiator Co.

	Remote, Air-cooled System	Price for Complete Installation
2	24,000	2000.00 to 2200.00
3	36,000	2500,00 to 2700.00
5	60,000	4500.00 to 5000.00
	Self-contained, Water-cooled System	
2	24,000	2300.00 to 2500.00
3	36,000	3500.00 to 3700.00
	Self-contained, Air-cooled System	
2	24,000	2600.00 to 2800.00
3	36,000	4500.00 to 4800.00
5	60,000	7000.00 to 7500.00

Room Size Air Conditioning Units.   The cost of portable room size air conditioning units vary according to size, ranging from ½-Hp., which cools room areas up to 400 sq. ft., to 2-Hp., for spaces up to 1,200 sq. ft.

All models are for window installation and include automatic thermostat controls.

Net prices run from $225.00 for a ½-Hp. unit to $600.00 for 2-Hp. units. If electric wiring is necessary, add extra for installation.

STEAM AND HOT WATER HEATING

Because of different conditions surrounding the installation of heating apparatus, it is impossible to give any set rule that can be accepted, without modification, for all kinds of buildings to be heated. It is necessary to take into consideration all of the conditions in and around any building, and additions or deductions made to suit the requirements, no matter what rule may be used for figuring.

Methods of Computing Heating.   The most advanced method of figuring heating and the one that is generally used by heating engineers is the Btu Method. This method is based on replacing the heat loss through exposed walls, doors and windows, floors, ceilings, etc., and uses so many factors, based on the type of construction that it is impossible to go into detail in a book of this kind.

Approximate Prices on Copper Tubing

Prices on copper tube and fittings are subject to wide fluctuations due to the fluctuations in the price of copper. Always check prices before submitting bids.

Copper Tubing

Price per lin. ft.	¼"	⅜"	½"	⅝"	¾"	1"	1¼"	1½"
Type "K"................................	$0.40	$0.65	$0.85	$1.00	$1.46	$1.80	$ 2.25	$ 2.90

Table Giving Number of Square Feet of Surface in Exposed
Walls of Various Lengths and Heights

Height of Ceiling	Running Feet of Exposed Wall Without Regard to Window Openings																		
	6	7	8	9	10	11	12	13	14	15	16	17	18	19	20	21	22	23	24
8	48	56	64	72	80	88	96	104	112	120	128	136	144	152	160	168	176	184	192
8½	51	60	68	76	85	94	102	110	119	127	136	145	153	162	170	178	187	195	204
9	54	63	72	81	90	99	108	117	126	135	144	153	162	171	180	189	198	207	216
9½	57	66	76	86	95	105	114	123	133	142	152	161	171	181	190	200	209	218	228
10	60	70	80	90	100	110	120	130	140	150	160	170	180	190	200	210	220	230	240
10½	63	73	84	94	105	115	126	136	147	157	168	178	189	199	210	220	231	242	252
11	66	77	88	99	110	121	132	143	154	165	176	187	198	209	220	231	242	253	264
11½	69	80	92	104	115	126	138	149	161	172	184	195	207	218	230	241	253	265	276
12	72	84	96	108	120	132	144	156	168	180	192	204	216	228	240	252	264	276	288
12½	75	87	100	112	125	137	150	162	175	187	200	212	225	238	250	262	275	287	300
13	78	91	104	117	130	143	156	169	181	195	208	221	234	247	260	273	286	299	312
14	84	98	112	126	140	154	168	182	196	210	224	238	252	266	280	294	308	322	336

Height of Ceiling	25	26	27	28	29	30	31	32	33	34	35	36	37	38	39	40	41	42	43
8	200	208	216	224	232	240	248	256	264	272	280	288	296	304	312	320	328	336	344
8½	212	221	230	238	246	255	263	272	280	289	298	306	315	323	332	340	349	357	366
9	225	234	243	252	261	270	279	288	297	306	315	324	333	342	351	360	369	378	387
9½	237	247	256	266	275	285	294	304	313	323	332	342	351	361	370	380	389	399	408
10	250	260	270	280	290	300	310	320	330	340	350	360	370	380	390	400	410	420	430
10½	262	273	283	294	305	315	325	336	346	357	367	378	388	399	409	420	430	441	451
11	275	286	297	308	319	330	341	352	363	374	385	396	407	418	429	440	451	462	473
11½	287	299	310	322	333	345	356	368	379	391	403	414	426	437	449	460	471	483	494
12	300	312	324	336	348	360	372	384	396	408	420	432	444	456	468	480	492	504	516
12½	312	325	337	350	362	375	387	400	412	425	437	450	462	475	487	500	512	525	537
13	325	338	351	364	377	390	403	416	429	442	455	468	481	494	507	520	533	546	559
14	350	364	378	392	406	420	434	448	462	476	490	504	518	532	546	560	574	588	602

Table Giving Number of Square Feet of Area in Window Openings of Various Sizes

Width Glass (In.)	Width Open'g (Ft. In.)	Height Glass																		
		18"	20"	22"	24"	26"	28"	30"	32"	34"	36"	38"	40"	42"	44"	46"	48"	50"	52"	54"
	Height Open'g	3'-6"	3'-10"	4'-2"	4'-6"	4'10"	5'-2"	5'-6"	5'-10"	6'-2"	6'-6"	6'-10"	7'-2"	7'-6"	7'10"	8'-2"	8'-6"	8'-10"	9'-2"	9'-6"
16	1- 8	5.8	6.4	7.0	7.5	8.0	8.6	9.2	9.7	10.3	10.8	11.4	11.9	12.5	13.0	13.6	14.2	14.7	15.2	15.8
18	1-10	6.4	7.0	7.6	8.2	8.9	9.5	10.1	10.7	11.3	11.9	12.5	13.1	13.7	14.3	15.0	15.6	16.2	16.8	17.4
20	2- 0	7.0	7.7	8.3	9.0	9.7	10.3	11.0	11.7	12.3	13.0	13.6	14.3	15.0	15.6	16.3	17.0	17.7	18.3	19.0
22	2- 2	7.6	8.3	9.0	9.7	10.5	11.2	11.9	12.6	13.4	14.0	14.7	15.5	16.2	17.0	17.7	18.4	19.2	19.8	20.6
24	2- 4	8.2	8.9	9.7	10.5	11.3	12.0	12.8	13.6	14.4	15.1	15.9	16.7	17.4	18.2	19.0	19.8	20.6	21.4	22.2
26	2- 6	8.7	9.6	10.4	11.2	12.0	12.8	13.7	14.6	15.4	16.2	17.1	17.9	18.7	19.5	20.4	21.2	22.0	23.0	23.8
28	2- 8	9.3	10.2	11.1	12.0	12.9	13.8	14.7	15.5	16.4	17.3	18.2	19.1	20.0	20.8	21.8	22.6	23.5	24.4	25.3
30	2-10	10.0	10.8	11.8	12.8	13.7	14.6	15.6	16.5	17.5	18.4	19.3	20.3	21.2	22.2	23.2	24.0	25.0	26.0	27.0
32	3- 0	10.5	11.5	12.5	13.5	14.5	15.5	16.5	17.5	18.5	19.5	20.5	21.5	22.5	23.5	24.5	25.5	26.5	27.5	28.5
34	3- 2	11.0	12.1	13.2	14.3	15.3	16.4	17.4	18.5	19.5	20.6	21.6	22.6	23.7	24.8	25.8	27.0	28.0	29.0	30.0
36	3- 4	11.7	12.8	13.9	15.0	16.1	17.2	18.3	19.5	20.5	21.6	22.8	23.8	25.0	26.1	27.2	28.3	29.4	30.5	31.7
38	3- 6	12.2	13.4	14.6	15.8	16.9	18.0	19.2	20.4	21.6	22.7	24.0	25.0	26.2	27.4	28.6	29.8	31.0	32.1	33.2
40	3- 8	12.8	14.0	15.3	16.5	17.7	18.9	20.1	21.4	22.6	23.8	25.1	26.2	27.4	28.7	30.0	31.2	32.4	33.6	34.9
42	3-10	13.4	14.7	16.0	17.3	18.5	19.8	21.0	22.4	23.6	24.9	26.2	27.4	28.6	30.0	31.3	32.6	33.8	35.0	36.4
44	4- 0	14.0	15.3	16.7	18.0	19.3	20.7	22.0	23.4	24.6	26.0	27.3	28.6	30.0	31.3	32.6	34.0	35.3	36.5	38.0
46	4- 2	14.6	16.0	17.4	18.8	20.1	21.5	23.0	24.4	25.6	27.1	28.4	29.8	31.2	32.6	34.0	35.5	36.8	38.2	39.6
48	4- 4	15.2	16.6	18.0	19.5	20.9	22.4	23.8	25.3	26.7	28.1	29.5	31.0	32.4	34.0	35.4	36.8	38.3	39.6	41.0
50	4- 6	15.7	17.2	18.7	20.3	21.8	23.2	24.8	26.2	27.7	29.2	30.7	32.2	33.7	35.2	36.7	38.2	39.7	41.2	42.6
52	4- 8	16.3	17.9	19.4	21.0	22.5	24.0	25.6	27.2	28.7	30.3	31.8	33.4	35.0	36.5	38.0	39.6	41.2	42.7	44.2
54	4-10	16.9	18.5	20.1	21.8	23.4	25.0	26.6	28.2	29.8	31.4	32.9	34.6	36.2	37.8	39.5	41.0	42.7	44.3	46.0
56	5- 0	17.5	19.3	20.8	22.5	24.2	25.8	27.5	29.0	30.8	32.5	34.0	35.8	37.5	39.8	40.8	42.5	44.2	46.0	47.5

Standard Sizes of Two-Light Windows.

Courtesy American Radiator Co

Copper Tubing
Nominal Size

Type "L"......................	.37	.50	.75	.90	1.10	1.50	1.45	2.50
Price Per lin. ft.	**2"**	**2½"**	**3"**	**3½"**	**4"**	**5"**	**6"**	
Type "K"......................	$4.35	$6.20	$8.50	$12.00	$15.00	$35.00	$50.00	
Type "L"......................	3.75	5.40	7.25	9.80	12.00	28.00	38.00	

When purchased in quantities of more than 2,000 ft. or lbs., whichever is greater, deduct 12 percent from above prices.

Prices of Brass Solder-Joint Valves

These valves are made for use with copper tubing and can be used for steam or water service.

Size in Inches

Description of Fitting	½"	¾"	1"	1¼"	1½"	2"
Gate valve..............................	$11.15	$14.25	$17.25	$23.00	$29.75	$41.75

Approximate Quantity of Solder and Flux Required to Make 100 Joints

Size, Inches	⅜"	½"	¾"	1"	1¼"	1½"	2"	2½"	3"	3½"	4"	5"	6"	8"	10"
Solder, Lbs........	½	¾	1	1½	1¾	2	2½	3½	4½	5	6½	9	17	35	45
Flux, Oz.	1	1½	2	3	3½	4	4	7	9	10	13	18	34	70	90

Estimating the Cost of Pipe and Fittings.   —To estimate the cost of pipe and fittings required for any heating plant, obtain the total number of square feet of radiation in the job (based on cast iron radiation) and figure at $1.20 to $1.35 per square foot. This is based on prices of pipe as given on the previous pages.

For one story residences having short pipe runs, figure the cost of the pipe and fittings at $1.25 per square foot of radiation (based on standard cast iron radiation).

An example of the method used in estimating the cost of pipe and fittings is as follows: For a job containing 1,400 square feet of standard radiation, take 120 per cent of 1,400 gives 1680, or the pipe and fittings would cost approximately $1700.00.

The above allowances for pipe and fittings do not include radiator valves, floor and ceiling plates, boiler fittings, expansion tanks, etc., but only the pipe and fittings required for roughing-in the job.

LABOR INSTALLING HEATING PLANTS

The labor cost of installing steam, hot water, vapor and vacuum heating systems is usually figured on the basis of the number of radiators or convectors (commonly termed units) in the job, and estimated at a certain price per unit. This allowance includes all necessary labor to rough-in the job, set and connect boiler, set and connect radiators, convectors or baseboard radiation, and complete the job ready to operate.

This allowance varies with the type of heating system, whether a one or two-pipe system and the class of building in which it is installed.

Labor Installing One-Pipe Heating Systems in One Story Houses. To install one-pipe heating systems in one story houses, it will require about 7 hours steam fitter per unit (per radiator), and the labor cost per unit should average as follows:

	Hours	Rate	Total	Rate	Total
Steam fitter or plumber	7	—	—	$20.55	$143.85

Labor Installing One-Pipe Heating Systems in Two Story Residences. When installing one-pipe heating systems in two story residences, it will require about 10 hours steam fitter time per unit (per radiator), and the labor cost per unit should average as follows:

	Hours	Rate	Total	Rate	Total
Steam fitter or plumber	10	—	—	$20.55	$205.50

Labor Installing One-Pipe Heating Systems in 2 or 3-Story "Flat" or Apartment Buildings. When installing one-pipe heating systems in 2 or 3-story "flat" or apartment buildings, figure about 8 hours steam fitter time per unit (per radiator), and the labor cost per unit should average as follows:

	Hours	Rate	Total	Rate	Total
Steam fitter or plumber	8	—	—	$20.55	$164.40

Labor Installing One-Pipe Steam Heating Systems in Stores, Theaters, Public Garages, One Story Factory and Warehouse Buildings. When installing one-pipe steam heating systems in any of the buildings listed above, figure about 16 hours steam fitter time per unit (per radiator), and the labor cost per unit should average as follows:

	Hours	Rate	Total	Rate	Total
Steam fitter or plumber	16	—	—	$20.55	$328.80

Labor Installing Two-Pipe Hot Water Heating Systems in One Story Houses. When installing two-pipe heating systems such as mentioned above in one story houses, figure about 14 hours steam fitter time per unit (per radiator), and the labor cost per unit should average as follows:

	Hours	Rate	Total	Rate	Total
Steam fitter or plumber	14	—	—	$20.55	$287.70

Labor Installing Two-Pipe Hot Water Heating Systems in 2 or 3-Story Apartment Buildings. When installing two-pipe heating systems in 2 or 3-story apartment buildings, figure about 14 hours steam fitter time per unit (per radiator), and the labor cost per unit should average as follows:

	Hours	Rate	Total	Rate	Total
Steam fitter or plumber	14	—	—	$20.55	$287.70

Labor Installing Two-Pipe Hot Water Heating Systems in Residences and Other Types of Buildings. When installing two-pipe heating systems in residences or other types of buildings not specifically mentioned, figure 16 hours steam fitter time per unit, and the labor cost per unit should average as follows:

	Hours	Rate	Total	Rate	Total
Steam fitter or plumber	16	—	—	$20.55	$328.80

SECTION III/Exteriors

CHAPTER 12

ROOFING, GUTTERS AND DOWNSPOUTS

Although the demand, as well as use, of conventional shingles continues, fiberglass based asphalt shingles are experiencing an upsurge and over the next few years could become the leading product in the industry.

Among the reasons cited are the availability of raw materials and manufacturing control. The basic raw material, silica, or sand is virtually unlimited. And costs of silica are stable compared to those of the wood fiber and paper used in organic mat shingles. In addition to requiring less energy to manufacture, the process is more consistent thus assuring a more uniform product.

For the remodeling contractor this means three things: Fiberglass shingles are 75 percent more weatherproof than organic mat shingles; warranties are five to 15 years longer than for most conventional shingles and fiberglass shingles carry an A fire rating instead of C.

Thus, fiberglass shingles which for a long time were relegated to the sunbelt, because they become brittle as they aged, are moving northward, their brittleness eliminated by new manufacturing processes.

For the high-quality remodeling job cedar shingles are still available. Furthermore, through a new process by which they are treated with fire-retardent chemicals, they now carry a UL class C fire rating and are moving toward B. Now, however, wherever a C rating exists, contractors have the option of offering their more affluent clients a higher quality product.

Selecting Materials for Re-Roofing.   Obviously, it is best to use the same type of materials as on the original roof. However, if a change is dictated, a number of factors should be considered. Such as:

- Will the new material be as weatherproof and compatible with the pitch of the existing roof?

- Is color and pattern compatible with other architectural features?

- Can the existing framing support the new material?

- How do installation and costs compare?

Any material can be used on a high-pitched roof. Lower than 1/2 pitched roofs limit the choice of materials. In general, wooden shingles, shakes and asbestos cement shingles are seldom used for a pitch less than 1/5. For a pitch of 1/6, asphalt shingles are generally used since they lie flatter than wooden or asbestos cement shingles.

ROOFING SHINGLES AND ROOFING TILES

Roofing is estimated by the square containing 100 sq. ft. The method used in computing the quantities will vary with the kind of roofing and the shape of the roof.

The labor cost of applying any type of roofing will be governed by the pitch or slope of the roof, size, plan of same (whether cut up with openings, such as skylights, penthouses, gables, dormers, etc.), and upon the distance of the roof above the ground, etc.

Rules for Measuring Plain Double Pitch or Gable Roofs.   To obtain the area of a plain double pitch or gable roof as shown in Figure 1, multiply the length of the ridge (A to B), by the length of the rafter (A to C). This will give the area of one-half the roof. Multiply this by 2 to obtain the total sq. ft. of roof surface.

Example: Assume the length of the ridge (A to B), is 30'-0" and the length of the rafter (A to C), 20'-0". By multiplying (A to B), 30'-0" by (A to C), 20'-0" equals 600. The area of one-half the roof is 600 sq. ft. 600x2=1,200 sq. ft. of roof.

Rules for Measuring Hip Roofs.   To obtain the area of a hip roof as shown in Figure 3, multiply the length of the eaves (C to D) by 1/2 the length of the rafter (A to E). This will give the number of sq. ft. of one end of the roof, which multiplied by 2 gives the area of both ends. To obtain the area of the sides of the roof, add the length of the ridge (A to B) to the length of the eaves (D to H). Divide this sum by 2 and multiply by the length of the rafter (F to G). This gives the area of one side of the roof and when multiplied by 2 gives the number of sq. ft. on both sides of the roof.

To obtain the total number of sq. ft. of roof surface, add the area of the two ends to the area of the two sides. This total divided by 100 equals the number of squares in the roof.

Example: Assume the length of the eaves (C to D) is 20'-0" and the length of the rafter (A to E) is 20'-0". Multiply (C to D) 20'-0" by 1/2 of the length of the rafter (A to E), or 10'-0" equals 200 sq. ft., the area of one end of the roof. To obtain the area of both ends, 200 x 2=400 sq. ft.

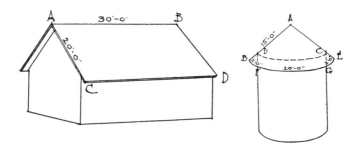

Fig 1. Plain Double Pitch or Gable Roof   Fig 2. Conical Building and Roof

To obtain the area of the sides of the roof, the length of the ridge (A to B), is 10'-0" and the length of the eaves (D to H), is 30'-0". Add (A to B) 10'-0" to (D to H) 30'-0", and the result is 40'-0". By taking ½ the combined length of the ridge and eaves, ½ of 40'-0" - 20'-0", the average length of the roof. Assuming the length of the rafter (F to G) as 20'-0", 20'-0" x 20'-0"=400 sq. ft. the area of one side of the roof, which multiplied by 2 equals 800 sq. ft., the area of both sides of the roof.

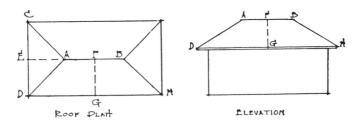

ROOF PLAN   ELEVATION

Fig 3. Hip Roof

Adding the area of the two ends and the area of the two sides equals 1,200 sq. ft. of roof area.

The area of a plain hip roof running to a point at the top is obtained by multiplying the length of the eaves (B to E) by ½ the length of the rafter (A to F). This gives the area of one end of the roof. To obtain the area of all four sides, multiply by 4.

Example: Multiply the length of the eaves (B to E), which is 30'-0", by the length of the rafter (A to F), 10'-0", and the result is 300 sq. ft., the area of one end of the roof. 300 x 4 = 1,200 sq. ft., the area of the 4 sides.

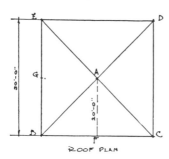
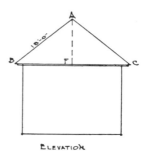

ROOF PLAN   ELEVATION

Fig 4. Hip Roof

Rules for Measuring Conical Tower Roofs and Circular Buildings. To obtain the area of a conical tower roof as shown in Figure 2, multiply ½ the length of the rafter (A to B) by the distance around the eaves at B. As an example, assume the length of the rafter (distance from A to B) is 15'-0" and the diameter of the building at B is 20'-0".

To obtain the distance around the building, multiply the diameter by $3_{1/7}$ or 3.1416. If the eaves project beyond the outside walls, and the diameter is given only to the outside walls of the building, add the length of the roof projection on both sides of the building to obtain the correct diameter. Example: If the diameter of the building (C to D) is 20'-0" and the eaves project 2'-0" on each side, the diameter of the building at the eaves would be 24'-0".

Multiplying 24'-0" (B to E), the diameter of the building at eaves, by 3.1416, gives 75.3984, or approximately 75'-5" around the eaves at projection (B to E).

To obtain the area of the roof, multiply ½ the length of the rafter (A to B), which is 15'-0", (½ of 15 is 7½) or 7'-6" by the distance around the eaves at B and E, which is 75'-5" or 75.4 feet, and the result is 565.5 or 565½ sq. ft., the area of the roof.

To obtain the area of a cylindrical or circular building, multiply the height by the circumference, or the distance around the building, and the result will be the number of sq. ft. to be covered. The circumference is obtained by multiplying the diameter (C to D) of the building by $3_{1/7}$, or 3.1416. To obtain the area of the outside walls of a cylindrical building whose diameter is 20'-0" and the height 15'-0", 20 x 3.1416-62.832, or 62'-10". Multiply 62.832 ft. (the distance around the building) by 15 ft. (the height of the building) = 942.48, or 942½ sq. ft., the area of the outside walls.

A SHORT METHOD OF FIGURING ROOF AREA

To obtain the number of square feet of roof area, where the pitch (rise and run) of the roof is known, take the entire flat or horizontal area of the roof and multiply by the factor given below for the roof slope applicable and the result will be the area of the roof.

Always bear in mind, the width of any overhanging cornice must be added to the building area to obtain the total area to be covered.

Example: Find the area of a roof 26'-0" x 42'-0", having a 12" or 1'-0" overhanging cornice. Roof having a ¼ pitch or a 6 in 12 rise and run.

To obtain the roof area, 26'-0"+1'-0"+1'-0" = 28'-0" width. 42'-0"+1'-0"+1'-0" = 44'-0" length. 28x44 = 1232 or 1,232 sq. ft. flat or horizontal area.

To obtain area at ¼ pitch or 6 in 12 rise and run: multiply 1,232 by 1.118=1377.376 or 1,378 sq. ft. of roof surface.

Add allowance for overhang on dormer roofs and sides.

Pitch of Roof	Rise and Run	Multiply Flat Area by	Lin. Ft. of Hips or Valleys per Lin. Ft. of Common Run
1/12	2 in 12	1.014	1.424
1/8	3 in 12	1.031	1.436
1/6	4 in 12	1.054	1.453
5/24	5 in 12	1.083	1.474
1/4	6 in 12	1.118	1.500
7/24	7 in 12	1.158	1.530
1/3	8 in 12	1.202	1.564
3/8	9 in 12	1.250	1.600
5/12	10 in 12	1.302	1.612
11/24	11 in 12	1.357	1.685
1/2	12 in 12	1.413	1.732

Hips and Valleys.   The length of hips and valleys, formed by intersecting roof surfaces, running perpendicular to each other and having the same slope is also a function of the roof rise and run. For full hips or valleys, i.e. where both roofs intersect for their full width, the length may be determined by taking the square root of the sum of the rise squared plus twice the run squared.

Using the factors given in the last column of the above table, the length of full hips or valleys may be obtained by multiplying the total roof run from eave to ridge, (not the hip or valley run), by the factor listed for the roof slope involved.

Your total estimate should include the following: The cost of the roofing materials and underlayment, nails, roof coatings, plastic roof cements, flashing materials, equipment rentals, replacing any boards at the edge of the roof and repair, if required, of sheathing.

WARNING. KEEP CLEAR OF ELECTRICAL POWER LINES AND TELEVISION AERIALS THAT ATTACH TO THE ROOF.

Removing Roofing Materials. Take care not to damage flashing on chimneys, vents and valleys. Use the old flashing as a pattern to cut the new. To remove asphalt shingles, figure one roofer and one laborer working together can strip around 20 squares per 8-hr. day. To this, add 2 hours to remove debris and clean up.

To remove eaves flashing and drip edges, figure one roofer can remove 50 linear ft. per hour.

To remove chimney and vent flashing, figure one roofer can remove and clean in preparation for replacement, 3 hours for a chimney and one hour for a vent pipe. Add 1 hr. to remove debris and clean up.

PREPARATION FOR NEW ROOFING

Installing Underlayment. *Note: Do not use underlayment for wooden or shake shingled roofs. Moisture trapped between the underlayment and the sheathing will cause the shingles to decay or be attacked by fungus.* A roofer and laborer should be able to install 2500 sq. ft. of underlayment per 8-hr. day at the following cost per 100 sq. ft.

	Hours	Rate	Total	Rate	Total
Roofer	.32	—	—	$21.25	$ 6.80
Laborer	.32	—	—	14.10	4.51
Cost per 100 sq. ft.		—	—		11.31
Cost per sq. ft.			—		.11

If using 15 lb. asphalt saturated roofing paper as underlayment, figure $11.95 per roll (432 sq. ft. Roll).

To Install Drip Edges. Drip edges are usually made of aluminum, galvanized steel or copper. Use nails of the same materials to prevent corrosion. Space nails 1" from edge, no more than 10" apart. Where two drip edges meet, seal with asphalt roofing cement. Figure materials costs as follows: aluminum, $0.30 per ft.; galvanized steel, $0.28 per ft.; copper, $1.50 per ft. A roofer should be able to install 60 linear ft. per hr.

To Install Eaves Flashing. Eaves flashing strips are made from 65 or 90 lb. mineral surfaced roll roofing material.

Ninety-pound material is preferred since it will last longer. In areas of moderate to heavy snowfall install a double thickness. Material costs are $12.55 for 50 lb. material and $14.66 for 90 lb. material. Figure one roofer can install 60 lin. ft. per hr. or, figure as follows:

Single Thickness. Install with a minimum of 6" head lap until the top of the eaves flashing is at least 12" (24" if pitch is 1/6 or less) past the inside wall line of the house. Space nails 1" from top edge and 24" apart. Bend flashing to overhang. Apply roofing lap-cement and nail flashing to roof. Start 1" from drip edges and space nails 4" apart. Apply lap-cement to nail heads. One roofer should be able to install 60 lin. ft. per hour at a cost of $0.35 per linear ft.

Installing Chimney Flashing. Using the old pieces as patterns, a local sheet metal shop can cut and shape new flashing. Nail flashing to sheathing taking care to use nails of the same material as the sheathing. Apply a clear butyl or aluminized compound to the back of the cap flashing and press into place. Caulk all edges of cap flashing and mortar joints. Figure one roofer can replace 15 ft. per hour providing a satisfactory raggle exists. If a raggle has to be chiseled, figure one laborer can cut 8–10 lin. ft. per hour. With an electric saw, figure 12–15 lin. ft. per hour.

Chimney Flashing Table

No. of Brick		Inches		Pitch of Roof		
Wide	Long	Wide	Long	To 1/3	To 1/2	To 3/4
					Lin. Ft. of Flashing	
2	2	18"	18"	11'	11'	12'
2	21/2	18"	22"	12'	12'	13'
2	3	18"	26"	13'	13'	15'
2	31/2	18"	30"	13'	14'	16'
2	4	18"	34"	14'	15'	17'

Installing Valley Flashings. *Composition Flashings.* Composition roofing valley flashing is constructed the same way for both open and closed valley flashings. NOTE: DO NOT LEAVE STRIPS OF ROOFING ON LAWN IN SUN. ABSORBED HEAT WILL BURN LAWN. Use old flashing as pattern. Cut 18" width of material to fit valley, allowing 4" to 7" for overhang of drip edges. Place strip mineral side down, apply roofing lap-cement to the underside of the vee at the drip edge and nail to sheathing 1" from edge of material 12" apart.

Using the same pattern, cut a 36" wide strip of material 30" longer than valley centerline to fit valley. Cut vee using old pattern and place mineral side face up on 18" strip. Fasten with roofing lap-cement and nails. Figure one roofer can install 40 lin. ft. per hour at a cost of $0.53 per lin. ft.

Metal Flashing. Metal flashing is installed the same way as open or closed valley flashing except that it is usually installed over 30 or 65 lb. composition roll roofing. With metal flashing when the pitch is ½ or more, the flashing must extend at least 7" on each side of the valley centerline. Less than ½, the pitch must extend at least 10" per side.

Installing Vent Pipe Flashings. These can be purchased from most building materials suppliers in ready-to-install form. Vent pipe flashings should have flanges which extend 8" on top of the vent, 6" on each side and 4" below. Figure one man can install such flashings at a rate of 0.5 hours per unit.

Flashing Between Roof and Vertical Walls. These flashings are made from 65 or 90 lb. composition material. If the vertical wall has lap siding, it is best to use flashing strips 12" long bent to slide 4" up under the siding. Since these strips are installed as roofing is applied, add 10 minutes per course labor for the total job.

NOTE: It is best not to use asphalt roofing cement on side of flashing strips which will come in contact with wood or shake shingles. The wood will draw the oil out of the cement and cause the shingles to warp or split.

Flashing Vertical Walls Without Lap Siding. Cut an 8" wide strip of 90 lb. composition roofing material equal to the length to be flashed. Apply asphalt roofing cement to underside and place flush against vertical wall. Nail, spacing nails 1" from edge and 10" apart, and coat heads with roofing cement. Apply thick bead of roofing cement to edge of flashing against vertical wall. Figure one man can apply 40 lin. ft. per hr. at a cost of $0.53 per lin. ft.

INSTALLING NEW ROOFING

Asphalt Shingles. Asphalt shingles come in several different styles. Strip shingles are furnished in three tab square butt strips, two tab hex strips and three tab hex strips. Installation is the same for all three, except when installing shingles as a starter course and starting subsequent courses. Individual asphalt shingles are furnished and laid in exactly the same manner as wood shingles.

Estimating Quantities of Asphalt Shingles. When measuring roofs of any shape, always allow one extra course of shingles for "starters" at the eaves, as the first course must always be doubled. An alternate method is to use composition roll roofing as the starter course. In this case, decrease the number of squares required accordingly.

For roof measurements use the roofing diagram on Page 227. Measure the length of all hips, valleys and ridges figuring each at 1'0" wide. Multiply and add to total for roof. Many roofing contractors do not measure hips, valleys and ridges. Instead they prefer to add a predetermined percentage to cover material and waste. Percentages commonly used are: Gable roofs, 10 percent; hip roofs, 15 percent; hip roofs with dormers and valleys, 20 percent.

High winds can blow asphalt shingles loose if they are not properly nailed. Six nails to the strip, nailed right to the cutout is recommended.

In addition to self-sealing shingles, most manufacturers produce a shingle designed for high wind areas which interlock in such a manner that all shingles are integrated into a single unit.

Interlocking shingles are available in single coverage for reroofing and double coverage for new construction. When using asphalt shingles for roofs, roll-asphalt-roofing of the same material is often used for forming valleys, hips and ridges.

Nails Required for Asphalt Shingles. When laying individual asphalt shingles use 12 ga. galvanized nails, 1 1/2" long with 7/16" heads. For laying over old roofs, 1 1/4" long. When laying square butt strip shingles, use 11 ga. galvanized nails 1" long and for laying over old roofs 1 1/4" long.

Sizes and Estimating Data for Asphalt Shingles

Kind of Shingle	Size	No. Shingles per Sq.	Expos. Inches	Length Nails	No. Nails per Shingle	Lbs. Nails per Sq.
3-in.-1 strip	12"x36"	80	5	1	4	1
3-in.-1 strip	15"x36"	80	5	1	4	1

Approximate Prices of Mineral Surfaced Asphalt Shingles

Kind of Shingle	Size	Weight per Square	Price per Square
3-in-1 strip	12"x36"	235 lbs.	$19.00
3-in-1 strip	12"x36"	300 lbs.	27.00
3-in-1 strip	15"x36"	325 lbs.	38.00
3-in-1 strip	15"x36"	350 lbs.	43.00

Most asphalt shingles carry an Underwriters Class "C" rating. Using fiberglass, an "A" rating can be achieved. Class "A" 235 lb. shingles are approximately $26.50 per sq., and 300 lb., $65.00 per sq.

Starter Course Using Composition Roll Roofing. Cut starter course 12" wide, 3/4" longer than length of roof from 90 lb. material. Place face down. Allow ends to extend 3/8" beyond gables and eaves. Secure with asphalt cement and nail, spacing nails 8" apart and 1" in from top and sides. Figure one man can lay the preceeding at a rate of 40 linear ft. per hour.

Installing Three Tab Butt Strip Shingles. Start course with partial shingle strip. Place face down, allowing 3/8" overhang at gable and eaves. Nail through drip edge. Continue starter course using full size strips four nails per strip. To install first course, place whole strip at a gable corner, mineral side up and tabs down. Place daubs of cement over nail heads and press strip into position.

NOTE: DO NOT HEAT ASPHALT ROOFING CEMENT OVER FIRE. EXPLOSION OR FIRE COULD RESULT. AN ACCEPTABLE METHOD IS TO PLACE CAN IN WARM WATER.

Nail strip in place with six galvanized nails on a line just above the ends of the shingle slots. Place subsequent courses centering tabs so that alternate courses are in alignment. A roofer will lay one square of asphalt shingles in two hours on double pitched roofs with no hips, valleys or dormers. Figure about 35 lin. ft. per hour for fitting hips, valleys and ridges. Hip and ridge material is usually cut on the job from regular composition roll roofing.

Estimating Asphalt Roofing Materials

Roofing Material	Shingles Per Sq.	Nails Per Shingle	Nail Length	Nails Per Sq.	Estimated Lbs. Per Square 12 ga., 7/16" Hd.	11 ga., 7/16" Hd.
Roll Roofing (new)			1"	252(1)	0.73	1.12
Roll Roofing (over old)			1 3/4"	252(1)	1.13	1.78
3 tab Sq. Butt (new)	80	4	1 1/4"	336	1.22	1.44
3 tab Sq. Butt (over old)	80	4	1 3/4"	504	2.38	3.01
Hex Strip (new)	86	4	1 1/4"	361	1.28	1.26
Hex Strip (over old)	86	4	1 3/4"	361	1.65	2.03
Giant American	226	4	1 1/4"	479	1.79	2.27
Giant Dutch Lap	113	2	1 1/4"	236	1.07	1.39
Single Hex	82	2	1 3/4"	172	0.79	1.03

(1) Spaced 2" apart.

Asphalt Shingles

Dimensions, Weights and Exposure

Roofing Material	Length	Width	Packages Per Square	Shingles Per Square	Weight Per Sq. Lbs.	Exposure
2 & 3 tab sq. Butt............	36"	12"	3	80	235	5"
2 & 3 tab Hexagonal........	36"	1 1/3"	3	86	195	5"
Individual Staple and Individual Lock	16"	16"	2	80	145	
Giant American	16"	12"	4	226	330	5"
Giant Dutch Lap..............	16"	12"	2	113	165	10"

Recommended Nails/Asphalt Shingles

Installation	1" Sheathing	3/8" Plywood
Re-roofing over asphalt roofing	1½"	1"
Re-roofing over wood shingles	1¾"	
New roofing strip or individual shingles	1¼"	7/8"

Cedar Shakes

Estimated Coverage Per Square

Size	Shake	Estimated Sq. Ft. Coverage Exposure								
		5½"	6½"	7"	7½"	8"	8½"	10"	11½"	13"
18½"x½" to ¾"	Handsplit & resawn	55(1)	65	70	75(2)					
18¾"x¾" to 1¾"	"	55(1)	65	70	75(2)					
24"x½" to ¾"	"		65	70	75(1)	80	85	100(2)		
24"x¾" to 1¼"	"		65	70	75(1)	80	85	100(2)		
32"x¾" to 1¼"	"							100(2)	115	130(2)
24"x½" to ⅝"	taper-slit		65	70	75(1)	80	85	100(2)		
18"x⅜"	st.-split	65(1)								
24"x⅜"	"		65	70	75(1)					

(1) Recommended for 3-ply construction
(2) Recommended for 2-ply construction

Cost of 100 Sq. Ft., 300 lb. Strip Asphalt Shingles
On Plain Double Pitch or Gable Roofs

	Hours	Rate	Total	Rate	Total
1 Sq. Strip Shingles	—	—			$29.70
1 lb. galvanized Nails	—	—			.75
Roofer				$21.25	$21.25
Cost per 100 sq. ft.				—	$51.70
Cost per sq. ft.				—	5.17

- On roofs having gables, dormers, etc., add 15 min. per sq.

- On difficult constructed hip or English type, add 12 minutes per sq.

- If shinglers are experienced, deduct 10 minutes from above.

Cost of 100 Sq. Ft., 325 lb. Strip Asphalt Shingles
On Plain Double Pitch or Gable Roofs

	Hours	Rate	Total	Rate	Total
1 Sq. Strip Shingles	—	—			$41.80
1 lb. Roofing Nails	—	—			.75
Roofer	—	—		21.25	21.25
Cost per 100 sq. ft.				—	$63.80
Cost per sq. ft.				—	6.38

- On roofs having gables, dormers, etc., add 12 minutes.

- On difficult hip or English type, add 10 minutes.

- If shinglers are experienced, deduct 15 minutes.

Roofing Material Costs

Roll Roofing

90 lb. Slate Coat (100 sq. ft. coverage - 4 colors)	$14.66 roll
50 lb. Smooth (100 sq. ft. coverage)	12.55 roll
Selvedge Edge (50 sq. ft. coverage)	12.33 roll
15 lb. felt (432 sq. ft. coverage)	13.88 roll
30 lb. felt (216 sq. ft. coverage)	13.88 roll
9" starter (36')	5.22 roll
18" valley (36')	9.33 roll

Aluminum Flashing

14" x 10"	$ 7.19	20" x 10"	$ 9.77
14" x 50"	31.55	20" x 50"	30.95
5 x 7 Step shingles .14 ea.			

Roof Edge (10' aluminum)

	White	$ 2.39 ea.
	Brown	2.99 ea.
Rake Edge (10' white)		2.99
Plastic Roof Cement 1 gal.		4.29
5 gal.		16.55

WOODEN SHINGLES AND SHAKES

Wooden shingles are still very popular in California, as well as other pockets throughout the country where building codes permit their use. They are, however, a premium product, and price, more often than not, is the deciding factor in their application.

They are usually sold by the square, which covers 100 sq. ft. and contains 1000 shingles. Widths range from 4" to 14". Widths more than 8" are generally halved and used as separate shingles. When re-roofing, always use the same shingles and exposure. The following exposures are generally used:

Standard Shingle Exposures

Single Length	1/5 Pitch or More	1/5 Pitch or Less
16"	5 "	33/4"
18"	1/2"	41/4"
24"	71/2"	53/4"

The labor cost of laying wood shingles will vary with the type of roof, whether a plain gable roof, a steep roof or one cut up with gables, dormers, etc. Also with the manner in which they are laid, whether with regular butts, irregular or staggered butts, or thatched butts.

The costs given on the following pages are based on the actual number of shingles a man will lay per day and not upon the number of squares covered, as this will vary with the spacing of the shingles. It does not make any particular difference to the shingler whether the shingles are laid 4", 4 1/2" or 5" to the weather, as he will lay practically the same number either way. It does make considerable difference in the number of sq. ft. of surface covered, which will vary from 10 to 40%.

The number of shingles laid will vary with the ability of the workman and the class of work, as ordinary carpenters will not lay as many shingles as carpenters who specialize in shingle laying. On the other hand, experienced shinglers usually demand a higher wage rate than ordinary carpenters.

Some carpenters claim to be able to lay 16 bundles (3,200 shingles) per 8-hr. day, but this is unusual and is generally found only on the cheapest grade of work where only one nail is driven into each shingle instead of two that are necessary to secure a workmanlike job.

Estimating the Quantity of Wood Shingles. Ordinary wood shingles are furnished in random widths, but 1,000 shingles are equivalent to 1,000 shingles 4" wide.

Dimension shingles are sawed to a uniform width, being either 4", 5" or 6" wide.

Wood shingles are usually sold by the square based on sufficient shingles to lay 100 sq. ft. of surface, when laid 5" to the weather, 4-bundles to the square.

When estimating the quantity of ordinary wood shingles required to cover any roof, bear in mind that the distance the shingles are laid to the weather makes considerable difference in the actual quantity required. There are 144 sq. in. in 1 sq. ft. and an ordinary shingle is 4" wide. When laid with 4" exposed to the weather, each shingle covers 16 sq. in. or it requires 9 shingles per sq. ft. of surface. There are 100 sq. ft. in a square. 100 x 9=900, and allowing 10% to cover the double row of shingles at the eaves, waste in cutting, narrow shingles, etc., it will require 990 shingles (5 bundles) per 100 sq. ft. of surface.

Number of Shingles and Quantity of Nails Required Per 100 Sq. Ft.

Distance Laid to Weather	Area Covered by One Shingle Sq. In.	Add for Waste Per Cent	Acutal No. per Square Without Waste	Number per Square With Waste	No. of 4-Sq. Bdls Required	Pounds 3d Nails Req'd.
4 "	16	10	900	990	5.0	3.2
4 1/4"	17	10	850	935	4.7	2.8
4 1/2"	18	10	800	880	4.4	2.5
5 "	20	10	720	792	4.0	2.0

Distance Laid to Weather	Area Covered by One Shingle Sq. In.	Add for Waste Per Cent	Acutal No. per Square Without Waste	Number per Square With Waste	No. of 4-Sq. Bdls Required	Pounds 3d Nails Req'd.
5 1/2"	22	10	655	720	3.6	1.6
6 "	24	10	600	660	3.3	1.5

How to Apply Shingles for Different Roof Slopes.   Roof pitches are computed in fractions, such as 1/8, 1/3, 1/2 pitch. In this cross-section, the steepness of distances AB and BC constitutes pitch. Distance AC, extending from one eave-line to the other, is known as the span. One-half of this span, distance AD or DC, is called the run, and distance BD is called the rise. The relationship of the rise to run obviously affects the slope of AB or BD; in fact, roof pitches are computed from the ratio of rise to run. Therefore, the first step is to determine length of the run (AD or DC) and the rise (BD).

Wood shingles are manufactured in three lengths — 16-inch, 18-inch, and 24-inch. The standard weather exposure (portion of shingle exposed to weather on roof) for 16-inch shingles is 5", for 18-inch shingles, it is 5 1/2", and for 24-inch shingles, it is 7 1/2". These standard exposures are recommended on all roofs of 1/4 pitch and steeper (6" rise in 12" run). On flatter roof slopes, the weather exposure should be reduced to 3 3/4" for 16-inch shingles, 4 1/4" for 18-inch shingles and 5 3/4" for 24-inch.

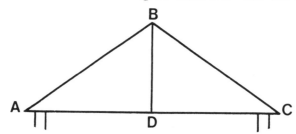

This diagram shows at a glance, the weather exposure to be used for various roof pitches. For example, if a roof has a rise of 8" in a run of 12", it can be seen that this is 1/3 pitch and that an exposure of either 5", 5 1/2" or 7 1/2" should be employed, depending upon the length of the shingles used.

Refer to the first part of this Chapter for table headed "Lengths of Common, Hip, and Valley Rafters Per 12 Inches of Run" and "To Obtain Area of Roofs for Any Pitch" to obtain the number of square feet of roof surface to be covered with shingles at varying roof pitch.

To Install Wooden Shingles.   Starter shingles are placed at corner where gable and eave meet, over-hanging 3/4" at gable and extend 1 1/2" beyond sheathing. Nails should be 1 to 1 1/2" above exposure and 1 1/2" in. on gable side.

NOTE: BE SURE NAILS DO NOT GO THROUGH SHEATHING.

Labor Laying One Square (100 Sq. Ft.) Wood Shingles

Class of Work	Mechanic	Number Laid per 8-Hr. Day	Distance Shingles are Laid to Weather					
			4"†	4¼"	4½"	5"	5½"	6"
Plain Gable or Hip Roofs	Carpenter	2,000–2,200	3.8	3.6	3.4	3.0	2.8	2.5
	Shingler	2,750–3,000	2.8	2.6	2.5	2.3	2.0	1.9
Difficult Gable Roofs, cut up with gables, dormers, hips, valleys, etc.	Carpenter	1,700–1,900	4.5	4.2	4.0	3.6	3.3	3.0
	Shingler	2,200–2,500	3.4	3.2	3.0	2.7	2.5	2.3
Difficult Hip Roofs, Steep English Roofs, hips, valleys, etc.	Carpenter	1,300–1,500	5.7	5.4	5.1	4.6	4.2	3.8
	Shingler	2,000–2,200	3.8	3.6	3.4	3.0	2.8	2.5
Shingles Laid Irregularly or with Staggered Butts on Plain Roofs.	Carpenter	1,700–1,900	4.5	4.2	4.0	3.6	3.3	3.0
	Shingler	2,400–2,700	3.1	3.0	2.8	2.5	2.3	2.1
Shingles Laid Irregularly or with Staggered Butts on Difficult Constructed Roofs.	Carpenter	1,100–1,300	6.7	6.3	6.0	5.4	4.9	4.5
	Shingler	1,600–1,800	4.7	4.5	4.2	3.8	3.4	3.1
Shingles with Thatched Butts.*	Shingler	800–1,000	8.9	8.4	8.0	7.1	6.5	6.0
Plain Sidewalls.	Carpenter	1,300–1,500	5.7	5.4	5.1	4.6	4.2	3.8
	Shingler	1,700–1,900	4.5	4.3	4.0	3.6	3.3	3.0
Difficult Sidewalls, having bays, windows, breaks, etc.	Carpenter	1,100–1,250	6.8	6.4	6.0	5.4	5.0	4.5
	Shingler	1,400–1,650	5.2	5.0	4.6	4.2	3.8	3.5

To obtain number of bundles of shingles required, divide number of shingles as given above by 200, and the result will be the number of bundles required, i.e. 2,200 shingles ÷ 200 equals 11 bundles;   1,000 ÷ 200=5 bundles;   800 ÷ 200=4 bundles, etc.

*Shingles with thatched butts require 25% more shingles than when laid regularly.

†Use 4" column for carpenter or shingler time per 1,000 shingles. (5 bundles).

The above table is based on using 2 nails to each shingle and 10 per cent waste.

NAIL FLUSH WITH SURFACE. DO NOT CRUSH SHINGLE. EARLY DECAY CAN RESULT.

Install second shingle at other end of course. Nail chalk line to butt ends of placed shingles and nail several shingles, aligned with chalk line, randomly in between end shingles. Nail, using two nails per shingle, ¾" from side of shingle. Install remaining shingles, by aligning with placed shingles, allowing ¼" between shingles to permit swelling when wet.

The first course of shingles is placed on the starter course so that the gaps between shingles are offset from gaps in the starter course by 1½". Nail using two nails per shingle. A roofer and helper can install 4 to 6 squares of wooden shingles per 8-hr. day at the following cost per 100 sq. ft.:

	Hours	Rate	Total	Rate	Total
1 Sq. Wooden Shingles		—	—	$80.00	$ 80.00
4 lbs. Nails		—	—	3.00	3.00
Roofer	1.3	—	—	21.25	27.65
Helper	1.3	—	—	14.10	18.35
Cost per 100 Sq. Ft.				—	129.00

Do not install shingles in valleys. Go only to valley chalk-line. To cut and fit shingles next to valley, figure one roofer can install 20 lin. ft. per hour.

Hip and ridge shingles can be bought prefabricated. Their length should be twice the exposure. One roofer can usually lay 35 lin. ft. per hour.

Installing Wooden Shakes. Shakes are installed the same as shingles, with the following exceptions: Shingles are used as the starter course for shakes. Thus you should order enough shingles for a starter course and add this cost to your estimate. Since shakes are hand split, the sides will be uneven, and the gap between shingles should be about ¼" to ⅜". Shakes are generally applied over 1"x4" roofing sheathing which requires an underlayment of roofing paper, as noted below.

The first shake in a course at a gable edge should extend 1" beyond the edge. An additional labor factor is that shakes call for an underlayment between the first and succeeding courses. Use an 18" wide strip of 30 lb. roofing paper covering the top of the shakes and sheathing above. The paper is placed twice the exposure from the butt and parallel to butt ends. Add 0.3 hr. per sq. for roofer and 0.3 hr. per helper for placing this material.

ROLL ROOFING

Composition roll roofing material, at 3 ft. wide and 36 ft. long, is designed to cover 100 sq. ft. of roof with 6" vertical and horizontal laps.

Standard rolls weigh 87 lbs. and are called 90 lb. roofing. When installing roll roofing, underlayment and the eaves flashing strip are not required.

Roll roofing can be installed horizontally or vertically with nails exposed or concealed. However, on roofs with a pitch of 7/12 it should be installed horizontally, on lower pitched roofs, vertically.

Roll roofing should be applied in warm weather. In cool weather, materials may crack. Install on dry surfaces only, otherwise decay can occur. Avoid walking on it at all times. Rolls left in sun on lawn can absorb sufficient heat to burn lawn.

Installing Roll Roofing Vertically. Measure from eaves to ridge, allowing extra 4¾" for overhang at eaves and ridges. Place strip parallel to gable, extending 4" beyond ridge and ¾" beyond eave. Tack strip in place and nail using ⅞" galvanized roofing nails 1" in from edge and 2" apart. Mark sheathing cracks lightly and space nails in next strip to avoid cracks. Overlap next strip 6" and coat lap with roofing lap cement and nail vertical lap 4" apart, 1" in from edge. Nail bottom 2" apart 1" up from eave. Succeeding strips are installed in the same manner. The 4" extension at the ridge is bent over the ridge and nailed to sheathing, spacing nails 8" apart and 1" up from end of strip. At gables and eaves, nail to sheathing 6" apart. Apply molding strips to overhang of both eaves and gables. A roofer and helper should be able to install 1900 sq. ft. of roll roofing per day vertically at the following cost per 100 sq. ft.:

	Hours	Rate	Total	Rate	Total
1 Sq. Roll Roofing		—	—		14.66
lbs. Nails		—	—		0.75
Roofer	0.4	—	—	21.25	8.50
Helper	0.4	—	—	14.10	5.65
Cost per 100 sq. ft.			—		$29.56
Cost per sq. ft.			—		2.95

If course ends at a valley add, 20 minutes per strip.

If course ends at hip, add 20 minutes per strip.

See end of next application for ridges.

Installing Roll Roofing (Horizontally). Although the application procedure to apply roll roofing horizontally is approximately the same as installing it vertically, it tends to take longer because of the difficulty working on a greater pitch. Figure a two-man crew, roofer and helper, can lay 6 to 8 squares of horizontal roofing per 8-hr. day at the following cost per 100 sq. ft.:

	Hours	Rate	Total	Rate	Total
1 Sq. Roll Roofing		—	—		14.66
1 lb. Nails		—	—		0.75

	Hours	Rate	Total	Rate	Total
Roofer..	0.5	—	—	21.25	10.65
Helper	0.5	—	—	14.10	7.05
Cost per 100 sq. ft..........................			—		$33.11
Cost per sq. ft..............................			—		3.31

Hips and Ridges. To finish hips and ridges figure one man can lay 100 lin. ft. of roll roofing material per hr.

GUTTERS AND DOWNSPOUTS

The most popular types of gutters are made from galvanized steel and aluminum. Each comes finished or unfinished. Those coming with baked on finishes offer a range of colors which can match or compliment the existing siding. The advantage of such finishes in addition to complimenting the decor is that they need little or no maintenance and have a considerably longer life span than unfinished products. On the other hand, unfinished products can be painted to match exact color of the house. Unprotected galvanized steel gutters and downspouts are inexpensive. However, unless they are primed and painted they will rust and corrode. Although aluminum is more expensive, it forms its own protective coating giving it a considerably longer service span.

Typical Components
  1   End Cap
  2   Outside Miter
  3   End Piece with Outlet
  4   Gutter Section
  5   Slip Joint Connector
  6   Inside Miter
  7A Elbow-Style A
  7B Elbow-Style B
  8   Downspout or Conductor Pipe
  9   Pipe Strap
  10 Expansion Joint

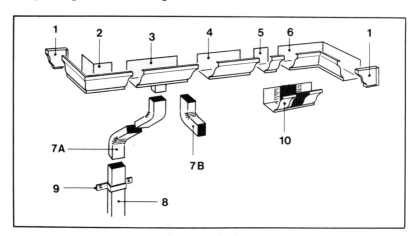

Courtesy Architectural Aluminum Mfg. Assoc.

Typical gutter and downspout components.

Because it is lighter, aluminum is easier to install. However, since it lacks the rigidity of steel, greater care must be used in handling it or dents and nicks will occur.

New to the scene are gutters and downspouts made from polyvinyl chloride, requiring very little maintenance. However, PVC will expand and contract as temperatures change and unless an allowance is made for these physical changes, it can bend and pull away from the roof.

Approximate Materials Costs
Gutters, Downspouts and Hardware*

Unit		Minimum Quantity	Aluminum
Gutters	.027/5"x20"	1	.55 ft.
	.032/6" custom	1	.81 ft.
	.032/6"x20"	1	.75 ft.
Downspouts	3"x8'/3'x10'	160	.29 ft.
		200	
	4"x8"	80	
	4"x10'	100	.49 ft.
Inside & Outside Miters	5"	20	1.29 ea.
	6"	20	3.83 ea.
Strip Miters			.63 ea.
End Caps	5"	50	.18 ea.
	6"	"	.50 ea.
Elbows	3"	30	.33 ea.
	4"	16	.58 ea.
Outlets	3"	50	.24 ea.
	4"	36	.49 ea.
Pop Rivets		1000	8.00M
Gutter Sealer		12	.85 ea.
Gutter Mastic		10	.72 ea.
Gutter Guard	5"	(75 pcs.) 225 ft.	53.82 pkg.
Ferrules	5"	500	.03 ea.
	6"	400	.04 ea.
Spikes	7"	500	.07 ea.
	8"	500	.08 ea.
Pipe Bands		100	.12 ea.
Drip Edge	3"	500 ft.	.15 ft.

Custom Gutters

Gutters	$ 1.90 Lin. Ft.
Downspout...	1.90 Lin. Ft.
4" Downspout	2.50 Lin. Ft.
Bay Cuts	5.00 Each Cut
Tie-Ins — Funnels..	7.50
Gutter Guards (Labor & Material)	.60

Divertors 3"...	18.00
4"..	21.00

Each labor accordingly above 30"

Estimated Labor & Materials Combined

Gutters	Per Lin. Ft.
8' box for flat roofs	$ 6.50
5" O.G. molded for pitched roof...	3.00
For O.G. gutters over 20' above grade add	2.25
5" 1/2 Rd. for pitched roofs	2.25
Over 20' above grade add...	2.25
All miters..	10.00
Elbows - 3")2.00; 4")2.50; 5")5.00; 6")...	6.00
Downspouts	
6" for large gutter	3.50
5" for L.G. with 1/2 rd...	2.00
4" for 1/2 rd.	$ 1.50
3" for 1/2 rd.	1.25
Funnels	8.00
Min. charge	100.00

    Above prices for ordinary straight jobs — any unusual conditions involving acessability and height or numerous ends, tubes on large hangers or elbows, must be charged at a higher cost per unit.

Add 50% over 20' high from grade

Removing Old Gutters and Downspouts. Begin at one end of gutter run and work to other end. Runs of more than six feet will require a helper. Try to prevent damage as some sections may be re-used, and the old installation can be used as a pattern to install the new material. Remove sheet metal screws in drop outlet, straps and downspouts. For strap hangers, use tin snips to cut straps at edge of roof. If bracket hangers cannot be disconnected, also cut with tin snips. Use block and pry bar for spike fasteners. Continue until all gutter sections are removed. Check fascia for damage or decay. Fill nail holes and cracks with wood putty. A sheet metal worker and helper should remove 50 lin. ft. per hour at the following cost per 100 lin. ft.

	Hours	Rate	Total	Rate	Total
Sheet Metal Worker	2	—	—	$20.75	$41.50
Helper	2	—	—	14.10	28.20
Cost per 100 lin. ft................................		—			$69.70
Cost per lin. ft.				—	.70

Installing Gutters and Downspouts. Mark slope of gutter run, 1/16" to 1/4". Figure a downspout for each corner. However, downspouts are required for every 40 ft. of run and runs longer than 40 ft. need one at each end.

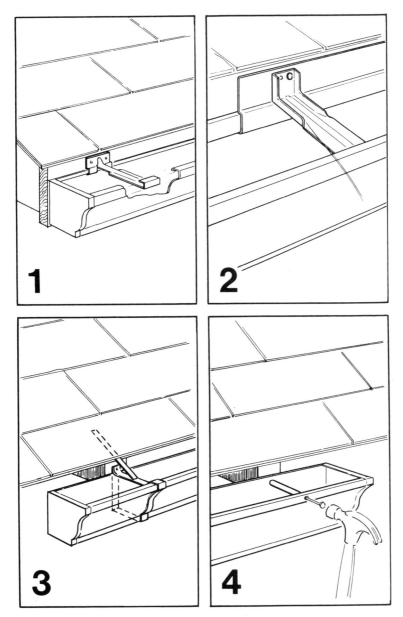

Courtesy Architectural Aluminum Mfg. Assoc.

Various gutter hangers. 1. Combination hanger with a free-floating gutter system. 2. Variation of (1) features a combination bar hanger and fascia apron. 3. Traditional wrap-around hanger with roofing strap. 4. Spike and ferrule mounting.

Cut gutters to exact length using old gutters as a pattern and allowing for connectors at each end. Cut unfinished gutters with a hacksaw, enameled gutters with tin snips to avoid chipping. Apply rust-preventative primer to cut edge.

If using spikes and ferrules, do not use old spike holes. Using old gutter as pattern, locate new holes 1" on either side of old hole. Apply mastic to joints and assemble sections. Attach assembled sections to fascia.

Assemble downspouts using elbows to reach wall of house. Drill two holes at backside of all joints and fasten with two sheet metal screws or pop-rivet. On wood or vinyl or aluminum siding, strap downspouts to wall using 2 penny aluminum or galvanized nails.

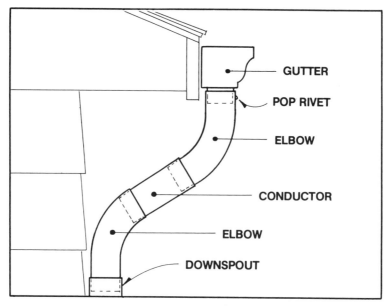

Courtesy Architectural Aluminum Mfg. Assoc.

Downspout should be flush with wall for maximum support, and pop-riveted for maximum strength.

A sheet metal worker and helper should attach 1000 lin. ft. of downspouts and gutters per 8-hr. day at the following cost per 100 lin. ft.:

	Hours	Rate	Total	Rate	Total
Sheet Metal Worker	8	—	—	$20.75	$166.00
Helper	8	—	—	14.10	112.80
Cost per 1000 lin. ft.			—		$278.80
Cost per 100 lin. ft.			—		27.88

To attach downspouts for stucco walls using toggle bolts, add 5 min. time per hour for worker.

To attach downspouts to brickwalls using lead anchors, add 15 min. time per hour for worker.

QUICK REFERENCE CHART # 6

Labor Factors for Insulation

Item	Unit	Factor	
		16" oc	24" oc
R 30 Batt	SF	.00444	.00400
R 22 Batt	SF		.00286
R 19 Batt	SF	.00267	.00235
R 11 Batt	SF	.00235	
1½" CPVB	SF	.00333	
3½" CPVB	SF	.00286	
Stick Clip	EA	.00533	
Weld Pin	EA	.00533	
Thermostud	SF	.00667	
On concrete	SF	.01332	
Styrene			
Glued	SF	.08000	
Nailed	SF	.00533	
Batts w/wire			
R 3.5 Batt	SF	.00400	
R 5.9 Batt	SF	.00320	
R 11 Batt	SF	.00267	
R 13 Batt	SF	.00286	
R 19 Batt	SF	.00267	
R 30 Batt	SF	.00533	
R 38 Batt	SF	.00533	

QUICK REFERENCE CHART # 7

Labor Factors For Roofing

Item Description	Unit	Factor	
235# Seal Tab Shingles		New	Reroof
Plain Gable	SF	.0111	.0100
Plain Hip	SF	.0118	.0105
Gable w/dormer	SF	.0125	.0111
Hip w/dormer	SF	.0125	.0111
Gable w/intersecting roof	SF	.0125	.0111
Hip w/intersecting roof	SF	.0125	.0111
Gable w/dormer & inter. roof	SF	.0133	.0118
Hip w/dormer & inter. roof	SF	.0133	.0118
Replace shingles	Each		.0400
Replace tabs	Each		.0333
90# Mineral Roll Roofing			
Plain Gable-nails exposed	SF	.0077	.0077
Plain Hip-nails exposed	SF	.0083	.0083
Plain Gable-nails concealed	SF	.0091	.0091
Plain Hip-nails concealed	SF	.0099	.0099
Wood Shingles on plain gable or hip w/ridge, hip and valleys included			
16" w/5" exposure	SF	.0250	
18" w/5" exposure	SF	.0250	
24" w/53/4" exposure	SF	.0217	
16" w/41/2" exposure	SF	.0278	
18" w/41/2" exposure	SF	.0278	
24" w/61/2" exposure	SF	.0189	
16" w/4" exposure	SF	.0313	
16" w/33/4" exposure	SF	.0333	
18" w/51/2" exposure	SF	.0227	
24" w/71/2" exposure	SF	.0164	
24" w/7" exposure	SF	.0175	
24" w/61/2" exposure	SF	.0189	

QUICK REFERENCE CHART #8

Labor Factors For Sheet Metal

Item Description	Unit	Factor				
FLASHINGS						
Aluminum	SF	.05333				
Copper	SF	.05333				
Zinc	SF	.05333				
Fabric backed copper	SF	.02500				
Fabric backed aluminum	SF	.02500				
Mastic backed copper	SF	.02500				
Mastic backed aluminum	SF	.02286				
Fabric	SF	.02222				
Plastic	SF	.02762				
GUTTERS						
Galvanized steel	LF	.08000				
Aluminum	LF	.08000				
Copper	LF	.08000				
DOWNSPOUTS						
Aluminum	LF	.05333				
Copper						
3"	LF	.05333				
4"	LF	.06400				
2" x 3"	LF	.05333				
3" x 4"	LF	.06400				
Galvanized steel	LF	.05333				
LOUVERS						
Aluminum eave vents	LF	.04571				
Attic vent 12" x 24"	EA	.72727				
Foundation vents	EA	.16000				
Brick vents	EA	1.33333				
CAULKING		1/2 x 1/2	3/4 x 3/4	3/4 x 1	1/4 x 1/2	3/8 x 3/4
Butyl	LF	.04000	.04444	.05000		
Polysulfide	LF	.04000	.04444	.05000		
Silicone	LF				.05714	.06957
FLASHING						
Valley	LF	.06667				
Window & Door	LF	.06667				
Ridge/Hip	LF	.05714				
GUTTERS	LF	.08000				
DOWNSPOUT	LF	.08000				
RIDGE ROLL	LF	.08000				

CHAPTER 13

SIDING AND EXTERIOR PAINTING

The siding market for the remodeler has been changing for the better. The choices have never been greater. Not only in variety, but price.

The direction is on the wood-look including sidings made from aluminum and vinyl. Modern coatings permit texturing aluminum to look like wood creating rich, long-lasting colors and warranties up to 40 years. New developments in vinyl have created products which never need painting with a wide variety of wood colors and a molding process which can duplicate every detail of real stone, brick and shake.

On the other hand, new developments in hardboard and plywood offer excellent alternatives at prices cheaper than wood boards or shakes.

Hardboards are available in prefinished panels. The colors are rustic and the panels are not easily vandalized. A feature easily translated to low-income housing where many homes need residing. One company's hardboard siding comes in a stain base, a benefit not previously available.

And plywood, that work horse of the industry is now available in fir, pine, cedar and redwood siding.

And last there's cedar. It's still the premium product on the market. But, because of its cost, manufacturers are focusing on custom and high-quality remodeling jobs where the money exists to justify its use.

WOOD SIDING

Wood siding comes in a variety of sizes and shapes, as well as woods. Included are pines, redwood, cypress, hemlock, spruce, cedar and poplar.

Among the classification of wood siding are bevel, drop and board. There are also shingles and shakes. An advantage to wood is that it is a natural insulator. Before application, the wood should be treated with a water repellent, if it has not already been pretreated by the lumber mill. Even so, there will be considerable cutting on the job-site, and it is important that cut surfaces should be treated before installation.

Shingles, Shakes and Siding

Redwood Bevel Siding

½" x 6" C Redwood	$0.45 ft.	(500M)
½" x 8" C Redwood	.60 ft.	(900M)
½" x 10" C Redwood	.83 ft.	(1000M)

Wood Siding
1" x 6" #1 & 2 Spruce (T & G, rough sawn).. .28 ft. (560M)
1" x 8" #1 Pine (Channel Lap)... .44 ft. (640M)

Rough Sawn Cedar
⅞" x 12", 8' to 16' (Interior/Exterior, Bd. & Batten) .... .69 ft.

Cedar Shingles and Shakes
Handsplit Shakes (resawn)..$104.55 sq.
Sidewall Shakes (18" machine-grooved).. 69.95 sq.
#1 Wood Shingles... 99.00 sq.

Plywood & Aspenite Siding

TEXTURED			INVERTED BATTEN		
(3/8" Grooves, 8" O.C.)			(1½" Grooves, 12" O.C.)		
Type	**4x8⅝"**	**4x9⅝"**	**Type**	**4x8⅝"**	**4x9⅝"**
Pine	$20.55	—	Pine	$20.95	—
Fir	22.55	$25.55	Fir	22.95	$26.95
Aspenite	10.95	—	Aspenite	10.95	—

Rough Sawn Fir Plywood (4" x 8" O.C.)
48 x 96.. $21.40 ea.

Asbestos Siding
12" x 12⁵/₃₂"... 57.95 ea.

Primed Lap Hardboard Siding
12" wide, 10" exp. (80 sq. ft. bundles, 5 pieces 16" long) .... Per bundle $35.95 (450M)

Sheathing (Asphalt impregnated)
4 x 8½".. $3.59 ea.
4 x 8²⁵/₃₂"... 5.19 ea.

Aluminum Siding
White Horizontal (8"x12' lengths)
  Smooth.. $65.95 sq.*
  Rough Sawn .... 57.95 sq.*
White Vertical (12"x10' lengths) .... 73.95 sq.*
*add $2.00 sq. for color
Soffit (12"x12')... 9.95 ea.

Aluminum Siding Accessories
Snap-on Outside

Corner Post (10')............................	$9.95 ea.	Starter Strip (12'6")	$2.22 ea.
Outside Corner Post (10')................	9.95 ea.	Crown Moulding (12')	4.49 ea.
Individual Corners	.69 ea.	Western Sill (10')	6.89 ea.
Inside Corners (10')	5.79 ea.	Brick Mold Casing (10')....................	6.33 ea.
Sill Trim (12'6")...............................	3.77 ea.	Backer Plate......................................	.08 ea.
"J" Channel (½", ⅝", ¾", 1-⅛", 12")......................	2.59 ea.	Siding Nails......................................	3.59 lb.
"L" Channel (12'6")..........................	2.99 ea.	Trim Nails...	5.89 lb.
"F" Channel (12').............................	6.49 ea.	Casing & Header Cover (12')	5.29 ea.

Bevel and Drop Siding. The labor cost of placing bevel or drop siding will vary with the class of work and the method of placement. In the least expensive method, only one end of the siding is squared and the ends of the corners are left rough and covered with metal corner pieces. This method is used extensively in the South because the long summers and intense heat can cause mitered wood corners to open up.

Where a better quality appearance is desired, it is necessary to cut and fit each piece of siding between the window casing and the corner boards. Two masons or carpenters usually work together, as it is necessary to square one end of the siding, then measure and cut each board separately to insure a snug fit.

This also applies where the siding is mitered at the corners.

Another method of finishing off exterior corners for bevel or drop siding is to install corner boards. These boards are generally made from 1" or 1¼" material depending on the thickness of the siding. They can be plain or molded, depending upon the architecture of the house.

Corner boards can be applied to the sheathing and the siding fitted tightly to the narrow edge of the corner board. When this method is used, the joints between the siding and corner boards should be caulked or treated with water repellent. Corner boards can also be applied over the siding which minimizes water infiltrating the ends of the siding. This latter method is better for paneling.

Interior corners are butted against a corner strip consisting of 1" or 1¼" material, depending upon the thickness of the siding.

Bevel siding should have sufficient lap to prevent wind-driven rain from working behind the boards. FHA standards require a minimum of 1".

Quantity of Bevel Siding Required Per 100 Sq. Ft. of Wall

Measured Size Inches	Actual Size Inches	Exposed to Weather	Pattern	Add For Lap	Ft. B.M. Req. per 100 sq. ft. Surface
½ x 4	½ x 3¼	2¾	Regular	46%	151
½ x 5	½ x 4¼	3¾	Regular	33%	138
½ x 6	½ x 5¼	4¾	Regular	26%	131
½ x 8	½ x 7¼	6¾	Regular	18%	123
⅝ x 8	⅝ x 7¼	6¾	Regular	18%	123
¾ x 8	¾ x 7¼	6¾	Rabbetted	18%	123
⅝ x 10	⅝ x 9¼	8¾	Rabbetted	14%	119
¾ x 10	¾ x 9¼	8¾	Rabbetted	14%	119
¾ x 12	¾ x 11¼	10¾	Rabbetted	12%	117

The above quantities include 5% for end cutting and waste.

Weight per 1000 ft.—½" thick 800 lbs. Red cedar 600 lbs.; ⅝" thick 1,000 lbs. Red cedar 750 lbs.; 1" thick 1,200 lbs. Red cedar 900 lbs.

Quantity of Drop Siding Required Per 100 Sq. Ft. of Wall

Measured Size Inches	Actual Size Inches	Exposed to Weather	Add for Lap	Ft. B.M. Req. per 100 Sq. Ft. Surface	Weight per 1000 Ft.
1x6	¾ x5¼	5¼	14%	119	1800
1x8	¾ x7¼	7¼	10%	115	2000

The above quantities include 5% for end cutting and waste.

Quantity of Shiplap Required Per 100 Sq. Ft. of Surface

Measured Size Inches	Actual Size Inches	Add for Lap	Ft. B.M. Req. per 100 Sq. Ft. Surface	Weight per 1000 Ft.
1x 8	¾ x7¼	10%	115	2200
1x10	¾ x9¼	8%	113	2200

The above quantities include 5% for end cutting and waste.

Quantity of Dressed and Matched (D & M) or Tongued and Grooved (T & G) Boards Required Per 100 Sq. Ft. of Surface

Measured Size Inches	Actual Size Inches	Add for Width	Ft. B.M. Req. per 100 Sq. Ft. Surface	Weight per 1000 Ft.
1x6	¾ x5¼	14%	119	2100
2x6	1⅝ x5¼	14%	238	2300

The above quantities include 5% for end cutting and waste.

To prepare exterior walls for new siding, the following work may be necessary. To remove existing stucco, per 1000 sq. ft.:

	Hours	Rate	Total	Rate	Total
Labor.............................	1.25	—	—	$16.65	$20.81

To add ½" plywood sheathing over existing boards, per 100 sq. ft.:

	Hours	Rate	Total	Rate	Total
105 sq. ft. sheathing.............................		—	—		$32.00
1 lb. nails.............................		—	—		.03
Carpenter.............................	1.0	—	—	$20.60	20.60
Helper.............................	.3	—	—	$15.67	5.00
110 sq. ft. felt.............................		—	—		3.47
Carpenter.............................	.4	—	—		8.24
Cost per 100 sq. ft.............................			—		$70.14
Cost per sq. ft.............................			—		.70

Installing Plain Bevel Siding. It is particularly important to have the first course level. If the first course is not level and uniform, succeeding courses will also be off.

The position of the first course is determined by measuring down from the bottom of the soffit at 2' intervals across the entire wall to 1" below the bottom plate. This will usually be on the foundation. Snap a horizontal chalk-line. A ⅜" furring strip is nailed along the chalk-line to provide support for the starting course.

The butt edge of the first course is laid over the furring strip aligned with the chalk line. Start at one side and work to the other.

The first course is nailed to the bottom plate at points just below each stud to mark nailing locations for subsequent courses.

Overlap is measured at the top of the siding to be lapped and a chalk-line placed to show the position of the butt edge of the second course.

The second course is also started at the wall's end, and nailed with a single nail at each stud, tapped flush with the siding face. Siding should fit snug, but not tight. Vertical joints should be staggered and positioned so that they fall on studs.

Under a window sill, siding should be cut to fit the groove on the bottom of the sill. Over doors and windows, siding should be set on the drip cap.

Labor Placing Bevel Siding

Measured Size Inches	Actual Size Inches	Exposed to Weather Inches	Class of Workmanship	Feet B.M. Placed per 8-hr. Day	Carpenter Hours per 1000 Ft. B.M.
4	3¼	2¾	Rough Ends	350-400	21.3**
4	3¼	2¾	Fitted Ends	240-285	30.5
4	3¼	2¾	Mitered Corners	200-240	36.3
5	4¼	3¾	Rough Ends	415-460	18.2**
5	4¼	3¾	Fitted Ends	285-330	25
5	4¼	3¾	Mitered Corners	240-285	30.5
6	5¼	4¾	Rough Ends	475-525	16*
6	5¼	4¾	Fitted Ends	325-375	23
6	5¼	4¾	Mitered Corners	265-310	28
8	7¼	6¾	Rough Ends	570-620	13.4**
8	7¼	6¾	Fitted Ends	375-415	20
8	7¼	6¾	Mitered Corners	300-350	24
10	9¼	8¾	Rough Ends	650-700	12**
10	9¼	8¾	Fitted Ends	440-480	17.5
10	9¼	8¾	Mitered Corners	375-425	20
12	11¼	10¾	Fitted Ends	475-525	16
12	11¼	10¾	Mitered Corners	400-450	19

**Where an electric handsaw is used to square both ends of the siding before placing and leaving the exposed corners rough to be covered with metal corner pieces, deduct 1 to 1½ hours time per 1,000 ft. b.m.

Labor Placing Drop Siding

Measured Size Inches	Actual Size Inches	Class of Workmanship	Feet B.M. Placed per 8-hr. Day	Carpenter Hours per 1000 Ft. B.M.
6	5¼	Rough Ends	525-575	14.5*
6	5¼	Fitted Ends	350-400	21.4

Measured Size Inches	Actual Size Inches	Class of Workmanship	Feet B.M. Placed per 8-hr. Day	Carpenter Hours per 1000Ft. B.M.
6	5¼	Mitered Corners	285-325	26.3
8	7¼	Rough Ends	600-650	12.8*
8	7¼	Fitted Ends	415-460	18.2
8	7¼	Mitered Corners	325-375	23.0

*Where an electric saw is used to square both ends of the siding before placing and leaving the exposed corners rough to be covered with metal corner pieces, deduct 1 to 1½ hours time per 1,000 ft. b.m. from the costs given above.

Estimated Nail Quantities

	Length		No. per Lb.		Lbs. Per 1000 B.F.	
Size	Alum.	Gal.	Alum.	Gal.	Alum.	Gal.
6d	1⅞"	2 "	560	190	2	6
7d	2⅛"	2¼"	460	170	2½	6½
8d	2⅜"	2½"	320	120	4	9
10d	2⅞"	3 "	210	100	5½	11

SHINGLES AND SHAKES

Shingles like vertical siding and paneling can be applied over old siding. If the siding is uneven, a 1" x 4" nailing strip is applied horizontally as a nailing base for the shingles. Spacing of the nailing strips will depend on the length and exposure of the shingles. Shingles should be applied with rust resistant nails.

Shingles come in 16", 18" and 24" lengths. They also come in random widths of 3" to 14" as well as uniform widths of 4", 5" and 6". The latter shingles are called Dimension shingles and are applied with tight fitting joints. The wider shingles are applied with ¼" to ⅛" spacing between joints to allow for expansion during weather changes.

Either can be applied by two basic methods: Single-course or double-course.

Single-Course Method. This method consists of simply laying one course over the other the same as in bevel siding. However, greater exposure is permitted allowing the use of second-grade shingles since only ½ or less of the butt is exposed. The spacing for shingles is determined the same as for bevel siding. A carpenter and helper can apply approximately 500 sq. ft. of single-course wood shingles per 8-hour day at the following cost per 100 sq. ft.

	Hours	Rate	Total	Rate	Total
Carpenter	8	—	—	20.60	164.80
Laborer	8	—	—	15.67	125.36
Cost per 100 sq. ft.				—	58.03

Double-Course Method. This method consists of applying an undercourse of shingles and nailing a second course over it with ½" or ¾" projection of the butt over the lower course. In this method the top course should be first grade, while the undercourse can be third course or undercourse grade. All joints must be broken so that the vertical butt joints of the top course are 1½" from the joints of the undercourse.

A carpenter and laborer can apply 300 sq. ft. of double-course shingles per 8-hr. day at the following cost per 100 sq. ft.

	Hours	Rate	Total	Rate	Total
Carpenter	8	—	—	$20.60	$164.80
Laborer	8	—	—	15.67	125.36
Cost per 100 sq. ft.				—	96.72

Weather Exposure/Shingles
Maximum Exposure

Size	Single Course	Double Course 1st Grade	2nd Grade
16"	7½"	12"	10"
18"	8½"	14"	11"
24"	11½"	16"	14"

Shakes. Shakes are somewhat longer than shingles and come in lengths of 18, 24 and 32 inches. Of the three kinds, Handsplit and Resawn are hand-cut and machine finished, while Tapersplit and Straightsplit are mostly hand-cut and finished. Any of the preceding can be applied by the two basic methods of application, single-course or double-course. Nails should be rust-resistant. In the single-course method, it's customary to blind nail the shake by placing the nail 1" above the butt line of the next course. Since they are longer, shakes generally have greater weather exposure than shingles.

Weather Exposure/Shakes
Maximum Exposure

Size	Single Course	Double Course Resawn/Taper	Straight
18"	11½" 8½"	14"	16"
24"	11½"	20"	22"
32"	15"		

A carpenter and laborer can apply 600 sq. ft. of single-course shakes per 8-hr. day at the following cost per 100 sq. ft.:

	Hours	Rate	Total	Rate	Total
Carpenter	8	—	—	$20.60	$164.80

	Hours	Rate	Total	Rate	Total
Laborer..	8	—	—	15.67	125.36
Cost per 100 sq. ft................................			—		48.36

Grades And Sizes/Cedar Shingles

Three Grades	Sizes	Bundles Per Square	Lbs. Per Square
1, 2 and 3	Each Grade comes in 24", 18" and 16" shingles	Each Grade contains four bundles per square	Each Square per grade weighs 192 lbs., 158 lbs., and 144 lbs. respectively

Wood Shingles
Estimated To Cover 100 sq. ft.*

Exposure	No. of Shingles Required	Nails Required (lbs.)	
		3d	4d
4"	990	3¾	6½
5"	792	2	5¼
6"	660	2½	4¼

*includes 10% wastes

Grades And Sizes/Cedar Shakes

Grade	Dimensions	Bundles Per Square	Lbs. Per Square
No. 1	18"x½" to ¾"	4	220
Handsplit &	18"x¾" to 1¼"	5	250
Re-sawn	24"x½" to ¾"	4	280
	24"x¾" to 1¼"	5	350
	32"x¾" to 1¼"	6	450
No. 1 Tapersplit	24"x½" to ⅝"	4	260
No. 1 Straightsplit	18"x⅜"	5	200
	24"x⅜"	5	260

Recommended Nails/Wood Shingles

Size	Length	Gauge	Head	Shingles
3d	11/4"	14½	7/32"	16" & 18"
4d	11/2"	14	7/32"	24"
5d	13/4"	14	7/32"	16" & 18"
6d	2"	13	7/32"	24"

3 & 4d nails are used for new construction;
5 & 6d nails are used for re-roofing.

In the double-course method, the second course is nailed 2" above the butt-line. A carpenter and laborer can apply 400 sq. ft. of double-course shakes per 8-hr. day at the following cost per 100 sq. ft.:

	Hours	Rate	Total	Rate	Total
Carpenter	8	—	—	$20.60	$164.80
Laborer	8	—	—	15.67	125.36
Cost per 100 sq. ft.			—		72.54

HARDBOARD SIDING (LAP AND PANEL)

Hardboard lap siding comes in various sizes including 8", 10" and 12" widths by 16' long. Hardboard panels come in 4' x 8' and 4' x 9' sizes, or up to 4' x 16' if required.

When stored on the job-site, the material should be placed on stringers, avoiding direct contact with the ground and covered with a waterproof covering to prevent direct exposure to the elements.

Courtesy Boise Cascade

Careful job-site storage is a "must" for hardboard siding.

As with all wood building materials, hardboard siding should never be applied where excessive moisture conditions exist, such as drying concrete, plaster or over wet sheathing materials. Where such conditions exist, the building should be allowed to dry before application proceeds.

Vapor barriers of 1 perm or less (polyethylene film or foil-backed gypsum board, for example) are required on the warm side of the wall in all heated or insulated buildings.

Hardboard siding should never be installed in direct contact with the ground or where water may collect and contact the siding. Allow at least 6" to 8" of space between the siding and the ground or anywhere where water is apt to collect.

The application table below shows the recommended nailing procedure. REMEMBER NAILS SHOULD PENETRATE A MINIMUM OF 1½" INTO THE FRAMING MEMBER. ALWAYS USE CORROSION RESISTANT NAILS.

| SIDING | FRAMING (2" x 4") MAXIMUM SPACING | NAIL SIZE | NAIL SPACING | | JOINT GAP | GAP AROUND OPENINGS |
			SIDING ONLY (1)	RACKING STRENGTH REQ'D (2)		
LAP SIDING DIRECT TO STUDS	16"o.c.	8d	16"o.c.	Not Applicable	Moderate Contact	1/8"
OVER SHEATHING	16"o.c.	10d	16"o.c.	Not Applicable	Moderate Contact	1/8"
SQUARE EDGE PANEL SIDING DIRECT TO STUDS	24"o.c.	6d	6"o.c. Edges 12"o.c. Intermed.	4"o.c. Edges 8"o.c. Intermed.	1/16"	1/8"
OVER SHEATHING	24"o.c.	8d	6"o.c. Edges 12"o.c. Intermed.	4"o.c. Edges 8"o.c. Intermed.	1/16"	1/8"
SHIPLAP EDGE PANEL SIDING DIRECT TO STUDS	16"o.c. (3)	6d	6"o.c. Edges 12"o.c. Intermed.	4"o.c. Edges 8"o.c. Intermed.	Moderate Contact	1/8"
OVER SHEATHING	16"o.c. (3)	8d	6"o.c. Edges 12"o.c. Intermed.	4"o.c. Edges 8"o.c. Intermed.	Moderate Contact	1/8"

(1) Racking resistance per FHA Circular 12 provided by sheathing or corner braces.
(2) Racking resistance provided by siding.
(3) Some manufacturers permit application to studs spaced 24"o.c. and should be consulted for their recommendations.

Installing Hardboard Lap Siding. Hardboard lap sidings are recommended for wood framed structures such as homes and apartments. They are not recommended for use as mansard roofing. The stud spacing should be a minimum of 16" o.c. When application is direct to studs or over wood board sheathing, a breather-type, not a vapor-barrier, building paper should be used behind the siding. This can be eliminated if moisture resistant panel sheathing has been used, unless, however, it is required by local code or regulations.

A ⅜" x 1½" cant strip is used to start the first course. This is nailed along the bottom of the wall framing as shown in the illustration below.

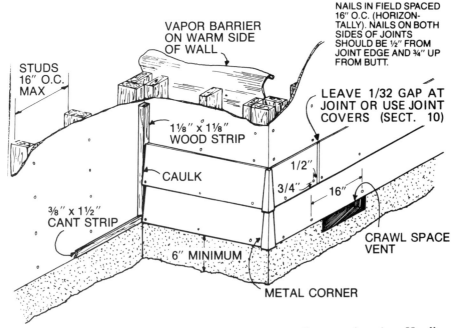

NAILS IN FIELD SPACED 16" O.C. (HORIZONTALLY). NAILS ON BOTH SIDES OF JOINTS SHOULD BE ½" FROM JOINT EDGE AND ¾" UP FROM BUTT.

VAPOR BARRIER ON WARM SIDE OF WALL

STUDS 16" O.C. MAX

1⅛" x 1⅛" WOOD STRIP

LEAVE 1/32 GAP AT JOINT OR USE JOINT COVERS (SECT. 10)

CAULK

½"

¾"

16"

⅜" x 1½" CANT STRIP

CRAWL SPACE VENT

6" MINIMUM

METAL CORNER

Courtesy American Hardboard Assoc.

The bottom of the first course is positioned overlapping the cant strip ¼" to 1" and nailed, placing nails 16" apart, through the siding and cant strip into the joint, header or sill. Plastic hammer caps are suggested to minimize hammer marks. Nailing should proceed from one end to the other leaving the nail heads slightly above the surface.

Do not set or drive nails especially when siding is installed over soft material such as plastic foam sheathing.

Each course of siding must overlap the previous course by 1". Nails are placed along the bottom edge 16" apart at stud locations about ¾" above the bottom edge.

Vertical joints must be centered over framing members and the siding nailed on each side of the joint.

The use of metal joint covers will permit speedier application and offer a more professional appearance and more weather-tight wall. If joint covers are not used, all joints should be caulked. Siding ends should be spaced 3/16" apart with the joint cover centered, or, corner boards may also be used.

Where siding is notched out around windows, doors and other openings, shims should be installed behind the siding for continuous support. Nails should be 16" apart through siding and shim. Where siding butts against window, door and other vertical members, there should be a 1/8" space left for expansion. All areas where siding butts around doors, windows and other openings should be caulked.

Outside corners can be covered with metal corners covered or butted against 1 1/8" thick wood corner boards.

Courtesy Boise Cascade

Individual outside corner caps maintain continuity of siding in traditional clapboard style.

At inside corners, a metal inside corner is installed or the siding is butted against a 1⅛" sq. piece of wood leaving a ⅛" gap which is caulked.

Good building practices call for keeping siding at least 6" above the finished grade and out of contact with roofs, slabs and places where moisture tends to collect.

A professional sider can usually apply 450 sq. ft. of hardboard lap siding per 8 hr. day at the following cost per 100 sq. ft.:

	Hours	Rate	Total	Rate	Total
Carpenter	1.77	—	—	$20.60	$36.46
Laborer	1.77	—	—	15.67	27.74
Cost per 100 sq. ft.:			—		64.20

Installing Hardboard Panel Siding. The uses for hardboard panel siding are the same as for hardboard lap siding. The same conditions for moisture also apply and hardboard panel siding should never be applied over wet sheathing.

A vapor barrier, 1 perm or less, must be installed on the warm side of the wall in all heated or insulated buildings. If plastic foam sheathing is installed on the cold side of the studs, particular attention should be given the vapor barrier because of the low vapor permeability of foam materials. Check the manufacturer's recommendation when applying vapor barriers.

The following application procedure describes installing vertical groove, reverse board and batten and plain hardboard panel siding.

When applying vertical grooved or reverse board and batten panels, studs must be 16" o.c. maximum. Plain panels, ungrooved, may be applied over studs 24" o.c. if building codes permit. Unless local codes or building regulations dictate otherwise, building paper may be omitted behind panel sidings having shiplap joints or battens.

Vertical grooved and reverse board and batten panels must be installed with the grooves running vertically. Panel must butt over framing members. The position for nails is shown in the illustration below.

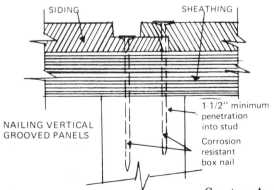

SIDING   SHEATHING

NAILING VERTICAL GROOVED PANELS

1-1/2" minimum penetration into stud

Corrosion resistant box nail

Courtesy American Hardboard Assoc.

Nails are spaced as indicated in the chart below. The heads should be left slightly above the surface. IT IS IMPORTANT TO NOT SET OR OVERDRIVE THE NAILS.

Type of Panel	Stud Spacing inches	Racking resistance provided by sheathing or diagonal bracing		Racking resistance provided by siding panels	
		Edges	Center Studs	Edges	Center Studs
Vertical Grooved and Reverse Board & Batten	16	6(1)	12(1)	4(2)	8(2)
Plain Panels without Grooves	16	6(1)	12(1)	4(3) 6(2)	8(3) 12(2)
	24	6(1)	12(1)	6(2)	12(2)

Nail Spacing, inches

(1) Corrosion resistant box nails, 6d or longer if siding is direct to studs without sheathing, or long enough to penetrate 1" or more into studs if applied over sheathing. Colored nails supplied as a siding accessory are preferred for prefinished sidings. Plastic hammer caps are recommended to minimize hammer marks on nails and prefinished sidings.

(2) Siding applied direct to studs with 8d galvanized box nails.

(3) Siding applied direct to studs with 6d galvanized box nails.

Square-edge ungrooved panels may be applied over sheathing or direct to studs with the panel edges centered over the studs. Nails are placed 3/8" from panel edges and should penetrate framing at least 1". A gap of 1/16" to 1/8" is recommended between square edge panels, which is covered with a batten strip nailed to the stud.

If siding is to provide racking resistance, nails must be spaced 4" around the perimeter of the panel and 8" at intermediate supports. When applied over structural sheathing, nailing must be spaced 6" at the edges and 12" at intermediate supports.

Panels with shiplap edges can also be applied over sheathing or direct to studs. Shiplaps are available in two widths, ⅜" and ¾". When nailing, a ⅜" shiplap must be nailed ⅜" from the edge on both sides of the shiplap. For ¾" shiplap, nailing must be ⅜" from the edge through the underlap *and* the overlap.

All horizontal joints should have solid wood blocking behind them, and made weather tight. When panels are stacked as in two and three story homes, a metal "z" flashing should be applied to the top of the first course to provide a waterproof joint. Clearance between these panels must be at least ⅜" to ½" depending on joist depth and moisture content.

Courtesy Boise Cascade

A good way to gap hardwood panels is with a quarter.

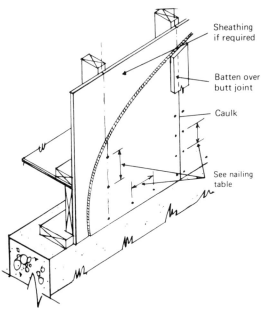

Sheathing
if required

Batten over
butt joint

Caulk

See nailing
table

Courtesy American Hardboard Assoc.

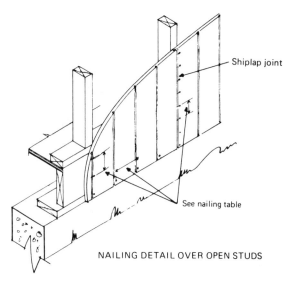

Shiplap joint

See nailing table

NAILING DETAIL OVER OPEN STUDS

Courtesy American Hardboard Assoc.

Outside corners are generally finished off by applying corner boards as shown in Figure 1. There are several methods for finishing off inside corners as illustrated in Figure 2, 3, and 4.

A carpenter and laborer can usually apply 800 sq. ft. of hardboard panel siding per 8-hr. day at the following labor cost per 100 sq. ft.:

	Hours	Rate	Total	Rate	Total
Carpenter	8	—	—	$20.60	$164.80
Laborer	8	—	—	15.67	125.36
Cost per 100 sq. ft.:			—		36.27

VINYL SIDING/VERTICAL AND HORIZONTAL

Vinyl siding is one of the newer siding products to come along in the past few years. Its increasing popularity can be traced to a number of things, not the least of which are its long, transferable warranties and the fact that it is virtually maintenance free.

It is as applicable to remodeling as it is to new construction and its adaptability and ease of application are just two of its many features. Others are, in addition to its solid color, it won't peel, blister, flake or rot. It is impervious to insects, termites and other insect pests. It does not require painting and does not show scratches.

Horizontal vinyl siding comes in two styles, "Double" 4" clapboard and single 8" clapboard. Both come in 12'6" lengths with 8" exposure. Each comes in a variety of colors suited to all types of homes. When applied

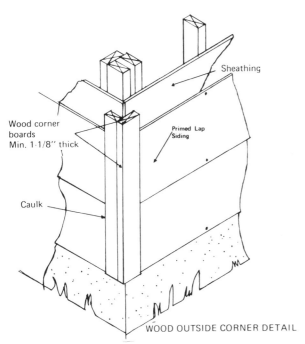

Sheathing

Wood corner
boards
Min. 1-1/8" thick

Primed Lap
Siding

Caulk

WOOD OUTSIDE CORNER DETAIL

Fig. 1

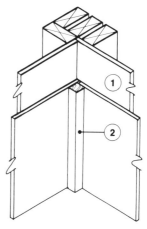

panel siding
1. sheathing or building paper if
required.
2. wood inside corner.

Fig. 2

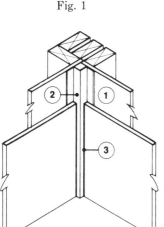

panel siding
1. sheathing or building paper if
required.
2. metal inside corner.
3. caulking or sealant.

Fig. 3

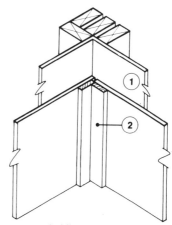

panel siding
1. sheathing or building paper if
required.
2. battens.

Courtesy American Hardboard Assoc.

Fig. 4

all framing shown for illustration purposes only.

with foam polystyrene or fiberboard backerboard, vinyl siding has the added value of thermal and accoustical insulation.

Vertical vinyl siding has the same properties as horizontal. It's primarily used to highlight such areas as doorways, porches, porch ceilings and gable ends of homes. It comes in a "Double" 5" panel, 10' long with 10" exposure.

A wide variety of installation accessories are available for both horizontal and vertical vinyl siding including starter strips, undersill trim, window and door channels, inside and outside corner posts, window and door caps, etc.

Warranties of up to 40 years are offered.

In cold climates—many carpenters do not recommend vinyl because it tends to become brittle and when jarred or hit, will crack and break.

Installing Horizontal Siding.   In remodeling, remove shutters and downspouts, and outside electrical fixtures. Replace any rotted boards and nail down any loose boards. If old siding has been removed, apply waterproof sheathing paper. If walls and base are not level and plumb, they should be furred out where necessary. Strapping may be required on uneven outer walls and masonry walls.

Nails should be placed in the center of the slots, not set or flush. A minimum of ¼" clearance should be left at all "J" channels and corner posts to allow for normal expansion and contraction. Below 32°, leave ⅜" clearance. Nails should be aluminum or other corrosion resistant metal 1½" to 2" long, plain shank, 0.12" dia. and 5/16" flat head.

Snap chalk line for starter strip. Nail starter strip every 8", alternating rows of nailing slots. Double nail at ends. Inside corner posts are positioned ¼" from top and nailed beginning at the top 12" o.c. Outside corner posts are installed in the same manner.

As installation reaches window and door caps, they should be furred out where necessary for alignment with adjacent panels. In remodeling, existing window head flashing is left in place.

"J" channels are installed over window-door caps. A ¼" tab is cut at each end of the cap and the cap is bent down over the "J" channel on each side to prevent water from running down behind the vertical "J" channel.

After the first panel is locked in the starter strip, backerboard is inserted bevel edge down and towards the wall. Panels are nailed 16" on center (not over 8" in areas where severe winds may be encountered). Nails should be centered in nailing slots. Panels should not be pulled up tight, but allowed to hang without strain.

Panels are lapped one-half of the factory notched cut-outs. The end of the uncut panel should always lap over the end of the notched panel. Laps should be staggered for best appearance. Undersill trim is fitted under window sills; at the tops of walls against soffits; moldings and to finish off trimmed and fitted cut edges of siding panels anywhere above the level of the starter strip. Caulking should be done whenever required or according to manufacturer's recommendations. When cutting siding to fit around windows and doors, a saw or sharp knife should always be used to cut locking detail and lower edge.

An experienced carpenter and helper should be able to install 500 sq. ft. of horizontal vinyl siding per 8-hr. day at the following cost per 100 sq. ft.:

	Hours	Rate	Total	Rate	Total
Sider	1.6	—	—	$20.60	$32.96
Laborer	1.6	—	—	15.67	25.07
Cost per 100 sq. ft.:			—		58.03

Installing Vertical Siding.   Corner posts, window and door channels and window and door caps are installed the same as for horizontal siding. A chalk line is run around the bottom side of the walls and vertical-base-flashing installed, nailed 8" o.c. Window and door cap is installed above all windows and doors not previously covered. Vertical panels are started from the center of the wall and installed working in both directions. A plumbline is dropped at the center of the wall and a double vertical starter strip nailed 8" o.c. at the top of the slot, $7/8$" to one side of the plumbline. Panels are nailed in the center of the nailing slots 16" o.c. An allowance of $3/8$" for expansion is left at the top of each panel. Fitting around windows and doors is accomplished the same as for horizontal panels. Gables are finished with $1/2$" inverted "J" channel fitted along the gable slope. An experienced sider and helper should be able to install 500 sq. ft. of vertical vinyl siding per 8-hr. day at the following labor cost per 100 sq. ft.:

	Hours	Rate	Total	Rate	Total
Sider	1.6	—	—	$20.60	$32.96
Helper	1.6	—	—	15.67	25.07
Cost per 100 sq. ft.:			—		58.03

Installing Aluminum Siding.   Aluminum siding, long a leading product in remodeling, has been improved so much in the past ten years, it is almost a new product. Advances in coating technology permit it to be manufactured in a variety of durable colors and finishes including simulated wood.

In answer to today's demand for energy-saving products, aluminum siding is also available with insulation laminated to its underside. Backerboard made of various insulating materials simply dropped behind the panel are also available.

Life expectancy of aluminum siding is 20 years or more in most situations. Styles include "Double" 4 and "Double" 5 and 8" for horizontal installation; board and batten, and v-groove in 8", 12" and 16" for vertical

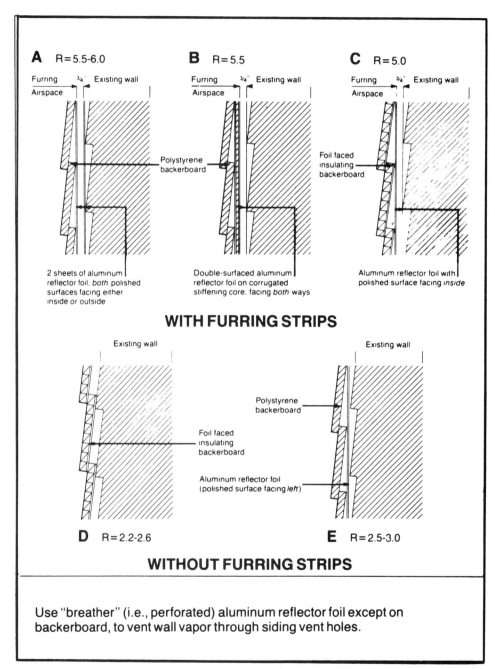

WITH FURRING STRIPS

WITHOUT FURRING STRIPS

Use "breather" (i.e., perforated) aluminum reflector foil except on backerboard, to vent wall vapor through siding vent holes.

Courtesy Architectural Aluminum Mfg. Assoc.

Various aluminum siding applications.

installation. Accessories similar to those offered with vinyl siding to facilitate installation and improve finished appearance are also available.

Pre-planning and proper preparation of the walls are essential to a smooth-running, quality-appearing job. Rotten boards should be removed and loose boards nailed firmly to framing members. Furring strips should be used to bring up low spots so that nailing surfaces are true and even.

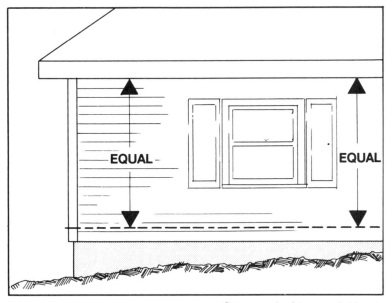

Courtesy Architectural Aluminum Mfg. Assoc.

By measuring equal distances down from the eaves, and establishing a straight reference line, the siding will appear parallel regardless of any actual settling of house from true level.

Backer-strips are used with 8" horizontal siding to provide panel support at key points. Outside corner caps are applied one at a time to complete the outside junction of panels. Inside corners are finished similar to those for vinyl.

Aluminum siding is hung on the nails, not nailed to the wall. Nails should not be set or driven flush. In remodeling, care should be taken that nails are holding securely and in firm, solid wood. Only aluminum nails should be used and they should be driven at right angles to the wall, avoiding angling the nail up or down.

Panels should overlap at least ½". Except for insulated panels, laps should be supported with backer-strips. Short pieces of siding, 20" or less, should be avoided. Joints or laps should be staggered for strength and appearance. Caulk should be applied around all openings where water has a chance of entering. An experienced aluminum sider and helper should be

Extra care should be taken on first course, because this course establishes base for all other courses.

Aluminum siding must be hung with aluminum nails through the center of the factory-slotted holes.

Nails must be driven into sound lumber.

Courtesy Aluminum Association Inc.

able to install 500 sq. ft. of aluminum siding per 8-hr. day at the following labor cost per 100 sq. ft.:

	Hours	Rate	Total	Rate	Total
Sider	1.6	—	—	$20.60	$32.96
Laborer	1.6	—	—	15.67	25.07
Cost per 100 sq. ft.:			—		58.03

Caulking. For caulking around doors and windows, a nozzle, ⅜" or larger should be used. Caulking materials can be classified according to two broad groups. The first group, having a life span of five to twenty years, are made from natural and synthetic rubber and are ranked in performance beginning at the low end with latex, followed by butyl, then neoprene, which offers the longest life. The high performance types include polyurethane, polysulfide and silicone. A building erected as late as 1970 and caulked with one of the natural rubbers could have a major problem today with infiltration. One man using a cartridge-type gun should be able to caulk about 400–450 lin. ft. per 8-hr. day at the following labor cost per 100 lin. ft.:

	Hours	Rate	Total	Rate	Total
Caulker	1.88	—	—	$15.67	$29.46
Cost per lin. ft.			—		.29

MASONRY REPAIRS

Cutting Out Old Brick Mortar Joints. Using a carborundum wheel 5" in diameter and ¼" thick for a cut to a depth of ½", the following cost per 100 sq. ft. may be assumed:

	Hours	Rate	Total	Rate	Total
Tuckpointer	2	—	—	$20.81	$41.62
Helper	1	—	—	16.90	16.90
Cost per 100 sq. ft.			—		$58.52
Cost per sq. ft.			—		.58

Repointing Mortar Old Brick Joints. After the mortar joints have been cut out, two tuckpointers working on the scaffold with one helper on the ground should point 400–500 sq. ft. of brick wall per 8-hr. day at the following labor cost per 100 sq. ft.:

	Hours	Rate	Total	Rate	Total
Tuckpointers	3.5	—	—	$20.81	$72.84
Helper	1.5	—	—	16.90	25.35
Cost per 100 sq. ft.			—		$98.19
Cost per sq. ft.			—		.98

Removal of Brick by Hand Chipping. A mason should hand chip around 200 pieces per 8-hr. day at the following labor cost per 100 pieces:

	Hours	Rate	Total	Rate	Total
Mason	4.5	—	—	$21.38	$ 96.21
Helper	1.0	—	—	16.90	16.90
Cost per 100 pieces			—		$113.11
Cost per brick			—		1.13

Removal of Brick by Pneumatic Pick. Where larger areas of brick are to be broken out, figure two men for each 100 sq. ft. of 12" thick wall, as follows:

	Hours	Rate	Total	Rate	Total
Labor	18	—	—	$15.67	$282.06
Pick Rental		—	—	40.00	40.00
Cost per 100 sq. ft.			—		$322.06
Cost per sq. ft.			—		3.22

In replacing masonry veneer, care should be taken to retain the original appearance. After removing all loose mortar and brushing the joint to remove dust and loose particles, the surface should be dampened. The mortar should be tamped well into the joint to achieve a good bond. Pointing should be the same as existing joints.

Care should be taken to keep mortar off the face of the brick or stone. Since older homes frequently used soft bricks and porous stone trim, the entire surface may require treatment with transparent waterproofing. Painted, stained or dirty brick can be cleaned by careful sandblasting, then repainted or waterproofed.

To Patch Face Brick. To patch 4" face brick, figure one mason and one helper can lay about 65 sq. ft. per day.

Labor Cost per 100 Sq. Ft.

	Labor	Rate	Total	Rate	Total
Mason	12	—	—	$21.38	$256.56
Helper	12	—	—	16.90	202.80
			—		$459.36
Labor Cost per sq. ft.					4.59

Removal Of Concrete Block. Block walls can usually be knocked down manually by laborers. For 12" or 8" block walls, figure 100 sq. ft. per 8 hr. day at the following cost per sq. ft.:

	Hours	Rate	Total	Rate	Total
Laborer	.008	—	—	$16.90	$1.35
Cost per sq. ft.			—		1.35

To remove 4" partition block, figure 100 sq. ft. as follows:

	Hours	Rate	Total	Rate	Total
Laborer	4.5	—	—	$16.90	$76.05
Cost per sq. ft.			—		.76

Removing Gypsum Tile.   Figure one laborer can remove 100 sq. ft. in 2.5 hrs. as follows:

	Hours	Rate	Total	Rate	Total
Laborer	2.5	—	—	$16.90	$42.25
Cost per sq. ft.			—		.42

To Patch Building Brick.   Where openings are closed up or otherwise patched out in small areas, one mason and one helper should lay about 30 cu. ft. of building brick per day.

Labor Cost to Patch 100 Sq. Ft. of 12" Building Brick Wall

	Hours	Rate	Total	Rate	Total
Mason	27	—	—	$21.38	$ 577.26
Helper	27	—	—	16.90	456.30
			—		$1033.56
Cost per sq. ft.			—		10.33

To Patch Concrete Block Partitions.   One mason and a helper should patch out 150 sq. ft. of 4" block partitioning per day.

Labor Cost to Patch 100 Sq. Ft. of 4" Block Partitioning

	Hours	Rate	Total	Rate	Total
Mason	5.5	—	—	$21.38	$117.59
Helper	5.5	—	—	16.90	92.95
			—		$210.54
Cost per sq. ft.			—		2.10

To Rebuild Chimneys.   On small chimneys one mason with a helper will lay about 500 bricks per day at the following cost per brick:

	Hours	Rate	Total	Rate	Total
Mason	8	—	—	$21.38	$171.04
Helper	8	—	—	16.90	135.20
			—		306.24
Cost per brick			—		.61

SOFFITS

Today's manufactured soffit systems offer not only convenience and ease of installation for the remodeling contractor, but beauty and long-life for the homeowner. Not only are they suitable for roof over-hang, but porches, covered walkways and patio over-hangs as well. The more popular manufactured systems are made either of aluminum or vinyl, and each comes with a complete line of accessories for ease of installation and an attractive finished appearance.

In aluminum, soffit panels come in 12" widths by 144" long. Vinyl panels are approximately 10" wide by 10' long. Both come in solid as well as perforated panels to permit proper breathing. At least 25 percent of the total installation should be perforated.

Installation.   When using the aluminum system, a 40' run of overhang will require 120 running feet of soffit of which 25 percent, or about 30 ft., should be perforated. The same measure will require 40 ft. of molding or frieze board, 40 ft. of fascia cap and fascia board and 1 lb. of 1½" siding nails and 1 lb. of white trim nails. (If the rafter sidewall is to be covered, figure the area allowing for some scrap.)

In remodeling, if the existing soffit is level, the rear soffit support can usually be hung so that it coincides with the bottom of the existing soffit. (Check manufacturer's instructions). At appropriate intervals throughout the run, determine the correct length of soffit pieces to be cut.

Slide the first piece of soffit into the rear soffit support and nail through the nailing flange into the bottom of the fascia board. Center nailing is not required in soffit lengths up to 4 ft. The exposed edge of the soffit will be covered by the fascia cover.

Subsequent soffit pieces are locked into place by pulling the piece toward the installer which locks it into the v-groove. Each fourth panel should be perforated. At corners the run can be mounted square, 90° or 45°.

One man should be able to handle 300 linear ft. of soffit per 8-hr. day at the following labor cost per 10 lin. ft.:

	Hours	Rate	Total	Rate	Total
Sider	2.67	—	—	20.60	55.00
100 lin. ft.		—	—		55.00
Cost per 10 lin. ft.			—		5.50

EXTERIOR FINISH CARPENTRY

Placing Corner Boards, Fascia Boards, Etc.   When placing wood fascia boards, corner boards, etc., on houses, a carpenter should place 175–225 lin. ft. per 8-hr. day at the following cost per lin. ft.:

	Hours	Rate	Total	Rate	Total
Carpenter	.04	—	—	$20.60	$.82
Cost per lin. ft.			—		.82

Placing Exterior Wood Cornices, Verge Boards, Etc. When placing exterior wood cornices, verge boards, fascia, etc., consisting of two members, two carpenters working together should place 150–175 lin. ft. per 8-hr. day at the following cost per lin. ft.:

	Hours	Rate	Total	Rate	Total
Carpenter	9.82	—	—	$20.60	$202.29
Cost per lin. ft.			—		2.03

When the exterior consists of 3-members (crown mold, bed mold, fascia, etc.), two carpenters working together should place 100–125 lin. ft. per 8-hr. day at the following labor cost per lin. ft.:

	Hours	Rate	Total	Rate	Total
Carpenter	14.29	—	—	$20.60	$294.37
Cost per lin. ft.			—		2.94

If a 4-member wood cornice is used, two carpenters working together should place 60–75 lin. ft. per 8-hr. day at the following cost per lin. ft.:

	Hours	Rate	Total	Rate	Total
Carpenter	23.53	—	—	$20.60	$484.72
Cost per lin ft.			—		4.85

The above quantities and costs do not include blocking out for fascia boards, cornices, etc. An extra allowance should be made for all blocking required.

Placing Brick Moldings. A carpenter should fit and set around 32 lin. ft. brick molding per hour at the following cost per lin. ft.:

	Hours	Rate	Total	Rate	Total
Carpenter	.03	—	—	$20.60	$ 0.62
Cost per 100 lin. ft.			—		62.00
Cost per lin. ft.			—		0.62

Placing Wood Cupolas. One carpenter should set a prefabricated pine cupola in around two hours.

	Hours	Rate	Total	Rate	Total
Carpenter	2	—	—	$20.60	$41.20

Time and material for flashing should be added to have the above cost.

METHODS OF MEASURING AND LISTING PAINTING QUANTITIES

When estimating quantities of paint and exterior finishing, the actual surface to be painted should be measured as accurately as possible from the plans or from measurements taken at the building. From these measurements it should be possible to estimate the quantity of materials required, but the labor quantities present a much more difficult problem, owing to the different classes of work and the difficulties encountered in applying the paint. For instance, the covering capacities of paint will be the same for a plain surface or a cornice, but the labor cost painting the cornice will be considerably more owing to the height of the cornice above the ground and the amount of "cutting" or "trimming" necessary. Care must be used when pricing any piece of work, as conditions on each job are different.

Clapboard or Drop Siding Walls. Obtain actual area of all walls and gables. Add 10 percent to actual surface measurement to allow for painting under edge of boards. Do not deduct for openings less than 10'-0"x10'-0".

Shingle Siding. Obtain actual area of all walls and gables and multiply by 1. Do not deduct for openings less than 10'-0"x10'-0".

Eaves. Plain eaves painted same colors as side walls, obtain area and multiply by $1_{1/2}$. If eaves are painted a different color than side walls, obtain area and multiply by 2.
Eaves with rafters running through, obtain area and multiply by 3.
Eaves over brick, stucco or stone walls, obtain area and multiply by 3.
For eaves over 30'-0" above ground, add $1/2$ for each additional 10'-0" in height.

Cornices, Exterior. Plain cornices, obtain area and multiply by 2. Fancy cornices or cornices containing dentils, etc., obtain area and multiply by 3.

Downspouts and Gutters. Plain downspouts and gutters measure the area and multiply by 2. For fancy downspouts and gutters, obtain area and multiply by 3.

Blinds and Shutters. Plain blinds or shutters, measure one side and multiply by 2. Slatted blinds or shutters, measure one side and multiply by 4.

Columns and Pilasters. Plain columns or pilasters, obtain area in sq. ft.; if fluted, obtain area and multiply by $1_{1/2}$; if paneled, obtain area and multiply by 2.

Lattice Work.   Measure one side and multiply by 2 if painted one side only; if painted two sides, obtain area and multiply by 4.

Porch Rail, Balustrade, Balusters.   If solid bulustrade, add one foot to height to cover top and bottom rail. Multiply the length by the height. If painted two sides, multiply by 2.

If balustrade consists of individual balusters and handrail, multiply length by the height, then multiply the result by 4.

Handrail only. If under 1'-0" girth, figure as 1'-0" by length and multiply by 2.

Moldings.   Cut in on both sides, figure 1 sq. ft. per lin. ft. if under 12" girth. If over 12" girth, take actual measurement.

Doors and Frames, Exterior.   Inasmuch as it costs almost as much to paint a small door as a large one, do not figure any door less than 3'-0"x7'-0". Allowing for frame, add 2'-0" to the width and 1'-0" to the height. For instance, a 3'-0"x7'-0" door would be figured as 5'-0"x8'-0", or 40 sq. ft.

If a sash door, containing small lights of glass, add 2 sq. ft. for each additional light, A 4-lt. door would contain 8 sq. ft. additional; a 12-lt. door, 24 sq. ft. additional, etc.

If painted on both sides, obtain sq. ft. area of one side and multiply by 2.

Door frames only, where no door is hung, allow area of opening to take care of both sides.

Windows, Exterior.   Inasmuch as it costs almost as much to paint a small window as a large one, do not figure any window less than 3'-0"x6'0". Add 2'-0" to both the width and height of the opening, to take care of the sides and head of the frame and the outside casing or brick mold, and multiply to obtain the area. For instance, a window opening 3'-0"x6'-0", add 2'-0" to both the width and height, making 5'-0"x8'-0", containing 40 sq. ft. of surface.

If sash contain more than one light each, such as casement sash, etc., add 2 sq. ft. for each additional light. A 6-lt. window would contain 12 sq. ft. additional; a 12-ft. window, 24 sq. ft. additional, etc.

Roofs.   For flat roofs or nearly flat, measure actual area. For roofs having a quarter pitch, measure actual area and add 25 percent; roofs having a one-third pitch, measure actual area and add 33⅓ percent; roofs having a half pitch, measure actual area and add 50 percent.

Fences.   Plain fences, measure one side and multiply by 2; picket fences, measure one side and multiply by 4.

Covering Capacity of Oil Base Paint on New Exterior Wood. In figuring the number of square feet a gallon of oil base paint will cover, a great deal depends upon the surface to be painted; that is, the kind of wood, the degree of roughness, etc. Some woods are more porous than other others and absorb more paint. Much depends on the way the paint is brushed out as some painters brush the paint out more and thus cover more surface.

The priming coat, properly applied, should cover 450 to 500 sq. ft. per gallon. The second coat should cover 500 to 550 sq. ft. per gallon and the third coat should cover 575 to 625 sq. ft. per gallon.

When estimating exterior trim painting, with measurements taken in accordance with standard methods as given on previous pages, the priming coat should cover 750 to 850 sq. ft. per gallon; the second coat should cover 800 to 900 sq. ft. per gallon and the third coat should cover 900 to 1,000 sq. ft. per gallon.

Bear in mind the above coverages are based on surfaced lumber, as the covering capacity will be greatly reduced when applied to rough boards.

Painting Old Exterior Wood Surfaces. When estimating repaint work on old exterior wood surfaces, if the existing surface is sound and in good condition, two coats should be sufficient to give a good job and paint coverages should be about the same as for the second and third coats on similar new work.

If the old surface shows cracking, blistering, scaling and peeling, the old paint should be removed by using either a paste or liquid paint remover of the slow drying type, or a blow torch and scraper.

If the old paint is removed completely, three coats of paint should be applied the same as recommended for new work.

Painting Wood Shingle Siding. Wood shingle siding should receive three coats of paint on new work. Paint coverages per gallon should be as follows: first coat, 300 to 325 sq. ft.; second coat, 400 to 450 sq. ft.; third coat, 500 to 550 sq. ft.

Wood shingles which have been previously painted with an oil paint and are in suitable condition for repainting, should receive two coats of paint. The first coat should cover 400 to 450 sq. ft. per gal. and the second coat 500 to 550 sq. ft. per gal.

Painting Exterior Wood Floors and Steps. When painting exterior wood floors and steps with oil base paint, material coverages per gallon should be as follows: first coat, 325 to 375 sq. ft.; second coat, 475 to 525 sq. ft.; third coat, 525 to 575 sq. ft.

Painting Brick, Stone, Stucco and Concrete. When painting masonry surfaces that are reasonably smooth, one gallon of oil base paint should cover

170 to 200 sq. ft. for the priming coat; 350 to 400 sq. ft. for the second coat and 375 to 425 sq. ft. for the third coat.

These quantities are subject to considerable variation due to the porosity of the surfaces to which the paint is applied, smoothness of walls, etc., as a rough porous surface will require considerably more paint than a smooth hard surface.

Painting Metal Work.   The area which any paint may be expected to cover on metal work will vary with the surface to be painted as badly pitted or rough metal will require more paint than a perfectly smooth surface. The covering capacity will also vary with the temperature, consistency of the paint and the effort behind the brush.

However, for ordinary smooth surfaces, one gallon of paint should cover 550 to 650 sq. ft., one coat.

Aluminum Paint.   Aluminum paint is used for both priming and finishing coats on metal surfaces.

The covering capacity varies with the condition of the surface but on smooth surfaces, one gallon should cover 600 to 700 sq. ft. with one coat.

COVERING CAPACITY OF PAINTS

It is difficult to say how many sq. ft. of surface one gallon of paint will cover, as there are several items that influence the covering capacity. By brushing the paint out very thin it will cover more surface than when applied thick. Dark paint will hide the surface better than light paint, and for that reason it can be brushed out thinner than the lighter colors. Also, a rough surface will require considerable more paint than a smooth surface.

Soft and porous wood will absorb more oil and require more paint than close grained lumber.

Another thing that must be considered are the ingredients entering into the paint. Different brands of paint vary in covering capacity or hiding power.

Shingle Stain.   When staining wood shingles after they have been laid, one gallon of good stain should cover 120 to 150 sq. ft. of surface, for the first coat.

The second and third coats will go farther, as the wood does not absorb as much stain as on the first coat and should cover 200 to 225 sq. ft. per gallon.

One gallon of good stain should cover about 70 sq. ft. of roof with 2-coats or 50 sq. ft. with 3 coats.

If the shingles are dipped in stain before laying, it will require 3 to $3\frac{1}{2}$

gals, of stain per 1,000 shingles. When dipping shingles in stain, only two-thirds of the shingle need be dipped, as it is unnecessary to dip the end of the shingle that is not exposed.

Covering Capacity of Oil and Spirit Stains. When staining finishing lumber, such as birch, mahogany, oak, gum, etc., one gallon of oil stain should cover 700 to 725 sq. ft.

One gallon of spirit stain should cover 500 to 600 sq. ft.

Covering Capacity of Oil Base Paint on New Exterior Wood. In figuring the number of square feet a gallon of oil base paint will cover, a great deal depends upon the surface to be painted; that is, the kind of wood, the degree of roughness, etc. Some woods are more porous than others and absorb more paint. Much depends on the way the paint is brushed out as some painters brush the paint out more and thus cover more surface.

The priming coat, properly applied, should cover 450 to 500 sq. ft. per gallon. The second coat should cover 500 to 550 sq. ft. per gallon and the third coat should cover 575 to 625 sq. ft. per gallon.

When estimating exterior trim painting, with measurements taken in accordance with standard methods as given on previous pages, the priming coat should cover 750 to 850 sq. ft. per gallon; the second coat should cover 800 to 900 sq. ft. per gallon and the third coat should cover 900 to 1,000 sq. ft. per gallon.

Bear in mind the above coverages are based on surfaced lumber, as the covering capacity will be greatly reduced when applied to rough boards.

The percentage for overhead and profit should be added to the costs listed on the following pages.

Cost of Burning Off Paint From 100 Sq. Ft. of Old Siding

	Hours	Rate	Total	Rate	Total
Painter	2.85	—	—	$17.52	$49.93

Cost of Sanding and Puttying 100 Sq. Ft. Plain Wood
Siding and Trim

	Hours	Rate	Total	Rate	Total
Painter	0.5	—	—	$17.52	$8.76

Cost of Sanding and Puttying 100 Sq. Ft.
Outside Trim Only

	Hours	Rate	Total	Rate	Total
Painter	0.86	—	—	$17.52	$15.07

Cost of 100 Sq. Ft. (1 Sq.) 2-Coat House Paint
Applied to Plain Wood Siding and Trim

	Hours	Rate	Total	Rate	Total
Priming Coat					
0.24 gal. paint		—	—	$17.75	$ 4.26

	Hours	Rate	Total	Rate	Total
Painter	0.95	—	—	17.52	16.64
Second Coat					
0.19 gal. paint		—	—	17.75	3.37
Painter	0.85	—	—	17.52	14.89
Cost 100 sq. ft..................................	1.80		—		$39.17

Cost of 100 Sq. Ft. (1 Sq.) 3-Coat House Paint
Applied to Plain Wood Siding and Trim

	Hours	Rate	Total	Rate	Total
Priming Coat					
0.24 gal. paint		—	—	$17.75	$ 4.26
Painter	0.95	—	—	17.52	16.64
Second Coat					
0.19 gal. paint		—	—	17.75	3.27
Painter	0.85	—	—	17.52	14.89
Third Coat					
0.17 gal. paint		—	—	17.75	3.02
Painter	0.75	—	—	17.52	13.14
Cost 100 sq. ft..................................	2.55		—		$55.33

Paint costs vary according to quality used, color and local material prices. Add for surface preparation.

Cost of 100 Sq. Ft. (1 Sq.) 3-Coat House Paint
Applied to Exterior Trim Only

	Hours	Rate	Total	Rate	Total
Priming Coat					
0.13 gal. paint		—	—	$18.77	$ 2.44
Painter	1.40	—	—	17.52	24.53
Second Coat					
0.12 gal. paint		—	—	18.77	2.25
Painter	1.12	—	—	17.52	19.62
Cost 100 sq. ft..................................	2.52		—		$48.84

Cost of 100 Sq. Ft. (1 Sq.) 3-Coat House Paint
Applied to Exterior Trim Only

	Hours	Rate	Total	Rate	Total
Priming Coat					
0.13 gal. paint		—	—	$18.77	$ 2.44
Painter	1.40	—	—	17.52	24.53
Second Coat					
0.12 gal. paint		—	—	18.77	2.25
Painter	1.12	—	—	17.52	19.62
Third Coat					
0.11 gal. paint		—	—	18.77	2.06
Painter	1.00	—	—	17.52	17.52
Cost 100 sq. ft..................................	3.52		—		$68.43

Cost of Applying 1-Coat House Paint to One Average
Wood Half-Screen (Screen Wire Not Painted)

	Hours	Rate	Total	Rate	Total
0.02 gal. paint		—	—	$17.75	$ 0.36
Painter	0.14	—	—	17.52	2.45
Cost per screen	0.14	—	—		$ 2.81

Cost of Apply 1-Coat House Paint to One Average
Wood 2-Lt Storm Sash

	Hours	Rate	Total	Rate	Total
0.04 gal. paint		—	—	$17.75	$ 0.71
Painter	0.29	—	—	17.52	5.08
Cost per storm sash	0.29	—	—		$ 5.79

For each additional cost, add same as above.

**Paint costs vary according to quality used, color and local material
prices. Add for surface preparation.**

Cost of 100 Sq. Ft. (1 Sq.) 2-Coat House Paint Applied
to Old Wood Surfaces in Good Condition

	Hours	Rate	Total	Rate	Total
First Coat					
0.19 gal. paint		—	—	$17.75	$ 3.27
Painter	1.0	—	—	17.52	17.52
Second Coat					
0.17 gal. paint		—	—	17.75	3.02
Painter	0.8	—	—	17.52	14.02
Cost 100 sq. ft..	1.8	—	—		$37.93

Cost of 100 Sq. Ft. (1 Sq.) 1-Coat Oil Paint
Applied to Brick or Smooth Concrete Surfaces

	Hours	Rate	Total	Rate	Total
0.54 gal. paint		—	—	$18.77	$10.14
Painter	0.93	—	—	17.52	16.29
Cost 100 sq. ft..	0.93	—	—		$26.43

Cost of 100 Sq. Ft. (1 Sq.) 1-Coat Oil Paint
Applied to Rough Plaster or Stucco Surfaces

	Hours	Rate	Total	Rate	Total
0.67 gal. paint		—	—	$17.75	$11.89
Painter	1.1	—	—	17.52	19.27
Cost 100 sq. ft..	1.1	—	—		$31.16

Labor and Materials Required for Various Painting Operations

Exterior Work—Residential Description of Work	Painter No. Sq. Ft. per Hr.	Painter Hours 100 Sq. Ft.	Material Coverage Sq. Ft. per Gal.
Sanding and Puttying Plain Siding and Trim	200-210	0.50	
Sanding and Puttying Outside Trim Only	115-120	0.86	
Burning Paint off Plain Surfaces	40-50	2.20	
Burning Paint off Wood Siding	30-40	2.85	
Exterior Brush Painting Plain Siding And Trim — Priming Coat	100-110	0.95	400-450
Second Coat	115-125	0.85	500-550
Third Coat	125-135	0.75	575-625
Exterior House Painting Rubberized Woodbond — One Coat	125-135	0.75	450-500
Exterior Trim Only — Priming Coat	65-75	1.40	750-850
Second Coat	85-95	1.12	800-900
Third Coat	95-105	1.00	900-1,000
Oil Paint—Shingle Siding* — First Coat	115-125	0.82	250-300
Second Coat	150-160	0.65	375-425
Oil Paint—Shingle Roofs* — First Coat	100-120	0.90	120-150
Second Coat	155-175	0.60	220-250
Stain—Shingle Siding* — First Coat	75-85	1.20	120-150
Second Coat	115-130	0.82	200-225
Stain—Shingle Roofs* — First Coat	145-155	0.67	100-120
Second Coat	190-210	0.50	170-200
*If surfaces are exceptionally dry, increase labor hours and decrease covering capacity.			
Asbestos Wall Shingles — First Coat	60-70	1.50	150-180
Second Coat	85-95	1.11	350-400
Brick Walls, Oil Paint — First Coat	100-120	0.93	170-200
Second Coat	140-160	0.67	350-400
Third Coat	155-175	0.60	375-425
Porch Floors and Steps, Oil Paint — First Coat	235-245	0.42	325-375
Second Coat	270-280	0.36	475-525
Third Coat	285-295	0.35	525-575

Labor and Materials Required for Various Painting Operations—Con't.

Exterior Work—Residential Description of Work	Painter No. Sq. Ft. per Hr.	Painter Hours 100 Sq. Ft.	Material Coverage Sq. Ft. per Gal.
Waterproof Cement Paint—Smooth Face Brick..........First Coat	175-185	0.55	90-110
Second Coat	260-270	0.38	140-160
Clear Waterproof Paint—Smooth Face Brick..........First Coat	200-210	0.50	500-510
Second Coat	200-210	0.50	590-610
Stucco, Medium Texture, Oil Paint..........First Coat	90-100	1.10	140-160
Second Coat	150-160	0.65	340-360
Third Coat	150-160	0.65	340-360
Stucco, Medium Texture, Wpf. Cement Paint..........First Coat	130-140	0.74	90-110
Second Coat	190-210	0.50	125-145
Exterior Masonry, Stucco, Asbestos Cement Board and Shingle Siding— Rubberized Flat Finish..........First Coat	100-120	0.91	325-375
Second Coat	165-175	0.59	375-425
Concrete Walls, Smooth, Wpf. Cement Paint..........First Coat	170-180	0.57	110-130
Second Coat	275-285	0.36	150-170
Concrete Floors and Steps—Floor Enamel..........First Coat	250-280	0.38	440-460
Second Coat	190-210	0.50	575-625
Third Coat	200-220	0.48	575-625
Cement Floors—Color Stain and Finish..........First Coat	350-370	0.28	475-525
Second Coat	280-300	0.35	450-500
Fences, Plain, Average..........First Coat	125-135	0.77	450-470
Second Coat	190-200	0.51	530-550
Fences, Picket, Average..........First Coat	140-150	0.70	630-650
Second Coat	160-170	0.60	650-675
Fences, Wire-Metal, Average..........First Coat	100-110	0.95	900-1,000
Second Coat	140-150	0.70	975-1,125
Shutters, Average, Each Coat..........No. of Shutters	2-3	0.40	11-13
Downspouts and Gutters, Paint..........First Coat	170-180	0.57	540-560
Second Coat	185-195	0.53	575-600
Screens, Wood Only, Average, Each Coat..........No. of Screens	6-8	0.14	45-55
Storm Sash, 2 Light, Average, Each Coat..........No. of Sash	3-4	0.29	23-27

Spray Painting—Residential Work

Description of Work	Painter No. Sq. Ft. per Hr.	Painter Hours 100 Sq. Ft.	Material Coverage Sq. Ft. per Gal.
Brick, Tile and Cement—Cement Water Paint ... First Coat	265-275	0.37	90-110
Second Coat	325-350	0.30	140-160
Brick, Tile and Cement—Oil Paint ... First Coat	240-260	0.40	250-275
Second Coat	240-260	0.40	400-450
Brick, Tile and Cement—Synthetic Resin Bound Exterior Paint ... First Coat	275-290	0.36	125-150
Second Coat	335-360	0.30	175-200
Rough Brick, Tile, Cement and Stucco*—Plastic Paint ... One Coat	265-275	0.37	65-75
Asbestos Wall Shingles* ... First Coat	100-110	1.00	150-175
Second Coat	150-175	0.60	225-250
Stucco*—Exterior Cement Water Paint or Synthetic Resin Bound Exterior Paint ... First Coat	200-225	0.47	90-100
Second Coat	265-285	0.37	125-150
Stucco*—Oil Paint ... First Coat	160-175	0.60	200-225
Second Coat	225-240	0.43	350-400
Shingle Roofs—Oil Paint ... First Coat	260-275	0.37	125-150
Second Coat	260-275	0.37	200-225
Shingle Roofs—Stain ... First Coat	275-300	0.35	125-150
Second Coat	275-300	0.35	200-225
Shingle Siding*—Oil Paint ... First Coat	160-175	0.60	125-150
Second Coat	175-200	0.55	225-250
Shingle Siding*—Stain ... First Coat	175-200	0.55	125-150
Second Coat	190-215	0.50	200-225

*Trim Must be Figured Separately as Hand Work

CHAPTER 14

WINDOWS AND DOORS

Energy efficiency is now coming in for its share of consideration when it comes to selecting windows and doors.

For the remodeling contractor this means selecting windows and doors by giving as much weight to energy efficiency as esthetics.

Windows in particular have been labeled the villain in residential energy losses.

However, manufacturers of windows and doors, recognizing this shortcoming, have upgraded the designs of their products to make them more energy efficient. Today there is a wide selection of energy efficient designs to fit traditional and contemporary decor for the contractor from which to select.

Energy loss through windows takes place in three ways: Infiltration, conduction and radiation. Radiation is not as serious as infiltration and conduction, since it works in two directions. Thus in winter there can be a desirable heat gain which exceeds the window's conduction loss. If radiation is still a problem, reflective film or tinted glass are good solutions. Having a window which can open or close is another.

Frequently, infiltration and conduction can be corrected simply by installing storm windows or weatherstripping. If the infiltration is really bad, replacement is the best answer.

Adding another layer of glass will reduce the conduction loss by 50 percent. A storm window added to an existing window with insulating glass will reduce conduction by 30 percent. If the existing windows must be replaced and there are no storm windows, thermalized replacement windows with double or triple insulating glass are an excellent solution.

As a result of the demand for energy conservation, double glazed units now account for over 60% of residential window sales, triple glazed over 20% and single glazed with storm windows 18-20%.

Window styles vary by geographical area. In the West, horizontal sliding windows are favored. In the Northeast, North Central and South, builders favor casement and double-hung windows. Single-hung windows are concentrated mainly in the deep South.

In window specifying, the width is always given first; then the height, then the number of pieces of glass (called lights); then the window style. For example: 28½ x 24", 2 Lts., DH means the window glass is 28½" wide, 24" high, there are two pieces of glass and the window is a double-hung unit.

COMMON WINDOW STYLES

Window style and size should take into account several things. Although in most cases window height is a standard 6'8", the same as door height, sill height will vary with the style and size of the window. A rule-of-thumb is 1' in living and family rooms, 2'6" for dining rooms and 3'6" for kitchens. Exterior viewing should be convenient whether a person is standing or sitting.

How many windows should a room have? As a rule the glass area of a room should be no less that 10% of the floor area. And, at least 4% of the same floor area should be devoted to windows that open and close for ventilation. There should also be a balance between fixed and operating windows.

How easy is it to clean? If it is to open and close, how is it for ventilation? Today, all of these requirements can be satisfied, depending on the manufacturer and how much money the householder wishes to spend.

When it comes to replacement, however, the news is good. In most cases, homeowners have done a 180 degree turn when they replace their windows. They want, if not the best, a window of considerably higher quality than what they presently have. Consequently, it is usually wise to recommend the best quality window and work down.

Authorities also suggest that the replacement of windows and doors is an undersold portion of the remodeling market. Siding jobs are the perfect opportunity to suggest a new entry door and windows. Not only do you increase your own profitability, you do a service to your client by giving them a chance to upgrade the appearance of their home which is probably what they wanted in the first place. Simply changing old windows for new ones cannot only give an old home a new look, by careful selection, it can give it a new architectural style without extensive changes.

Today, the trend is to use stock windows or "standards". Although "custom" windows are still made, in a cost conscious economy they are generally impractical.

However, some manufacturers do make what is called a "standard special". These windows are generally designed for a particular marketing area or housing development. For example: Say a tract builder developed an area containing 500 homes 15-20 years ago. Usually these are in large metropolitan areas. Some manufacturers recognizing the need for replacement windows in these developments have developed special stock windows designed for a particular development. Often, they are not listed in the catalog. If a contractor is bidding a job in a large, older development, and windows are involved, a query to his window supplier might show they have a special stock window for that particular development.

Thanks to the versatility of standards, as well as the variety of styles, most stock windows can be made to fit openings in older buildings through the use of accessories offered by many manufacturers.

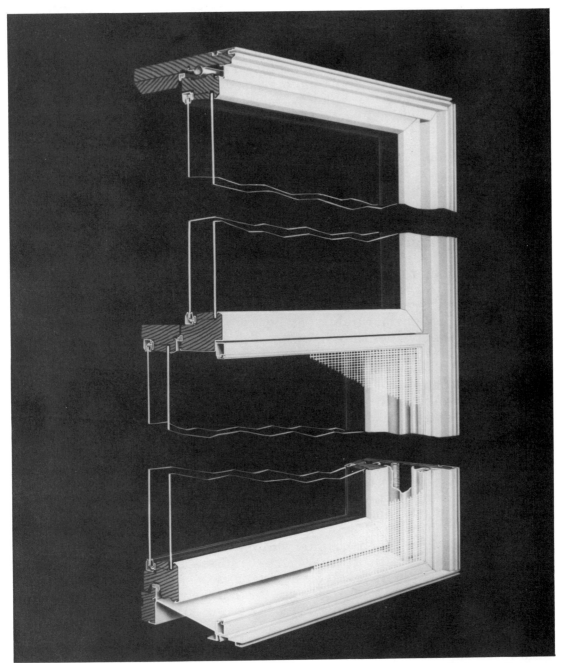

Courtesy Rolscreen Company

This cutaway of the Pella Traditional Double-Hung window shows wood construction, low maintenance aluminum exterior, double glazing, vinyl-wrapped foam weatherstripping, spring-loaded vinyl jamb liners and fiberglass screen.

Frame extenders of different widths adapt stock windows to a wide range of wall thicknesses, standard and odd size. Exterior vinyl and metal casings not only simplify installation but help seal a home against energy loss. Sill nose covers, jamb clips, and metal drip caps all contribute to the ease of installation and help make stock windows energy efficient and adaptable to most existing window openings.

WINDOW TYPES

Double Hung Windows. Double hung windows (verticle sliding) are still among the most familiar and popular. Each has two sashes which slide up and down vertically. The sashes are provided with springs, balances or compression weather stripping which help hold it in place in any location. A number of manufacturers offer windows in which the sash can be easily removed for cleaning, or painting. They can be grouped in a number of ways, double with mullion in-between, triple with a fixed window in the middle or even up to five to create a window wall. Many come with snap-in wood muntins to create a Colonial or Cape Code effect. Patterns include horizontal bars, divided lights or diamond lights. They have several limitations. Only half of the window can be open at one time for ventilation. If they are not removable, they're difficult to clean. Located over a sink or counter, they're not easy to open.

Casement Windows. Casement windows (side-hinged) swing out horizontally, generally with a crank. Utilizing a storm window or insulated glass, they're extremely energy efficient. Screens are located on the inside of outside swinging windows. They are generally factory assembled and come with all hardware in place. Their biggest advantage is that the entire window can be open for ventilation. Another is that they can be cleaned from the inside, unless the hinges are set so as to prevent access to the outside glass. Equally important, a casement window, by design, will be tighter than a double-hung window.

Horizontal Sliding. In horizontal sliding windows the sash moves sideways in metal or plastic tracks. Such windows can also be grouped if desired. If the sash is removable, they're easy to clean. Like their double-hung counterpart, only half of the window can be used for ventilation and they are not always easy to clean.

Awning Windows, and Hopper Windows. If a window is top-hinged it's called an awning window, bottom hinged a hopper window. Both can have one sash operable and one fixed, or both operable. The awning window swings out, while the hopper window swings in. Both have an upward airflow. Open outward, the awning type will direct air upward; however, if

SIZE SELECTION

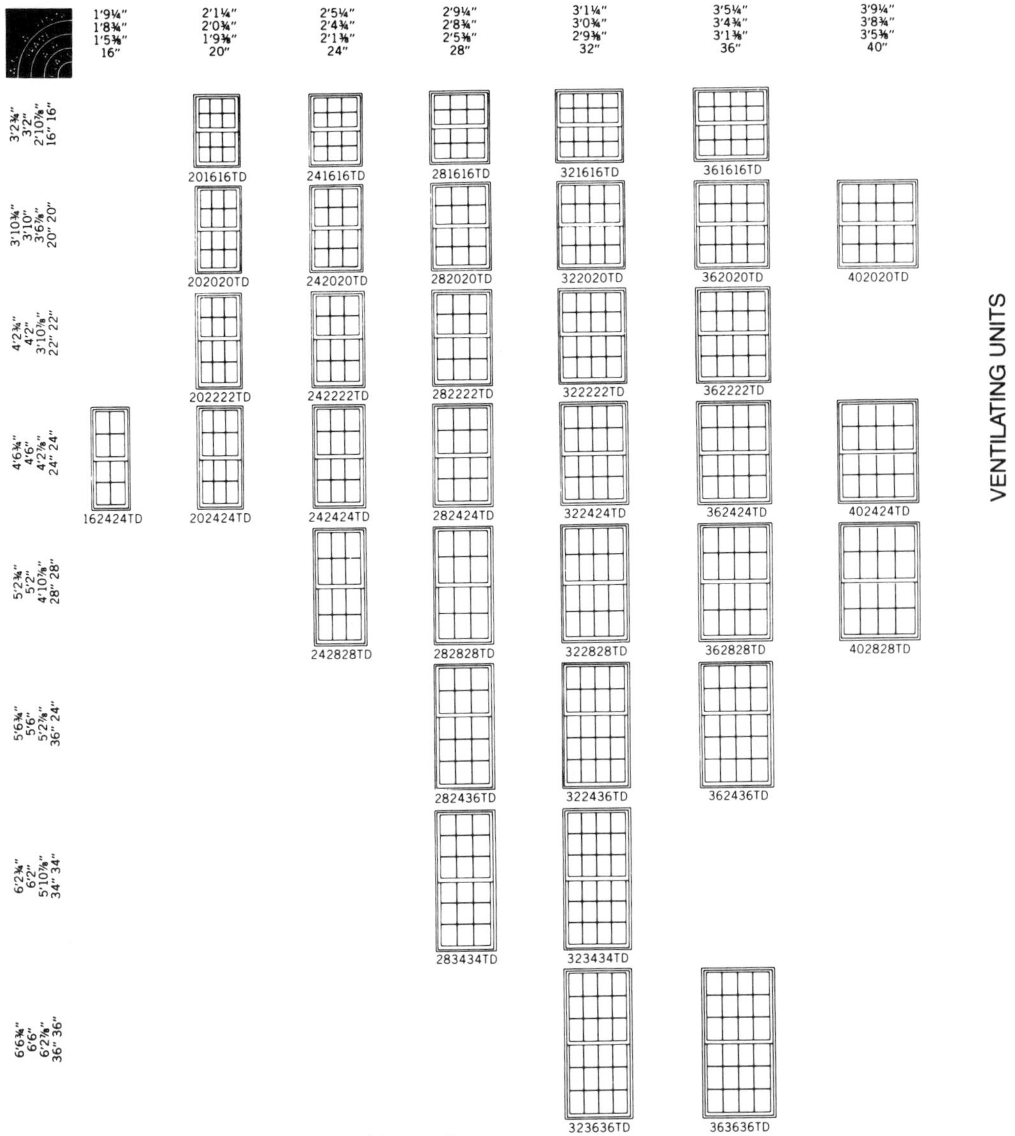
1'9¼" 1'8¾" 1'5⅜" 16"
2'1¼" 2'0¾" 1'9⅜" 20"
2'5¼" 2'4¾" 2'1⅜" 24"
2'9¼" 2'8¾" 2'5⅜" 28"
3'1¼" 3'0¾" 2'9⅜" 32"
3'5¼" 3'4¾" 3'1⅜" 36"
3'9¼" 3'8¾" 3'5⅜" 40"
3'2¾" 3'2" 2'10⅞" 16" 16"
3'10¾" 3'10" 3'6⅞" 20" 20"
4'2¾" 4'2" 3'10⅞" 22" 22"
4'6¾" 4'6" 4'2⅞" 24" 24"
5'2¾" 5'2" 4'10⅞" 28" 28"
5'6¾" 5'6" 5'2⅞" 36" 24"
6'2¾" 6'2" 5'10⅞" 34" 34"
6'6¾" 6'6" 6'2⅞" 36" 36"
201616TD
241616TD
281616TD
321616TD
361616TD
202020TD
242020TD
282020TD
322020TD
362020TD
402020TD
202222TD
242222TD
282222TD
322222TD
362222TD
162424TD
202424TD
242424TD
282424TD
322424TD
362424TD
402424TD
242828TD
282828TD
322828TD
362828TD
402828TD
282436TD
322436TD
362436TD
283434TD
323434TD
323636TD
363636TD
VENTILATING UNITS

All specifications subject to change without notice.

Courtesy Rolscreen Company

Pella's new energy-efficient double-glass insulation system.

it opens inward it will direct the air downward. The hopper window which only opens inward directs the airflow upward. The awning type is operated with a push-bar or crank, while the hopper generally has a simple lock handle at the top. Both windows can be grouped and easily cleaned from the inside unless the hinges interfere with arm-room. Bottom hinged windows are generally located low in the wall and therefore are not considered viewing windows.

Jalousie Windows. Jalousie windows consist of series of horizontal clear or opaque glass slats which usually open outwards with a crank. Because of their low insulating value, in colder climates they require a full storm window. They have good ventilation characteristics and cleaning can easily be done from the inside.

Fixed Windows. Fixed windows do not open. Consequently, they do not require screens or hardware, nor do they provide ventilation. Since they can be made as big as 6' or 8' across, they are excellent for viewing and provide a lot of light. Cleaning, however, necessitates a trip outside. They are frequently used in combination with a double-hung window on each side. Usually they consist of single light of insulated glass or double glazed in a wood sash.

They can, however, be installed without sash by simply setting the glass into rabbeted frame members and held in place with stops. Double-hung and casement windows also come with metal sash made of aluminum or steel. However, they're cold in the winter and radiate heat in the summer. They also sweat, causing the paint to peel, necessitating considerable upkeep. Steel sash should be treated to make it rust resistant. Installation varies according to the manufacturer.

Glass blocks are another type of fixed window commonly used in bathrooms and basements. They come in both light-diffusing and light-directing styles. All are 3-7/8" thick and have face sizes of 6"x6", 8"x8" and 12"x12". Blocks add privacy and cut off unpleasant views, reduce disturbing noises and can accent decorative schemes. Regular masonry tools are used for installation.

REMODELING USING STANDARD WINDOWS

In replacement windows the basic rules of good construction apply. Usually, one dimension will "be on the money". However, if it isn't, there are many accessories to make standard windows fit odd-size openings. Frame expanders and expander receptors make it possible to adapt standard windows to fit different wall thicknesses. Metal jamb fastening clips and rigid vinyl auxilliary casing can also be used to expedite installation. Odd-shaped openings can be blocked with 2 x 4s. Nailing trimmer studs at one or both sides will frequently shorten the width of a rough opening to size.

Today, windows are being looked upon as an adjunct to air conditioning. People want windows that open and close, as much as they want light and a view. Cleaning, accessibility and ease of opening and closing are also points to consider when replacing windows. So too, is noise.

Obviously, windows are no longer a simple consideration. Remodeling contractors who want a first class job should contact a window manufacturer. Many employ architects or architectural representatives. Not only will they assist in selecting type and style, they can help with any structural or installation problems.

WINDOW REMOVAL

Removing Sash and Frame.   *Single, Double Hung Window.* Where frame removal is not required or desirable, removing only the sash will minimize the cost of replacement. All that is required is remove the stops, cut sash cords, remove parting strip and cord pulleys. Wire brush opening and remove any storm window hardware. Allow 30 minutes per window. *Removing Complete Frame.* If the complete frame is removed, add 30 minutes to the preceding.

Closing Old Window Openings.   Place 2 x 4 studs 16 inches on center aligning with existing studs under window. Toenail to old header and sill using eight or tenpenny nails. Install sheathing and insulation and apply vapor barrier to inside face (warm side) of framing being sure to overlap any existing vapor barrier. Figure one man can enclose 20 sq. ft. of wallspace per hour at the following cost per sq. ft.:

	Hours	Rate	Total	Rate	Total
Carpenter	1	—	—	$20.60	$20.60
Cost per sq. ft.:			—		1.03

For finishing off interior and exterior wall surfaces, see Chapters 7 and 8 for interiors and Chapter 13 for exteriors.

INSTALLING REPLACEMENT WINDOWS

Without Reframing.   Where blocking is required, the blocking is secured to the frame using 16d nails. Be sure blocking is level and plumb. Standard window installation clips are used to set the window through opening. Insulate around all sides. Install new stops and interior trim. Caulk and install exterior trim. Allow 1.5 hrs. for one carpenter to complete the preceeding. If opening and closing hardware are required, add 15 minutes per window to the preceeding.

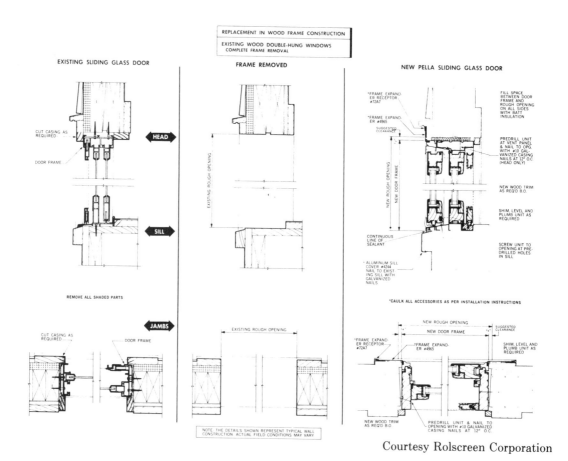

Courtesy Rolscreen Corporation

Raising Sill Height. In older windows sometimes the jamb dimensions are such that the width of a standard replacement window will fit, but the height is too short, The opening can be resized by removing the old apron, stool and sill. Measure down from the top of the window opening equal to the new window height and install a rough sill and cripple studs to the required height. A new subsill is installed on the rough sill and the replacement window installed using standard installation technique.

Allow one carpenter about 2 hrs. to complete such an installation.

Complete Reframing. Window suppliers generally have tables from various manufacturers showing individual glass, sash and rough opening size. However, window sizes vary from manufacturer to manufacturer.

When the manufacturer is known, it is best to follow their recommendations. Otherwise additional blocking and/or shimming may be required.

If the manufacturer isn't known, rough openings can be figured as follows: For a single, double-hung window add 6 inches to the total glass width for the rough opening width and 10 inches to the total glass height for rough opening height. For double-sash casement windows add 11¼ inches to the total glass width and 6⅜ inches to the total glass height.

For combination windows figure the total width of the multiple opening by adding the width of the individual sash opening to the width of the mullions plus 2 inches for the overall rough opening.

However, a window manufacturer or distributor should be consulted before any window replacement is bid regardless of the kind of opening to be filled.

Where the desired opening is larger than the existing opening, complete reframing is generally necessary. If the wall is load-bearing, the opening will require temporary support and a new header (3½ feet or more). To eliminate inside patching on one side of the new opening, one side should be positioned 1½ inches from an existing stud. Corners should be avoided and enough room allowed for trim. The position for new studs can be determined by adding the frame width of the new window plus 3½ inches.

The new header is installed, supported by jack studs nailed to the existing studs. Header length should be new window frame plus width dimension plus 3½ inches. The opening is finished off to height size by installing a new rough sill on cripple studs as described previously. One carpenter should be able to reframe 20 sq. ft. per hour at the following cost per sq. ft.:

	Hours	Rate	Total	Rate	Total
Carpenter	1	—	—	$20.60	$20.60
Cost per sq. ft.			—		1.03

Although header size will vary, the following can be used for estimating.

Span (Feet)	Header (Inches)
3½	2, 2x6s
5	2, 2x8s
6½	2, 2x10s
8	2, 2x12s

Most replacement windows are factory assembled and ready for installation. The general procedure is the same regardless of style or manufacturer. However, it is important that the manufacturer's procedure be checked for any specific instruction. For example, one might suggest removing the sash from the frame, Another, may recommend that sash, frame and bracing be installed as a unit before cross-bracing is removed. When siding is applied over sheathing, the window is installed first and then the siding reapplied.

Strips of 15 lb. asphalt felt should be slid between the sheathing and siding around the opening, if the siding is horizontal. If the casing does not have built-in caulking, a bead of caulking should be placed over the siding behind the head and side casing.

Generally, the frame and sash are inserted as a unit, squared and shimmed, if necessary, then nailed in place with tenpenny nails. Double-hung windows should be checked for operation while nailing to be sure the sash works freely.

It's customary when installing a window over a panel siding to run a bead of caulk at the junction of the siding and sill and install quarter-round over the caulking. Figure one carpenter can complete the above installation in 2 hrs. time. However, if the window is on the second story, double the installation time. For larger windows or difficult locations figure 2 men, thus doubling the installation time.

Labor To Install Windows

	Average Conditions
Replace windows and frame existing opening:	
Frame building	4 hrs.
Masonry building	6 "
Replace sash only (per pair)	2 "
For one sash	2 "
Picture window	12 "
Install mullion window and frame opening	8 "
Frame new opening:	
Single	4 "
Mullion	6 "
Windows with liners, masonry frame, add	2 "
Trim interior, any window, add	2 "

Double Hung Window and Frame Prices*

(One lite, top and bottom/glazed single strength)

For Frame or Masonry

24x24x 1⅜"	$65.00
26x26x 1⅜"	75.00
28x28x 1⅜"	78.00
30x34x 1⅜"	95.00
32x16x 1⅜"	60.00
32x32x 1⅜"	90.00
32x34x 1⅜"	95.00
For divided sash, add per lite	$ 2.50
For removable sash, add	10.00
For 1¾" sash, add	100%
For R.E. interior trim, add	15.00
For window for 12" mason wall, add for liners	15.00
For colonial or hardwood trim, add	15.00

*Above prices are a composite and do not reflect any specific manufacturer

DOORS/EXTERIOR

Doors are equally as guilty as windows when it comes to contributing to energy loss, particulary infiltration. Like windows, manufacturers have already begun to address themselves to the problem. As a result the remodeling contractor has a variety of energy efficient doors to choose from. Made from either wood or metal, they are available in several styles in a wide variety of designs and patterns.

When it comes to insulation efficiency, steel clad doors seem to have the edge. R-values in the 15 plus range are not uncommon. These are achieved by using polyurethane foam and honeycomb cells as the core.

Other features include adjustable thresholds, various types of factory installed weatherstripping and strike plates which can withstand impacts of up to 500 lbs., lessening the chance of breaking and entering.

Steel adapter frames which fit into existing frames also add to the security. Special thresholds also prevent frost buildup. Thermal breaks or barriers divide the outside from the inside of the door eliminating the possibility of any frost or condensation on the inside face of the door.

Factory finishing helps to keep maintenance costs down, and being metal, all are guaranteed to never warp, crack, shrink or swell. Metal doors also have excellent fire ratings, up to 1½ hour B.

Although most wood doors do not have the high R-values of insulated metal, advances in wood technology have given them new stability, and problems of distortion are not as great as they once were.

Flush Doors. Wood flush doors are made with plywood or other wood type facing applied over a frame. The core can be hollow or solid. Solid cores are generally woodblock or particle board. Solid core doors are preferred for exterior doors because their construction minimizes warping and distortion.

Metal flush doors are generally made from steel facing with the core being filled with polyurethane and some type of honeycomb for insulation.

Panel Doors. Panel doors also come in wood and metal. Wood panel doors have solid vertical members called stiles, solid cross members called rails and thin strips which divide the stiles and rails into panels. In addition to the flush style, metal doors also come in embossed designs. Both types come with glass panels.

Glazed Doors. Glazed doors are usually french doors. The rails and stiles are divided into lights by muntins. They are frequently used as patio, porch or terrace doors. They can be hung in a variety of ways, such as singly or in pairs. Snap-in muntins can be added to create a traditional appearance and provide ease of maintenance.

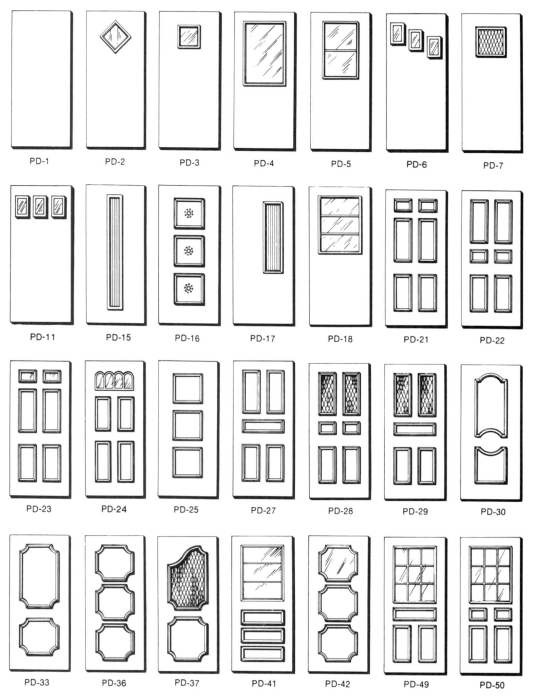

PD-1 PD-2 PD-3 PD-4 PD-5 PD-6 PD-7

PD-11 PD-15 PD-16 PD-17 PD-18 PD-21 PD-22

PD-23 PD-24 PD-25 PD-27 PD-28 PD-29 PD-30

PD-33 PD-36 PD-37 PD-41 PD-42 PD-49 PD-50

Courtesy Perma-Door by American Standard

Perma-Door steel doors with deeply drawn galvanized panels, inside and out.

Exterior doors are 1¾" thick and 6'8" high. The recommended size for entrance or front doors is 3' wide, while side or rear doors can be 2' 8" wide to 3' wide. Jambs can be wood or metal. Although wood has been the traditional material, steel and aluminum have been gaining in popularity. Jamb widths vary according to the material and the kind of wall into which they will be set. Wood jambs are usually 5¼" for lath and plaster and 4½" for drywall. However, they can be easily cut down or expanded to fit most openings. Stock metal jambs are manufactured in variety of widths and recommended for specific applications. Standard widths are made for lath and plaster, concrete block, brick veneer and drywall. These are 4¾", 5¾", 6¾" and 8¾". Drywall, however, is sized differently. Common widths of metal jambs available for this application are 5½" and 5⅝".

Although most sills are made of oak, when softer woods are used, the assembly should include a metal nosing and wear plate.

Removing Old Doors.   A clean rough opening is mandatory if a new door is to function properly. After removing the old door from hinges, remove inside casing and outside brickmold. Side jambs are generally removed by cutting in half and prying away from studs. If nails are too long, either cut with hacksaw or drive flush and sink. Pry off head jamb and sill. Check sub-floor to be sure it is level and flush. If not, it must be filled in. Plumb opening to be sure it will accept new unit.

Figure one carpenter can accomplish the preceding allowing 1.5 hours per door. For cleanup and removal, add 20 minutes.

INSTALLING NEW DOORS

Relocating Doors.   It may be desirable to move a door to a new location. Openings are closed by installing 2 x 4 vertical studs spaced no more than 16" apart, preferably placing them in line with existing studs. Toenail new studs to old door header and to the floor using three eightpenny or tenpenny nails at top and bottom. Replace sheathing using same material or material of similar composition and thickness. Add insulation and apply a vapor barrier over the inside face of the framing. (Warm side of wall). Be sure the vapor barrier covers the rough framing and overlaps any existing barrier already installed. Figure one carpenter can complete the preceding in 4 hours at the following cost per opening.

	Hours	Rate	Total	Rate	Total
Carpenter	4	—	—	$20.60	$82.40

To finish off interior and exterior walls, see Chapters 7, 8 and 13.

CUTTING NEW OPENINGS

Rough Framing. If the opening is new or not square, it will probably have to be rough-framed with a header and "cripple or door buck studs". The rough opening should be approximately 2" to 2¼" higher and 2½" to 3" wider than the door to be installed. For the header, double 2 x 6's are nailed to the studs on each side of the opening. "Door buck" studs are nailed on each side of the opening with twelvepenny nails, spaced about 16" apart and staggered. The sill should rest on the floor framing, which in most cases must be cut out to a depth which will place sill even with the top of the finished floor. After the sheathing and paneling have been placed over the framing, leaving only the rough opening, the door frame is ready for installation.

A carpenter should be able to rough-frame a standard 3' x 6'8" door including the necessary cutouts in 3 hours at the following cost per door opening:

	Hours	Rate	Total	Rate	Total
Carpenter..	3	—	—	$20.60	$61.80

Installing Doorframe. Apply a bead of caulk on both sides and top of cutout or install 15 pound asphalt felt. Tip frame into place and brace, using wood shingles as wedges. Square up until true and plumb. Place nails ¾" in from outer edge 16" on center and set with nail set. Nail casing to the front edge of jamb with 10d casing nails spaced 16" on center. Figure one carpenter can install a conventional exterior frame and casing with oak sill in approximately two hours.

	Hours	Rate	Total	Rate	Total
Carpenter..	2	—	—	$20.60	$41.20

Hanging The Door. After determining the hand of the door, mark both door edges and corresponding jambs accordingly. To operate easily, the door should conform to the shape of the finished opening, less 1/16" clearance at the sides and top. If there is no threshold, bottom clearance should be 1/16". With Threshold, 1/8" bottom clearance above the threshold, Check the jambs for trueness and transfer any irregularities to the door. Any trimming to reduce the door width should be done on the hinge side. Bevel the lock edge so that it will clear the door when it is closed. Exterior doors, unless otherwise specified, are hung with three hinges. The top of the top hinge is installed 7" from the top of the door. The bottom of the bottom hinge is installed 11" from the bottom of the door. The center hinge is centered between the bottom of the top hinge and the top of the bottom hinge. Both the door and jambs are mortised for setting the hinges. The hinges most commonly used are 3½" or 4" loose-pin butt mortise hinges.

Since most doors come already cut out for hardware, all that remains is to install the lock-set and striker on the door jamb. Figure one carpenter can size the door, install the hinges and lockset, including strike plate in about 1.5 hours.

	Hours	Rate	Total	Rate	Total
Carpenter	1.5	—	—	$20.60	$30.90

Weatherstripping.   Today, all doors and windows should be weather-stripped regardless of climate. This includes new units as well as old. Some metal clad doors feature a magnetic weatherstrip which seals much like a refrigerator. The most accepted procedure is to caulk around the frame or jamb using latex caulking compound and applying a ¼ " bead. Figure a carpenter can caulk 200 lin. ft. per hour at the following cost per linear ft.:

	Hours	Rate	Total	Rate	Total
Carpenter	1	—	—	$20.60	$20.60
Cost per lin. ft.					.10

Storm Doors.   Energy costs being what they are, so-called "storm doors" are as practical in warm climates as they are in cold. A combination storm and screen door requires approximately 1.5 hours for installation.

	Hours	Rate	Total	Rate	Total
Carpenter	1.5	—	—	$20.60	$30.90

Sliding Glass Doors.   There are many types of sliding glass doors including metal, wood and metal-covered-wood called metal clad with a factory applied finish. In addition to there being a style to fit almost any type of architecture, today's sliding glass doors are specifically designed to save energy.

Most are manufactured in frame sizes to fit existing openings and consequently are ideal for remodeling. Furthermore, they are specifically designed to replace thermally inefficient aluminum sliding glass doors. Options such as double glazing and tinted glass provide additional energy savings. They also come with one, two and three side lights.

If space allows for hinged swinging doors, a new popular replacement for sliding doors is an atrium or concept door. These doors fit the same opening, but one panel is hinged rather than sliding. The seal is much tighter and to some extent, they also provide better security.

Removing Old Doors.   Since most new frames are sized to take advantage of the existing rough opening, it's best to remove the entire frame. After lifting out the screen, remove any existing trim on the outside. The oper-

Courtesy Rolscreen Company

The installation of Pella Sliding Glass Doors helped transform what was once a screened patio into this year round living space.

ating panel is moved to the middle of the frame, raised and pulled out of the track. Stationary panels are detached by removing the holding plates, then moved to the center and lifted out in the same manner as the operating panel. The frame is generally held in place with screws or by a holding flange underneath the siding. Sometimes a power saw is required to cut the flange after the frame has been removed. Clean the rough opening and check for plumb, level and square. Check rough opening dimensions. Figure one man can complete the preceding steps in 2 hours.

	Hours	Rate	Total	Rate	Total
Carpenter..	2	—	—	$20.60	$41.20

If the existing rough sill requires replacement in order to provide continuous sill support for the new door, add 1 hr. to the above.

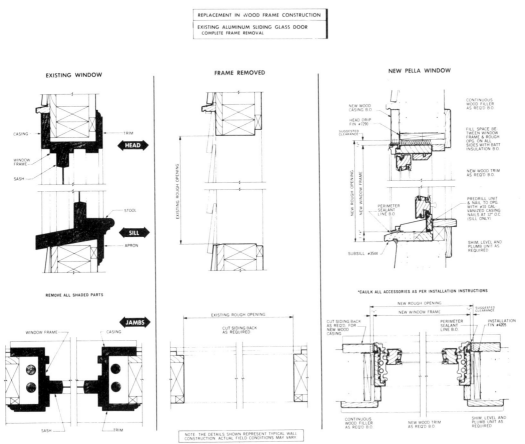

Courtesy Rolscreen Corporation

Labor To Install Doors

	Average Conditions
Inside door and jamb	½ day
Exterior door and frame	½ "
Trim door	¼ "
Cut-out for window:	
Masonry wall	1½ "
Frame wall	½ "
Perfatape wall, interior	¼ "
Pocket doors (pair)	½ "
Replace interior door in existing frame	½ "

Electronic door openers take little over 2 hours to install:

	Hours	Rate	Total	Rate	Total
Electrician	2.25	—	—	$20.60	$46.35

Material Prices

Jambs and Frames (A-Grade) White Pine
Interior jambs (32" headers)
Clear/drywall (for staining) ....$16.95 each
Clear/plaster (for staining) .... 17.95 each
"B"/drywall (for painting) .... 9.95 each
"B"/plaster (for painting) .... 11.95 each

Exterior frames
With oak sill (36" header) .... 37.95 each
Without sill (36" header) .... 26.95 each
Oak Sills
32".. 10.55 each
36".. 10.95 each
Sliding door... 46.95 each

Flush Doors (1-⅜" Hollow Core)

Size	Lauan	Birch
24" x 80"	$18.22	$22.55
26" x 80"	19.22	23.55
28" x 80"	19.22	23.55
30" x 80"	19.22	23.55
32" x 80"	20.55	24.95
36" x 80"	21.95	26.55

Exterior (1-¾")

Size	Lauan		Birch	
	Hollow	Solid	Hollow	Solid
30" x 80"	$21.95	$36.95	$28.95	$44.95
32" x 80"	23.95	37.95	29.95	45.95
36" x 80"	23.95	38.95	31.95	47.95

Pre-Hung Doors (1-⅜" hollow-core Lauan)
Includes one-side casing (17L) and stop and hardware.

24" x 80"	$51.55
28" x 80"	52.95
30" x 80"	52.95
32" x 80"	53.95
36" x 80"	54.95

Add: Ex. side of casing, $6.99; keyed lockset, $6.00.

Locksets and Hinges

	Style A	Style B	Style C
Passage.......................................	$ 6.39	$11.22	$11.22
Privacy	7.49	13.66	13.66
Entry	14.55	18.55	18.55
Hinges	1.89 pr.		

Bi-fold Doors
Lauan flush doors (2-panel)

24" x 80½"	$31.55
30" x 80½"	33.95
36" x 80½"	38.95

Lauan flush doors (4 panel)

48" x 80½"	51.95
60" x 80½"	53.95
72" x 80½"	57.95

Mirror

	Clear	Bronze	Smoked Antique	Gold Vein
Two-panel				
24" x 80¾"	$ 75.55	$ 94.55	$ 99.95	$102.95
30" x 80¾"	86.55	111.95	118.95	122.95
36" x 80¾"	113.55	121.95	133.95	148.95
Four-panel				
48" x 80¾"	143.95	185.95	194.95	202.95
60" x 80¾"	178.95	217.95	277.95	241.95
72" x 80¾"	191.95	273.95	258.95	277.95

Steel

Two-panel			**Four-panel**	
24" x 80¾"	$34.95		48" x 80¾"	$55.95
30" x 80¾"	37.95		60" x 80¾"	66.95
36" x 80¾"	41.95		72" x 80¾"	75.55

Hemlock Sash Doors

One Light	1⅜"	1¾"
2'6" x 6'8"	$84.95	$90.95
2'8" x 6'8"	86.95	91.95
3'0" x 6'8"	89.95	96.95
Three Light		
2'6" x 6'8"	90.95	93.95
2'8" x 6'8"	91.95	94.95
3'0" x 6'8"	96.95	99.95

Combination Doors (Wood)
Four Lights (1⅛" thick) with screen

30" x 80"	$129.95
32" x 80"	133.95
36" x 80"	137.96

Colonial (1⅛" thick) with storm and screen

32" x 80"	$149.95
36" x 80"	149.95

Bottom Crossbuck (Wood)

9 Square Lights (1¾")		**12 Diamond Lights**
2'8" x 6'8"	$139.95	$159.95
3'0" x 6'8"	139.95	159.95

Screen Doors (Wood)
1⅛" Hemlock

30" x 80"	$34.95
32" x 80"	34.95
36" x 80"	35.95

Combination Doors (Aluminum)

Mill Finish (1")	**White Enamel (1¼")**	**Colonial Crossbuck**
30", 32", 36, $54.95	32", 36" $73.95	32", 36" $89.95

Wood Patio Doors (Wood)
74¼" x 80⅝" $499.95
94¼" x 80⅝"   599.95
Steel Entrance Doors Range from $149.00 to $189.00

DOORS/INTERIOR

Interior doors generally consist of two styles, flush and panel. However, there is an increasing use of sliding and bifold doors. Still another, growing in use, is the accordian fold door.

Flush and panel doors are usually 1⅜" thick, while folding and sliding doors are usually 1⅛" thick. Accordian folding doors range in thickness based upon weight, size and material which varies from cloth to wood. Flush doors are usually hollow core, consisting of a light frame covered with plywood or hardboard. Finishes come in various woods, such as oak, birch or mahogany which are generally finished naturally. Hardboard and non-selected grades are usually painted.

Panel doors have solid stiles, rails and panels of various types. The folding louvered door is generally used for closets because of its ventilation characteristics. Folding and sliding doors are also used for wardrobes and pantries.

Pocket doors or doors which slide into the wall are used where space to swing is limited or would block a hallway, etc.

Door widths can be subject to building regulations, so it may be advisable to check to see if any exist before a door is installed. Minimum widths are usually 2'6", bedrooms and other rooms; 2'4", bathrooms and 2'0" for small closets or linen closets.

Standard interior door height is 6'8" for first floor doors, while doors of 6'6" are frequently used on second floors, basements or in homes which are a story-and-a-half.

Hanging Interior Doors. For new or added doors, the opening should be rough framed in manner similar to exterior doors. Hinged doors should open and swing in the direction of entry, preferably toward a blank wall. They should not be obstructed by other swinging doors or swing into a hallway.

For framing figure 2½" plus the door width for horizontal, and 2" plus the door height for vertical. Where wood casing is used, the head and side jambs are the same widths as the overall wall thickness. Where metal casing is used with drywall, the jamb width is the same as the stud width.

Jambs can be purchased in precut sets or complete with stops and the door hung in the frame. The prehung door is the simplest and most economical to install.

Usually, the stops are temporarily nailed in place until the door is hung. These are usually 7/16" thick and can be from 3/4" to 2 1/2" wide. They are mitered and installed at the junction of the head and side jambs. A "sanitary stop" consisting of a 45° bevel cut at the bottom of the stop 1 1/2" above the floor will make cleaning or refinishing of the floor easier.

When installing the new door frame, the hinge side of the frame is fastened first. Shingle wedges are used between the side jamb and the rough door buck to plumb the jamb. Additional wedges are placed at the hinge and latch locations and along the top. The jamb is nailed using two eightpenny nails at each wedge, and after installation, the wedges are trimmed flush with the wall.

The door is fitted to the frame using the following clearances: 1/8" for the knob-side and top, 1/16" on the hinge side and 1/2" or more at the bottom, particularly if it is to swing over carpeting. The hinges should be the proper size for the door they will support. For 1 3/8" doors, the best size is 3 1/2" x 3 1/2". Two hinges are sufficient for most hollow-core doors. However, if the door is heavier, three are better.

Locks come in three styles.

- Entry lock sets. These are keyed and decorative.

- Bath or bedroom lock sets. Called "privacy lock sets". They have an inside lock control and a safety slot for opening the door from the outside.

- Passage or latch set. There is no locking device.

Lock sets are usually purchased with the door and may even be already installed. If not installed, the manufacturer provides directions which should be carefully followed. Lock sets should be installed so that the doorknob is 36" to 38" above the floor.

The stops which were temporarily nailed, can now be permanently installed. Casing is positioned about 3/16" from the face of the jamb and nailed, spacing nails about 16" apart.

Metal casing can be nailed to the door buck and the drywall inserted and then nailed to the studs. Or the casing can be fitted to the drywall and the drywall attached by nailing through the casing and the drywall into the stud.

Generally, one carpenter can complete the above procedure, including framing and installing the door, hinges and hardware in 1.5 hours at the following labor cost per door.

	Hours	Rate	Total	Rate	Total
Carpenter..	1.5	—	—	$20.60	$30.90

Bypass Sliding Doors. Bypass sliding doors can be used to enclose a variety of storage areas. Their advantage is no floor space is lost to door swing.

Installation is usually in a standard door frame, to which an upper track is hung and concealed behind a piece of trim mounted below the head jamb. The rough opening is framed in the same way as for a conventional swinging door. The doors, which contain rollers, are guided on the floor by a small guide track. The rollers are adjustable so that the door may be aligned and plumb with the opening. Standard sizes are $1_{3/8}$" thick, 6'8" or 7'0" high and any width. Be sure to consult the installation instructions as the rough opening sizes vary from manufacturer to manufacturer. One carpenter can usually hung a bypass door 6'8" x 6', including hardware, at the following cost per installation:

	Hours	Rate	Total	Rate	Total
Carpenter..	3	—	—	$20.60	$61.80

Bifold Doors. Bifold doors come in a variety of widths and heights. Their advantage is that when they are open, the entire storage area is accessible. Wood and metal are the types most commonly used. Bifold doors can be installed in regular door frames, and openings are framed the same as for a swinging door. Bifold doors operate on upper and lower tracks. A single carpenter can install a four-panel bifold door, including installing the tracks in about 2.3 hours at the following cost per installation:

	Hours	Rate	Total	Rate	Total
Carpenter..	2.3	—	—	$20.60	$47.40

Folding Doors. Folding doors come in a variety of materials and prices. Top of the line are the wood folding doors, offered in a choice of veneers, such as oak, birch, walnut or mahogany. They are available finished or sanded and ready to stain or paint. Frequently, they are used to close off laundry or storage areas. The better quality wood doors, however, can be used to divide rooms, and, when closed, look like paneling. Their most outstanding feature, in addition to convenience, is that they fold inside their own doorway, taking little room and allowing complete access to the area they enclose. Most come assembled with hardware. One manufacturer even supplies a wood head mold to conceal the track and a jamb mold for jamb enclosure.

Two-panel units will enclose areas up to 26½" wide, while four-panel units will enclose openings up to 72" wide. For larger openings or folding wall room dividers, widths up to 40'3" are available. Standard finished heights are 6'8", 7'6" and 8'.

Installation is reasonably simple and one man can generally hang a double folding door in a four-panel unit in 2 hours at the following cost per installation.

	Hours	Rate	Total	Rate	Total
Carpenter	2	—	—	$20.60	$41.20

Labor To Set Finish Hardware

Type	Hours/Each	Type	Hours/Each
Rim lock	.5	Surface door closer	1.0
Mortised lock	1.0	Concealed door closer	3.0
Cylinder lock	.5	Sash lift and lock	.5
Front Ent. cylinder lock	2.0	Kickplate	1.0

CHAPTER 15

PORCHES AND DECKS

For years "porch-sittin" during the summer months was a prime outdoor activity. For most, it was the means for escape from a hot, stuffy, non-air-conditioned home. Not infrequently, the main recreational feature, if the porch was covered, was a swing suspended from the ceiling. Porches were the forerunners of today's patios and decks. Today, whether it is in a small town or big city, many older homes and urban two-flats and three-flats are "alive and well" with porches front and rear, still functional elements to the residents of housing to which they are attached.

Modern patios and decks are an extension of yesterday's porches. However, they are highly functional compared to the utilitarian aspects of older porches. Today they are more of an extension of living space. Not only are meals served on them, meals are frequently prepared on them. They're for parties, social gatherings and above all, the setting for this country's leading summer recreational pastime—sunbathing.

PORCHES

The labor placing porch work is a highly variable item owing to the vast differences in the style and construction of porches and the amount of detail involved. Consequently, this section has several approaches to assist the reader in estimating porch remodeling and repairs.

In the midwest, there is a standard charge of $125.00 for the permit fee.

Labor To Wreck Porch (Average)

1 Story	1 day
2 Story	3 days
3 Story	4 days

Add For Debris Removal

1 Story	$ 70.00	(Minimum)
2 Story	$100.00	”
3 Story	$130.00	”

Replacement

Rear Open Porches/Labor Only
(under average conditions)

Size: 7'x20'

1 Story	8 days
2 Story	12 days
3 Story	16 days

Add ½ day for all intermediate landings and winders.

Porch Repairs/Labor Only

6" x 6" column (not over 12')..4 hrs.
6" x 6" lookout...4 hrs.

Stairs

Front (not over 7 risers, 5' wide)..8 hrs.
Rear (per run, not over 8 risers)...8 hrs.
   Winders: Add 50%
   Oversize: Add 25%

Joists

Single Face (not over 16')...2 hrs.
Single Regular (not over 16')...2 hrs.
Complete Replacement (7' x 12')...4 hrs.

Rails (per lin. ft.)

Picket...10 min.
Three member ....6 min.
Front Chippendale with ⅓ balustrade...15 min.

Materials (Approximate Cost Midwest)

6" x 6" Posts (12' lengths)...$35.00
Lookouts (9' lengths)..$25.00
Boxed Columns (12' length)..$30.00
Joists (2" x 8")...$0.70 per lin. ft.
Fir Flooring...$1.50 per sq. ft.
Railings
   Rear Picket...$3.00 each
   Rear 3-member ....$2.50 each
   Front (Molded top, 1⅜") Balustrate...$6.00 each

Typical Porch Replacement Costs
(Materials and Labor)

Stoops. Size: 4' x 6'. No roof, average seven steps including rails and pickets: Total: $530.00. For larger sizes, figure $15.00 per sq. ft. additional.

Rear Open Porch/Type I

(see illustration below)

Includes:

Size: 7' x 22'
Steps
1" x 4" T & G Flooring
2" x 8" Joists and Rafters
Roof Deck: ⅝" plywood
Roll Roofing
6" x 6" Columns and Lookouts
Picket Railings

1 Story $2120.00
2 Story $3375.00
3 Story $4940.00
Note: Add 6% for each
foot in width over 22 ft.
Smaller widths, no credit.

Add for:
Winders......................................$ 10.00 each
Hot Roof....................................$150.00
Piers ....$ 50.00 each

Debris Removal:
1 Story ....$ 70.00 (minimum)
2 Story ....$100.00   "
3 Story ....$130.00   "

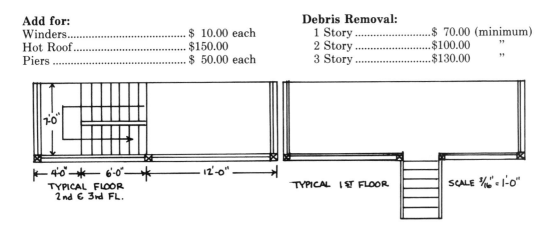

Rear Open Porch/Type II

(see illustration below)

Size: 7' x 22'
Materials, Add-ons and
Debris Removal same as
for Type I.

1 Story $2120.00
2 Story $4185.00
3 Story $5800.00

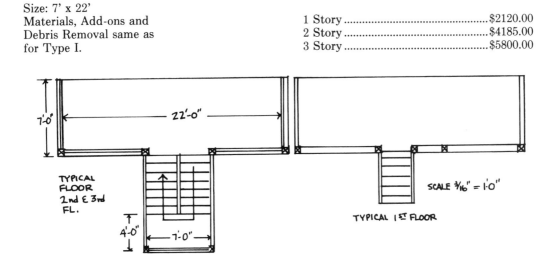

Placing Plain Porch Columns. When placing plain square or turned porch columns, such as commonly used for rear porches and other inexpensive porches, a carpenter should place one post in about ¾ hrs., at the following labor cost:

	Hours	Rate	Total	Rate	Total
Carpenter..	0.75	—	—	$20.60	$15.45

Placing Porch Top and Bottom Rail and Balusters. When placing wood top and bottom rail and wood balusters, such as used on front porches, a carpenter should complete 15–20 lin. ft. of rail per 8-hr. day at the following cost per lin. ft.:

	Hours	Rate	Total	Rate	Total
Carpenter	0.46	—	—	$20.60	$ 9.48

When placing top and bottom rails with open balusters or using matched and beaded ceiling, such as is often used for less expensive grades of work, a carpenter should complete 35–45 lin. ft. of rail per 8-hr. day at the following cost per lin. ft.:

	Hours	Rate	Total	Rate	Total
Carpenter	0.2	—	—	$20.60	$4.12

Framing and Erecting Exterior Wood Stairs For Rear Porches. When framing and erecting outside wood stairs for rear porches on two-and three-flats, etc., where the stringers are 2" x 10" or 2" x 12", with treads and risers nailed on the face of the stringers, it will require 18–22 hrs. carpenter time per flight of stairs. This is for ordinary stairs having 14–18 risers extending from story to story.

The labor cost per flight should be as follows:

	Hours	Rate	Total	Rate	Total
Carpenter	20	—	—	$20.60	$412.00

If the stair consists of 2 short flights with an intermediate landing between stories, it will require 12–13 carpenter hours per flight, or 24–26 hrs. per story, including platform, at the following labor cost:

	Hours	Rate	Total	Rate	Total
Carpenter	25	—	—	$20.60	$515.00

Framing and Erecting Wood Stairs Having Winders. Where the wood stairs to rear porches have 4–6 winders in each story, figure 24–28 hrs. carpenter time, at the following labor cost per story:

	Hours	Rate	Total	Rate	Total
Carpenter	26	—	—	$20.60	$535.60

Clear Ponderosa Pine Porch Material

Kind of Molding	Size in Inches
Square Baluster Stock	1⅛" x 1⅛"
Square Baluster Stock	1⅜" x 1⅜"

Square Baluster Stock.. 1⅝" x 1⅝"
Balustrade Cap... 3⅝" x 1⅝"
Balustrade Shoe.. 3⅝" x 1⅝"
Rabbeted Porch Jamb... 1½" x 3½"
Plowed Porch Shoe... 1½" x 3½"
Top Rail.. 3" x 2¼"
Top Rail.. 3¾" x 1¾"
Bottom Rail... 3½" x 1¾"

WOODEN PATIOS AND DECKS

An increasingly popular way to add living space to an existing home is the addition of a deck or patio to create outdoor living space. These structures become an extension of the home itself, inviting the outdoors in and the indoors out.

The size and structure of a deck is limited only by the imagination of the planner—and the budget. It can be simple and square, or elaborate and multi-level. Pools and hot tubs can be surrounded by the deck, or pleasant garden areas included. Seats that double as railings, tables that double as seats, stairs leading off to another "room"; all can be part of a well thought out plan.

Because they are outdoor rooms, patios should cooperate with nature and existing structure to the extent possible. Mature trees can provide welcome shade; a hillside can provide a dramatic view; a door can make the deck an extension of a dining room or even a bedroom. When the structure must face South or West, an awning or cover may be needed; lattice work or a wall may be desirable to hide an unwanted view.

If the land near the house is uneven, and a paved patio is not practical, the deck can be built near ground level with short posts overcoming the uneven ground. The low-level deck can also be built to cover a concrete patio that has cracked or become unsightly.

In preparing an estimate for construction of a deck, be sure to consider three basics that can affect the total time needed to build the deck.

(1) *Location*: Is the deck near the front of the house, or in the back? Since the location is often the back of the house, allow adequate time to move all building materials from their delivery point to the area where you will be working.

(2) *Level*: Will the floor be at ground level or elevated to an upper level of the house? The floor level will influence the size of lumber needed for beams and joists, length of the posts and the time necessary for moving material.

(3) *Structure*: How elaborate will the finished structure be? Multiple levels, unusual shapes and sizes or other unusual features add to the time required for planning, cutting and placing the material during construction. Making a detailed diagram is wise, because it will aid in planning for material quantities and in building the deck.

Planning should also include careful consideration of the types and sizes of material to be used for posts, beams and joists, and the decking. Some useful guidelines follow.

Posts.   Usually 4" x 4" lumber, or they can be metal pipe. To avoid sinking, they should be set in concrete to an adequate depth that freezing will not affect them (6" below frost line). Where the ground is solid, they may be set on concrete pads or pre-formed concrete anchors.

Beams and Joists.   Steel beams can be used or 2" x 6" lumber for beams up to 16' in length. Many carpenters prefer 2" x 6" for joists, set on 24" centers; centers can be up to 36", and 16" centers can be used for extra strength.

Decking.   Usual choices include construction grade lumber, cedar, redwood or specially pressure-treated lumber for outdoor use. 2" x 6" lumber is often preferred for strength; 1" x 6" can be used if joists are 16" on center. Galvanized nails should be used to prevent corrosion.

For estimating construction time, use the following guidelines; they are approximate times for each of the major steps in building an average 16' x 16' deck at the second story level.

Posts: Figure about one hour per post to dig the hole, set in concrete and brace it to assure plumb. A power auger will often be needed at a cost of about $40 per day.

Beams: Allow approximately one hour per beam (three 16' beams would be needed for a 16' x 16' deck) including placing the beam, leveling and bolting in place.

Joists: For the deck described placing all joists on 24" centers figure about 5 hours, including placing the necessary facia.

Decking: Allow 8 hours to cut and nail all the decking lumber and trimming the ends. If joists are placed on longer or shorter centers, more cutting time may be necessary.

Railing: To cut and place railing on three sides of the deck, allow about 8 hours, including bolts where needed.

Stairs: For an upper level deck, a set of outdoor stairs will usually be included. Figure 8 hours to cut and place on full flight with a railing.

Door: If the deck is added outside a room where no door exists, allow 8 hours to frame and install a standard door. Sliding glass doors will require 12 to 16 hours, depending upon how much reinforcing must be done.

The estimate should include approximately 8 hours of time for a helper who will be needed to place heavy items and to move material. For the typical 16' x 16' deck with all items as listed, estimate labor as follows:

	Hours	Rate	Total	Rate	Total
Carpenter	49	—	—	$20.60	$1009.40
Helper	8	—	—	$15.45	$ 123.60
Cost per square foot:					$ 4.45
(Incl. door and stairs)					

When the deck is constructed at ground level, growth of vegetation beneath the deck should be prevented. A simple and effective method is to fill the area with pea gravel over a heavy plastic sheet to prevent growth of grass and weeds.

Deck And Patio Lumber Prices

Deck and patio lumber. Pressure treated, can be stained, painted or left natural.

Size	Per Lin. Ft.	Size	Per Lin. Ft.
2 x 4 (8' x 10')	$0.30	2 x 10 (12' x 16')	$ .94
2 x 4 (12' x 14')	.34	2 x 12 (12' x 16')	1.25
2 x 4 (16')	.35	4 x 6 (8'–14')	.94
2 x 6 (8' x 14')	.50	4 x 6 (16')	.99
2 x 6 (10', 12', 16')	.53	4 x 6 (18' x 20')	1.09
2 x 6 (18' x 20')	.56	4 x 6 (22' x 24')	1.29
2 x 6 (T & G)	.55	6 x 6 (8'–14')	1.40
2 x 8 (8' x 10')	.64	6 x 6 (16')	1.55
2 x 8 (12'–16')	.69	6 x 6 (18' x 20')	1.65
4 x 4 (8')	.63	6 x 6 (22' x 24')	1.95
4 x 4 (10' x 16')	.69	1 x 6 Fencing	.27

Deck and Patio Accessories

Step Brackets (7" rise–10" tread)	$ 5.99 ea.
Step Brackets (6" rise–16" tread)	7.79 ea.
Rail Post Bracket	3.39 ea.
Metal Post Bracket	5.49 ea.
Translucent Roofing (White or Green)	
26" x 8' corrugated	7.33 ea.
26" x 10' "	9.95 ea.
26" x 12' "	11.95 ea.

Porch Flooring (1 x 4 P/L)
T & G, kiln-dried, sanded

$.20 ft. (600M)

Ornamental Iron Railing

4' railing	$10.95 ea.
5' railing	13.95 ea.
6' railing	16.55 ea.
Newel Post	4.79 ea.
Adj. Fittings	3.19 ea.

Floor flanges	$ 2.44 ea.
Lamp tongue	2.44 ea.
Flat column	11.77 ea.
Corner column	27.95 ea.

Vapor Barrier (.004)

6 x 100	$15.95 roll
8 x 100	18.95 roll
10 x 100	19.95 roll
12 x 100	24.95 roll
16 x 100	30.95 roll

20 x 100	$36.95 roll
20 x 100 (blk)	37.95 roll
10 x 25	8.19 roll
15 x 25	11.95 roll
20 x 25	14.95 roll

INDEX

A

	Page
Air cleaners, electronic	203
Air conditioning	214
cost per installation	215
labor to install	215
Alarms, household	202
Aluminum siding	269
(see Siding)	
Ampacity of insulated copper conduction	190
Asphalt shingles, estimating quantities	232
installation	233
nails required	233
Attics, conversion	43

B

Base cabinets, removal	13
replace	20–23
Baths, combined labor material costs	32
Bath fixtures, installation dimensions	27
Bathtubs	179
Bathtubs, removal	27
roughing in plumbing	28
Bidet, install	28, 181
Brick, repairs	273, 274, 275

C

Cabinets, bath, install	28
kitchen install	15–22
kitchen remove	12
Carpentry, exterior finish	276
Cedar shakes, estimating coverage	235
grades and sizes	258
Ceilings, to remove	123
to install	124–126
Ceiling fans	202
Chimneys, to rebuild	275
Chimney flashing	231
Concrete, slabs	58
Concrete block, repairs	274, 275

D

	Page
Conduit electrical	186
Corner boards, to place	276
Cornices, to place	277
Cupolas, to place	277

D

Decks	317
labor to install	318, 319
Dishwashers	182
Doors	289
exterior	299
labor to install	305
sliding glass, to install	305
sliding glass, to remove	303
to install	301, 303
to remove	301
Doors	
bifold to install	310
bypass sliding, to install	310
folding, to install	310
hardware, labor to set	311
interior	308
to install	308, 310
Door openers, electric	306
Dormers, add	46–48
Drip edges, to install	230
Drywall	
required thicknesses	111
taping	119
to install	116, 119
Ductwork, install	20

E

Eaves flashing, to install	230
Electrical	185
basements, attics	203
distribution	195
estimating, basic circuit	192, 193
grounding circuits	204
installing service entrance	193–95
labor per circuit, one connection	192
labor per circuit, through studs	192

Page

material prices.............................. 204–206
rewiring, labor to install............. 196–202
to determine power needs......... 189, 190
Excavating, sewer pipe...................... 172

F

Flashing, roofing 230–232
Flooring, estimating material.................. 91
    estimating labor 92, 93
    sanding 93–95
    staining/sealing 95, 96
    hardwood, labor to install.................... 92
    oak block.. 99
    parquet 98
    tile and sheet............................... 99–103
Flooring, removal............................... 13, 90
    blocking 44
    sleepers 49
Furring strips, masonry walls.......... 51, 114

G

Garbage disposal, install................ 24, 183
Grounding circuits 204
Gutter and downspouts................. 225, 242
    installation 244–247
    material costs.................................... 243
    removal 244

H

Hardboard siding................................. 259
Hardware, labor to set......................... 311
Heaters, auxilliary, bath.................. 31, 202
    electric 178
    gas 178
Heating systems 207
    costs, installed 213–214
    estimating costs............................... 208
    estimating labor costs 220–222
    hot water 217
    labor to balance............................... 213
    loads 208
    warm air..................................... 209–211

Page

I

Insulation, basements............................. 52
    room additions 55–56

K

Kitchens, design of............................ 5–12

L

Lavatories, removal 30
    installation 30, 180
Lighting, low voltage............................ 203
    outdoor fixtures................................ 203
Lumber, estimating quantities.......... 59–69

M

Masonry repairs.................................. 273
Moldings, removal 126
    replace... 126–133

N

Nails, quantities and kinds............... 69–75
    for asphalt shingles.................... 233, 235
    for hardboard siding 260

P

Paint, estimating interior
    dimensions............................... 142–145
    covering capacity, interior 145–147
    estimating labor 147–154
    hardwood floors 154
    walls and ceilings 155–158
Painting, estimating exterior
    dimensions............................... 278–281
    covering capacity, exterior 281–282
    estimating labor costs 282
    labor and material tables.................. 285
    labor to burn off.............................. 282
    sanding and puttying 282
Parquet, to install 98
Pipe fittings, estimating quantities of ... 173
Pipe sizes and prices.................... 175–177
    gas, to install.................................. 211
    smoke, to install............................. 211

	Page
Plaster walls	110
combined labor/material costs	111
Plenum chambers, to install	212
Plumbing, estimating labor	
roughing in	173
fixtures, labor placing	173
preparing detailed estimates	174
Plumbing, estimating	171
Plywood paneling, materials	
estimating	112
to install	116
Porches, labor to wreck	313
days to replace	313
debris removal	313
labor costs to repair	315–316
labor to repair	314
typical replacement costs	314, 315

R

Range tops, removal	13
hoods, install	23
Registers, heating	212
Roofing	225
estimating material required	234
install underlayment	230
labor to install asphalt shingles	235
roll, to install	240–242
to measure roof size	226–230
Rooms, additions	55
conversions	43

S

Sanding and puttying	282
Sheathing, labor to apply	59
Shingles and shakes, wooden,	
roofing	236
application for different slopes	238
estimating quantities	237
to install	238, 239, 240
Shingles and shakes, wooden,	
siding	256
grades and sizes	258
labor to install	256–257

	Page
weather exposure	257
Shower stalls	179
Shut-off valves, install	12
Siding, aluminum	269
to install	269–273
Siding, hardboard	259
nailing table	260
to install	260–265
Siding, vinyl	266
to install, horizontal	268
to install, vertical	269
Siding, wood	251
beveled siding, quantities required	253
drop siding, quantities required	254
labor placing, bevel siding	255
labor placing, drop siding	255
ship lap, quantities required	254
T & G, quantities required	254
Sink removal	12
install	23, 181
Skylights, install	45
Soffits	275
to install	23, 276
Stairways, types	79
custom, spiral and disappearing	86–88
labor to construct	80–83
removal	80
Sub-flooring, remove	90
replace	90

T

Taping, drywall	119
Tile, install	37–42, 120–123
Toilets, remove	27
install	27, 181

V

Valley flashing, to install	231
Vanities, removal	30
install	30
Vent pipe flashing to install	232
Ventilators, bath	31
Vinyl siding	266

W

	Page
Walls, estimating sq. ft. of exposure	218
Walls, labor to frame	58
replaster	110
stripping	110
Walls, new partitions	46
Wall cabinets, hanging	14
Wall cover, Flexwood	168–169
Canvas	168
Vinyl	169
Wallpaper, hanging	166–168

	Page
Warm air ducts	212
Waterproofing	49–50
Weather exposure, shingles and shakes	257
Windows, install	44
Windows, to remove	295
close opening	295
to install	295–298
Window openings, various sizes	219
Window styles	290
Window types	291
Wiring, removal	188

MENSURATION

The information on the following pages will enable contractors and estimators to estimate quantities and costs accurately and in a minimum of time.

In a number of tables, the quantities are stated in decimals, as by using decimals, it is possible to state the fractional parts of inches, feet and yards, in a smaller space than where regular fractions are used.

For the contractor or estimator who is not thoroughly familiar with the decimal system, complete explanations are given covering the use of all classes of decimal fractions, so they may be used rapidly and accurately.

Estimating is nearly all "figures" of one kind or another, so it is essential that the contractor and estimator possess a fair working knowledge of arithmetic, if his estimates are to be accurate and dependable.

Most of the estimator's computations involve measurements of surface and cubical contents and are stated in lineal feet (lin.ft.), square feet (sq.ft.), square yards (sq.yds.), squares (sqs.) containing 100 sq. ft., cubic feet (cu.ft.), and cubic yards (cu.yds.). These quantities are often further reduced to thousands of brick, feet of lumber, board measure (b.m.), etc.

The rules on the following pages will enable the user to compute areas in square feet or cubical contents easily, accurately and quickly.

The following abbreviations are used throughout the book to make all tables brief and concise and to insert them in the smallest possible space :

	Abbreviation	Symbols
Inches	= in.	= ''
Lineal feet	= lin. ft.	= '
Feet and inches	= ft. in.	= 2'-5''
Square feet	= sq. ft.	= □'
Square yards	= sq. yds.	= □yds.
Squares	= sqs.	
Cubic feet	= cu. ft.	
Cubic yards	= cu. yds.	
Board measure	= b. m.	

Linear Measure

12	inches	=12 in.=	12''	=1 foot	=1 ft.	=1'-0''
3	feet	= 3 ft.=	3'- 0''	=1 yard	=1 yd.	
16½	feet	=16½ ft.=	16'- 6''	=1 rod	=1 rd.	
40	rods	=40 rds.		=1 furlong	=1 fur.	
8	furlongs	= 8 fur.		=1 mile	=1 mi.	
5,280	feet	=1,760 yds.		=1 mile	=1 mi.	

Square Measure or Measures of Surfaces

144 square inches	= 144 sq. in.	= 1 square foot = 1 sq. ft.
9 square feet	= 9 sq. ft.	= 1 square yard = 1 sq. yd.
100 square feet	= 100 sq. ft.	= 1 square = 1 sq. (Architects' and Builders' Measure.)
30¼ square yards	= 30¼ sq. yds.	= 30.25 sq. yds. = 1 square rod = 1 sq. rd.
160 square rods	= 160 sq. rds.	= 1 Acre = 1 A.
43,560 sq. ft.	= 4,840 sq. yds.	= 1 Acre = 1 A.
640 acres	= 640 A.	= 1 square mile = 1 sq. mi.

Cubic Measure or Cubical Contents

1,728 cubic inches	= 1,728 cu. in.	= 1 cubic foot	= 1 cu. Ft.
27 cubic feet	= 27 cu. ft.	= 1 cubic yard	= 1 cu. yd.
128 cubic feet	= 128 cu. ft.	= 1 cord	= 1 cd.
24¾ cubic feet	= 24¾ cu.ft.	= 24¾ cu. ft. =24.75 cu. ft.	= 1 perch* = 1P.

*A perch of stone is nominally 16½ ft. long, 1 ft. high and 1½ ft. thick, and contains 24¾ cu. ft. However, in some states, especially west of the Mississippi, rubble work is figured by the perch containing 16½ cu. ft. Before submitting prices on masonry by the perch, find out the common practice in your locality.

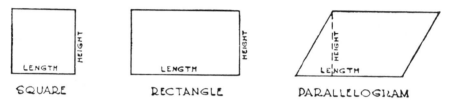

SQUARE   RECTANGLE   PARALLELOGRAM

To Compute the Area of a Square, Rectangle or Parallelogram.—Multiply the length by the breadth or height. Example : Obtain the area of a wall 22 ft. (22'-0") long and 9 ft. (9'-0") high. 22x9=198 sq. ft.

To Compute the Area of a Triangle.—Multiply the base by ½ the altitude or perpendicular height. Example : Find the area of the end gable of a house 24 ft. (24'-0") wide and 12 ft. (12'-0") high from the base to high point of roof. 24 ft. x 6 ft. (½ the height)=144 sq. ft.

To Compute the Circumference of a Circle.—Multiply the diameter by 3.1416. The diameter multiplied by 3₁/₇ is close enough for all practical purposes. Example : Find the circumference or distance around a circle, the diameter of which is 12 ft. (12'-0"). 12x3.1416=37.6992 ft. the distance around the circle or 12x3₁/₇=37.714 ft.

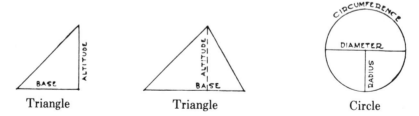

Triangle   Triangle   Circle

To Compute the Area of a Circle.—Multiply the square of the diameter by 0.7854 or multiply the square of the radius by 3.1416. Example : Find the area of a round concrete column 24 in. (24" or 2'-0") in diameter. The square of the diameter is 2x2=4. 4x0.7854=3.1416 sq. ft. the area of the circle.

The radius is ½ the diameter. If the diameter is 2 ft. (2'-0") the radius would be 1 ft. (1'-0"). To obtain the square of the radius, 1x1=1. Multiply the square of the radius, 1x3.1416=3.1416, the area of the circle.

To Compute the Cubical Contents of a Circular Column.—Multiply the area of the circle by the height. Example : Find the cubical contents of a round concrete column 2 ft. (2'-0") in diameter and 14 ft. (14'-0") long.

From the previous example, the area of a circle 2 ft. in diameter is 3.1416 sq. ft. 3.1416x14 ft. (the height)=43.9824 cu. ft. or for all practical purposes 44 cu. ft. of concrete in each column.

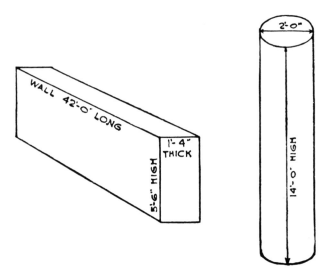

To Compute the Cubical Contents of any Solid. —Multiply the length by the breadth or height by the thickness. Computations of this kind are used extensively in estimating all classes of building work, such as excavating, concrete foundations, reinforced concrete, brick masonry, cut stone, granite, etc.

Example : Find the cubical contents of a wall 42 ft. (42'-0") long, 5 ft. 6 in. (5'-6") high, and 1 ft. 4 in. (1'-4") thick, 42'-0"x5'-6"x1'-4"=308 cu. ft. To reduce cu. ft. to cu. yds. divide 308 by 27, and the result is 11 11/27 or 11½ or 11.41 cu. yds.

How to Use the Decimal System of Numerals in Estimating.—In construction work nearly all figures are either feet and inches or dollars and cents but inasmuch as it is convenient to use the decimal system in making many computations, a brief description of this system is given for the use of contractors and estimators who are not familiar with it.

A decimal is a fraction whose denominator is not written, but is some power of 10. They are often called decimal fractions but more often simply a decimal.

Example: We know 50 cents is 50/100 or 1/2 of a dollar. Writing the same thing in decimals would be $0.50.

Numerator	50
Denominator	100

When written as .50 or .5, it is a fraction whose denominator is not written, it being understood to be 10 from the fact that 5 occupies the first place to the right of the decimal point.

Therefore we have the following :

0.5	means	5/10, for the	5 extends to the	10th's place;
0.25	means	25/100 , for the	25 extends to the	100dth's place;
0.125	means	125/1000, for the	125 extends to the	1000dth's place.

The names of the places are, in part, as follows :

Thousands	Hundreds	Tens	Units	(Decimal Point)	Tenths	Hundredths	Thousands	Ten-Thousandths
1	3	4	5	.	2	7	6	5

This number is read "one thousand three hundred forty-five and two thousand seven hundred and sixty-five ten thousandths." The orders beyond the ten thousandths are hundred thousandths, millionths, ten millionths, etc., but in figuring construction work it is seldom necessary to carry the figures beyond three or four decimal points.

A whole number and a decimal together, form a mixed decimal. Example : 2.25 is the same as $2_{25/100}$ or $2\frac{1}{4}$.

The period written at the left of tenths is called the decimal point. Example. 0.5 = 5/10;   0.25 = 25/100 = ¼;   0.375 = 375/1000 = ⅜, etc.

It is not necessary to write a zero at the left of the decimal point in the above examples, for 0.5 means the same as .5. The zero is often written there to call attention more quickly to the decimal point.

In the construction business, decimals are used chiefly to denote feet and inches, hours and minutes, the fractional working units of the various kinds of materials, and in money, which is dollars and cents or fractional parts of 100.

Table of Feet and Inches Reduced to Decimals

The following table illustrates how feet and inches may be expressed in four different ways, all meaning the same thing.

1	inch = 1 " = 1/12th	foot	=0.083
1½ inches = 1½" = 1/8th		foot	=0.125
2	inches = 2 " = 1/6th	foot	=0.1667
2½ inches = 2½" = 5/24ths		foot	=0.2087
3	inches = 3 " = 1/4th	foot	=0.25
3½ inches = 3½" = 7/24ths		foot	=0.2917
4	inches = 4 " = 1/3rd	foot	=0.333
4½ inches = 4½" = 3/8ths		foot	=0.375
5	inches = 5 " = 5/12ths	foot	=0.417
5½ inches = 5½" = 11/24ths		foot	=0.458
6	inches = 6 " = 1/2	foot	=0.5
6½ inches = 6½" = 13/24ths		foot	=0.5417
7	inches = 7 " = 7/12ths	foot	=0.583
7½ inches = 7½" = 5/8ths		foot	=0.625
8	inches = 8 " = 2/3rds	foot	=0.667
8½ inches = 8½" = 17/24ths		foot	=0.708
9	inches = 9 " = 3/4ths	foot	=0.75
9½ inches = 9½" = 19/24ths		foot	=0.792
10	inches =10 " = 5/6ths	foot	=0.833
10½ inches =10½" = 7/8ths		foot	=0.875
11	inches =11 " = 11/12ths	foot	=0.917
11½ inches =11½" = 23/24ths		foot	=0.958
12	inches =12 " =1	foot	=1.0

Example : Write 5 feet, 7½ inches, in decimals. It would be written 5.625, Which is equivalent to $5_{5/8}$ feet.

Table of Common Fractions Stated in Decimals

The following table gives the decimal equivalents of common fractions frequently used in estimating :

$$1/16 = \frac{6\frac{1}{4}}{100} = 0.0625 \qquad 7/16 = \frac{43\frac{3}{4}}{100} = 0.4375$$

$$1/8 = \frac{12\frac{1}{2}}{100} = 0.125 \qquad 1/2 = \frac{50}{100} = 0.5$$

$$3/16 = \frac{18\frac{3}{4}}{100}\ \ 0.1875 \qquad 9/16 = \frac{56\frac{1}{4}}{100} = 0.5625$$

Table of Common Fractions Stated in Decimals—Cont'd.

$$1/4 = \frac{25}{100} = 0.25 \qquad\qquad 5/8 = \frac{62\,1/2}{100} = 0.625$$

$$5/16 = \frac{31\,1/4}{100} = 0.3125 \qquad\qquad 11/16 = \frac{68\,3/4}{100} = 0.6875$$

$$3/8 = \frac{37\,1/2}{100} = 0.375 \qquad\qquad 3/4 = \frac{75}{100} = 0.75$$

$$13/16 = \frac{81\,1/4}{100} = 0.8125 \qquad\qquad 15/16 = \frac{93\,3/4}{100} = 0.9375$$

$$7/8 = \frac{87\,1/2}{100} = 0.875 \qquad\qquad 8/8 = \frac{100}{100} = 1.0$$

Annexing zeros to a number does not change its value; 0.5 is the same as 0.500.

Table of Hours and Minutes Reduced to Decimals

The following table illustrates how minutes may be reduced to fractional parts of hours and to decimal parts of hours.

Number of Minutes		Fractional Part of an Hour		Decimal Part of an Hour	Number of Minutes		Fractional Part of an Hour		Decimal Part of an Hour
1	=	1/60th	=	0.0167	31	=	31/60ths	=	0.5167
2	=	1/30th	=	0.0333	32	=	8/15ths	=	0.5333
3	=	1/20th	=	0.05	33	=	11/20ths	=	0.55
4	=	1/15th	=	0.0667	34	=	17/30ths	=	0.5667
5	=	1/12th	=	0.0833	35	=	7/12ths	=	0.5833
6	=	1/10th	=	0.10	36	=	3/5ths	=	0.60
7	=	7/60ths	=	0.1167	37	=	37/60ths	=	0.6167
8	=	2/15ths	=	0.1333	38	=	19/30ths	=	0.6333
9	=	3/20ths	=	0.15	39	=	13/20ths	=	0.65
10	=	1/6th	=	0.1667	40	=	2/3rds	=	0.6667
11	=	11/60ths	=	0.1833	41	=	41/60ths	=	0.6833
12	=	1/5th	=	0.20	42	=	7/10ths	=	0.70
13	=	13/60ths	=	0.2167	43	=	43/60ths	=	0.7167
14	=	7/30ths	=	0.2333	44	=	11/15ths	=	0.7333
15	=	1/4th	=	0.25	45	=	3/4ths	=	0.75
16	=	4/15ths	=	0.2667	46	=	23/30ths	=	0.7667
17	=	17/60ths	=	0.2833	47	=	47/60ths	=	0.7833
18	=	3/10ths	=	0.30	48	=	4/5ths	=	0.80
19	=	19/60ths	=	0.3167	49	=	49/60ths	=	0.8167
20	=	1/3rd	=	0.333	50	=	5/6ths	=	0.8333
21	=	7/20ths	=	0.35	51	=	51/60ths	=	0.85
22	=	11/30ths	=	0.3667	52	=	13/15ths	=	0.8667
23	=	23/60ths	=	0.3833	53	=	53/60ths	=	0.8833
24	=	2/5ths	=	0.40	54	=	9/10ths	=	0.90
25	=	5/12ths	=	0.4167	55	=	11/12ths	=	0.9167
26	=	13/30ths	=	0.4333	56	=	14/15ths	=	0.9333
27	=	9/20ths	=	0.45	57	=	19/20ths	=	0.95
28	=	7/15ths	=	0.4667	58	=	29/30ths	=	0.9667
29	=	29/60ths	=	0.4833	59	=	59/60ths	=	0.9833
30	=	1/2	=	0.5	60	=	1	=	1.0

Example: Write 4 hours and 37 minutes in decimals. It would be written 4.6167.

Now find the labor cost for 4.6167 hrs. at $7.50 an hr.

$$
\begin{array}{r}
\text{Hours,} \quad 4.6167 \\
\text{X Hourly Rate,} \quad \$7.50 \\
\hline
2308350 \\
323169 \\
\hline
\end{array}
$$

Total Cost, $34.625250 or $34.63

Similar Decimals.—Decimals that have the same number of decimal places are called similar decimals. Thus, 0.75 and 0.25 are similar decimals and so are 0.150 and 0.275; but 0.15 and 0.275 are dissimilar decimals.

To reduce dissimilar decimals to similar decimals, give them the same number of decimal places by annexing or cutting off zeros. Example, 0.125, 0.25, 0.375 and 0.5 may all be reduced to thousandths as follows : 0.125, 0.250, 0.375 and 0.500.

To Reduce a Decimal to a Common Fraction.—Omit the decimal point, write the denominator of the decimal, and then reduce the common fraction to its lowest terms.

Example : 0.375 equals 375/1000, which reduced to its lowest terms, equals 3/8.

$$
25 \left| \frac{375}{1000} \right. = 5 \left| \frac{15}{40} \right. = \tfrac{3}{8}
$$

How to Add Decimals.—To add numbers containing decimals, write like orders under one another, and then add as with whole numbers. Example, add 0.125, 0.25, 0.375, and 1.0.

The total of the addition is 1.750, which equals 1 750/1000, and which may be further reduced to 1¾

$$
\begin{array}{r}
0.125 \\
0.25 \\
0.375 \\
1.0 \\
\hline
1.750
\end{array}
$$

How to Subtract Decimals.—To subtract one number from another, when either or both contain decimals, reduce to similar decimals, write like orders under one another, and subtract as with whole numbers.

Subtract 20 hours and 37 minutes from 27 hours and 13 minutes, both being written in decimals, The difference is 6.6000 or 6.6 hours, which reduced to a common fraction is 6 3/5 hours or 6 hours and 36 minutes.

$$
\begin{array}{r}
27.2167 \\
20.6167 \\
\hline
6.6000
\end{array}
$$

How to Multiply Decimals.—The same method is used as in multiplying other numbers, and the result should contain as many decimal points as there are in both of the numbers multiplied.

Example: Multiply 3 feet by 6 inches by 4 feet 9 inches

4 ft. 9 in.=4'-9"=4¾ ft.=4.75 Mutiplicand
3 ft. 6 in.=3'-6"=3½ ft.=3.5 Multiplier
To multiply, proceed as illustrated

$$
\begin{array}{r}
4.75 \\
3.5 \\
\hline
2375 \\
1425 \\
\hline
\end{array}
$$

Product   16625 or 16.625

In the above example, there are 2 decimals in the multiplicand and 1 decimal in the multiplier. The result or product should contain the same number of decimals as the multiplicand and multiplier combined, which is three. Starting at the right and counting to the left three places, place the decimal point between the two sixes. The result would be 16.625, which equals 16 625/1000= 16 5/8 sq. ft.

Practical Examples Using Decimals

The quantities of cement, sand and gravel required for one cu. yd. of concrete are ordinarily stated in decimals. For instance, a cu. yd. of concrete mixed in the proportions of 1 part cement ; 2 parts sand ; and 4 parts gravel, is usually stated 1: 2 : 4 and requires the following materials :

1.50 bbls. cement=150/100 bbls. =1½ bbls. =**6** sacks.

0.42 cu. yds. sand=42/100 cu. yds.=21/50 cu. yds. =**1**1½ cu. ft.

0.84 cu. yds. gravel=84/100 cu. yds. =**2**2⅔ cu. ft.

There are 4 sacks of cement to the bbl., and each sack weighs 94 lbs. and contains approximately 1 cu. ft. of cement.

There are 27 cu. ft. in a cu. yd.; to obtain the number of cu. ft. of sand required for a yard of concrete, 0.42 cu. yds=42/100 cu. yds.=21/50 cu. yds. and 21/50 of 27

$$\text{cu. ft.} = \frac{21\times27}{50} = \frac{567}{50} .567\div50=11.34 \text{ or } 11\frac{1}{3} \text{ cu. ft. sand.}$$

To find the cost of a cu. yd. of concrete based on the above quantities, and assuming it requires 2¼ hrs. labor time to mix and place one cu. yd. of concrete, proceed as follows :

1½ bbls. cement	= 1.50 bbls. cement	@	$9.00 per bbl.	= $13.5000
11⅓ cu. ft. sand	= 0.42 cu. yd. sand	@	5.75 per cu. yd.	= 2.4150
22⅔ cu. ft. gravel	= 0.84 cu. yd. gravel	@	5.75 per cu. yd.	= 4.8300
2¼ hrs. labor	= 2.25 hrs. labor	@	9.80 per hr.	= 22.0500
Cost per cu. yd.				$42.7950

You will note the total is carried in four decimal places. This is to illustrate the actual figures obtained by multiplying. The total would be $42.80 per cu. yd. of concrete.

In making the above multiplications you will note there are 2 decimals in both the multiplicand and the multiplier of all the amounts multiplied, so the result should contain as many decimals as the sum of the multiplicand and multiplier, which is 4. You will note all the totals contain 4 decimal places. Always bear this in mind when making your multiplications because if the decimal place is wrong it makes a difference of 90 percent in your total. You know the correct result is $42.7950 but suppose by mistake you counted off 5 decimal places. The result would be $4.27950 or $4.28 per cu. yd. or just about 1/10 enough; or if you made a mistake the other way and counted off just 3 decimal places, the result would be $427.950 or $427.95 per cu. yd., or just about 10 times too much. Watch your decimal places.

The same method is used in estimating lumber. All kinds of framing lumber are ordinarily sold by the 1,000 ft., b.m., so 1,000 is the unit or decimal used when estimating lumber.

Suppose you buy 150 pcs. of 2"x8"-16'-0", which contains 3,200 ft. b.m. This is equivalent to 3200/1000=32/10=3⅕ thousandths or stated in decimals it may be either 3.2 or 3.200. The cost of this lumber at $230.00 per 1,000 ft. b.m., would be obtained by multiplying 3.200 ft. at $230.00 per 1,000 ft. b. m., as follows :

3.200 M ft. of lumber @ $736.00000 or $736.00.

Note there were 3 decimal places in the multiplicand and 2 decimal places in the multiplier, so the result should contain 5 decimal places, but inasmuch as all the decimals are zeros, drop all but two of them to designate 736 dollars and no cents.

Things to Remember When Using Decimals

.	at the left of a figure indicates a decimal.
.6	indicates tenths, thus .6=6/10=.60=60/100=.600=600/1000
.06	indicates hundredths, thus .06=6/100=.060=60/1000
.006	indicates thousandths, thus .006=6/1000
.0006	indicates ten thousandths, thus .0006=6/10000

When multiplying decimals always remember that the result or product must contain as many decimal places as the sum of the decimal places in both the multiplicand and the multiplier ; thus : Find the cost of 3 hrs. 20 min. laborer's time at $9.80 an hr.

3 hrs. 20 min. equal 3/⅓ hrs. =3.3333 Multiplicand
7 dollars 50 cents an hr. = 9.80 Multiplier

There are 3 decimals in the multiplicand and 2 decimals in the multiplier, so the result or total should contain as many decimals as the sum of the multiplicand and multiplier, which is 5.

2666640
299997
32666340=32.666340=$32.67

Be sure your decimal point is in the RIGHT place and the rest is easy.

Conversion Factors
S. I. Metric - English Systems

Multiply	by	to obtain
acres	0.404687	hectares
"	4.04687×10^{-3}	square kilometers
ares	1076.39	square feet
board feet	144 sq in. X 1 in.	cubic inches
" "	0.0833	cubic feet
bushels	0.3521	hectoliters
centimeters	3.28083×10^{-2}	feet
"	0.3937	inches
cubic centimeters	3.53145×10^{-5}	cubic feet
" "	6.102×10^{-2}	cubic inches
cubic feet	2.8317×10^{4}	cubic centimeters
" "	2.8317×10^{-2}	cubic meters
" "	6.22905	gallons, Imperial
" "	0.2832	hectoliters
" "	28.3170	liters
" "	2.38095×10^{-2}	tons, British shipping
" "	0.025	tons, U.S. shipping
cubic inches	16.38716	cubic centimeters
cubic meters	35.3145	cubic feet
" "	1.30794	cubic yards
" "	264.2	gallons, U. S.
cubic yards	0.764559	cubic meters
" "	7.6336	hectoliters
degrees, angular	0.0174533	radians
degrees, F (less 32 F)	0.5556	degrees, C
" C	1.8	degrees, F (less 32 F)
foot pounds	0.13826	kilogram meters
feet	30.4801	centimeters
"	0.304801	meters
"	304.801	millimeters
"	1.64468×10^{-4}	miles, nautical
gallons, Imperial	0.160538	cubic feet
" "	1.20091	gallons, U. S.
" "	4.54596	liters
gallons, U.S	0.832702	gallons, Imperial
" "	0.13368	cubic feet
" "	231.	cubic inches
" "	0.0378	hectoliters
" "	3.78543	liters
grams, metric	2.20462×10^{-3}	pounds, avoirdupois
hectares	2.47104	acres
"	1.076387×10^{5}	square feet

Conversion Factors (Cont'd)

Multiply	by	to obtain
hectares	3.86101×10^{-3}	square miles
hectoliters	3.531	cubic feet
,, ...	2.84	bushels
,, ...	0.131	cubic yards
hectoliters	26.42	gallons
horsepower, metric	0.98632	horsepower, U. S.
horsepower, U.S.	1.01387	horsepower, metric
inches	2.54001	centimeters
,, ...	2.54001×10^{-2}	meters
,, ...	25.4001	millimeters
kilograms	2.20462	pounds
,, ...	9.84206×10^{-4}	long tons
,, ...	1.10231×10^{-3}	short tons
kilogram meters	7.233	foot pounds
kilograms per m	0.671972	pounds per ft
kilograms per sq cm	14.2234	pounds per sq in.
kilograms per sq m	0.204817	pounds per sq ft
,, ,, ,, ,, ...	9.14362×10^{-5}	long tons per sq ft
kilograms per sq mm	1422.34	pounds per sq in.
,, ,, ,, ,, ...	0.634973	long tons per sq. in.
kilograms per cu m	6.24283×10^{-2}	pounds per cu ft
kilometers	0.62137	miles, statute
,, ...	0.53959	miles, nautical
,, ...	3280.7	feet
liters	0.219975	gallons, Imperial
,, ...	0.26417	gallons, U.S.
,, ...	3.53145×10^{-2}	cubic feet
,, ...	61.022	cubic inches
meters	3.28083	feet
,, ...	39.37	inches
,, ...	1.09361	yards
miles, statute	1.60935	kilometers
,, ,, ...	0.8684	miles, nautical
miles, nautical	6080.204	feet
,, ,, ...	1.85325	kilometers
,, ,, ...	1.1516	miles, statute
millimeters	3.28083×10^{-3}	feet
,, ...	3.937×10^{-2}	inches
pounds, avoirdupois	453.592	grams, metric
,, ,, ...	0.453592	kilograms
,, ,, ...	4.464×10^{-4}	tons, long
,, ,, ...	4.53592×10^{-4}	tons, metric
pounds per ft	1.48816	kilograms per m

Conversion Factors (Cont'd)

Multiply	by	to obtain
pounds per sq ft..............	4.88241	kilograms per sq m
pounds per sq in..............	7.031×10^{-2}	kilograms per sq cm
" " " "	7.031×10^{-4}	kilograms per sq mm
pounds per cu ft..............	16.0184	kilograms per cu m
radians............................	57.29578	degrees, angular
square centimeters...........	0.1550	square inches
square feet.......................	9.29034×10^{-4}	ares
square feet.......................	9.29034×10^{-6}	hectares
" "	0.0929034	square meters
square inches...................	6.45163	square centimeters
" "	645.163	square millimeters
square kilometers.............	247.104	acres
" "	0.3861	square miles
square meters..................	10.7639	square feet
" "	1.19599	square yards
square miles.....................	259.0	hectares
" "	2.590	square kilometers
square millimeters...........	1.550×10^{-3}	square inches
square yards.....................	0.83613	square meters
tons, long..........................	1016.05	kilograms
" "	2240.	pounds
" "	1.01605	tons, metric
" "	1.120	tons, short
tons, long, per sq ft.........	1.09366×10^{-4}	kilograms per sq m
tons, long, per sq in........	1.57494	kilograms per sq mm
tons, metric.....................	2204.62	pounds
" "	0.98421	tons, long
" "	1.10231	tons, short
tons, short	907.185	kilograms
" "	0.892857	tons, long
" "	0.907185	tons, metric
tons, British shipping......	42.00	cubic feet
" " "	0.952381	tons, U. S. shipping
tons, U. S. shipping.........	40.00	cubic feet
" " "	1.050	tons, British shipping
yards...............................	0.914402	meters